Lola Montez

Lola Montez

Her Life & Conquests

JAMES MORTON

PORTRAIT

Visit the Portrait website!

• •

Portrait publishes a wide range of non-fiction, including biography, history, science, music, popular culture and sport.

Visit our website to:

• read descriptions of our popular titles
• buy our books over the internet
• take advantage of our special offers
• enter our monthly competition
• learn more about your favourite Portrait authors

VISIT OUR WEBSITE AT: www.portraitbooks.com

First published in 2007 by **Portrait**
an imprint of
PiatkusBooks Ltd
5 Windmill Street
London W1T 2JA
e-mail: info@portrait.co.uk

The moral right of the author has been asserted

A catalogue record for this book is
available from the British Library

ISBN 0 7499 5115 X

Edited by Steven Gove
Text design by Paul Saunders

Typeset by Phoenix Photosetting, Chatham, Kent
www.phoenixphotosetting.co.uk
Printed and bound in Great Britain by
William Clowes Ltd, Beccles, Suffolk

For Dock Bateson, with love
and
Bruce Seymour, with admiration

Picture Credits

⤞⤝

Contents

→>-<←

Acknowledgments

-+->-<+-

Apart from my debt to Bruce Seymour my thanks are also due to Pauline Bateson, Jeremy Beadle, J. P. Bean, Alan Brooke, Veronique Delpierre, John Duncan, Mary Ewing, Steve Gove, Jill Grey, who generously shared her papers on Savile Morton and Lola's time in Paris, Loretta Lay, Barbara Levy, Alison Sturgeon, Denise Dwyer, Richard Whittington-Egan, Susan Goldstein, City Archivist and the staff of the San Francisco History Center, the California History Society, San Francisco, David Kestler and the staff of the Bancroft Library, University of California, Berkeley, the staff at the National Archives at Kew, the Monacensia-Saammlung, Stadtbibliothek, Munich, the King Ludwig I Archiv in the Bayerische Staatsbibliothek, Munich, the Bibliothèque Nationale, the Bibliothèque Historique de Ville de Paris, the British Library and the Newspaper Library at Colindale, the New York Public Library, the Direction and Staff of the Doris Foley Library for Historical Research, Nevada City, the Harvard Theatre Collection, the Houghton Library, Harvard, the Boston Public Library, the New York Public Library, the New York Historical Society, the Performing Arts Library and Museum in San Francisco, the Mitchell Library in Sydney, the State Library of Victoria and the Ballarat Historical Society.

As is always the case, the book could not have been begun, let alone finished, without the constant support, advice and help of Dock Bateson.

Introduction

➤➤◄◄

THE FIRST I EVER HEARD of Lola Montez was when, aged fifteen, I went to see the film made of her life by the great director Max Ophuls. The 1848 revolutions across Europe were not part of my school's history curriculum, and even had they been, the troubles of King Ludwig of Bavaria would have been shunted to one side as we learned how Palmerston kept England and the monarchy on a steady course, dispatching gunboats over the Mediterranean. History was not always taught with a spirit of inquiry in those days.

Although I was a great admirer of Ophuls with his 360-degree panning and track work, the reason for seeing the film was not his technique, nor any great interest in Lola. It was to see the beautiful, if rather wooden, pre-Brigitte Bardot French actress Martine Carol, who had a great reputation in the 1940s and early 1950s. In real life she had been courted by the gangster Pierre Loutrel and, so claimed my friends who sneaked into the cinemas of Notting Hill Gate, bared her breasts on screen; a sight which in the early fifties was something usually denied to teenagers. She may have done so in the French cinemas but those bits never crossed the channel to the Continentale, the Paris-Pullman and the cinemas off the Edgware Road which were then the homes of X-rated films. In those days the most flesh one was allowed to glimpse was of a nudist volleyball game in long shot in films with titles such as 'Naked as Nature Intended'. Now the story was that when Martine as Lola appeared before King Ludwig of Bavaria, she tore her dress revealing all. I may tell you she did not. Or if she did, the censor had out not only his scissors, but needle and thread, in no time at all.

At the time the film itself was not highly regarded and was a box-office failure. It was a very Brechtian exercise. Peter Ustinov, as Lola's manager and ringmaster, controlled a series of scenes from her life, with a cast of dwarves acting out tableaux before the screen dissolved into the action. Anton Walbrook was King Ludwig, Oskar Werner a student and Will Quadflieg was Franz Liszt. By the final scenes – in which Lola leaps from a platform and, having survived the jump, is kissed by men from the audience paying a dollar a time for the privilege – I was hooked. But just what was true?

Certainly not the dive, unless that was a symbolic representation of her life. The kissing? There were stories in the press that men queued to shake her hand for a dollar a time. The dress tearing? Very possible. Was Liszt her lover? Certainly. Some years later, in a second-hand bookshop in Worthing on the south coast, I found a copy of her wildly inaccurate and self-promoting autobiography. She claimed in that volume to be the subject of more biographies than any other living woman, adding that none of them came any nearer to being an accurate biography of her than they did 'to being an authentic history of the man in the moon'. That was probably because she told so many people so many lies.

So just what was the truth behind the stories of her nationality and parentage, of the suicides and ruin of her lovers (twenty-five and counting), of her court appearances (at least twenty), of duels, of her often disastrous theatrical performances, of her relationships with Liszt and Alexandre Dumas senior, of her elopement at the age of fourteen, of her three or more marriages (all but one of them bigamous), of the enslavement of Ludwig I, of the horsewhipping of men who displeased her, of bandit lovers, of her contracting syphilis at an early age, of the mountebanks and rogues she knew and used and who in turn cheated her, of her death in poverty or in the comforting arms of religion before she was forty?

What made her the darling of the news pages of the broadsheets of the time, so that the *New York Daily Times* of 14 January 1853 could report in the same breath and paragraph: 'Interesting news is told of Queen Victoria . . . Mr Heald, the husband of Lola Montez, was drowned at Lisbon by the upsetting of a yacht'? Anything to do with her was valuable: 'We regret to learn from a North West contemporary that Captain James of Kolah contingency, is so seriously ill that his life is dispaired [sic] of. This gentleman is, we believe, the husband of the celebrated Lola Montez, from whom he has never been divorced.'[1]

A good example of Lola's status in newsprint, even late in her career – or perhaps of the provincialism of some of the papers – comes from the *Pittsfield Sun*:

> The Steamship *America* arrived at Boston on Monday with Liverpool dates of the 2nd. Among the passengers were Madame Lola Montez, who has been married to the Prince of Shalfosky at Paris, and Thomas Allibone, of Philadelphia. There is no later intelligence from India and the principal interest centers in the Chinese news. The London *Times* says that probably Canton has been attacked and captured.[2]

Had she played her cards in a slightly different order Lola could have become one of the great feminist icons, but over the years she has become rather isolated from, even discarded by the movement. This is not really surprising. She was far too great an individualist for adoption by those whom she spent a good deal of time mocking. Life was, for her, too much of a personal struggle to become involved in the greater scheme of things. If women in general benefited by her actions, so well and good, but it was more by chance than intention.

It is perhaps a little unkind to describe her as a sociopath but there is no doubt she displayed many of the traits of one – recklessly deciding on courses of action from which there was to be no turning back, irrespective of how damaging they might be to herself or others. It is not surprising that Lola developed the characteristics she did. A criminologist would have a fine time picking over the reasons behind her behaviour. There was, in her early life, more or less every incident which has been used at one time or another to explain social deviance. Her illegitimate mother and grandmother; the death of her natural father at a very young age; her unwanted transportation from the warmth of India to a dour Scots community; being deposited in the house of the choleric General Sir Jasper Nicolls, old enough to be her grandfather, and who, to mix services, ran a very tight ship; a boarding school away from even that home – there is no evidence she was invited to other girls' homes or even that Nicolls had her back in the holidays; years of separation from her mother and her stepfather, Patrick Craigie, who does appear to have been fond of her; the sudden arrival of her mother bringing the threat of an arranged marriage to a much older man; marriage to a man well down the social pecking order in hidebound India.

It is hardly surprising that she saw herself as an unwanted outsider, desperate to break into the closed circle of English and Continental society, and that she invented stories to improve her station in life. Looking at her pictures it is probable that she also possessed that physical quality of abundant pubic hair which the early criminologist, Caesare Lombroso, attributed to women likely to become prostitutes.

Lola was always the outsider trying, and generally failing, to be accepted in turn by society, the world of theatre and dance, and the general community, until she found inclusion in religion. Even then she was used as a circus pony to boost repentance rather than as an integral part of the movement. Before that she had been the wife of an impoverished low grade soldier, 'pretty Mrs J', to whom discarded dresses were handed out by the gentry and who, as a treat, was allowed to ride on an elephant with them. Of an evening she might be the belle of the ball but, when dawn came, the coachmen had once more turned into mice. She might have been the plaything of the nobility but she was not invited to their dining tables with their wives.

She was shown to be a fake when she danced in London and her lack of talent was cruelly exposed when she danced in Paris. When she was there with her lover Dujarier she was accepted in the bohemian circles in which he moved, but she would never have achieved the respectability of marriage. In Munich she joined the long line of women who had been the King's mistress, but even when she was ennobled the Bavarian nobility turned its collective back on her.

Calling cards were rarely returned, and when they were it was with abusive writing on them.

On her return to London she again moved in shabby society. Lord Brougham may have been the Lord Chancellor but he was not highly regarded socially, and at best she was someone to be taken to the opera. Her 'marriage' to the young officer Heald was an unmitigated disaster and effectively shut her out of England for the better part of a decade. By the time she returned to Paris the great literary salons were no longer open to her. Her acting was well enough received but she must have known she would never be the equal of the Booths, of Laura Keene or even Caroline Chapman. When she turned to lecturing she was in the hands of the 'dissolute whale of a New York bay', Chauncey Burr, exploited by him and later by an old school friend, Mrs Buchanan, and the Reverend Francis Hawks. Yet she was the darling of a louche society; wealth and men went through her hands like sand.

What did Lola look like? Everyone agreed that whatever she lacked in talent on the stage, she more than made up for in her looks and personality. She had

> an exceedingly willowy figure, being rather above the average height of women, magisterial in her manner, with eyes of liquid fire, large and dark brown, such as are seen on rustic beauties of the Emerald Isle; delicately moulded features, lovely teeth, beautiful white hands, with pink nails and taper fingers, and an air of refinement which attracted others like a magnet.[3]

Indeed, with very few exceptions, whatever people thought of Lola's background, temper and manners everyone agreed that, of her time, she was a stunning beauty, perhaps the most beautiful woman in the world. And she had the temper to go with it. 'Lola's beauty, particularly the splendour of her breasts, made madmen everywhere,' thought the German biographer Edward Fuchs. Her friend, the writer Edward DeLeon, thought she had the most wonderful eyes he ever saw and that 'she spoke most eloquently with them when her lips were silent'. Another wrote of her 'fiery eye, the beautifully formed nose, her profile, and her beautifully arched eyebrows'.[4]

Others spoke of her 'mice teeth', then said to be the height of love-liness, of her thick eyelashes which made her eyes seem darker than they were. A Polish critic said that Lola possessed twenty-six of the twenty-seven points on which a Spanish writer insists as essential to feminine beauty. The only point on which she failed to score were her eyes, which should be black. He personally would not change them.[5]

There were, naturally, her detractors. Whoever provided the notes on which the Englishman Albert Vandam based his stories did not like Lola: 'Her gait and carriage were those of a duchess for she was natu-rally graceful but the moment she opened her lips the illusion van-ished – at least to me . . . though not devoid of wit, her wit was that of a pot-house, which would have not been tolerated in the smoking room of a club in the small hours.'[6] A disgruntled member of her troupe with whom she travelled to Australia in 1855 thought:

> Frivolous, naughty as a little child; can charm with a wink; woe to him who falls into her disfavour. She has a very excitable nature and for the slightest reason her whole body will tremble and her eyes flash lightning. For this reason one has to treat her very carefully because she is the most courageous and foolhardy woman who ever walked this earth.[7]

What did she sound like, this woman who throughout her life passed herself off as the daughter of Spanish nobility? The critic of the *Cour-rier de la Louisiane* thought she spoke English with a mixture of Irish and Spanish accents.[8] According to the French critic Théophile Gautier, 'she gabbles Spanish indifferently, French hardly at all and English passably'. Even towards the end of her life people were capti-vated by her voice. The journalist Mary Clemmer Ames saw her lec-turing and gushed: 'Rarely a man, and very rarely a woman, holds so complete a control over the modulation of voice as did Lola. Ever changing, its intonations were perfect and sweet as they were infinite. In her physique, in the perfect abandon of her manner, in her voice, were hidden the secrets of her power.'[9]

Camille Paglia once suggested that 'The prostitute is not, as feminists claim, the victim of men, but rather their conqueror, an outlaw.' One may disagree with that as a general proposition, but there is little doubt that it was true in the case of Lola Montez until her last years, when she was in the grip of the Evangelical church. Lola was a predator but sadly one who rampaged almost for the sake of it. Even when she was on to a good thing in the shape and form of King Ludwig she pushed her luck that bit too far. She could have been an *éminence grise*, but that was not her style. She had to be there in the front row of the dress circle and as a result she ended outside the stage door exit: 'but half civilised – splendid creature of lust, not of metaphysical refinements. Here lay the fatality of her attractions. Lorelei Montez ... was as much a man in the attributes of physical courage, wilfulness, heedlessness of general opinion, dedication to purpose as any man she knew.'[10]

What is the tally of her lovers? Twenty can be identified with some or even absolute certainty; there is good evidence to name another twenty, and that does not begin to include the men who paid her hotel bills, her rent and living expenses when she was without an immediate protector, who gave her gaming counters, cash itself or presents readily convertible into cash.

It would be impossible to write any sort of biography of Lola Montez without acknowledging a huge debt to the monumental research of the Californian lawyer Bruce Seymour. He appeared on the highly popular intellectual American game show *Jeopardy!*, winning sufficient money to allow him to spend the early 1990s researching her life. As a result he was able to correct many of the misapprehensions and false tales about her. Not content with that feat, he generously donated his papers to the Bancroft Library at the University of California, Berkeley for the benefit of all future researchers. In them he has written that he hopes someone will make use of them to write a better book. Despite the advice, encouragement and support he has given me I would not dare to make that claim, but I hope I have cast some new light on her and have expanded her story to include the lives of the men and women she loved and cheated, with whom she fought and very often whom she ruined.

Throughout, for the sake of consistency, I have spelled her name Montez although a number of contemporary books, magazines and newspapers have her as Montes. In the bibliography, however, I have used the spelling adopted by the author.

CHAPTER ONE

Lola in Bud and Under Siege

E VEN AT THE END of her life, when she was supposedly in the grip of an Evangelical religious fervour and had slumped at the foot of the cross, Lola Montez could not stop lying. She lied about her parents and her upbringing. She lied about her relationships with men, her social status, her marriages and anything else about which she considered it expedient to prevaricate. Even when it was wholly unnecessary she would lie for the sake of it.

Many of us have, from time to time, improved our social status for the benefit of our listeners – or at least have wished to – but surely nobody has turned it into such an art form as did Lola Montez. Her name was Maria Dolores de Porres y Montes. That is if it wasn't Rosanna Gilbert, or Betsy Watson – something she always denied – or Betty or Eva James, or Mlle Marie Marie, or Mrs Burton, or Mrs Heald, or – at the very end of her life – Fanny Gibbons. She was born in Calcutta, if it wasn't Madrid or Constantinople, Geneva, Lucerne, Havana, or Limerick or Sligo, or more prosaically, Montrose in Scotland.

Over the years she regularly changed her parents' nationality and with it their station in life. Most often her mother was Spanish – there was some partial truth in that – sometimes Señora Oliveres de Montalo; and her aunts were the Marquise de Panestra and the Contesse de Villa-Palma – no truth in that at all. Sometimes her mother was a Cuban noblewoman, occasionally a Dublin actress. Sometimes her father – occasionally Gilbert but often Patrick Oliver – was a Spanish grandee; quite often he was an executed leader of the Carlists, as was a non-existent husband. On other occasions the Gilbert family were descendants of the explorer, Sir Humphrey Gilbert.

Some thought her father to be either an Indian rajah, the Sultan of Turkey, or the King of the Cannibal Islands. Others believed she might be the illegitimate daughter of Lord Byron – whom she was thought to resemble – from a coupling with a Scots washerwoman, and she did not always disabuse them. Another putative father was the celebrated Spanish matador Francisco Montez, whose real name was José Redondo and who fought as Paquito. When approached on the subject he indicated he was flattered by the attribution but that unfortunately it was false. Sometimes she was stolen as a child and brought up by gypsies who taught her to sing and dance.[1]

The truth was rather different and less romantic. Perhaps one key to her character is that her mother, Elizabeth, and grandmother were both illegitimate. Her mother was the daughter of Charles Silver Oliver, a former High Sheriff of Cork and a Member of Parliament, a pillar of Ireland's ruling Protestant class. Before he married at the then late age of forty, he had fathered four children by a Mary Green, who was indeed part Spanish. The youngest of them was Elizabeth. In his fashion Oliver took care of the four children; the boys John and Thomas were apprenticed to grocers and Elizabeth and her sister Mary were bound to a milliner, Mrs Hall in Cork. When he died in 1817 each was left the not inconsiderable sum of £500, to be paid at the age of twenty-one. Naturally, the seven legitimate children he subsequently sired did rather better.

At the age of fourteen Elizabeth Oliver met Edward Gilbert, an ensign in the 25th Foot, later the King's Own Scottish Borderers, became pregnant and moved out of the city. According to Lola she was born around Valentine's Day 1820 but sometimes, when it suited her, as late as 1825. Nor was her mother averse to shaving a few years off her own age.

In fact her parents married on 29 April 1820 in Christ Church, Cork and Lola was baptised Elizabeth Rosanna Gilbert at St Peter's, Liverpool on 16 February 1823. Almost certainly she was born on 17 February 1821 at Grange, County Sligo, the same year a two-year famine began in Ireland.[2]

One puzzle has been whether Lola was illegitimate like her mother and grandmother before her. Finding an answer has been made no easier by the conflicting dates of her birth given throughout her life. After her wedding at the fashionable Christ Church in Cork Elizabeth's mother cocked a snook at the local gentry by placing a marriage notice, which appeared on 6 May 1820:

> Married in Cork, Edward Gilbert, Esq, 25th Regiment to Eliza, daughter of late Charles Silver Oliver, Esq, of Castle Oliver, MP[3]

But was it in fact a double whammy in that this 'reputed' daughter of Charles Oliver had already had an illegitimate daughter to go with her impudence? Probably not. It is clear that Lola was baptised on 16 February 1823 in Liverpool and the question of her legitimacy seems to have been solved by the discovery of a note, possibly written by her mother, on the back of her baptismal certificate, stating that Elizabeth Rosanna Gilbert was born at Grange in the County of Sligo on the seventeenth day of February 1821. Apparently Lola's mother filed a copy of the baptismal certificate when she applied for a widow's pension on Gilbert's death.[4] Of course, she might simply have been improving events *post hoc* but on this occasion she should probably be given the benefit of the doubt.

In support of this evidence, Gilbert's regiment was stationed in the Sligo area at what would have been the time of Lola's birth. If the certificate is correct it is clear that Lola was legitimate, but it also means it would be doubtful whether she had any serious memories of her father. The question remains as to why Lola was not baptised for so long after her birth. It certainly does not support the argument that the family was Catholic, a 'fact' on which she traded for most of her life.

On 14 March, a month after Lola's baptism, Gilbert and his family sailed to rejoin his regiment in India. A passage in a small cabin cost £110 on an East India Company boat. There was no facility for washing of clothes at sea and as a result a dozen and a half single nightcaps and a similar number of nightshirts were required, but there was generally an excellent band for dancing. Ships docked at Diamond Harbour, some ninety miles from Calcutta, and another boat had to be hired for the remainder of the journey, which would last twelve to eighteen hours.

Gilbert, together with his family, was immediately sent to rejoin his regiment at Dinapore, a cantonment founded by Warren Hastings, near Patna on the Ganges and 530 miles from Calcutta. It was a difficult journey. Six years later Captain Christopher D. Aplin of the 33rd Native Infantry recorded his own experiences. Aplin left Calcutta on 1 December 1829. After Kishanaghur, which he reached on 5 December, there was no European station for the next fortnight. At the beginning of the journey the average speed made was one and a quarter miles an hour but things improved on 16 December when he covered fourteen and a half miles. The day before he noted that they had eaten no meat for nine days and the bread was eight days old. By 29 December he had covered 374 miles. On 13 January he reached Patna, where the Ganges was used as a burial ground. He bought 100lb of potatoes for a rupee.

On 17 January after a total of six weeks en route he arrived at Dinapore, situated in a wide sandy plain interspersed with mango topes which he thought cheerful and imposing. He was impressed with what he saw. There were bungalows around a square and a regimental band was playing on a turfed parade ground, around which there was a fashionable evening drive. It was estimated that even a cadet could live on 100 rupees a month, then worth £25. If he 'chummed' with another officer they could keep six servants for 40 rupees a month. A horse and groom would cost another 16 rupees. Pay and allowances were 200 rupees a month. In 1827 Bessie Fenton described it as a very gay – in the old-fashioned sense of the word – station with dances, parties and plays. On Shrove Tuesday there was a masked ball.[5]

It must have been very similar when Gilbert, a desperately ill man, finally arrived at the cantonment in September 1823. Within days, on 22 September, he died from cholera and was buried in the compound's Cemetery No. 2. His death was by no means unusual. The mortality rate was high in Dinapore: on 27 September that year the twenty-year-old wife of a drum major died, to be followed by her daughter three days later. Thirty-five more had died by the end of 1824. Bessie Fenton's first husband was another who died there.

All Gilbert's effects – including his dog, a concert flute, ten volumes of *New British Theatre*, eighteen pairs of socks, a French grammar and twenty-one false collars – were sold, realising a very respectable £460 2s. Mrs Gilbert was paid £60 4s 1½d by the regiment and given a widow's pension.[6]

In later life Lola had a rather rose-tinted and romantic view of a death she could not possibly have remembered: 'There was a young and gallant officer by the name of Craigie, whom her father loved, and when dying and too far gone to speak, he took his child and wife's hand and put them in the hand of this young officer, with an imploring look, that he would be kind to them when death had done its work.'[7]

Now, apart from returning with a young girl to England or Ireland and the drudgery there, something she cannot have considered to be much of an option, the widow Gilbert had no choice but to remarry in short order. There is little doubt that she was a handsome woman and there were plenty of suitors. Even Lola, who never had any time for her mother, thought so: 'The hearts of a hundred officers, young and old, beat all at once with such violence for her, that the whole atmosphere for ten miles round fairly throbbed with the emotion.'[8]

On 16 August 1824, Elizabeth Gilbert married her former husband's brother officer, Captain Patrick Craigie, whose father had been a chemist in, and provost of, Montrose. Lola infinitely preferred her stepfather to her mother who, she maintained, was far too interested in balls and parties. Now she was left with the ayahs to run around pampered but barefoot, growing increasingly wild. One story which may have some truth is that she would creep up behind the villagers and push them into the creek. 'She was a Badmash but she was always kind to me,' one villager is reputed to have told the writer Sir Walter Lawrence. She was wilful, disobedient and fearless. Forbidden to bathe in a creek because of snakes, she did exactly that. She had, she said, been told that cobras only attacked those who were afraid of them.[9]

Finally, Craigie and her mother decided Lola must be sent back to Scotland to be educated by his brother David and other relatives in Montrose. There was one last Christmas in India and then on Boxing Day 1826 Lola left for England, sailing from Diamond Harbour on the *Malcolm* with Lieutenant-Colonel William Innes and his wife Eliza, who had agreed to look after her. Two days later the captain and the purser came on board and on 2 January the pilot was dropped. By the end of January the vessel left Madras. From then on the journey was not a wholly smooth one. Water was rationed to five pints per day with an extra pint on pea soup days. Immediately they ran into squalls and rain and on 3 February there was a monsoon. Within the month the first of the privates going home died. There were more storms at the end of February and on 4 March it was too stormy for divine service. Five days later a second private died. They reached St Helena and an invalided private was unloaded to be court-martialled. At the end of the month wet bales were discovered in the hold and it was decided to alter the trim by hoisting water butts. On 6 April another seaman died. On 18 April Third Officer Betts died nearly a month before Land's End was sighted. The journey ended as it began when, on 22 May, the baggage was unloaded in heavy rain.[10]

It is difficult to think of a much more troublesome uprooting and transplanting than Lola – and no doubt many children before and after her – suffered. Later she wrote rather winsomely, 'The peculiarity of her dress, and I dare say not a little eccentricity in her manners, served to make her an object of curiosity and remark . . .'[11] Others remembered she had amused herself in church by sticking flowers in the wig of an elderly worshipper in the pew in front of her.[12] She wrote to Craigie asking to be allowed to return to India but her plea was ignored.

In 1831, at the age of eleven, she moved from Montrose to live in Durham where her relations opened a school. There she was taught drawing by a J. G. Grant. With the gift of hindsight and writing a trifle lasciviously, he remembered that she was:

at that time a very elegant and beautiful child of about ten or (perhaps) eleven; of stature rather promising to be tall than actually for her age, but symmetrically formed with a flowing graceful carriage, the charm of which was only lessened by an air of confident self-complacency – I might almost say haughty ease – in full accordance with the habitual expression of her else beautiful countenance, namely, that of indomitable self-will – a quality which I believe had manifested itself from early infancy. Her features were regular but capable of great and rapid changes of expression. Her complexion was orientally dark, but transparently clear, her eyes were of deep blue, and, as I distinctly remember, of excessive beauty although bright with less indication of the gentle and tender affections of her sex than of more stormy and passionate excitements.

Even then she had a temper and a half:

The mouth, too, had a singularly set character, far more allied to the determined than the voluptuous, and altogether it was impossible to look at her for many minutes without feeling convinced that she was made up of very wayward and troublesome elements. The violence and obstinacy, indeed, of her temper gave too frequent cause of painful anxiety to her good kind aunt; and I remember, upon one occasion it was necessary, before Eliza could receive her lesson, to release her from solitary durance, in which she had been kept all the previous part of the day for some rebellious outbreak of passion. The door was opened, and out came the incipient Lola Montes looking like a little tigress just escaped from one den to another![13]

On 14 September 1832 she was sent south to live near Reading with the family of Sir Jasper Nicolls, who had joined the army in 1793. It was not an arrangement which particularly pleased the frequently irritable man: 'Today arrived from Durham Capt Craigie's sister, with Mrs C's daughter whom they request us to put to school for them. I shall have a fine number of children to look after if they increase in this manner.'[14]

It was always unlikely that this ill-matched pair would get on. Nicolls was then fifty-four years old. He had served in the Peninsular War and had received a Gold Medal for his part in the retreat from Corunna. At the siege of Bhurtpore in 1825, where Craigie had been the baggage manager of Brigadier General Schuldhorn's division,

Nicolls had led his division, marching expressly on his orders to the tune of 'The British Grenadiers'. Nicolls had returned to England two years earlier on leave and was living in some comfort surrounded by a number of daughters.

Although this was undoubtedly a step-up in the British class system for Lola she thought Nicolls cold and silent. In turn he thought she would come to no good. It was only a matter of time before she was sent to a boarding school run by the Misses Aldridge in Camden Place, Bath. There were around fifteen girl pupils aged from ten to seventeen or eighteen. All the arts were taught – singing, dancing, piano playing, drawing and sewing, but also Latin and French. Although she certainly could pick up a language, Lola rarely became fluent in them. In later life she invented a Paris education for herself but this was simply another of her embellishments. There is no record that she made friends or that she was anything but a year-round boarder.

And if Nicolls did not care for Lola at first sight, eighteen months later he showed no greater affection for her mother:

> At last we have heard from Mrs Craigie who was I suppose constrained to answer our numerous letters tho' she heard from us 6 times before this effect was produced – I felt greatly surprised – not a little vexed – and in some degree repented of having so easily undertaken an unpleasant and apparently thankless task. I likened her to a tortoise who buries her eggs lightly in the sand, and leaves them to sun and to chance.[15]

As for Lola, her troubles really began when on 2 November 1836 her mother sailed from Calcutta on the *Orient* to take her back to India. It was a wearisome journey and Nicolls was relieved when she landed: 'A load has been lifted from us by the arrival of Mrs Craigie – she had a very tedious voyage of five months and eleven days, as bad as our own. The North East winds have kept all shipping from entering the Channel and the Orient anchored at Penzance.'[16]

That was by no means the worst of things. On board was thirty-year-old Lieutenant Thomas James from the East India Company, returning to England for his health. The company paid his homeward passage but he would have to pay the cost of his return. He was taken ill again during the voyage and was nursed by the handsome Mrs Craigie. Shipboard romances were not uncommon and perhaps the handsome Mrs Craigie flirted with the younger officer. Certainly, somewhat surprisingly, she continued to see him after they landed.

Mrs Craigie went to London and on 26 April was there visited by Nicolls. Three days later they set off to see Lola in Bath, where rather curiously they were joined by James. From the moment mother and daughter met after some ten years' separation they took a cordial dislike to each other. According to Lola her mother's first words were how badly her daughter's hair had been dressed. Now Mrs Craigie began steps to remove her from the school. In the background is a suggestion that a music master may have become too close to Lola but it seems that, over the years, Mrs Craigie had marked Lola either as the future wife of the elderly Abraham Lumley or for one of his bachelor sons. Now she wanted the marriage made. In her memoirs Lola, opting for the former as her potential husband, thought of him as a 'gouty old rogue', and claimed he was a Supreme Court judge in India. More likely he was Craigie's commanding officer.

The *New York Times* in its obituary of Lola interpreted the incident as follows:

> Mamma, with the usual foresight of her kind had contracted a match for the budding Lola . . . The chosen swain was a very rich and very yellow Nabob, who had expressed a desire to have a young wife shipped to him, and expected her in due course with his next lot of blue pills and bitter beer. Lola exploded with anger and Mamma refused to be comforted. Conciliation being impossible Lola determined to call in the advice of a military friend. That gentleman deliberated on the matter, and the next day eloped with her, as the wisest thing that could be done under the circumstances.[17]

James had also been introduced to Lola by Mrs Craigie. She first sought his advice and then promptly eloped with him in a carriage and pair. Clearly at that stage there was some physical attraction because later she described him as being of 'average height, blue eyes, rather attractive brown hair, sparkling white teeth in an era when teeth were rarely white and seldom sparkled, low brow and searching eyes'. There was also both the sense of adventure and the opportunity to spite her mother. If indeed Mrs Craigie and James had only made eyes at one another, it was still a desperate snub.

Lola had, she said, expected James 'to love her like Papa'. James, unsurprisingly, had more carnal ideas. Thirty miles up the road, 'he was no longer my Papa'. Of herself she wrote, 'The maid was no longer innocent. She awoke, besmirched by a guilt that she neither sought nor understood.' In her more sober days towards the end of her life it was not a course of conduct she recommended: 'Run-away matches, like run-away horses are almost sure to end in a smash-up. My advice to young girls who contemplate taking such a step is that they had better hang themselves just one hour before they start.'[18]

Nicolls was naturally both displeased with the affair and not a little pleased with his own foresight:

> I am not a bad prophet as to the figure which young people will make in life – I always predicted the vanity and lies of EG would bring her to shame – She has started very badly, if not worse, for leaving school in June, she married a Company officer without a penny, in two or three weeks – Her mother I fear cannot be blameless – at all events the 1,800 or 2,000£ expended on her education and her mother's voyages is lost.[19]

For the moment, however, James had serious difficulties. There was no problem with the age of consent but he had seduced a brother officer's daughter. There was also the possibility of Lola being made a ward of court, with the accompanying scandal. A rapprochement with the mother was essential. James's sister went to see Mrs Craigie and succeeded in convincing her that since Lola was no longer *intacta* further resistance was pointless.

Finally the pair went to Co. Meath where they were married by James's brother, the Reverend John James, on 23 July 1837 at Rathbeggan, a parish between Dublin and Eniskillen. But by then Lola was already bored. Life in the Irish countryside did not appeal to her. For her it was an unremitting diet of 'hunting, eating, hunting, tea'. Nicolls was kept posted:

> We have now heard from E. Gilbert from three quarters – all very, very unsatisfactory both regarding her and her husband – however Mrs

Craigie introduced the Gentl, and must bear the results as well as she can – She asked Lady N's advice thro' Mrs Rae, and we have told her to let her daughter write, but not to return her to confidence imm' – nor to see her – They are full of contrition already – but I fear that they want to draw on Craigie's funds by that means, which we have warned her against.[20]

For the moment the unhappy couple remained in Ireland living at Ballycrystal, of which Lola wrote: 'I wished for nothing more intensely than to be abducted once more, but this time not by a potential husband but by anything or anyone who would rescue me from the deadly monotony of this eternally repetitive life, from these cold English faces . . . no smiles, no friendly glances, no kind words.'[21] Later the pair took rooms in Westmoreland Street, Dublin, something which was rather more to her taste. Indeed there was a ball at Dublin Castle at which, she later claimed, Lord Normanby, then the Viceroy of Ireland, flirted with her.[22]

On 25 November her mother returned to India on the *David Scott*, arriving on 30 April 1838. It would take many months and a good deal of negotiating and wheedling before she would agree to see the errant Eliza. Nicolls was ecstatic:

Mrs Craigie having lost all her spirit's comfort by the frauds of her silly child, & encouraged by Craigie, means to return to Calcutta in a few days. Hers has been a lot much to be pitied – a kind step-father has lavished L1000 on her child's education & the dirty ungracious whelp has thrown it all away on the first man she met – The day of punishment surely awaits from some source – her husband's fraud & falsehood, and her own . . .[23]

James eventually made his peace with the East India Company. He borrowed the passage money from Craigie's friend Browne Roberts, a retired Indian civil servant, and on 18 September 1838 the pair sailed from Liverpool on the *Bland* bound for Calcutta. The journey was desperately long and often very uncomfortable. There was no Suez Canal to shorten the voyage and stops were made at Madeira (on 12 October), St Helena and the Cape.

A handbook published on the year of the voyage listed the

inventory now required of a lady travelling to India. The author, Miss Emma Roberts, thought it should include seventy-two chemises, seventy pocket handkerchiefs, thirty pairs of drawers or combinations, fifteen petticoats, sixty pairs of stockings, forty-five pairs of gloves, at least twenty dresses of different texture, twelve shawls and parasols, three bonnets, fifteen morning caps, biscuits and preserves and a dozen boxes of aperient pills. French stays were also required. They were the best and at least six pairs were to be taken. This huge amount of clothing was necessary because 'It is not prudent to depend upon any opportunity of getting clothes washed at the Cape.' And even if they were washed they would be badly done or stolen. As for bathing on the voyage, water was strictly rationed.

Other advice included taking the upper poop cabins, despite some disadvantages such as the chicken coops outside them. The after cabins on the lower deck were likely to be infested with rats. An abundance of feather pillows, a couch and cot were essential, as was a large-sized dressing glass to be screwed against the cabin walls. Pianos should be kept in the hold; there was nothing worse for the other passengers than having four or five indifferent pianists practising different tunes simultaneously. A quantity of brandy was desirable to be used as a form of tipping of the crew who would then be happy to do odd jobs.[24]

Later Lola claimed that on the voyage her new husband drank too much porter in the daytime and snored like a boa constrictor at night. If, which is highly unlikely, she was ever in love with him as opposed to enjoying the excitement of thwarting her mother, the emotion had almost certainly evaporated by the end of the voyage: 'The spirit and the feet lose their patience.'[25]

She later wrote: 'A long trip suffocates love even on the honeymoon. Travel by coach makes one weary and sleepy. You go to sleep from boredom and awake bored.' Given her apparent dislike of travel it is curious just how much of her life she spent in a coach or at sea. 'The sea makes women sick and men extraordinarily unpleasant. In the marital cabin you are constantly bumping into one another. You can't turn around without unwillingly embracing one another.'[26]

This time the journey took just over four months with a stop at

St Jago on the Cape Verde Islands. The captain observed her flirting with some of the male passengers and remarked, 'Love is a tune to be danced until the age of eighteen, smoked until forty and then turned into ashes until the funeral.' The Jameses arrived in Calcutta on 25 January 1839 and when James reported to the East India Company the next day he was sent to join the 21st Native Infantry at Karnal.

In 1835 George Eden, the second Lord Auckland, had been appointed Governor-General of India. His unmarried sisters Emily and Fanny, who lived with him after the death of their parents, were accustomed to a society life in the great English country houses. Now they would have to accompany him to Calcutta. It was a very different life.

On one side were the great balls, receptions and dinners, set against a background of princes whose horses had emerald-studded capes and whose temples were sheeted in gold. In the Northwest there was a society in which men killed their wives without question, wives sold their children for a handful of rice and where there was human sacrifice to appease the gods at seeding time. Years later, when lecturing, Lola would tell of a grand reception where the British officers were presented with dancing girls but were made by their commanding officer to return them. If not strictly accurate it ensured a *frisson* in her audience.

It was into this life that James brought Lola. But now the marriage had only a few months to run. If Lola is to be believed, James was a martinet. He had a diary in which he wrote her mistakes and faults and then lectured her about them. There were other problems. A commission in the East India Company was very much inferior socially to a regular commission and James was by no means a rich man. The life of an Englishwoman in India at the time was strictly controlled socially, and heading the hierarchical structure was Lady Emily Eden. It was not until 5 September that year that Lola and James were to meet the great lady, who had been lobbying Mrs Craigie to consent to see her daughter. During the hot season the ladies retired to the more bearable Simla and it was there Lola finally joined her mother for a month.

There had been a certain amount of apprehension in the Craigie camp about the arrival of the wilful Lola. For a start Mrs Craigie, herself the belle of the campus, had shaved a few years off her own age; Lola spelled danger to her on this and a number of other fronts. Simla was also a hotbed of affairs. To look a moment too long at a man was a dangerous sign of interest and to dance twice with the same person was regarded as the height of indiscretion.

But when she did meet Lady Eden, the minx was on her best behaviour. At the time she was representing herself as being only seventeen and her mother was certainly not going to contradict her. The thought of her arrival had caused sufficient consternation among her mother's party but in the event things went well enough. James was both handsome and respectful enough to pass muster. In her letters to her sister, Lady Eden wrote:

> Simla is much moved just now by the arrival of a Mrs J., who has been talked of as a great beauty all the years, and that drives every other woman, with any pretensions in that line, quite distracted ... Mrs J. is the daughter of a Mrs C., who is still very handsome herself, and whose husband is deputy-adjutant-general, or some military authority of that kind. She sent this only child to be educated at home, and went home herself two years ago to see her. In the same ship was Mr J., a poor ensign, going home on sick leave. Mrs C. nursed him and took care of him, and took him to see her daughter, who was a girl of fifteen at school. He told her he was engaged to be married, consulted her about his prospects, and in the meantime privately married this child at school. It was enough to provoke any mother, but as it now cannot be helped, we have all been trying to persuade her for the last year to make it up, as she frets dreadfully about her only child. She has withstood it till now, but at last consented to ask them for a month and they arrived three days ago. The rush on the road was remarkable, and one or two of the ladies were looking absolutely nervous. But could be more unsatisfactory than the result, for Mrs J. looked lovely and Mrs C. had set up for her a very grand jonpaum, with bearers in fine orange and brown liveries and the same for herself.

James, as well he might be, was also on his best behaviour:

> J. is a sort of smart-looking man, with bright waistcoats and bright teeth, with a showy horse, and he rode along in an attitude of respectful attention

to 'ma belle mère'. Altogether it was an imposing sight and I cannot see any way out of it but magnanimous admiration. They all called yesterday when I was at the waterfalls, and F. thought her very pretty.

And she was well-behaved enough to be invited for dinner on the Monday:

Mrs J. is undoubtedly very pretty and such a merry unaffected girl. She is only seventeen now, and does not look so old, and when one thinks that she is married to a junior lieutenant in the Indian army, fifteen years older than herself, and that they have 160 rupees a month and are to pass their whole lives in India, I do not wonder at Mrs C.'s resentment at her having run away from school. Are regimental ladies in India nowadays expected to keep in seclusion while their husbands are on active service? I think not.[27]

Certainly Lola had no intention of doing so. They met again in November when Lady Eden had travelled to Kurnaul and made camp there. The belle of the 'at home' she gave on 13 November was undoubtedly Lola: 'except that pretty Mrs J. who was at Simla, and who looked like a star amongst the others, the women were all plain'. Something must have happened, for she added, 'I don't wonder that if a tolerable-looking girl comes up the country that she is persecuted with proposals.'

On Saturday 16 November Lady Eden was on her way:

We left Kurnaul yesterday morning. Little Mrs J. was so unhappy at our going, that we asked her to come and pass the day here, and brought her with us. She went from tent to tent and chattered all day, and visited her friend Mrs —, who is with the camp. I gave her a pink silk gown, and it was altogether a very happy day for her, evidently. It ended in her going back to Kurnaul on my elephant with E.N. by her side and Mr J. sitting behind, and she had never been on an elephant before, and thought it delightful.

But now she had fears for the girl:

She is very pretty and a good little thing apparently but they are very poor and she is very young and lively, and if she falls into bad hands, she would soon laugh herself into foolish scrapes. At present the husband and wife are very fond of each other, but a girl who marries at fifteen hardly knows what she likes.[28]

And she was right to have those fears. Quite who next did what to whom depends upon the teller. Lola claimed that her husband took up with a Mrs Lomer, whom she described as the wife of a captain in the 21st Native Infantry stationed at Bareilly. According to her the pair eloped to the far distant Neilghany Hills, nearly a thousand miles away. It was a story she repeated throughout her life. Much doubt has been cast on it and there are suggestions that it was a convenient invention by Lola to explain the failure of her marriage and come out smelling of attar of roses. There were certainly two Lomer brothers in the regiment at the time. Owen Lomer was a captain and the regimental adjutant, and his wife was in her early thirties. Militating against the story is the fact she had several small children, but she would not have been the first woman to abandon hearth and home. On the other side, there were also stories that it was Lola who had become too close to a local potentate.

There is, sadly, no further reference to Mrs J. in the Eden letters. If either the affair with Mrs Lomer or her own with a potentate happened then it is surprising that this woman who had a great ear for scandal and gossip did not record it.[29] Lola herself wrote that she cried a little and laughed a lot over her husband's departure.

The suggestion of a possible court-martial for James, as Lola would have liked, seems extremely doubtful, but certainly the break-up of the marriage caused ructions in the camp. Lola was first placed under the protection of a Mrs Palmer and then sent to her mother who, according to her, shut her away from society. Meanwhile it was put about that she had suffered a back injury. It took her mother some months to obtain a face-saving medical certificate stating that, after a fall from a horse at Meerut which was not responding to treatment, Lola needed to return to England for her health. The story of the James–Lomer elopement must have been another of Lola's fancies, for on 5 August James took personal leave to visit Calcutta and there the marriage was discussed with Craigie. It was arranged that, for the present, James would pay an allowance to Lola. The break-up of the marriage does not seem to have harmed his career. In all probability the other wives and single women were quite pleased to see such a dangerous siren removed.

On 3 October 1840 both Craigie and James were at the quay to see Lola off as she sailed on the *Larkins*. She would say that, including the money Craigie gave her and her own jewellery, she set off with the not inconsiderable sum of $10,000. Lola remembered that tears rolled down her stepfather's face as he saw her on board. The caring and prescient Craigie urged the captain, Charles Ingram, and his wife Anne, as well as an American couple, the Sturgises, to watch over his stepdaughter. It was, however, a case of *la fille mal gardée*.

CHAPTER TWO

Lola in India, London and on Her Toes

THROUGHOUT HER LIFE Lola seems to have believed men's hearts were situated somewhere below the fourth waistcoat button. One of the first in whom she discovered this anatomical phenomenon was the ADC to Lord Elphinstone, Captain George Lennox, whom she met returning to England in 1841 on the *Larkins*.[1]

When she left India the intention was that she should lodge with her stepfather's relations in Scotland. The good-hearted man did what he could to ensure she was not exposed to the perils of London. Other relations were instructed to meet her off the boat. But by the time it docked in Portsmouth it was all too late and Lola was long past redemption. Lennox had boarded at Madras and almost immediately they began an affair.

Even by her later standards, her conduct was scandalous and ill-advisedly flagrant. She did not even bother to take elementary precautions to avoid being observed and refused to attend Sunday morning service, remaining below deck with Lennox. The cabin door was not secure and Caroline Marden, a spying servant, later told the Consistory Court how Lennox went to Lola's cabin after breakfast and remained there until tiffin, sitting on the sofa and kissing. Inconveniently for Lola, 'rolling of the ship sometimes opened the door and I have seen them together only in her stays and petticoats. More than once I have seen Lennox lacing up Mrs James' stays.'

On 20 October when the *Larkins* docked it was too late to travel to London and the pair spent the night in separate rooms in the Star and Garter.[2] The following morning it was on to the Imperial Hotel, Covent Garden where crucially they took a room together.

From the affidavits and files of the Consistory Court it is possible to piece together what happened in the days after Lola landed. The eighth allegation of their behaviour on 21 February at the Imperial Hotel was the crucial one: 'Retired on the night of said twenty-first of February to the said Bedroom in the same and there lay naked and alone in one and the same bed there being but one bed in the said Bed Room and there had the Carnal use and knowledge of each others Bodies and committed Adultery together.'[3]

For the next day or so Richard and Elizabeth Walters, the proprietors of the hotel, saw a series of comings and goings. Craigie had asked a former brother officer, Major Robert McMullen, to see Lola off to Scotland and while she was out walking he called to invite her to dine. She refused. In turn McMullen spoke to Browne Roberts, who also called at the Imperial and invited her to stay with him and his wife at 23 Dorset Square. Again she was adamant that she was staying where she was. After Lennox left on the following day to visit his relations, Lola was asked to leave for what the divorce papers described as 'a number of reasons', one of which was the different names on the luggage.

Giving the name of James and saying, quite correctly, that her husband was in India, Lola took rooms at 7 Great Ryder Street. There was now another effort by the family to reclaim her. Sarah Watson, Captain James's sister, called at the Imperial and was directed to Ryder Street. She asked Lola to go to live with Craigie's sister, Catherine Rae, but again Lola demurred, saying 'with an oath' she would never go to any friend of Major Craigie. A few days later both Sarah Watson and Catherine Rae went to see Lola to tell her she could go to Blackheath until she was prepared to go to Scotland – anything to get her out of this louche life. Lola had had one dose of Montrose and she was not having another. She again refused, and for Mrs Watson's pains used her name in some of her escapades around London over the following months.

Meanwhile, Lennox visited her every day, paying the rent and staying from nine in the morning until shortly before midnight. Lola told Annie Martin, her new landlady, that she expected to marry him, but after a month he was reclaimed by his family. From then on Lola was on the move on a regular basis. From Great Ryder Street, in June it was to 8 Half Moon Street where she lived under the name Eva James, and at the end of July she moved in a downward spiral across Piccadilly to 13 Duke Street. At the beginning of August she could be found in Chapel Street to the north of Oxford Street, and towards the end of the month out in what was then the country in Almond Cottage, Hornsey Road, Islington. She stayed there until the end of October, when she left for Leeds and then travelled on to Edinburgh. There she finally joined Craigie's sister Catherine Rae at 15 Nelson Street. For the moment she had run out of money and protectors. Meanwhile her maid, Charlotte Haddon, stayed at the cottage until a notice to quit expired.[4]

Lola does not appear to have been a great letter writer and, apart from her protests to newspapers and her correspondence with Ludwig of Bavaria, only a bare two dozen of her letters survive. One which does is an undated letter, written from Edinburgh probably in February 1842 and signed E., to a Mr Lons or Louis. As was the case throughout her life, Lola had money troubles. The Charlotte referred to is the former maid:

> I received the trunks quite safe yesterday and am exceedingly obliged by yr trouble in sending them. I send Charlotte a character she wrote to me the other day to send her some money. I have it not myself and am writing at this moment to several of my friends to obtain a sum sufficient to enable me to return to London which if I get will see me back again. I am heartily tired of Edinburgh and have been advised by several people to return to London. I shall when ever I have it. Send Charlotte something for she has a good and honest heart. I am in great expectations of a cousin of mine a Spanish lady coming to this country. If she does I shall

be more comfortable than I am at present. I shall enclose in an envelope
Charlotte's character and believe me

Very truly Yours E. James.[5]

It is likely that Lola did have some Spanish cousins on her mother's
side but although in later years she elevated them to the nobility, it is
very doubtful they were great ladies.

Then on 18 March 1842, still in Edinburgh, Lola was served with
divorce papers by the bailiff Thomas Innes. A divorce was not easily
or cheaply attained. The procedure was to bring an action in damages
against the wife's seducer, to be followed by a divorce *a mensa et thoro*
and then a private Act of Parliament. The whole expensive and
lengthy procedure could cost £1,000.

Given that he had not the money to bring a private Act for divorce,
what realistically was left open to James was the divorce *mensa et
thoro*. While dissolving the marriage, this was in effect a judicial separation – neither party could remarry during the lifetime of the other.
The alternative was an action against Lennox for damages for what
was known as criminal conversation; or both proceedings could be
taken. James took this third route. In March 1842 he both filed for
divorce and sued Lennox in the Queen's Bench Division.

An action for damages for criminal conversation – which was
neither criminal nor a conversation but simply adultery – was highly
popular at the time for aggrieved husbands and highly expensive for
erring gentlemen. Jurors themselves were a 'special jury of gentlemen
of fortune', twenty-four men selected from freeholders of substance,
knights and urban gentry. They were generally thought to be more
inclined to value the honour of gentlemen than the usual juror.

Once damages were awarded – and they could be as high as
£15,000, often awarded in a matter of minutes[6] – the defendant either
paid up, came to an arrangement with the husband or was arrested,
his goods seized and he was put in prison. An 1836 Act allowed the
defendant to apply for his release after twelve months. Before that the
period had been ten years.[7] One escape route was to flee to France and
live an impoverished life in Calais or Boulogne. When it came to it
Lennox did not need to flee.

The Solicitor-General and Mr J. W. Smith appeared for James with Mr Thesiger and Mr Ball for Lennox, whose defence was what was known as a 'rolled-up' plea. First, there had been no criminal conversation, and if there had, there had been no marriage. Smith for James opened the case gently. It was not a bad case of criminal conversation and there were no aggravated circumstances; undoubtedly there had been no violated friendship and hospitality to add to the injury inflicted on the plaintiff, but they were brother officers. The defendant had been introduced to the plaintiff's wife as to the wife of a brother officer; and, as he had been guilty of this act of adultery with her, he must take the responsibility for his criminal conduct.

Now common sense prevailed. Thesiger had a brief conversation with the Solicitor-General and he took over the proceedings. He believed inquiries of this description were generally of a disagreeable and sometimes very painful kind, and he was desirous, so far as he was able, to do justice and yet to prevent an investigation, which, though it must be painful to all, must otherwise take place. He had proposed an amount to his learned friend which he believed was satisfactory to him, and if that was so, this painful case might terminate without further delay. His learned friend thought the proposed sum of £100 to be fair and just between these parties. It was all very well mannered and in the circumstances Lennox escaped quite lightly.

There was a report of James v Lennox in the *Morning Herald* and a short note in *The Times*,[8] but Lola was then an unknown. There were far more fascinating cases in the offing, such as the action brought later that month by Lord William Paget, second son of the Marquis of Anglesey, against Lord Cardigan over his affair with Lady Frances, Paget's wife.[9] Another six months and it would be Lola who made the headlines.

The James divorce action followed a few days later, when Caroline Marden, the servant on the *Larkins*, gave her evidence and Anne Eastmond Ingram, the captain's wife, was suitably shocked: 'Within a few days of Lennox's arrival I observed Mrs James conduct towards him was unguarded and flighty ... The intimacy between them soon allowed him to visit her in her cabin. I saw her go into his cabin and vice versa ...' In fact Mrs Ingram's worry was more that they might overturn the lamps in the cabin than commit adultery. Nevertheless, 'I found it necessary in consequence of what I considered misconduct in Mrs James to discontinue associating with her and to exclude her from invitations in my cabin.' As for Ingram himself, he had never 'seen more improper conduct in a married woman. At landing I saw Mrs James and George Lennox walking arm in arm to the baggage warehouse in Portsmouth.'[10]

If the story of James's elopement with Mrs Lomer and her husband is true, why did Lola not cross-petition on the grounds of her husband's adultery? Simply, the remedy was not available to her. He had to have been cruel as well. Snoring like a boa constrictor and diarising her faults may have been annoying but this would certainly not constitute cruelty in the 1840s.

Lennox subsequently returned to India, sailing on 28 December 1843, and died there the following year, the first of a string of Lola's men to die at an early age. He took fever on the march from Secunderbad to Trichnopoly begun on 6 March 1844 and died near the village of Ootatoor on 2 May. He was just twenty-three.

As for Lola and society, if not a 'ruined woman' already she certainly was now. So what was open to her, since she could not remarry? There was her mother's trade of milliner, but that clearly would not suit her lifestyle. A governess? No more appealing. Some three years later, an advertisement by A.B. which appeared in *The Times* – promptly seized on by *Punch* – showed the downside from the governess's position: 'A lady wishing for a situation as Governess in a gentleman's family residing in the country, to instruct two little girls in music, drawing and English; a thorough knowledge of the French language is required.'

The position offered 'a comfortable home' but no salary. *Punch* wanted to know, 'Does he regard the governess as a horse that he would work like one, and in terms corresponding to keep and stabling?'[11] And when the two little girls grew up it was not likely to be out to pasture but more a question of the knacker's yard. In any event, what respectable household and sensible wife would have a woman such as Lola under their roof? Think of the risk that a straying husband or an elder son might be lured into a difficult situation.

What about the theatre? That was much more promising. It is pos-sible that even before the divorce Lola had already determined on a career on the boards. While in Scotland she 'was an unsuccessful peti-tioner to Mr Murray for leave to try her fortune as a performer on the boards of the Edinburgh Theatre'.[12] She would also claim that while on the *Larkins* she had met a Lord Arbuthnot who encouraged her to get to know as many titled men as she could, something that would help her in the theatre.

And the $10,000 – if it was anything but a convenient explanation of how she survived for so long in London – soon evaporated. But where did it go? Some of it no doubt went on a handsome pair of matched greys and a phaeton in which she drove through Hyde Park, that happy hunting ground of the high-class prostitute. Indeed an anonymous and undated letter to King Ludwig I of Bavaria suggested that she had danced naked under the name Cochrane and, at the time, that anyone with twenty francs could have had her.[13] It is more likely that she was under the protection of one or more of the many gay blades of London.

So how did Lola and the other courtesans keep themselves from becoming pregnant? It may be that she was barren, but otherwise there were a variety of devices which they could use without reliance on the creation of Colonel Condom or Cundum (or possibly Dr Conton or Gabriello Fallopio). There were a number of herbal reme-dies designed for what could delicately be described as promoting menstruation. Saxifrage, rue, sage and feverfew were all commonly used. Pennyroyal could be boiled and drunk. A number of different pessaries could also be used. At the time of Lola's birth, Francis Place, the self-educated London tailor who himself had fifteen children, was advertising for the working classes sponges 'as large as a green walnut or small apple' designed not to 'diminish the enjoyment of either party'. It was thought preferable to use them when damp and a little warm. The middle classes were to have a sponge one inch square attached to a double thread, while in his pamphlet *To the Married in Genteel Life* he suggested a soft and moistened sponge in the shape of a small ball attached to a narrow ribbon.[14]

Certainly, for part of the time Lola studied drama under the retired

actress Frances Maria 'Fanny' Kelly, the only woman to whom the
novelist Charles Lamb screwed up the courage to propose – she
refused because of the insanity in his family. Fanny Kelly made her
debut on the stage at the age of seven when she appeared in her uncle
Michael's production of *Bluebeard* at Drury Lane. She was highly
regarded in all Shakespearean roles as well as comedy and melodrama,
and was one of the first to play an entire scene with her back to the
audience when she appeared as Lisette in *The Sergeant's Wife*, John
Banim's melodrama. On 8 June 1835 she made her stage farewell at the
age of forty-five, and with her savings in 1840 opened her own theatre
and an academy for training young actresses at 73 Dean Street, Soho.
The theatrical venture was not a success. The new-fangled, cumber-
some and noisy stage machinery designed by Macdonald Stephenson
broke down disastrously. The actors could not be heard and the
theatre which had taken her life savings closed within a week. For a
time the school was a different matter and flourished. If anyone could
teach Lola stagecraft it was Fanny Kelly, and possibly it was here that
Lola met her later patron Lord Brougham, the one-time Lord Chancellor. Very much a man who liked to loll in theatrical and light circles,
he later advised Fanny when she fell further into debt and her theatre
school was seized by the landlord.[15]

Lola's theatrical pupillage was not, however, a success. Her voice
was too small for the theatre and her accent wobbled, while she
showed little aptitude as a dancer. What she did have was outstanding
beauty, presence and a fine figure. 'She has the legs of a doe but she
does not know how to use them, least of all for dancing,' thought
Charles Morice.[16] It was clearly far too late for her to be trained as a
ballet dancer proper. For the moment, however, things Spanish were
fashionable and even the great ballerinas would present a fandango or
an Oleana as an encore or a one-off piece. A Spanish dancer she would
have to be.

Naturally, later in her life Lola had a different and more engaging
version of how she learned Spanish dancing. She had, she said, been
taken by her Irish grandfather to a gypsy encampment and had been
taught there. The truth, however, was that after four months' tuition
and a short trip to Spain she metamorphosed into Lola Montez,

Spanish Dancer. Or to give her full title, Donna Maria Dolores de Porris y Montez. Some years later William Bennett, writing in the *New York Herald*, had a wonderfully garbled account of Lola's training. He claimed that after the Jameses' divorce she set herself up as a *femme de chambre* to an old roué and travelled with him to Spain. She left him there and he cut his throat. She then travelled with the matador Montez, perfecting her knowledge of her mother tongue.[17]

In the spring of 1843 Lola's investments paid a dividend when she came under the protection of James Howard Harris, the 3rd Earl of Malmesbury, himself an inveterate traveller and another who was partial to light ladies. Just how did she meet him? Both agreed in their respective recollections that it was on a train from Southampton to London, but for once Lola may have been telling more of the truth. The married Lord Malmesbury's self-whitewashing version is the more improbable of the two.

According to his memoirs he first met her when she returned from Spain where she had been taking dancing lessons. On his way to London from his country seat at Heron Court in Hampshire the train halted at Southampton, where he was asked by the Spanish consul to look after a well-born young lady who had just landed. Gentleman that he was, he did so. She told him – in poor English – that she was the widow of Don Diego Leon, who had been shot by the Carlists, and that she was going to London to sell her property and give singing lessons. Quite how a Spanish consul was deceived by Lola's fractured Spanish into thinking she was a well-born lady is questionable. Nor does it make sense that Malmesbury, who had supported the losing side in the Carlist war, would be taken in by her.[18]

The other, and more plausible, version of the story is that Malmesbury had met her rather earlier. He may have known her during the post-Lennox months in London and very likely had paid for at least part of her trip to Spain, during some of which he travelled with her. What is certain is that, charmed by her bad English if nothing else, he organised a benefit concert for her at his London house, 19 Strafford Place, at which she sang Castilian ballads and sold veils and fans 'to the party present and received a good deal of patronage'. It was he who introduced her to the solicitor turned impresario Benjamin Lumley who ran the Theatre Royal, Haymarket, specialising in Italian opera.

The Age had little doubt what had happened: '[Lola Montez] stands in an equivocal position with the Earl of Malmesbury and that in a moment of too much interest and excitement he introduced under his roof a person not in any respect qualified to make her appearance there.'[19]

But those thoughts came later. Meanwhile Lola's debut at the Haymarket theatre was keenly anticipated. This was the era of the popularity of the operas of Donizetti and Rossini and quality singers such as Julia Grisi.[20] It was also a time when there was either an entr'acte or a ballet or dance at the end of the performance, popularised by the great Fanny Elssler, some of which were highly inappropriate and certainly unrelated. One example was on 2 September 1843 when Lola danced the Bolero de Cadix in Berlin during the interval of *Fidelio*. For her debut on 3 June, however, Lola was to dance the Cachucha, 'El Oleano', this time appropriately enough between the acts of *The Barber of Seville*. Lumley certainly knew how to advertise his wares. He arranged that there should be an interview with the beautiful señora and, written by the elderly and captivated 'Q', a series of puffs duly appeared in the *Morning Post*: 'Her figure was even more attractive than her face, lovely as the latter was . . . Her foot and ankle were almost faultless.' But it was her conversation that really captivated him:

> Now, who is there, you will let me ask that had ever had half an hour's conversation with the Donna Lola, that can, for an instant doubt, but he has spoken with a sparklingly brilliant creature. I at any rate certainly do not. She is probably enough of that genius, which in England, is invariably called 'fast' but her speed is indubitably that of talent.

Lola told him 'anecdote after anecdote of Spanish life, many of them very "fast" ones indeed with a verve and entrain which were irresistible'.[21] It was hardly surprising that the audience, which included the Duke of Wellington, the Duke and Duchess of Cambridge and Lord Brougham, read like an edition of Debrett.

Everyone was seeing new clothes, for the newspapers on the

following Monday were almost unanimous in their praise, even if some expressed certain reservations. The *Morning Post*, of course, led the chorus of approval:

> Her wonderfully supple form assumed attitudes that were not dreamt of – the line of beauty being still preserved, in spite of the boldness of her movement. At one moment she bent down to the ground, moving her arms as if she were gathering roses in a parterre – and at the next moment starting to her feet, and raising her arms playfully in the air, as if she were showering the flowers on a lover's head. At one moment, her dancing represented seduction and entreaty – and next, she suddenly stamped her feet on the ground, placing her hand on her hip with a look of pride and defiance, like a fencer bidding his antagonist to come on if he dare and meet his doom.

The *Morning Herald* summarised, 'The young lady came, saw, and conquered', and its critic even dared to compare Lola's skills with the classical ballerinas:

> She is evidently a superior pantomimist, and understands the expression which may be evolved by bodily action and the gesticulation of the limbs. Her play with her arms is quite beautiful, and the inflection of her wrists is free and graceful in the extreme ... She has not quite the refinement of Fanny Elssler in her mode of executing character steps, but she has an equal buoyancy of manner, and can present phrases of satire and frolic to the eye just as happily.

The Times was grateful at last to have seen 'a Spanish dance by a Spaniard, executed after the Spanish fashion'. Its critic wrote, 'Her dance is not characterised by buoyancy, by remarkable grace, but it may be said to have much intensity.' The critic of the *Evening Chronicle* was able to analyse the reason for the sensation in some detail:

> Donna Montez is not a *dancer*, in the general acceptation of the word. She has (or at least displays) none of the *execution* of the art – no pirouettes, no entrechats, no wonderful displays of agility. Her dancing is little more than a gesture and attitude, but every gesture and attitude seems to be the impulse of passion acting on the proud and haughty mind of a

beautiful Spaniard; for she is exquisitely beautiful, in form and feature, realizing the images called up by a perusal of Spanish romance. Her dancing is what we have always understood Spanish dancing to be – a kind of _monodrama_ – a representation of various emotions succeeding each other with great rapidity, but with coherence and consistency.

Reviewing the event the _Era_, which over the years was to be ambivalent towards Lola, on this occasion thought: '[The] only fault was it was far too short for the 1,000 admirers; Donna Lola enchanted everyone . . . We never remember seeing the habitués both young and old taken by more agreeable surprise than this bewitching lady excited.' The _Weekly Dispatch_ thought the performance to be 'a real Spanish dance performed by a real Spaniard, Donna Montez who gave it a different character to Spanish dancing, imparted dignity to it'.[22]

But the jig was up even before the reviews appeared. The story which has passed into legend is that a spurned admirer, Lord Thomas Ranelagh, who had met Lola at Fanny Kelly's, revenged himself on her by calling out, 'Look, it's Betty James' and so ruining her performance.[23] It is very doubtful that the Ranelagh incident ever took place. It was never mentioned by the critics and Benjamin Lumley's memoirs give the lie to the tale. The writer 'Q', who is often blamed for the Ranelagh story, is more or less innocent. He merely wrote that there was whistling while she danced, which may very well have been true. There were usually pro and anti-Lola claques whenever she danced. What is much more likely is that immediately after the performance a number of men gathered around the unfortunate Lumley explaining to him that Lola was no more Spanish than they were. Within days the story that Lola was indeed the absent Lieutenant James's wife swept through _le tout_ London.

As was always the case when cornered, Lola mounted a spirited counter-attack. On 13 June Donna Lola, or someone on her behalf, began her career as a letter writer to the newspapers, a hobby she pursued with enthusiasm for the rest of her life. This time she wrote to the _Era_ saying she was

> cruelly annoyed by reports that I am not really the person I pretend to be but that I have long been known in London as a disreputable character.

I am a native of Seville and in the year 1833 when ten years old was sent to a Catholic lady at Bath where I remained seven months and was then taken back to my parents.

Her imperfect English was learned at Bath from an Irish nurse who had for many years been in her family. She had, she said, never seen London before she arrived on 4 April that year. She had referred the matter to her solicitors.

The *Morning Post* duly reported that two Spaniards had interviewed her. One said she came from Seville and the other from Manilla. The paper thought she should be given the benefit of the doubt and should dance again.[24] Others, with some accuracy, thought she had taken her name from the matador Francisco Montez.

The Age was, however, particularly displeased with her. She arrived unannounced at their offices where she remained for four hours, during much of which she perched on a desk. The paper thought, 'she knows more of Clarges Street or thereabouts than she does of the Teatro Real, Sevilla', identifying her as 'Mrs James whose pony-phaeton and pair of greys rendered her some time since a very conspicuous lady in the drives of Hyde Park'. As every respectable Spanish grandee should be, Lola was accompanied by a duenna. Unfortunately hers was in the form of a Mrs Clarke, an 'ancient member of the Opera Corps de Ballet' whom the paper also knew well as 'lately of the prime locality of George Street, Adelphi and subsequently of Chandos Street':

> We do not believe one syllable of this story which is undoubtedly an emanation from some *mauvaise langue*; but one thing there is no disputing – that Mrs James, under the designation of Donna Lola Montez *did* dine at the table of Lord and Lady Malmesbury; and the only conclusion to come to is that if it were possible for the world's scandal to be true, his LORDSHIP is a villain; and if it be false he is a victim.[25]

After all, while a man in society could and probably should have an actress or dancer under his protection, under no circumstances should she be introduced to his wife. Malmesbury sprang to his own defence:

My attention has just been drawn to a prominent paragraph in the last *Age* newspaper which states that I introduced the Spanish dancer Montez, to Lady Malmesbury at my table.

You will oblige me much by allowing me, through the medium of your journal, to declare this assertion to be scandalous falsehood.

The person in question brought some Spanish fans and lace to my house, which we bought of her, believing her to be what she stated – a refugee from Seville, desirous to obtain an engagement at some theatre in London.[26]

There was a little support for Lola. A Mark Barnard of 28 Southampton Street, Strand wrote in her favour saying that any doubt should be resolved in favour of a débutante. The *Era* regretted it had not received the letter early enough for it to have been published in its first edition and so, for a fortnight, Donna Lola faded from the newspapers. She never again appeared at the Haymarket and Lumley wrote in his memoirs: 'And it is certain that I acted wisely, though I had to exercise the virtue of self-denial: as there is little doubt from the reception that she met with at the first night, that the lovely lady would have drawn large sums to my treasury, for some time at least.'[27]

'Q' wrote that Lola disappeared from her lodgings and vanished that night, but he was wrong. On 10 July she appeared in London on the stage for the last time when she danced the Oleano and La Sevillana at a benefit night at Covent Garden. Benefits were then regular features of the stage. Throughout her life Lola, in common with many others on the stage, was to be generous in her appearances at such events. The beneficiary was expected to pay the artistes or persuade them to appear without fee and he or she bore the cost of hiring the theatre, something that could cost two or three hundred pounds. As a result they were not something to be undertaken lightly. The dramatist and librettist Edward Fitzball had been in the process of arranging one for himself but despaired of finding performers to draw the crowds. In Regent Street he met the popular singer Stretton and complained about his problem. Stretton suggested, 'You could secure the Lola Montez,' adding that she had turned down £50 to appear at his own benefit. Nevertheless Fitzball went to see her at her home, where she was sitting for her portrait. She thought not but added, "'I will however ask my mamma" – I think she said mamma – "what she thinks of it; give me your address, I will write to you". When he returned home the next day he found Lola sitting on the sofa chatting with his wife 'as familiarly as if they had known each other for years'.

It was announced that she would be making this one appearance. 'Next Thursday she departs for St Petersburg.' Lola arrived for his benefit in a splendid carriage accompanied by her maid and, unsurprisingly, Fitzball was another who was captivated by her: 'I have seen some sylphs appear and female forms of the most dazzling beauty in ballets and fairy dramas but the most dazzling and perfect form I ever did gaze upon, was Lola Montez, in her splendid white and gold attire studded with diamonds that night.'

After her performance, when he went to thank her, she 'held up her hand in graceful remonstrance . . . she was all that was generous, lady-like and gentle'. Fitzball never saw her again.[28] It was the first of many benefits she gave over the years, without seeking payment, to help other artistes, but the performance was reported as being thinly attended.

And what did her mother and stepfather think of her new career? According to Lola her mother put on mourning and sent out notices announcing her daughter's death. If she did, this would be in line with the attitude of families to actresses in early Victorian times. But none of the death notices survive, and Lola was always a consummate liar and fantasist when it suited her. On this occasion she was persuading Ludwig that as an 'orphan' she needed special love and care.[29]

Meanwhile Lola had new admirers. One of them apparently was Lord Arbuthnot, whom she claimed to have met on the *Larkins* and who later introduced her to the German princeling Heinrich Reuss-Lobenstein-Ebersdorff LXXII (all the men in the family were named Heinrich, which accounts for his high number).[30] Heinrich had two eminently desirable qualities – he was both wealthy and elderly. Apart from the family's curious habit of naming and numbering its sons, Heinrich's great gift to German culture is the word *Prinzipienreiter*, meaning a man obsessed with principles. It stems from a speech to his subjects telling them they should address his officers by their titles and that for twenty years he had been 'riding about on a principle'.

In June and July Heinrich was in London on a semi-state visit, staying at the Coburg Hotel, Charles Street, Grosvenor Square, dining with Victoria and Albert, attending Hampton Races, a Grand Ball at the French Embassy and the Duke of Wellington's Ball on 6 July, and being taken on a special train to see the Italian opera. Certainly someone introduced Lola, for Heinrich paid her debts and – much as one might say, 'Oh, do look me up if you are ever in Germany' – gave her a loose invitation to visit his court. The invitation was something upon which she immediately seized and which almost as immediately he came to regret deeply.[31]

·CHAPTER THREE·

✦

Lola in Europe

So, TOWARDS THE END OF July 1843 Lola descended on Prince Heinrich, if not quite uninvited, at least unexpected. Her visit was not a success. His was a tiny princedom with some 20,000 subjects, and while he may have been able to deal adequately with the local gentry and serving girls, like many and more experienced men after him he had no idea how to cope with the little panther who pounced on him and his household. According to her memoirs Lola had first travelled to Hamburg, which she had disliked, and so she sent the Prince a letter telling him she was in Leipzig and was looking forward to seeing him. She arrived at Ebersdorf on the Saale, where the unsuspecting Heinrich ruled.

From the start she proved to be difficult. Heinrich had sent a six-horse coach to meet her. Bored by the journey and with no conversation available since his servants spoke little French, she decided she would take the reins. Sensibly the coachman refused, saying the horses were inexperienced. He received a blow for his pains.

A reception for her that evening went well enough but, as the days passed, she became increasingly bored and tiresome, making ill-received jokes about her host. Worse, while walking his St Bernard dog, Turk, in the gardens, she cut off the heads of his carefully cultivated flowers, wove them into a garland and put them round the head of Heinrich's favourite horse. The Prince was not amused.

At a picnic arranged at his hunting lodge he was even less amused. She mocked the efforts of a band brought to play for the guests and then, when some local children were pressed into singing a folk song, she covered her ears, told the Prince to get rid of them and promptly left the table. The Prince went after her and took her wrist. Instantly she went for the dagger she kept, realised in time what she was doing and smiled an apology. But there was worse to come. One of the choirboys began to climb a tree and Lola set Turk on him. The boy was pinned down by the drooling dog and the Prince himself had to pull the animal away.

Now it was only a matter of minutes before the visit would end. An introduction to the concertmaster in Dresden was hastily drafted and, in an envelope rather nastily addressed to Mrs James, was handed to Lola by an aide who told her the Prince wished her to leave that day. It is possible Heinrich may also have given her a pourboire to help her on her way. She more or less kidnapped the aide, who was forced to drive with her, and insisted he come to her room at Ebersdorf where she gave him a pair of castanets. The waiting coach then took her, *sans* aide, to Dresden where she arrived on 7 August and booked into the Hotel de Wien.

By now her father had become General Don Diego Leon and, for the first and probably the only time in her life, she had several brothers, all of whom were officers in the service of Don Carlos. Two days later she danced at the court theatre. She appeared twice more in the week but her audience was divided. The young men were enthralled, the critics and the remainder of the audience less so. She certainly acquired more letters of introduction, although probably not the one she claimed to have received from the Queen of Saxony to be presented to the Queen of Prussia. And it was on to Berlin.[1]

By October Lola was reported to be in that city with her mother and sister – who can they possibly have been? – where she was 'bewitching the lions of the capital'. 'She is only 19 years of age and is said to be the daughter of a General of Brigade who died at Cadiz in 1841. Query: Is this the Donna Lola who obtained one night's popularity at the Italian theatre last season in London?' asked the *Era*.[2]

Among Lola's admirers there were bound to be undesirables. Accosted in the street one night, she was saved by the thirteen-year-old Hans von Bülow, son of the writer Eduard, who invited her to the hotel where he was staying with his father. Eduard was entranced and later wrote a short story, 'Die neue Melusine', about a ballerina. It told how she danced a Spider Dance and lived in a hotel where she ate little and spoke bad French. Even those who suffered from her temper soon forgave her. She not only held court at breakfast but also at late-night smokers where, when the conversation became blue, she would affect not to have heard what was said. Melusine was clearly Lola.[3]

As for Lola's dancing, it was more of the same. She debuted in the Oleano but her reception was mixed. Her beauty was beyond compare but her dancing was not. One critic thought that 'the great Taglioni wrote world history with her feet but Lola writes Casanova's Memoirs with her whole body'.[4] She danced twice more in public, in Berlin and then at the City Theatre in Potsdam where she performed the Oleano before King Friedrich Wilhelm IV.

It was in Berlin that the first of her celebrated public outbursts occurred. As with all Lola's stories, there are a number of versions differing in the extent to which they hold her culpable. She had either brought two fine Andalusian horses from Spain – which seems unlikely, given her adventures and the short time between leaving London and arriving in Berlin – or more likely had rented them and was riding one at a parade in honour of the state visit of the King's brother-in-law, Czar Nicholas I of Russia.

On 17 September the Czar and the King were due to take the salute in the Friedrichfelde. It was to be a massive display with the Prussian army appearing in newly designed ceremonial uniforms. The public began arriving at 5 am for the parade, and very soon efforts by the police to hold back the massive crowds were under siege. Regularly riders and drivers broke the lines and mingled with the soldiers to get a better viewing position. Lola rode into an enclosure near the King reserved for the nobility. The charitable view is that she found herself there when her horse shied at the sound of ceremonial gunfire: 'the young artist repaired thither on horseback, and there held herself at a respectful distance from the suite of their Majesties but the moment the artillery began to fire Mlle Montez' horse took fright and galloped with its rider in the midst of Staff of the two Sovereigns and suddenly stopped there'.[5]

The less charitable view is that she was anxious to make an impression on either a current or potential lover. Again there are two accounts of what happened next; whichever is preferred, from then on matters escalated. The more favourable to Lola, probably put about by herself, is that a gendarme hit her horse with the side of his sword. Lola would never tolerate what she saw as cruelty to animals and, in reply, she slashed the man with her whip. The less favourable is that he had merely tried to grab hold of the bridle to restrain the horse.

Whichever is correct, there were immediate and serious repercussions and the incident raised a number of problems. A man attacked in this way by another man of equal social status could seek a duel. If the attack had been by a social inferior then a whipping could have been administered. But an attack by a woman? It was not even that she was defending her honour, in which case public opinion would have been on her side.[6] The answer in Lola's case was a summons to appear in one of the lower criminal courts.

This was delivered the next day by a *huissier*. Lola, no lover of the police or authority in general, promptly flew into a tantrum. This was a standard tactic to be repeated throughout her life and throughout the world – Warsaw, Munich, London, New Orleans, Sydney. She simply tore up the summons, threw the pieces at the *huissier* and stamped on them when they fluttered to the ground. In an instant things had got out of hand. She was charged with contempt of the judicial process. Hitting the officer could have resulted in thirteen months but the moment she tore up the summons it suddenly became an affair worth between three and five years.

Lola must have had good connections to intercede for her and one of them may well have been Prince Albrecht, the King's brother, with whom she was said to have had a short affair while in Berlin.[7] There were stories that she had received four months' imprisonment and had to be pardoned by the King himself, and a variety of other stories that the gendarme had apologised for his behaviour, or that he had as a matter of gallantry asked for no action to be pursued. Over the years Lola generally had little to say on the matter. Later she would claim that the trouble had been over her smoking in the street. There is no doubt the story greatly helped her notoriety and reputation, which were, of course, not necessarily synonymous. But whichever version is correct – an apology made by Lola or on her behalf is much the most likely – it was time to move north. Leaving Berlin was probably the price she was obliged to pay if no sanctions were to be imposed on her. Next she headed for Poland, 'where she now is, and where, in all probability mindful of a lesson which might have been severer, she will henceforth show more temper and prudence'.[8] She did not.

As was often the case throughout the nineteenth century, Poland was in something of a political turmoil. Lola's arrival did nothing to calm things down. In 1831 an uprising by a group of young Polish officers had been cruelly suppressed. The university was closed in 1836, leading to the Great Emigration.

On the artistic front, Louis Thierry and Maurice Pion had been brought to Warsaw as, respectively, director and principal dancer of the ballet. In 1833 Pion had become director. He remained in the post until 1842 and succeeded in tightening up the performances, which had become increasingly slipshod.[9] Then on 1 September 1842 Ignacy Abramowicz was appointed as director. Handed a smooth-running machine, he somewhat incongruously combined his directorship with his other post as chief of police.

Unusually, there is a contemporary and relatively dispassionate memoir of Lola's time in Warsaw by Kazimierz Skibinski, a provincial actor and entrepreneur. Lola signed a contract for five appearances at 3,000 zlotys a performance. True to form, she immediately found a number of protectors including Count Zamoyski, a government minister named Turkull, Franciszek Potocki, and others including the banker Piotr Steinkeller. She also had the support of Antonini Lesznowski, the editor of *Gazeta Warszawska*. Skibinski thought that, in artistic terms, her first performance of the Cachucha was an affront to Mlles Wendt and Konstancja Turcynowic, the principal ballerinas of the company, but with the applause and claque organised by her protectors she was well enough received. At her second appearance there was a greater division of opinion and her reception was more blurred. As Lola would find time and time again throughout her career, there was a smaller audience for her third performance and now she refused to appear. The Italian singer Signora Assandri was sent for and performed an aria but by then the interval had lasted over an hour. The contract for Lola's last two performances was cancelled – the disinterested may think with some justification.

Lola appealed to Steinkeller and her other protectors, who suggested to Abramowicz that if he did not reinstate her she would speak ill of Poland when she continued her travels. Reluctantly, and as it turned out ill-advisedly, he did so. She then asked Steinkeller to provide a claque for her and he did, buying 100 tickets for blacksmiths from his factory. They were to watch him and when he applauded so should they. The performance started with hissing and the blacksmiths cheered. Now whistles were produced by the anti-Lola faction. She stopped dancing and went to the front of the stage where she gestured at the Abramowicz box. The curtain went down and his family went home.

Another version elaborates a little. After the whistling she stopped dancing and addressed the audience in French, saying that she knew they were not responsible for the noise and pointing at the box. The public then began demonstrating in her favour and now she reappeared, gesturing to the box once more, possibly deliberately pointing her backside at it.

There had already been bad blood between Abramowicz and Lola. Again accounts vary. It is clear that the man saw himself as having something of a *droit de seigneur* over ballerinas and after the first performance he took Lola back in his carriage to the Hotel Rzymski where she was staying. He made an approach to her, whereupon she pulled the cord, signalling the driver to stop, and ordered Abramowicz out. When he tried to argue she pulled her dagger on him and drove off, leaving him in the snow and wind. From then on he tormented her, arresting her servant and arranging the final hostile demonstration at the theatre.

In her lectures Lola claimed that it was Field Marshal Ivan

Fedorovich Paskevich at whom the invective was really directed. He was short in stature and when he laughed he threw back his head, exposing an artificial gold roof to his palate. 'A death's head making love to a lady could not have been a more disgusting or horrible sight.' She regarded him as gross. After the first performance he had invited her to his box and inspected her like a horse before remarking, 'Well, she is nothing special.' Her reply was, 'Your Grace, if you think that you have told me something new, you are mistaken. I heard it already in London and Berlin.' Undeterred, he had visited to proposition her in her dressing room after the third, aborted performance, offering a country estate and diamonds, and she had given him short shrift. It was he who ordered her expulsion. What is certain is that after the gesture in the direction of the director's box the crowd rose in her favour.

Students, possibly egged on by Steinkeller, unharnessed her horses and themselves pulled her carriage back to the hotel. From little acorns do great oak trees grow and now there were fears that she could actually spark a nationalist uprising. The next morning she was summoned by the military governor but refused to appear, demanding to see the Prince himself. When she tried to enter the Prince's quarters a policeman stood in her way. She struck out at him with her stiletto, fortunately hitting only his bandolier. Two gendarmes now replaced the policeman and a senior officer came to tell her that there was an order that she must accompany him to the border. No one could ever accuse Lola of cowardice, certainly not when her temper was up. She refused to go and when Abramowicz appeared she told him the same. The Spanish consul was sent for. She screamed at him, telling him that instead of protecting her he was conspiring against her. It is interesting how the consul went along with the fiction that she was the daughter of a Carlist general, for she still spoke the language poorly. Lola was put under arrest in her hotel room and in retaliation refused to come out when ordered.

Now Steinkeller was summoned and told that unless he had her at the border within the hour he would be held responsible for the previous evening's disturbance. He persuaded Lola to drive with him and his wife to their country residence, but by then the students were about to riot. Lola, Steinkeller and his wife set off for the border accompanied by an officer and two soldiers. The students now stormed the firehouses around the hotel and took forty sleighs to drive out with her. They were detained at the city's limits. When Steinkeller returned from depositing Lola at the Prussian border he was also arrested and spent the next month in prison. Some of the students received a flogging. A cartoon was circulated in Warsaw depicting a crucified Lola hanging between Steinkeller and Lesznowski, with Abramowicz on horseback piercing her side with a cossack pike.[10]

Some years later an account of the incident appeared in a letter to the *Boston Times*. Lola's conduct in Poland was given a vigorous defence by a pianist, S. M. A. Wolowski, who was in Warsaw at the time. He more or less confirms Lola's version of events:

> The eventful night arrived and when the Countess appeared before a splendid audience in the great theatre of Warsaw her performance was interrupted by the appearance of an officer of police who threatened that if she did not immediately proceed to meet the prince, who was waiting for her, he would insult her before the whole audience. The lady did not, for a moment, lose her presence of mind. With a degree of scorn and contempt impossible for me to describe she rejected the proposition and drawing her dagger, she exclaimed with the greatest energy, 'If you dare to approach one step as certainly as I am Lola Montez I'll kill you on the spot'.

She then gave an early version of her standard appeal for fair play and protection:

> 'However the Poles may be oppressed they will feel and resent this cruelty to an injured woman. Yes, I appeal to your chivalry – I place my personal security and my life under the protection of my audience the citizens of Warsaw.'
>
> The effect was magical – the audience rose en masse and the theatre rang with cheers and applause.[11]

So now it was another train north on what was becoming a seemingly endless journey to St Petersburg. She appeared twice in Stettin and then moved on to Danzig on 9 December, where she appeared three times. High prices were paid, not to observe her ability as a dancer but to see this already notorious woman herself. By early January she was in Königsberg, where again tickets sold at higher than usual prices and the reviews were generally favourable. It was then on to Riga.

It is not clear whether she ever reached St Petersburg. She claimed she was well received there and that she had an audience with the Czar and his ministers, but again something went wrong and now she decided to try Paris. Either there was a scandal or she realised she was not getting the bookings she needed. So it was back on a journey of which she wrote, 'If the journey to St Petersburg was boring, the trip back was more so. Nature had spread her white winding sheet over the countryside through which I travelled, giving it a stifling monotony.' Generals Winter and Boredom were firmly in command.

Then, at one of the stops to change horses, came a moment which could genuinely be described as life-changing. While waiting in an inn she saw in a newspaper that Franz Liszt, the great pianist and womaniser, was giving a series of concerts in Dresden and one in Dessau, on 24 February. Lola decided she simply had to meet him. And meet him she did. By the end of February Lola had become Liszt's latest conquest, or vice versa. Initially, being seen on the arm of the great pianist cannot have done Lola any harm whatsoever, but she soon found it was reflected glory, something that did not appeal to her. She was a personality in her own right.

In her heavily expurgated autobiography based on her American lectures, Lola is absolutely silent about her relationship with Liszt. But it was certainly short-lived and, given their mutually fiery temperaments, doubtless stormy. They were together in Dresden, where Liszt particularly wished to hear Wagner's *Rienzi*, a long and complicated account of fourteenth-century Rome. Liszt played a concert on 27 February which included Beethoven's 'Emperor' Concerto and two days later he took Lola to see the tedious five-hour masterpiece.

In one of the intervals Liszt and Lola went backstage to meet the composer and his lifelong friend Joseph Tichatschek, playing *Rienzi*, in the latter's dressing room. The meeting was not a success. Wagner wrote: 'Liszt's curious lifestyle at the time, which constantly surrounded him with distracting and annoying elements, kept us on this occasion from achieving any productive rapport.'

The distracting and annoying element was Lola, whom Wagner disliked intensely and immediately. He thought her almost too beautiful and too elegantly dressed and she seemed to look at him with insolent eyes.[12] Years later, hearing of her death, he was just as critical. His wife Cosima wrote:

> At table the conversation turns to Lola Montez. Describing her wretched ending, I say, 'The poor creature!' Richard admonishes me severely, saying that such heartless daemonic beings should not be grieved over, one should reserve one's pity for others. He is certainly right, yet badness seems to me always pitiable and nothing more worthy of our compassion than a wretched ending.[13]

Coming from Wagner, who was known as Lolus because of his relationship with Ludwig's grandson the Mad King of Bavaria, that could, in modern terms, be said to be a bit rich.

The relationship with Liszt could not and did not last. In the middle of March the pianist, as generous with his musical favours as Lola, gave a benefit concert in Dresden for the Italian tenor and composer Luigi Pantaleoni, whom he had befriended.[14] Concerts of the time bore little resemblance to those of the present day. There would be an overture, various songs by different singers punctuated by a piano or violin solo and then, to end, quite often an impromptu improvisation by the maestro. Naturally Pantaleoni appeared, but he sang poorly and too much in falsetto.

Afterwards, at a dinner – Lola says it was a breakfast – for Liszt, Lola was the only woman present. She found that Pantaleoni was not on the guest list and promptly invited him. Rather ungraciously, the tenor did not appreciate the gesture. He quarrelled with Gottfried Saemper, who had designed the Opera House, actually coming to blows, and he and Lola rowed violently and publicly. Pantaleoni said he was not a gendarme and Lola promptly slapped him. He then made such a rude gesture at her that – however unlikely it might seem – according to Lola, she fainted. That is Lola's version of events. Such newspaper reports as survive mention the quarrel. One suggested that

Dresden now added its name to the German and other cities from which she was expelled.[15]

Any thoughts of further travel with Lola to his engagements in the north were now abandoned by the pianist, who was said to be frightened of her temper. A story has grown up that Liszt paid the manager of a hotel for the furniture she would damage when she found he was gone. In a variation, Liszt paid the manager to lock her in her room for twelve hours so he could make good his escape. Probably neither is true, but that does not make them bad stories.[16] Possibly Liszt found that the demanding Lola was becoming wearisome; perhaps playing second fiddle to the handsome Hungarian was increasingly unacceptable for her. However short it may have been, the affair with Lola was sufficient for the comtesse Marie d'Agoult, Liszt's mistress and the mother of their three children, finally to break off their relationship. It also did the pianist considerable harm in the eyes of his public. From Lola's point of view there was one benefit. Whatever the reason for the ending of their relationship, he did at least provide her with letters of introduction to his friends in Paris. Throughout the remainder of their lives neither spoke ill of the other.

· CHAPTER FOUR ·

Lola in Paris

IN EARLY MARCH 1844, armed with her letters of introduction, Lola travelled to Paris, already the home of the great courtesans of her time. Almost exact contemporaries were the Russian-born La Païva and Alice Ozy. Born the same year as Lola, in her earlier days Alice had toured Russia and over the years was the lover of Théophile Gautier, Victor Hugo's son Charles and Gustave Doré, as well as the duc d'Aumont. Also in Paris were Marie Duplessis, the tragic Dame aux Camélias, loved by Liszt and immortalised by Alexandre Dumas junior; Apollonie Sabatier, known as La Présidente and the lover of Baudelaire; and Élisabeth-Céleste Vénard, known as Mogador, whom Lola would meet again in Australia.[1]

However unappealing it may be to Lola's twentieth-century admirers, it is an almost inescapable conclusion that, while she may not have been exactly on the streets during this and her later stay in Paris, in effect she was keeping herself by prostitution. Indeed in many ways Lola conforms to the stereotype of a prostitute – a lover of children and animals and happiness in the countryside, from where prostitutes often originated. She also comes into the category of fallen women who find themselves attracted to religious piety. 'Many of them refrain from all religious duties, on account of their unworthiness; although most of them are anxious for religious consolation when dangerous or fatal illness assails them.'[2]

During the first half of the nineteenth century, prostitution in Paris was carefully regulated. At the lowest end of the scale were the *filles soumises*, who were required to submit to regular checks for venereal disease. These girls could either have registered voluntarily or been registered after being stopped by the police. Girls might operate on their own – pimping at the time was not as we know it today, but a more relaxed affair in which a girl might choose and discard her protector – or in a brothel; the houses of highest class were those in the rue Le Peletier near the then Opera House and the Jockey Club.

There was also a strict order as to how approaches were to be made, depending upon the district in which the girl worked. Near the Bourse and the Opéra an approach was made by eye contact; in and around the Palais-Royale, Montmartre and Saint-Denis she should whisper in the man's ear. In the Latin Quarter she should address the man as *tu* and in the Cité, by no means the elegant area of today, she should accost the potential client and, taking his arm, drag him off by force.

The author Parent-Duchâtelet estimated that in 1836 there were as many as 18,000 working girls in Paris, of whom half were kept women or *femmes galantes*, outside the jurisdiction of the police. Because of the lack of controls he regarded them as the most dangerous of prostitutes.

During her first visit Lola probably worked as a *lorette*, a high-class prostitute living in the area of the rue Notre-Dame de Lorette, which runs from behind Gare St Lazare near the boulevard des Italiens up to Montmartre. The attraction of the area was that it had new and cheap housing and was near the grand boulevards and clients. The down side was the damp.

The life of a *lorette* was a complicated one – described by Henri Murger as having a boudoir, 'a counter where she slices pieces of her heart, as though they were slices of roast beef'. Her day required a carefully kept diary so that one lover did not happen upon another. There was also need for a hairdresser, a pedicurist and the inevitable piano-mistress, in reality her *éminence grise*.[3] In Lola's case the *éminence grise* was likely to have been the shadowy Madame Azam, who with her husband kept a hotel on the boulevard des Italiens and with whom for a time Lola stayed.

The likelihood is that until Lola found her protector in the form of the journalist Alexandre Henri Dujarier, she had worked as a *fille en carte*, a girl whose services were bought by a group of friends *en bloc*, each of whom would visit her on a different day. The great courtesan Marie Duplessis, La Dame aux Camélias, was said at the beginning of her career to have had a cupboard with seven drawers, in each of which she kept a shirt for her lover of that night. The benefit to the girl was a sort of stability, while to the men there was, in theory if not in practice, a diminution in the risk of catching venereal disease. Lola also worked as an artist's model, posing for Horace Vernet's painting *Prise de la Smalah d'Abdel Kader* which is now in the Musée National du Château de Versailles.

One of Lola's letters of introduction from Liszt was to the highly influential critic Jules Janin, and a flattering note appeared on her behalf on 18 March in *Le Journal des Débats*. Another was to the young journalist Pier-Angelo Fiorentino, born in Italy in 1806 and an uncredited part of the Dumas writing factory, who almost certainly was an early Parisian lover. Count Henri de Viel-Castel rather sniffily described him as 'Fiorentino et d'autres Bohèmes' and thought him to be the worst of the yellow-press journalists.[4] He had fled from Naples following a duel with an actor at the Théâtre Royal, San Carlo. Now he was working for the paper *Le Corsair* and he championed Lola. Described as most handsome, his only physical flaw was his mouth – his lips were said to be thick and red like the edge of a chamber-pot, but he covered them with a handsome moustache. He was soon enslaved and it was he who led the clamour for Lola to appear on the stage of the Opéra.[5] She had been taking lessons from Hippolyte Barrez, the ballet-master at the theatre, and Leon Pillet, the manager, was being pressured to engage her. A week after Janin's article, Fiorentino wrote in her praise and the same day the *Journal des Théâtres* suggested that if the Opéra would not have her there were other theatres which should. When Dumas spoke well of her, as did Pillet's protégé, the soprano Rosina Stoltz, she was booked.

Now, among others, she took as a lover Marius Petipa, creator of the ballets *Swan Lake*, *Sleeping Beauty* and *The Nutcracker*, who was engaged at the Opéra at the time. It was, by all accounts, another tempestuous relationship. A story about its end was that when Petipa said he was leaving, Lola told him that her ring contained a deadly poison which would kill them both. Petipa managed to send the ring to a chemist who said the grey powder was simply ashes. Unfortunately Lola also attacked Petipa's father, Jean, when he came to watch her rehearsing in a hall in the rue Victoire. She began to beat him and had to be pulled off the elderly man.[6]

On 27 March 1844 Lola made her Paris debut appearing at the Opéra, then at Salle Le Peletier, a short distance from the home of the Jockey Club. She was on stage after a performance of Weber's *Der Freischutz* in *Le Bal de Don Juan*. A short piece, this was one of many designed so that members of the Jockey Cub could see and admire the legs of their current girlfriends. The house was packed, and one of the enduring stories of her first appearance is that on her point she removed a garter and threw it into the audience. Variations are that she threw her underwear, but it seems that in fact she tossed a ballet shoe which was caught by an Alfred de Bellemont.[7] This incident apart, her dancing did not greatly please the spectators. They preferred Petipa and Mabille, and a polka, then the rage of Paris, danced by Coballi and Mlle Maria. When Lola returned for *Les Boleros de Cadix* as the final number she was not well received.

Three days later she repeated the roles after the premiere of Halevy's *Il Lazzarone*. Her name had already been blacked out on the posters. It was not a success and there was a good deal of hissing, although Fiorentino put the best possible interpretation on her performance: 'She astonished and charmed the public.' Other critics were by no means as generous. There were ironic suggestions that she would be appearing at the Circus and in a new ballet, the Bolero of the Whip, based on a Russian air. The unfortunate Leon Pillet, manager of the Opéra, came under fire for even allowing her near the place. Her contract was not extended.[8]

The next eleven months were, however, good ones for Lola. Within weeks she had become a *lionesse de Paris* with, among others, Fiorentino, on whom she could always rely for good notices, shouting her praises, 'bearing arms like Grisier, peppering the targets at Lepage's shooting gallery'.[9] It was a time of the lions of the city, who roamed within strict

social boundaries. They rose at ten and after their toilette and dinner
went to the Bois for the afternoon. There the lionesses drove in tilburys,
followed by gentlemen on horseback or in other carriages. It was impossible to drive with the women; their skirts did not allow the room. Then
it was to the restaurants on boulevard des Italiens, which had been pave-
mented in 1830. These *gants jaunes* only travelled to the chausée d'Antin,
to the passage de l'Opéra and perhaps just to the faubourg Montmartre.
It was regarded as very bad form to be seen any further afield. On Italiens they hardly ever strolled past the Café Anglais and never showed
themselves after the Variétés. Tortoni's, on the boulevard, was famous for
the ice creams sold there. 'Everyone who counted in Paris in the 1840s
used to pass there every day at about 5 o'clock,' wrote Henri de Villemessant. On the boulevard there was also the Maison d'Or, which opened in
1841. In it the restaurant le Grand Six was as famous as le Grand Seize at
the Café Anglais. Lola took to the life enthusiastically.

Lola may also have become a temporary mistress of Alexandre
Dumas senior. André Maurois argues that there is no hard evidence
for this, pointing to a letter she wrote some years later while in
Munich which, he suggests, shows Dumas hardly knew her. In fact her
letter was a reply to one from Dumas, and given the surveillance she
was under in the autumn of 1846 it is hardly likely she would write in
unguarded terms. She certainly knew the writer well. Given the sexual
appetites of both, it would not be in the least surprising if from time
to time she had ended in, or at least on, his purple bed.

There were occasionally glowing reports of her in the English
papers: Lola was a fine shot, and had left a card at Lepage's shooting
gallery perforated with pistol balls fired at double coups. The *Era*
announced that:

> the most famous Parisian shots allowed themselves vanquished by this
> prowess of the fair Andalusian. It is said that this dancer, little satisfied
> with the criticism of our dramatic editors who treated her, as she imag-
> ines, somewhat cavalierly at the time of her debts at the opera, has given
> them this significant hint to be more circumspect in the future. A hand-
> some woman, who has the aim sure, and the *coup d'oeil* of Mdlle Montez
> is certainly an actrice *à menager*.[10]

By the winter of 1844 Lola's constant lover was the editor and part owner of *La Presse*, Alexandre Henri Dujarier, who was regarded as being honourable, straightforward and generous in business. He spent his money freely but he had an aggressive way of speaking and he was also regarded as ill-spirited at the gaming tables. It is not clear where or how Lola met him. It could have been through her friend Fiorentino, who knew Dumas, who wrote for Dujarier's paper. In her book *The Woman in Black*; *The Life of Lola Montez* the somewhat unreliable Helen Holdredge suggests the introduction came from the journalist Gustave Claudin when Lola was in the Café de Paris with the writers François Méry, Théophile Gautier and Eugène Sue. The evidence is inconclusive but it is certainly possible, because she knew all three. Sue, at the time the roaring lion of the Paris literary scene, had just published *Mystères de Paris*. People paid an hourly fee to read the day's instalment in the papers, while illiterates would stand in doorways to have the novel read to them. With his fame he had become an inveterate snob who would no more go without a new pair of white kid gloves every evening than without his dinner. Highly unpopular with his fellow members of the Jockey Club, he overlooked his subscription and to their delight was expelled.[11] Lola admired him immensely.

Gustave Claudin was indeed another great admirer of Lola, describing her as very beautiful but by ill chance having absolutely no talent as a danseuse. 'The crowd went to see her dance not for her talent but for her very original beauty.' She had kept some sort of notebook and he wrote that they had discussed his writing her memoirs. She would wear 'enormous eccentric outfits which she carried off with jauntiness'. She told him that in India she had refused to dance with a man loaded with more diamonds than a snuff-box. When he asked why, she replied, 'Because this morning you hurt my foot.' The man was her chiropodist.[12] What militates against the story of the meeting with Dujarier is that Claudin makes no mention of it in his autobiographical sketches *Mes Souvenirs*. In fact Lola could have met him in any one of a dozen or more restaurants or cafés.

Writing later, Lola converted Dujarier from a lover into a fiancé and herself from a mistress to someone for whom marriage – *pace*

Thomas James – was a mere few weeks away. Indeed in her mind was a honeymoon in Spain with Méry and Dumas in attendance, something that sounds suspiciously like a *ménage à quatre*. What is certain is that she and Dujarier lived in the same house at 39 rue Lafitte. What is also certain is that Dujarier was by no means as steadfast in his affection for Lola as she wished and possibly even believed him to be. In reality Lola was in a pre-Dame aux Camélias situation. Dujarier might, as a young man, live with her, but there was no way in which he could subject his mother to the ignominy of having a courtesan as a daughter-in-law without the most dire social consequences.

More or less the same situation had occurred in the case of Élisabeth-Céleste Vénard, known as Mogador. A dancer at the Bal Mabille in the Champs-Elysées, she learned the then enormously popular and licentious polka from the dancer Brindidi, who gave her the nickname: so many men asked to dance with her, he said, that it had been easier to defend Mogador[13] in Morocco, recently captured by the French, than to fend off her admirers. Later she fell in love with Gabriel-Paul-Josselin-Lionel de Chabrillan, the heir to an estate near Châteauroux. His family expected him to marry for money and not a courtesan. De Chabrillan, ruined and disowned by his family, sailed for Australia in the late spring of 1852 to join in the gold rush. Through his efforts Mogador's name was taken off the list of public prostitutes on 27 April 1852 and on his return he offered to marry her. By now he had become the French consul-general in Melbourne. They married in London on 4 January 1854 and the next day sailed from Southampton. Mogador was completely reformed but de Chabrillan's family was unforgiving. This was the life Lola would have faced had Dujarier married her.

On 6 March 1845 Lola made her debut at the Théâtre Porte St-Martin, the one-time home of the great actor Frédéric Lemaître, appearing in *Dansomanie*.[14] Built on the site of a former circus in seventy-five days in 1781 to rehouse the cast from the Opéra-Royal, which had been destroyed by fire, the theatre seated 1,800 with orchestra stalls, *parterre-debut*, amphitheatre and four levels of boxes. By 1840, however, the Porte St-Martin was in decline. Its prices were half those of the Opéra and it was now alternating circuses with junk plays such as *La Duchesse de la Vanbanlière*. It was generally considered a much more suitable venue for Lola to appear at.

Her appearance, talked about since the previous September, had been eagerly awaited. The *avant-scènes* and balconies were full of fashionable young men and the first gallery with gentlemen riders and members of the Jockey Club. She appeared as Seraphie in *Dansomanie*, and the *Era* reported that the costumes combined elegance with perfect taste. She was wildly applauded in her first dance and 'nor was she less attractive nor less applauded in the Chachua'.[15]

On the whole the remainder of the press was reasonably kind. Another of Dujarier's friends, Charles de Boigne, thought that 'with a few more *battements*' her talent would be admired as much as her beautiful eyes. On the other hand, *Le Siècle* was sorry that her triumphant return had been spoiled by her attempt to dance. Naturally Fiorentino put a gloss on things, describing her costumes and the flowers she received without commenting on her dancing. She was, however, scheduled to appear in a new fairy ballet, *La Biche au Bois*. There may have been something of a joke in the title. 'Biche' was a synonym for courtesan and the Bois was the Bois de Boulogne.

The following night, 7 March, Dujarier was invited to a 55-franc pay-for-yourself dinner in the Trois Frères Provençaux, a restaurant in the arches of the Palais Royale which had been popular from the beginning of the century. It was to be a bohemian affair with journalists, a few lions, and actresses outnumbering the men by two to one. After the food there was to be dancing and a few hands of *lansquenet*, a German card game then popular in Paris and requiring absolutely no skill, in which the holder of the bank changed with each deal and had to match a card drawn by a player with one from the pack.

It seems that while it was a case of everyone paying for themselves, Dujarier was actually the guest of Anais Liévenne, an actress from the Vaudeville and one-time mistress of the Spanish ambassador. To complicate things she was then the current mistress of Alfred, comte de Flers, who was also present. Other women included courtesans Alice Ozy, Atala Beauchêne and Virginie Capon as well as a rather older and genuine actress, Louise Thénard. One of the men present was the man-about-town Roger de Beauvoir, whose novel *L'Écolier de*

Cluny gave Dumas père the plot for *La Tour de Nesle*. The editor and one-time director of the Opéra Dr Louis Véron, with whom Lola would later clash, is said once to have written a note to him, 'I expect you to dinner, dear boy. I have forgotten your Christian name but will ascertain it from one of your charming mistresses.'[16] Once when de Beauvoir was seen by Dumas kissing the author's rather plain wife, no duel or even reproach followed and Dumas is said to have commented wonderingly, 'And he had a choice.' Of de Beauvoir, Lola said he was 'one of the three men who kept Paris alive when I was there'. It was certainly to be a louche gathering.

Later Lola would claim she wanted to go but that Dujarier did not care for her to mix in this company, and in particular wished her to avoid a handsome twenty-four-year-old from Guadeloupe, Jean-Baptiste-Rosemond de Beaupin de Beauvallon. He was certainly louche and had once been charged with pawning his aunt's watch to pay for his costume for a fancy-dress ball. A man with an income of about 500 francs a month, he supported his lifestyle by consistently winning at cards. The real reason may be, however, that her lover wished to pay closer attention to La Liévenne than Lola would have allowed.

At the beginning of the evening de Beauvallon wanted to know why *La Presse* had not begun printing a serial he had written. Dujarier rebuffed him, saying he was not going to give precedence to anything over Dumas' articles, which were then appearing. Even at that early stage of the evening there was talk of a duel, but it appears that a drunken Dujarier was the one picking the quarrel. De Beauvallon said he never sought an affair – that is a duel – but sometimes it found him. After that little spat, Dujarier remarked to Liévenne that he would be in bed with her for 100 louis before a month was out. Even in these circles this was a serious social lapse. He apologised and kissed La Liévenne's hand.[17]

As the drink flowed, things became worse between the two men and the trouble does seem to have been of Dujarier's making. First, there was a dispute over a payout by the banker at the card table. That was smoothed over, but it was raised again at the end of the night when Dujarier found he owed de Beauvallon. Despite de Beauvallon saying there was no need, in what was taken as a deliberate slight Dujarier borrowed money from the other players to pay him out.[18]

The next day the genuine comte de Flers and the *soi-disant* vicomte d'Ecquevilley, de Beauvallon's seconds, called at the offices of *La Presse*.[19] They said they also represented de Beauvoir, whom Dujarier had insulted that night as well. Dujarier was not conciliatory in any way, reportedly saying, 'Grandvallon, Duvallon, Beauvallon. What does the gentleman want with me?' He was courting disaster and now de Beauvallon, pushed by his brother-in-law, Granier de Cassagnac, issued a challenge. In turn Dujarier appointed his seconds, Baron Pierre-Charles-Benôit de Boigne, a journalist and one of the founder members of the Jockey Club, and Arthur Bertrand, whose father had been one of Napoleon's marshals.

In *An Englishman in Paris* Albert Vandam wrote:

> ... for a man of social standing to refuse a challenge or to refrain from sending one, save under very exceptional circumstances, was tantamount to courting social death. They knew that every door would henceforth be closed against him; that his wife's best friends would cease to call upon her, by direction of their husbands; that his children at school would be shunned by their comrades; that no young man of equal position to his, were he ever so much in love with his daughter, would ask her to become his wife; that no parents would allow their daughter to marry his son. Is it surprising then, that with such a prospect facing him, a man should risk death rather than become a pariah.[20]

This was particularly true of a first appearance. One could decline a second encounter but not the first. Moreover, duels between editors and proprietors of newspapers and journals were not uncommon and there was already bad blood between *La Presse* and the republican *Le National*. Armand Carrel, editor of *Le National*, had been badly injured in the stomach during a sabre duel in 1833 with another journalist, Roux Laborie, who was regarded as having made a foul thrust. The seconds prepared to take up the duel themselves and only the intervention of the police prevented it. In July three years later Carrel fought Emile de Girardin, editor of *La Presse*, near St Mandé in a quarrel over the honour of the Duchess de Berri.[21]

Carrel shot first and wounded de Girardin. In turn de Girardin fired and hit Carrel near the old wound. Carrel died and Maurice Persat from the paper then issued a public challenge to de Girardin, who declined.[22]

Dujarier's immediate and ultimate problem was that he could handle neither a pistol nor a sword. Of the two he stood a better chance with the latter – duelling pistols had hair-triggers. On the other hand de Beauvallon, steeped in the duel, was talented in both disciplines. His father had been involved in four fatal encounters. Dujarier's seconds also thought things would be better if he fought de Beauvoir first, but he had left Paris to be with his ill mother. The meeting was set for 11 March.

Along with Alexandre Dumas, the seconds urged Dujarier to choose swords, for they had every reason to believe de Beauvallon would be content simply to disarm his opponent. But Dujarier decided on pistols. Dumas sent him with his son to the Tir de Gosset, where he managed to hit only two out of some twelve or fourteen – some say twenty-four – targets. Dujarier borrowed pistols from Dumas and de Beauvallon produced his own. De Beauvallon won the toss to decide whose pair would be used.

On the night before the duel Dujarier declined to attend the Théâtre Porte St-Martin to watch Lola dance. Instead he composed a letter to his mother:

> In the morning . . . an absurd reason for the most frivolous pretext and unless it is possible for my friends Arthur Bertrand and Charles de Boigne to avoid a meeting which my honour made me accept I am writing my last will . . .
>
> Honour is all; if you shed tears my good mother you will wish to shed them over a son as honourable as yourself than on a coward . . .

At 7 am Lola asked her maid to invite him to her rooms. Dujarier was already dressed and drinking some soup. This was inadvisable. It might keep out the cold but in general a bullet wound in the stomach was less difficult to treat if no food had been taken. Dujarier did not go to see Lola, instead he wrote a letter to her:

My dear Lola

I am leaving to fight with pistols. This explains why I wanted to sleep alone and also why I didn't come to see you this morning. I need all my composure and I must avoid the emotions that seeing you would have caused me. At ten, it will be all over and I'll run to embrace you, unless . . .

A thousand tendernesses, my dear Lola, my good little woman whom I love and will be in my thoughts. D. Tuesday morning.

He put on a coat and went downstairs to where his coachman and valet were waiting. De Boigne would go with him. Bertrand would come with the doctor. And off they set in light snow for the chemin de la Favourite in the Bois de Boulogne, the traditional home of the Parisian duel. Dujarier was never at his best in the mornings and the seconds had tried to persuade him to fight in the afternoon, but again he stubbornly refused.

The rules of engagement had already been set. He and de Beauvallon would stand thirty paces apart. At a signal of three handclaps they could advance five paces and then fire. Once one had fired the other must return fire immediately. The duel had been set for ten o'clock but by 11.30 there was no sight of either de Beauvallon or his seconds. Dujarier would have been well within his rights to go home, his honour satisfied. Instead he seems to have had something of a suicide wish, muttering that he would wait another hour. If he did not, he said, he would have to come out another day.

De Beauvallon and his party arrived at 11.35, proffering a variety of excuses. The traditional efforts were made by de Boigne to see if the matter could be settled. Neither party was willing to do so, and when Dujarier was shown how to hold the pistol he accidentally pulled the trigger and nearly shot de Boigne. It was clear that there was some powder around the muzzles of the pistols produced by de Beauvallon, but his second explained that they had been tested with a blank cap to ensure they were in working order.

It was of course hopeless. On de Boigne's signal Dujarier fired wildly into the air and then, instead of turning sideways to reduce the target, he stood face on. De Boigne and Bertrand would say they thought de Beauvallon had waited over half a minute before firing but onlookers would say it was four or five seconds. The bullet hit Dujarier in the face and he collapsed, dying almost immediately. His body was placed in the coach and driven back to rue Lafitte. Later Lola would maintain improbably that she knew nothing of the duel until that morning, but since it was the talk of Paris she must have heard something of it at the theatre. Whatever the truth, when she found Dujarier had left that morning she went in search and appealed to Dumas to tell her where the duel was taking place. He refused and she returned home in time for the arrival of the coach. She pulled open the door and Dujarier's body fell into her arms. Two hours later the police began an investigation into the circumstances surrounding the duel.

On 13 March a service was held at Notre-Dame de la Lorette and afterwards Dujarier was buried at Montmartre cemetery, with Balzac, Dumas, Méry and Emile de Girardin as his pallbearers. De Girardin gave the oration. There is no mention in the newspapers that Lola was present. Since Dujarier's mother was at the service it is highly unlikely that Lola attended.

In his will Dujarier left all his personal possessions to Alexandre Dumas and to Lola seventeen shares in the newspaper – a gift she would multiply many times in her mind over the years. Money, as throughout Lola's life, was now a serious problem. She could not get at her inheritance quickly enough and when it had not been paid to her during April she sued the executors. Unfortunately for her they were allowed forty days in law to distribute the estate and the court adjourned the case. Finally the shares were sold at 43 francs each, making a total after commission of 774 francs 99 centimes.[23] In fact, through a series of court cases brought against her Lola never received a franc. With no money from Dujarier, a new protector had to be found. As for his bequest to Alexandre Dumas, Dujarier's horses alone were worth around 14,000 francs and the furniture around 100,000.

But what was a girl going to do? In Lola's case it was to carry on as normal. The next night she appeared in *Dansomanie*, which she danced for a few more nights while continuing to rehearse *La Biche au Bois*. She also gallantly appeared at Longchamps for the first two days of the spring meeting. Her dancing career, however, was finished and she was dismissed from the Théâtre Porte St-Martin. A variety of explanations have been offered. One was the doubts over her nationality, but this seems highly unlikely. Another is that she had danced without a body stocking, a third that her notoriety was too great 'even for that theatre'. Most likely it was simply that she really was very bad and, more importantly, for the moment was without any protection.[24] She was thought to be moving to the Théâtre du Palais-Royal, regarded as an even more suitable venue for her limited talents. Indeed she may have danced the Cachucha there one night before what was described as the 'Lionnerie Parisienne', being applauded both 'as an original dancer and as a femme de la mode'.[25] If she did make that appearance, she never appeared again.

What she certainly did was attend the bal-jardins dancing the chahut, a sort of mixed quadrille version of the can-can, with the celebrated acrobat Jean-Baptiste Auriol at La Grande Chaumière at what is now the corner of the boulevards Montparnasse and Raspail. The dance itself was banned and anyone caught performing it could be fined or even imprisoned but, perhaps because of this, it became the rage of the dancehalls.

Then suddenly it was summer and time to move onwards, first to Belgium and then to the German spas. She was accompanied by Mme Azam, the wife of the hotel proprietor, while the good-hearted Fiorentino was prevailed upon to put a departure notice for her in *Le Corsair*.

→>◄←

CHAPTER FIVE

Lola on Her Travels

So Lola set off for a tour of Belgium and Germany with Mme Azam in tow, trawling her net to see what fish might swim into it. Just what were the precise arrangements for the journey depends upon whose version of the story is accepted. Most likely there was a third version which did credit to neither. Certainly they stopped in Brussels and then rested their caravan in the Belgian town of Spa, where Lola was turned away from the grand ball for not having an invitation.[1] A quarrel now broke out between the travellers and Mrs Azam returned to Paris on her own.

Lola promptly headed for Germany, doing some 'promiscuous gambling up and down the Rhine', when she decided to gatecrash the festival being held in Bonn, Beethoven's birthplace, to mark his seventy-fifth anniversary. Some suggest that this was an effort to restore her relationship with Liszt, who was there along with, among many others, the composer and conductor Louis Spohr, Jules Janin and Hector Berlioz, as well as 'Russian noblemen, English gentry, tight-waisted Prussian officers and here and there a spectacled and bearded head which might belong to a doctor of laws or of arts'.[2]

She arrived at the Golden Star hotel in Bonn, where both Liszt and her friend Fiorentino were staying, claiming that she had a reservation through the composer. No, she had not, and she was turned away. She may have failed to convince the proprietors of the Golden Star that she had a room booked but she did manage to insinuate herself into the grand dinner which followed the ceremony of the unveiling of a statue of Beethoven. The troubles at the banquet were not caused by Lola, but she certainly helped things along and behaved, as usual, in a most unladylike way.

Although there were over 400 guests, many were turned away and there had been hand-to-hand fighting to gain entry. At first Lola elbowed her way through, claiming to be a guest of Liszt, and then managed to persuade a local official to take her in, where she sat at an otherwise all-male table.[3] Generally women were placed near other women, but this in no way discomforted her; rather the reverse. The troubles started after the dinner, when toasts and speeches were made. It was extremely hot and clearly a considerable amount of drink had been taken. The Hungarian-born Liszt, who spoke French but never had a complete command of German, was pressed to reply to a speech. He proposed a toast to the monarchs of various countries, inadvertently omitting the French. Hippolyte Chélard, a Frenchman, called out, 'You've forgotten the French,' and a second diner shouted that it had been insulting to drink toasts to the King of Prussia and the Queen of England but not to the French King. An Englishman then yelled, 'Why not the Emperor of China and the Shah of Persia?' Professor Oscar Wolff of the University of Jena tried to calm things down and stood on a table to try to make himself heard. He was shouted down. Lola then stood on her table, appealing in French for Wolff to be allowed to speak or for him to speak up – some say she actually began to dance. The proprietor of the restaurant, fearful for his glass and china, ordered the band to strike up and the combatants moved outside the hall, only to be soaked by a sudden thunderstorm. An English divine who was present and who wandered near Lola during the dinner reported that 'Time had thinned her flowing hair.' He happily mentioned the baldness when he came back to the table as a precious fact to be noted.[4]

From there it was on to Baden-Baden, where two more unfortunate incidents led to Lola's expulsion. The first came when, demonstrating her agility and sense of balance in the Assembly Rooms, she lifted her foot on to a gentleman's shoulder. The second was when she lifted her skirt over her thigh to show the assembled gentlemen something which the papers chose not to print.[5]

Her movements for the next four months are unrecorded but by the end of the year she was back in Paris, where she had completely fallen out with the Azams. In December they sued her for 1,002 francs, the expenses Madame had incurred in the tour of Belgium. If Lola thought there was any money to come from her claim for Dujarier's legacy she was swiftly disabused. That was withheld by order of the third chamber.[6]

On 13 February 1846 Lola danced in a benefit for Mme Leontine at the Gaité. It was, said the *Revue des Théâtres*, her first appearance since 'an unfortunate event'. Unless there was yet another unfortunate event which has gone unrecorded, this rather contradicts the reports that she had appeared very shortly after Dujarier's death. Naturally people were curious to see her and her Lachucha went down well enough. Her quarrels with the Azams were by no means settled and now they obtained a judgment against her. For the moment, ignorant of John Jorrocks's advice, 'To 'ell with gifts what eats', they accepted a horse as security.

The most important event on Lola's horizon, however, was the forthcoming trial of de Beauvallon for the murder of Dujarier. The police had been busy with their inquiries and de Beauvallon, fearing his imminent arrest, had fled to Spain, from where he was retrieved. The trial itself, partly criminal and partly a claim by Dujarier's mother and sister for compensation, was moved to the Palais de Justice in Rouen.

At the hearing on 26 August 1846, Lola appeared all in black – in contrast to some of the *filles* who had been at the party, who were rigged out in their finest. She said she had wanted to go to the dinner at the Frères but Dujarier had dissuaded her, saying de Beauvallon was not somebody she should meet. At the reading of the letter Dujarier had written to her before he went to fight the duel, she burst into tears. The Englishman who supplied Albert Vandam with his information and who had watched the trial was impressed:

though the court was packed with men occupying the foremost ranks in literature, art and Paris society, no one attracted the attention she did. Even the sober president and assessors sat staring at her open-mouthed ... She was dressed in mourning – not the deepest, but soft masses of silk and lace – and when she lifted her veil and took off her glove to take the prescribed oath, a murmur of admiration ran through the court. That is why she had undertaken the journey to Rouen, and verily she had her reward.[7]

Lola attracted great sympathy. When she said she wished she had taken Dujarier's place in the duel it was not a wild boast. She had taken fencing lessons from the master Barrez and, also a fine shot, she was throughout her life forever issuing challenges to duels – quickly declined – to anyone who offended her.

Although in theory the evidence was overwhelming, no French jury of the time would convict on a charge of murder, provided the duel had been fought within the prevailing code. As a double insurance, however, de Beauvallon also had Pierre Berryer, the leading member of the criminal bar, appearing for him. The evidence was rigged, just as the duel had been. The fencing master Grisier was called to say de Beauvallon had approached him, asking to be taught a disarming movement. When Grisier had pointed out that it was very dangerous, de Beauvallon said it was worth trying, but then, of course, Dujarier had opted for pistols. The jury barely retired before they acquitted him. However, the trial was hardly over when a witness went to the police to say that de Beauvallon had been practising with the pistols on the morning of the duel, something which was against all the rules of duelling conduct and which he had denied at the trial.

Eighteen months later, on 8 October 1847, de Beauvallon received eight years for perjury. Sentenced with him was his second, the vicomte d'Ecquevilley. The pair were released or escaped during the 1848 revolution and some years later d'Ecquevilley wrote a self-serving book, protesting his lineage and claiming the conviction was unjust. It was really Dujarier's fault. When he had been to see the journalist all he wanted was for Dujarier to declare he had not intended to cause offence. It was he who had argued that swords or the less dangerous *pistolets d'Arçon* should be used, but he had been over-ruled. The choice of pistols had, he maintained, come after de Beau-vallon's had been tested, and anyway he had known of no rule that pistols must not have been tried.[8]

A suggestion by Vandam that the novelist Gustave Flaubert was at the first trial is discounted by some writers on the basis that his sister, to whom he was devoted, had died only a few days earlier. That may be right, but a funeral has rarely been allowed to come in the way of a good trial for an author. In fact the story of the outmatched duellist forms a basis for two incidents in Honoré de Balzac's *Comédie Humaine*, the first in *Le Père Goriot* and the second in *La Rabouilleuse*.

Lola was certainly still in Paris in May 1846, living at 95 rue Neuf des Mathurins, because from there she wrote to the Commissioner of Police in her bad French, complaining about an Adèle Bassolet of 20 place Pigalle, whom she maintained was harassing her, and asking for his help. But by August she was gone to Homburg, from where she wrote to the proprietress of the Hotel de Suède in Brussels asking for her trunks.[9] At the spa town the season was ending but there were still some important people in town, such as Prince Hohenzollern-Hechingen and the Marquis of Londonderry, the commanding officer of a future husband for Lola.[10] Homburg, like most of the resorts, put on a programme of summer entertainments, and it was announced that Lola Montez would dance there in the performance of 29 August, the last of the summer season.

She therefore missed a further hearing of the Azam case on 25 July in the Fifth Chamber when, while things may not have become clearer, both parties set out their respective stalls. 'Mlle Lola Montes is understood to have *bolted* from Paris,' laughed the *Sunday Times* about an earlier hearing; the paper opined that she had 'accrued no small pugilistic fame in Germany and various other parts of the Continent'.[11]

Mme Azam's case, put by Maître Chapon-Dabit, was that when Lola had failed at the Opéra and had to undergo training, she and her husband had taken her in – using the best sense of the word. In turn Lola had taken them in – with a rather different meaning. They had one of the finest *hôtels garnis* – hotels which provided lodgings but not board – in Paris, and a good deal of property besides. Sadly, Mme Azam had had a serious illness during the summer and wanted to take the waters. Lola persuaded her to go via Brussels, where Lola hoped to obtain an engagement, instead of going straight to Spa as she had intended. Mme Azam had paid all the expenses and advanced Lola money as well. At Baden there had been a complete breakdown in relations: '[Lola] was no longer a young artiste who was looking for work and studying her art in an honourable way. Salon gossip told everyone about the wantonness of her conduct. Madame Azam, an upright woman, could no longer regularise Lola's conduct by her presence.'[12]

There was also the question of the horse. Lola had not paid for its keep either. They had been obliged to put it out to livery and that had cost money as well. Horses, unlike Bordeaux wine, did not improve with age and it was an old horse anyway, said the Maître. As the *Sunday Times* wittily put it, 'the horse continued to eat his corn without regarding who had to pay for it'.

Naturally Lola's advocate, M. Cochery, put things in a different context. The Azams were Spanish, which was why Lola felt affection for them as fellow-countrymen. The illness was nonsense. What Mme Azam was thinking of doing was setting up a *hôtel garni* in Spa, and she was not at all vexed to have Lola along to give a touch of class to this proposed establishment. Lola, a true artiste, was generous, prodigal and paid the bills without thinking. On the other hand Mme Azam was tidy and well organised, as one would expect of a hotel proprietor. She left Lola to pay the bills. Brussels was merely a twenty-four-hour stopover; the real watering hole was Spa. What exactly had happened in Spa? It was better he did not say. What Lola had offered was to pay for the horse up to the time when the Azams refused to return it to her. And the tribunal agreed with him that would be the end of the matter. The real likelihood is that it was a question of Spaniard meeting Spaniard and that Lola had taken along Mme Azam as a cover and procuress.

But instead of attending court, where exactly had Lola been? By the early summer of 1846 she had acquired a new lover and they were off on their travels together. Francis Leigh, a former officer in the 10th Hussars, had sold out in that year and had met her in Paris; there she bought a riding costume and other clothes costing 372 francs and charged them to him. When he declined to pay, their relationship soured. Although they travelled to Ostend and Brussels, where they stayed at the Hôtel de Suède together in June, by August she was involved with Robert, the son of the former Prime Minister, Sir Robert Peel, and heir to the baronetcy. The small, foreign-looking – this showed the influence of his mother's Anglo-Indian family – and volatile Peel, then aged twenty-three, was a great disappointment to his parents. He had gone down from Oxford without a degree and had been found a position in the diplomatic service. After a spell as an attaché to the British legation in Madrid he was appointed secretary of the legation in Switzerland, from where he wrote home that he was 'bored with the dull monotony of Swiss seclusion'.[13] Lola must have been a godsend to him. Before meeting Peel, probably in July Lola had visited Heidelberg, a town renowned for the experience of its doctors in treating venereal diseases, and then gone travelling with the Latvian Count Meller-Zakomelsky, who would be an occasional companion for the next five years.

Lola paid for this reckless and flighty behaviour. By the middle of August 1846 she had split from Peel and was back looking for Francis Leigh. Told he still had a room at the Hôtel de Suède, she also took one, but by this time Leigh had had quite sufficient of her and locked her out of his room. In one final quarrel she took a shot at him. Given her skill with the pistol, it must have been an admonitory one. She was, as usual, in poor financial straits and her dog was running around begging for food. Within a few weeks, however, she had taken up with 'an old Englishman'.[14]

Once more there was help at hand. That month she wrote to a M. du Bois, Secretary of the Legation of Holland, to say that she had been invited by Peel to go to Stuttgart for at least part of the month-long wedding celebration of Crown Prince Karl of Württemberg and the Grandduchess Olga, and she was accepting.

By the end of the month, however, she had again temporarily broken with Peel. Now she was set, almost literally, for the crowning few months of her life – following the coach tracks made fifteen years earlier by the English adventuress Jane Digby to the court of King Ludwig I of Bavaria.

-+->-<-+-

CHAPTER SIX

Mr Wittelsbach – Luis y Lola

B Y THE AUTUMN OF 1846 Lola was once more out of both funds and
friends. Even if she did not get an offer to dance, Munich was a
good place to economise until she could recoup and possibly travel on
to Vienna. A year after her arrival the *Illustrated London News* thought
the city to be a contemporary Camelot:

> I confess that I am often astonished that more English do not perma-
> nently reside here. Thousands of English families to whom economy is
> an object, are to be found in other cities on the Continent where the
> living is dearer and there are not as many objects to interest the mind; but
> here, where a man can live for £50 a year and enjoy life for £100 – where
> there are works of art enough to occupy a lover of the arts for ever –
> where, during the greater part of the year, the finest music is to be had
> almost for nothing, and there is a perpetual scope for amusement –
> where a good lodging may be had for 12 shillings a month, and a man can
> live at an hotel, breakfast, dine, sup, drink his bottle of wine, and sleep for
> five shillings a day and have his stall at the opera for one shilling and eight
> pence a night . . .[1]

William Bennett, brother of James Gordon Bennett, the editor of the
New York Herald for which he wrote a column, had a slightly different
take on things: 'The number of illegitimate children born in Bavaria

is almost the same number as those born in wedlock. The beer is particularly excellent in Bavaria but their morals from the king down to the codger are as bad as they can be.'[2] This combination of cheap living and a lack of morality would prove a happy hunting ground for a predator such as Lola.

The king in question was Ludwig I. Although his Wittelsbach family had ruled Bavaria for nearly 1,000 years, at the time of his birth in 1786 in French-owned Strasbourg there was no real prospect of Louis, the godson of Marie Antoinette and later a very reluctant protégé of Napoleon and Josephine, becoming King Ludwig I of Bavaria. His father, Maximilian, was third in line for the position of Elector of Munich and that was it. Louis XVI gave little Louis a cache of diamonds, and the grenadiers in his father's regiment shaved off their beards to provide the stuffing for a pillow for the infant. When the presentation was made Maximilian said that while he was grateful, bearded officers were *de rigueur*, and he would be obliged if they would not do it again for future births.

With the beginning of the French Revolution in 1789, the family fled to Germany. In 1795 Charles, duc de Deux Ports, died childless, to be followed by the Elector of Hanover, Charles Theodore, four years later. So Maximilian became Elector and was crowned by Napoleon in 1805. On his death in 1825 Louis, now Ludwig, acceded to the throne.

In his youth Ludwig travelled extensively in Italy and Greece, attracted particularly to the latter. Even before his coronation what he wanted was to create a new Athens in Bavaria. Once he had taken the throne, he engaged the architect Leo von Klenze to create a series of temple-like Greco-Roman buildings, including the Valhalla Hall of Fame, a replica of the Parthenon, along the Bavarian Danube. He also acquired a wealth of paintings and sculptures for his Alt Pinakothek, which he presented to the nation. There were, of course, sacrifices to be made for this great expenditure and he kept a strict control on the family purse. His children ate black bread, while the royal cooks said they could not serve an extravagance such as onions on the budget allowed them.

In October 1810, for political reasons, Ludwig had married Princess Therese of Saxe-Hildburghausen, thought to be the best-looking

princess in Europe. At the time he was described as having soft features, a flushed face, a proud mouth and wide blue eyes, although his
face was pock-marked with the scars of smallpox which he had contracted at the age of eleven. He was also profoundly deaf and had a
bad stammer, something that affected him throughout his life. He
dressed like an eccentric professor, wearing an ill-fitting coat and carrying an umbrella.

The marriage – well received by the citizens and celebrated annu-
ally as the Oktoberfest – was marked and marred by Ludwig's serial
infidelity. The long-suffering Therese, who herself had eight children,
seems to have accepted this with something approaching compla-
cency. Throughout the marriage Ludwig flitted from one high-profile
affair to another; from aristocrat to actress to shop girl and back
again. His first long-term extra-marital relationship was with Mari-
anna, the Marchesa Florenzi, with whom he exchanged some 1,900
letters and poems during her two marriages. The stoical Therese
rarely took objection to a well-born mistress; it was the actresses who
caused the most talk among the subjects, and therefore the most distress. By the 1830s Ludwig could no longer be described as handsome.
By the time Lola arrived in Munich he was anything but, with an
unbecoming cyst on his forehead and a recurring skin rash.

Lola's intrigue with Ludwig very much followed the pattern of
Ludwig's earlier relationship with Jane Digby. He had met this
genuine adventuress at an Oktoberfest ball in 1832 and from the start
had been enchanted by her. She was, however, of a very different social
background from Lola. A great society beauty, she had been married
off at the age of seventeen to the middle-aged lawyer and rake Lord
Ellenborough. Her first affair was at the age of twenty with a librarian
and from then it was onwards and upwards. There was her cousin
Colonel George Anson, probably the father of her son born in 1828,
and then came the Austrian Prince Felix von Schwarzenberg. She took
little trouble to hide her relationship and the dénouement came when
they spent a night together in the Norfolk Hotel, Brighton on 7 February 1829. One of the servants recounted at the subsequent divorce
proceedings that – just as the maid would later say she had seen
Lennox lacing Lola – he had seen the Prince lacing-up Jane Digby. It

was seemingly standard evidence of the time. Ellenborough petitioned for divorce in the House of Lords and the Prince was posted to Paris. Jane followed post chaise.

The evidence was very clear but there was some sympathy for her – from, among others, Joseph Hume, coincidentally the member for Montrose – when the case came to the House in March 1830. It was no help. The bill for divorce was passed on 7 April that year. It was all a preview of Lola's situation – and that of many other women – a decade later.

Jane and Schwarzenberg had two children in Paris, but the affair cooled. She left them with him and headed to Munich. As with Lola fifteen years later, soon enough her portrait, by the chocolate-box court artist Joseph Stieler, joined those of the other beauties, including Ludwig's daughter and a number of mistresses, in his Schönheits gallery. To Ludwig, Jane was Ianthe and he Basily, from the Greek *basileus* meaning king. Following the pattern of his relationship with the Marchesa, so also Ianthe and Basily wrote each other poems and letters, and exchanged gifts.

It is unclear whether Jane was in love with her next husband, the somewhat staid Baron Carl-Theodore von Venningen, or whether the marriage on 10 December 1832 was principally a cover for the relationship with Ludwig. Their first child, Heribert, was born the next month and at least is said to have resembled the Baron. It is, however, possible that her next was Ludwig's. Bertha, born in September 1834, certainly had the mental instability of the Wittelsbachs and spent her adult life in an asylum. By 1835 Jane Digby had fallen in love with Count Spiridon Theotoky. After a duel with Venningen in which Theotoky was nearly killed, the pair left for Greece and the security of the court of Ludwig's son, King Otto.[3]

Over the years Ludwig ruled the kingdom benignly, his major problems arising from what was seen as an undue influence by the Jesuits with their ultramontane policies; they sought complete adherence to the Pope. By the 1840s there was a fear that the Catholic interests were obtaining political control of Bavaria, with its two-thirds Catholic and one-third Protestant population. No one disputed that Karl August von Abel, the Minister for the Interior, was anything but a fine politician, but the Protestant element now began campaigning against his increasingly strict control. Born on 17 September 1788, Abel – said when he was ten years old to have converted a woman on her deathbed – had in his early days fought an inconclusive duel with the Prince de Wallerstein. In 1836 he had married Friederike von Ronecker, a deeply religious woman who had a great influence on him. The following year he first took office, replacing Wallerstein, and he was quickly promoted to Minister of the Interior.

In the spring of 1844, while Munich was celebrating the marriage of Ludwig's third son, Luitpold, to the Princess Auguste of Tuscany and his fourth daughter, Hildegard, to the son of the Archduke Charles of Austria, there was discontent both over the Catholic influence and, more prosaically, the rise in the price of beer. On 2 May, while the royal party was at the theatre to see a performance of *Titus*, the breweries were stormed and barricades were built. The next day bakers' shops were looted.

Ludwig, like Jane Digby and Lola never less than personally courageous, drove through the streets the next day and on 5 May, with no guard or retinue, attended the annual fair in Au. He then left for Italy, wrote a bad poem about his former mistress the Marchesa – now a Mrs Waddington – and returned to Munich to find that the crowd had begun to champion the Crown Prince Maximilian, known to hold more liberal views. In Austria, Prince Metternich was also fomenting trouble, prophesying a religious war in Germany.

Two years later, in February 1846, there was serious discontent. The king was losing touch with the youth of Bavaria and also losing the support of his poorly paid officials and the army. Many members of the Chamber believed that Abel, with his dependence on Rome, was making Bavaria a political laughing stock and that the influence of Metternich and Austria was far too great. Ludwig was also afraid that his son Maximilian, who wished to holiday in Dieppe, would fall under French political influence. It was in the face of these problems that he and Therese took their annual summer holiday at Berchtesgaden.

It was raining in Munich at the beginning of October 1846 when Ludwig, Therese and their daughters returned. By the first day of the annual festival the weather had turned warm and on 5 October Lola Montez arrived with her dog Zampa, to be followed, if not joined, two days later by Robert Peel. Both stayed at the very smart Bayerischer Hof on Promenaden Platz. Now she was looking at worst for further engagements, but if possible for something rather better.

Six months later, in March 1847, she wrote to the *Pictorial Times* in London complaining that she had been having a hard time from the French newspapers: 'I left Paris in June last on a professional trip and amongst other arrangements decided upon visiting Munich where for the first time I had the honour of appearing before His Majesty and receiving from him marks of approbation which you are aware is not a very unusual thing for a professional person to receive at a foreign court.'[4]

For once Lola was being unduly modest and retiring. What Ludwig had encountered was a beautiful and untamed animal to whom the accepted standards and rules of behaviour did not apply. In just six months she had managed to achieve something far beyond the scope of the common or garden adventuress. She had taken such control of a monarch that, effectively, for a good part of the next year she had much of the day-to-day governance of his country in her hands. Indeed an early entry in the *Dictionary of National Biography* wrote of her, 'She now ruled the kingdom of Bavaria and, singular to say, ruled it with wisdom and ability. Her audacity confounded alike the policy of the Jesuits and of Metternich.'[5]

Actually, over the next seventeen months, considerably helped by his infatuation, stupidity, stubbornness and vacillation, she steadily, if unintentionally, destroyed Ludwig and his kingdom.

Another story which had circulated about her arrival was that Lola had been brought to Munich by a nobleman, an intelligence agent, with the express intention of ousting the Austrian influence in the kingdom. She was to be used to infiltrate Ludwig's court, which would lead to a revolution.[6] There can only be three candidates for the position of Lola-importer. First, there was Robert Peel. Second, there was the three-times widowed roué Heinrich von Maltzahn, who had known Lola either in London, Bonn, or most likely in Paris where he lived on the rue de la Madeleine. Later, when trouble broke out, he would protest that his arrival in Munich at the same time as Lola was simply coincidence and that he had come to enter his son at the university. Both are unlikely candidates. There is no evidence that it was British foreign policy at the period to try to foment trouble in Bavaria. And if Maltzahn had indeed brought Lola to the capital, possibly for his own self-preservation, he turned against her. Certainly within six weeks, frequently seen in her company, he was becoming known as 'the man who brought the Spanish woman to Munich'.

Yet another story that gained some currency came from Hineis, the Austrian Prince Metternich's police spy in Munich, who reported that Lola first lived with an Englishman whom she had met in Paris and who was her *souteneur*. Hineis was not always accurate in his information and indeed accepted that this and other incidents in his reports may simply have been current gossip, but if he is correct about the Englishman – although there is little evidence to support it – this could only have been Peel. A variation on the story is that it was the third candidate for Lola-importer, the strange and sinister Auguste Papon, who was pimping for her in her early days in Munich. This bogus captain, who claimed he was in the Croatian guard, had fake wounds to go with his self-appointed commission. Lola possibly met him first in Paris; certainly she knew him in Munich, where she called him her cuisinier, and after the 1848 debacle he joined her in Switzerland. It is also possible that she met him first when she was pursuing what the *Athenaeum* described as her 'reckless career as a gambler at the German Spas'.[7]

Over the years there have been numerous stories that Lola was a spy, but for whom she might have been working no one is quite clear and the names of her suggested paymasters vary. Candidates include the British Prime Minister Lord Palmerston, the Czar of Russia – probably on the basis that she had spent a few days in Russia and that her apparent interest in Polish uprisings was a diversionary tactic – the King of Prussia, the Austrian government and the police of Louis-Philippe. Certainly the French, who of course could see a foreign spy under every bedcover, thought she was a British agent while she was in Paris. She herself claimed that the Jesuits thought she was spying for freemasonry. Indeed, almost immediately she arrived in Munich there were rumours that she was there as an agent of English freemasons.[8]

The most likely choice – though without any real supporting evidence – is Palmerston. The British had a considerable interest in the difficulties of the monarchy in Greece, where Ludwig's extravagant, ostentatious and arrogant son Otto was a perpetual source of concern for Palmerston. King Otto had refused to repay the loans he had taken from Rothschilds and Palmerston was very keen to support the interests of British citizens if they clashed with those of the Greek government. In 1849, the year after Lola left Munich, Palmerston sent a squadron to Piraeus in an attempt to force a settlement of a claim of Don Pacifico, a British subject, whose house in Athens had been burned. Without doubt Lola would have been useful in passing on cushion, if not pillow, talk while she was in Munich, but there is no evidence that she did so.

It is just about possible, however, to make out a case that Robert Peel was running Lola as a spy. He was suspiciously close to her just before she went to Munich; he joined her almost immediately; and he was there to help pick up some of the pieces after the final debacle. There have been more unlikely stories.

Spy or not, after her arrival there was first the business of obtaining permission to dance at the Hoftheatre from the administrator, Baron August Frays, later to become a target of Lola's wrath. Munich normally attracted high-quality performers – that October Jenny Lind, the Swedish Nightingale, appeared in *La Sonnambula*. Permission for visiting artistes to appear was not readily granted, particularly if they wanted a high percentage of the box office. It was a matter Frays might think had to be referred to the King personally. Fortunately for Lola, Maltzahn was there to help. It was through him that Lola was able to obtain a private audience with the King, so bypassing Frays.

On 8 October she presented herself. Some reports have it that the King took an immediate liking to her. The private audience lasted far longer than was strictly necessary and Ludwig could be heard talking loudly in Spanish. It is at this point in their meeting that one of the great Lola legends has arisen. The King is said to have been fascinated by her bosom and wanted to know whether it was real or false. Whatever things were false about Lola, and there were many, her bosom was not among them. The story goes that Lola either took a pair of scissors and cut or simply tore her dress for the king's delectation.[9] An elaboration of the story is that she cut her dress much lower. Some suggest that it could not have happened: how, if she did so, could she have walked back to her hotel? The answer to that is simple – she could have been given a shawl with which to cover herself. But, true or false, the King was captivated. Frays suggested that she could dance for a third of the takings but Ludwig authorised her to appear for a half, adding a note that he should say the King was looking forward to seeing her dance.

Two days later, on Ludwig's thirty-sixth wedding anniversary, Lola made her debut between the acts of the comedy *Der Verwunschene Prinz*, 'The Enchanted Prince', by Johann von Plötz. She appeared dancing *Los Boleros de Cadix* after the first act and the Cachucha – the Oleana under another name and a prototype of her famous Spider Dance – after the second. There was enough applause, but again opinions about her talent were divided. Everyone, however, agreed upon her beauty. It would not have mattered if they had not. The most important viewer was the King, who like von Plötz's prince was certainly enchanted. Even if he had not been wholly captivated by the private audience two days earlier, he was now. He wrote in ecstatic terms to his old friend Baron Heinrich von der Tann telling him of his new love.

Ludwig was not the only person she captivated. There is the story that a child saw her in the street and ran home to tell her parents that she had seen a lady as beautiful as a fairy. 'That', observed her father grimly, 'must have been Lola Montez.'[10]

Ludwig was about to provide yet another example of the well-worn saw, 'There's no fool like an old fool'. First, he wanted Lola's portrait for his gallery of beauties. This would be an excellent cover under which they could meet. He had already discovered that in her four days in Munich she had attracted a small colony of admirers. They were mostly young officers, including most significantly Artillery Lieutenant Friedrich Nüssbammer, an orphan who had, it seems, intervened when she was insulted in the street. He quickly became devoted to her and she just as quickly ruined his life. The sittings for the court portrait painter Joseph Stieler would remove her from their attentions at least for an hour or so a day.

To those who conceive a monarch as being far removed from his or her subjects, the idea of Ludwig wandering around the streets of his capital as he did must seem very strange, particularly in an era when the well-guarded Queen Victoria was intermittently surviving assassination attempts. But, in some ways, he was a most informal monarch. He regularly went shopping and stopped to speak to people, often young and pretty girls, in the street. If he saw someone at a ball who he did not think had been invited he would question the man himself. Now he took to visiting Lola in her hotel of an afternoon or an evening and sometimes twice a day, once staying so late that the staff had locked up for the night. Maltzahn, who had aspirations for office, was often there and the three then spoke in French; otherwise the pair spoke in their rudimentary Spanish. Often she was seen in the company of Maltzahn alone. Letters between Ludwig and Lola over the next three years were in fractured Spanish. When Lola did not know a word she wrote it in French; when Ludwig did not know one he wrote in Italian or Latin.

She danced again on 14 October and already she had begun to polarise the audience. There were flowers enough on the stage but there was also some hissing. Lieutenant Axt of the gendarmerie was identified as a leading culprit and promptly sent by Ludwig to Regensburg. Now the portrait went ahead, Ludwig watching and Lola vamping him for all she was worth. Here, after weeks and months on the road and in a variety of unpromising beds, was the possibility of some stability and security. On 19 October she gave Ludwig a rose during the Stieler sitting. When the King left the flower behind by mistake he immediately sent a note to the artist saying it must be delivered at once in a bag. Lola had arranged to appear in Augsburg on 24 October and wrote to Frays requesting a copy of her music, but when the King heard of this a touching scene developed as a despondent Ludwig pleaded with her not to go. Finally, '*No puedo dejar Munic*,' she told him. 'I cannot leave Munich.' He was no longer simply enamoured; he was enslaved. Her appearance in Augsburg was cancelled, and so her dances on 14 October were the last the stage would see of Lola for some five years.

When the Stieler portrait finally appeared, the staunch Catholic Count Arco-Valley asked that the portrait of his own wife be removed from the gallery. Ludwig himself was not content with merely one portrait. He commissioned a second Stieler and in early 1847 also engaged Wilhelm von Kaulbach to paint Lola. By no means a chocolate-box artist like Stieler, he drew a sketch of her with a serpent around her waist, the clasp of her belt in the form of a skull, carrying a riding whip as, her hair loose, she mounted a scaffold. It also contained a newspaper with a headline of the Dujarier trial. Kaulbach was obliged to water down the image, but he still painted her posing like Mary Queen of Scots and with something of a sneer. Again Ludwig came to the sittings in Kaulbach's icy studio – as did Zampa, Lola's dog, which one day chased half a dozen peacocks kept by Kaulbach as models along with a number of other birds and animals. It is little surprise that Kaulbach did not like Lola, and the finished painting showed his dislike. Ultimately Ludwig rejected the finished portrait and for years it remained in Kaulbach's studio.[11]

There were, of course, financial rewards. Appropriately enough, on All Saints Day, within a month of her arrival, Lola had been placed on an annual allowance of 10,000 florins. At the time a university professor could expect to receive some 2,000 florins and a cabinet minister 6,000. One thousand florins was thought to be sufficient to lead an extremely comfortable life. Lola had already established herself as a conduit to the King's purse. When a dancer, Berta Thierry, complained that she and her sister Matilde were starving, and that she had not enough money for ballet shoes, she sought Lola's help. Lola obtained for her a grant of 200 florins, probably a year's salary for Berta.

The first sign that Lola was getting above herself and beginning to alienate the bourgeoisie came when, during the interval of a concert, Ludwig left Therese and went to speak to Lola in the stalls. She remained seated and it was with some difficulty that Ludwig made sufficiently explicit gestures to indicate she must stand.

There was another, worse incident on 15 November. For a woman who had spiritually given her heart to the King, Lola was physically far too close to Nüssbammer. She was certainly far too indiscreet. Shortly before midnight, along with her maid, she decided to go searching for the officer at his rooms at Frühlingstrasse 9. Clearly she was in a fine temper because she rang all the doorbells. When confronted by the landlady, who told her Nüssbammer was out, she again rang the bells before fortuitously fainting. She was taken to the house of a glazier who lived in the street, and was given a glass of wine and smelling salts before returning home. As if this was not sufficient, she turned up the next day, yet again ringing all the bells. The landlady screamed to her to stop, saying in French, 'I'm not deaf, Miss.' To this Lola replied that she was not 'Miss' but the King's mistress. Now Hineis reported that the pupils at a girls' school in Munich had been told to pray for the 'Mad King' that God would make him see reason and drive away his mistress.

It is said that Lola's renowned tempers were usually over in a flash, but it was not the case on this occasion. Horace Wyndham, another writer to fall in love with her legend, wrote of her: 'If she did many a foolish thing she never did a mean one.' In hindsight, given the servants whom she beat and sacked and who had no redress, it seems an over-generous epitaph. Life could be seriously disagreeable for those who fell foul of Lola, and with Ludwig backing her every demand, Nüssbammer was one of the first. That afternoon she complained to the King about him, alleging he had insulted her. Nothing would do but for him to be transferred. The unfortunate officer was ordered to leave for Würzburg by 7 pm the next day. He was not to return to Munich without the King's express permission. Nüssbammer called upon Lola to intercede and clearly they kissed and made up, because she told Ludwig the whole thing had been a misunderstanding. Nüssbammer's transfer was cancelled and he was given leave, but now Ludwig asked her to promise not to see the lieutenant again without telling him. It was not a promise she would keep. Ludwig would continually water down his request until it was agreed she could see Nüssbammer, but not too often. There is no evidence that she adhered even to that.

The Frühlingstrasse affair was not over yet. Someone had to pay for the insult to Lola. The next unfortunate was a policeman who investigated the incident and who had, very sensibly, questioned her staff. Lola had by now completely changed tack. It was not she who had been ringing doorbells late of an evening; someone was impersonating her; Ludwig must stop this. And he did so, giving her a note to take to the chief of police, Baron von Pechmann, in whose books she did not rate highly. Even before she came under the protection of the King she had refused to register with the police, as was required of all foreigners. When she deigned to do so, in the 'accompanied by' box she had helpfully written *un chien*. This, in fact, was her pug, Zampa. Von Pechmann had been making inquiries and without too much difficulty had discovered that she had been expelled from Baden-Baden, Berlin and Warsaw. There was also the *affaire* Dujarier to her discredit. Again, a story that she was willing to sell herself for a negligible amount – this time at the Bayerischer Hof – was in circulation. But the investigation into the Frühlingstrasse trouble went cold. No one could make a positive identification. In turn the Baron was positive she had bribed the glazier. On the King's instructions Lola went to Pechmann where, using as an interpreter Ambros Havard – the owner of the Goldener Hirsch, to which she had moved – she made a bitter complaint about the officer who was questioning her maid. At the end of November Ludwig ordered Pechmann to discontinue his inquiries into the matter. By then, however, there had been a number of other incidents.

On the same day that Ludwig had sent Lola to see the chief of police he added a codicil to his will: 'I would not be a man of honour, would be unfeeling if I made no provision for her who gave up everything for me, who has no parents, no brothers or sisters, who has no one in the wide world except me; nonetheless she has made no effort to have me remember her in my last wishes, and I do so totally on my own initiative.'[12] There was also a good measure of self-justification, for he added, 'Her friendship has made me purer, better. Therese, my dear, good, noble wife, do not condemn me unjustly.' Lola was to do rather better than she had by Dujarier's codicils. She was to receive the last portrait of her before his death, 100,000 florins as long as she had not married, and an income of 2,400 florins for life or until she subsequently married. All this within six weeks of meeting the King. Given that she was technically still married, the bequest was probably void from the outset. It would almost certainly have been challenged. Not that it would matter. Ludwig outlived her by many years.

On the down side, there had been an incident in a hat shop owned by a man named Schultz. Lola had ordered a white bonnet, but when she went to collect it said she did not like it. When Frau Schultz said she did not know how to make it any prettier, Lola tore it in two and threw the pieces under a table. As a result she was banned from the premises.[13]

Lola had still not learned that wandering about in her underwear did not constitute proper behaviour. She was said to have been measured naked for corsetry and clothing. Gertrude Arentz wrote of her, 'Her whole existence was a public performance and it never occurred to her to close shutters or draw curtains.'[14] Even worse, she was reportedly seen with five men, wearing only a shirt and slippers. Later Nüssbammer was allowed to stay and watch her try on dresses brought from another shop. Now rumours circulated that he would be married off to Lola to secure her status in Bavaria.[15]

Fifteen years earlier, Jane Digby had warned Ludwig about the contents of his letters to her becoming public knowledge. But, besotted with Lola, the King had learned no more from history than Lola. In any event, Lola was a very different kettle of fish from her predecessor. Jane was an adventuress in the strict sense of the word, Lola an adventuress in the financial sense. On 12 November Ludwig wrote, 'My dearest, my love Lolita', signing himself, 'Heart of my heart, your Luis.' This, along with his many other outpourings, would cost him dearly in both financial and emotional terms.

On 1 December Ludwig bought Lola a house at Barerstrasse 7, for which he paid 16,000 guilden and opposite which a protective gendarmerie post was set up. He might have to go without onions for dinner but he could not go without his Lola. The purchase was in her name, partly to conceal just from where the money came and partly because once she owned property she could apply for Bavarian citizenship. Already the previous month she had suggested to him that he abdicate and they go to live together in Spain. He did not take the suggestion seriously, but it inspired him to write some more bad poetry in her honour. Hineis reported that Ludwig was proposing to buy the property where Lola was presently living, as well as another plot of land on which to build her a third home.

There was, however, a great deal to be done by way of extension and refurbishment at the house, and for the time being Lola remained in her hotel. There were arguments over what building would be allowed. Typically, Lola was ignoring the required permits.

A year later the house was complete. Charles Francis, a journalist whom she knew from her London days, paid a visit and he provides a detailed and adulatory description. He peppered his article with phrases such as 'quite unique in its simplicity and lightness'. The slightly tinted muslin curtains were said to 'add a transparent, eggshell lightness to the effect'. She had, apparently, supervised the decoration with 'French elegance, Munich art and English comfort'. The walls of the chief room were painted from designs found in Herculaneum and Pompeii 'but selected with great taste'. The paintings included a Raphael. There was also a piano and a guitar, both of which she could play, and she was a talented embroideress. There was a rose-tinted bathroom – well in advance of her time, Lola advocated daily bathing – and a well-equipped kitchen, but 'her equipages are extremely modest and her household no more numerous or ostentatious than those of a gentlewoman of means'. There was a large flower garden 'in which, during the summer, most of the political consultations between the fair countess and her sovereign are held'.[16]

The house had been completed at some considerable cost, for throughout the autumn of 1846 Lola's expenditure knew few bounds. On Christmas Eve a plan for her monthly expenditure was conceived to prevent her exceeding her annual allowance of 10,000 florins, but it had no possible hope of succeeding. Already, since her arrival in Munich, Ludwig had spent thousands more on her. Maltzahn had returned to Paris, from where he had sent a coach costing 3,300 francs. The packing was extra and so were a pair of blue harnesses. The total of the extras came to just under another 1,000 francs.[17] In an effort to keep her extravagance under control, Ludwig had asked the formerly retired Carl Wilhelm, Baron von Heideck, to assist her, checking the bills under the guise of making sure she was not being swindled. Soon, to his deep regret, Heideck found that he was not only acting as purse keeper – or rather purse opener, because Lola had all bills sent to him – but also as a mask for Lola and Ludwig's regular meetings at tea parties at his home in the Briennerstrasse.

Throughout the autumn and early part of the winter of 1846, despite growing opposition to Lola subtly orchestrated by Abel, Ludwig remained blind to her faults and sins. Even when these were spelled out in words of one syllable, he stubbornly refused to accept advice that, for his own sake and that of the country, she must go. Pechmann now gathered his courage and approached Ludwig directly, pointing out the ill-feeling she was generating. Even when Lola did something for the good of the community it would turn sour. She had approached Ludwig on the subject of an increase in the wages of lowly paid teachers and he had approved such an increase. Unfortunately, not only did she leak the news a week before the official announcement, but people took her action as showing she had far too much influence.

Some weeks previously Pechmann had placed a spy in her household. Crescentia Ganser, who acted as interpreter for Lola, had in the past been used by the police as a not wholly reliable agent. Ganser once more brought up the name of Nüssbammer as one of the young men who visited her at night. Ludwig would have nothing of it in front of his police chief, but that evening he challenged Lola. There were accusations, denials, counter-accusations and finally a tearful reconciliation. Lola was jubilant and wrote a childlike but triumphant letter to Fiorentino:

> I left Paris at the beginning of June as a lady errant and raced about the world and *today* I'm on the point of receiving the title of *countess*! I have a lovely property, horses, servants, in sum everything that could surround the official mistress of the King of Bavaria.

She continued that the King loved her passionately (this was true) and that:

I am surrounded by the homage of great ladies, I go everywhere. All of Munich waits upon me, ministers of state, generals, great ladies [perhaps not quite so accurate] and I no longer recognise myself as Lola Montez. I do everything here. The king shows his great love for me. He walks with me. Goes out with me. Every week I have a great party for ministers etc. which he attends and where he can't do me enough homage.

But, as with every pot of ointment, there were flies:

although surrounded by all the glories and homage of my most ambitious hopes, alas, sometimes I dream, I think of Paris.

Dear Paris!

In truth, there isn't real happiness in grandeur. There is so much envy, so many intrigues. You always have to play the great lady and weigh your words to each individual. Alas! My joyful life in Paris! . . .

Farewell, dear friend. I send you a kiss. Thank God you aren't here because I can have neither friend nor . . . Grandeur is so difficult!

Your ever affectionate,

Lola.[18]

Even as she wrote the letter she was under pressure once more. Ganser went to see Pechmann, who advised her to go to the King directly, tell him everything she knew and provide him with the daily reports she had been keeping. There it was set out: the late-night visits by Nüssbammer and other men, Lola's spiteful and bragging remarks about others, including the actress Constanze Dahn, one of the King's earlier mistresses, and her comments that Hörmann, a provincial official, would never be a minister of state because he had interfered with her affairs.

The weeping King refused to accept the allegations. In another display of wilful blindness, coupled with a sense that she must be allowed to defend herself, he arranged that the unfortunate Heideck should put the points to her and obtain detailed answers. The meeting at his apartment was not a success. The little actress, very often far more convincing off stage than on, was enraged, swore on her father's grave that the allegations were false, tore at her clothes, reviled the King and wept, saying she would return to Paris at once. In true musical comedy tradition, Ludwig came into the room and instantly her fury was turned on him. Heideck now said she should beg the King's forgiveness and he again suffered her abuse and the destruction of a number of his teacups. So far as she was concerned an innocent woman had no need for forgiveness.

Ludwig desperately wanted to be convinced, and so he was. Another emotional reconciliation took place. Now Lola had him absolutely pinned. Later he would write that even had she confessed he would have forgiven her, such was his 'great passionate love' for her. Poor Heideck. He was not in love with Lola and had the wit to see just how dangerous she was and could be. Now he begged Ludwig not to see her again, but was told that was exactly what Ludwig proposed to do.

Another effort at the palace by the King's old friend Count Karl Sensheim, who was finance minister under Abel, simply served to convince the stubborn old fool that the whole thing was a plot against her and that he himself was being manipulated. Ludwig went to see her that evening and she once again convinced him that it was all lies. Now he decided that Lola must have a friend on whom she could depend. He wrote to Maltzahn in Paris asking him to return to Munich. Naturally there was a price. Maltzahn wanted a court appointment and Ludwig settled for adjutant. For all his apparent blindness, however, Ludwig did have an inkling of the problems. He wrote in his diary that Lola was meddling in affairs of state, that concessions merely brought demands for more concessions, and wondered where it would all lead: 'I hope I may never suffer again what my poor heart suffered last Saturday the 5th (a day which I will never forget to the end of my life) and what my darling Lola suffered. They tried to tear us asunder forever.'[19]

Concessions turned into humiliation. In an earlier, unguarded moment of passion Ludwig had suggested he might make her a countess. Now, to her wrath, he tried to downgrade the honour to that of baroness. Lola would have none of it. A countess, or departure from Munich. A countess it would have to be.

Within a few days of the Ganser debacle there was further trouble. This time Lola, her maid Jeanette, and her friend Berta Thierry created a scene in the post office. She had written to Nüssbammer and now wanted the letter back. The incident involved an assault on at least one official. Pechmann investigated once again, Lola complained once again. Pechmann was told by Ludwig that unless he himself inquired after his mistress, the King did not want to hear anything further from him about Lola. Pechmann continued his investigations, questioning the maid and Berthe. Lola immediately sent him a note saying that if he did not cease to trouble her she would complain to the King. Pechmann responded by issuing a summons to answer for her 'excessive behaviour in the postal building'.

The summons was returned by Lola with the answer that as she could not read German, she did not understand what the paper was all about, and that should be the end of the matter. Pechmann, to his credit but perhaps foolishly, refused to climb down. Bavarian documents were issued in German; if she could not read them then she must find a translator and, *en passant*, he was not going to let the matter rest without authorisation.

Lola was suffering from periodic cramps – something that seems to have troubled her throughout her adult life – and was not in the best of tempers. Given that she had not learned from history, it was bound to repeat itself. Back went the servant with the summons in pieces. Pechmann had the servant sign the investigation file as a witness. Lola had second thoughts – that, or the Thierrys explained to her that tearing up a summons was a serious matter. Berta's father, Ulrich, was despatched to make apologies. They were not accepted. It was all the stuff of which the second act of an operetta is made.

Part of a monarch's function is to help his subjects, particularly royal favourites, in distress and Ludwig was called on to undertake that task. In the early afternoon Pechmann received a note in peremptory terms. The King's dear Lola must not be bothered in future. She was not used to Bavarian ways. Leave her alone. Do not reply to this, simply obey.

Pechmann did not. He ordered an investigation of everyone involved. In turn the King ordered him to be transferred to Landshut.

'Freiherr von Pechmann has only himself to blame,' wrote Ludwig. 'It is time that the servants of the State learnt that they cannot with impunity oppose their king and neglect the consideration that is his due.'[20] The inquiry into Lola's conduct was dropped when she provided a doctor's certificate.

Quite apart from the official observations, Palmerston's nephew, Stephen Henry Sulivan, kept an eye on Lola, writing at irregular intervals to 'My dear Uncle'. The first of the letters is from the middle of November 1846 and contains only a brief reference. Paul, Baron de Bourgoing, the French envoy extraordinary and minister plenipotentiary at Munich, had tried to speak to Ludwig on the subject of the Spanish royal marriages but the King 'was not in the vein of business, and would talk of nothing but ballet dancers'.[21]

There was very much more about Lola in the next letter, which came a month later, and most of it was critical:

> She is handsome, ambitious to act the part of Madame de Maintenon, and with talent enough to gain ascendancy over the King who, instigated by her, is committing a series of arbitrary and unjust acts which will destroy the little popularity which the King has enjoyed. The King's ruling passion has always been to be an absolute sovereign, and anyone who encourages him is sure to gain great influence over him. This is the secret of the immense influence which Abel has acquired. As Lola proves to the King that he ought to be an absolute monarch and shows him how to be so, she is sure to gain and maintain her power, even if the King gets tired of her as a mistress.

Sulivan provided some examples of her behaviour to give an idea of the state of affairs in Munich. Lola imagined that the colonel of a regiment, whom he thought might be Pechmann, had laughed at her, so she called him names in front of several people. He complained to the King, but was told that he must overlook her outburst as it was the effect of her Spanish blood. The next day the colonel received an order to quit Munich.

He went on to say that Lola had a fancy to become a member of an arts club (the Kunstverein) where the members give a certain number of balls every year. She was told that the ballot was unfavourable – it was twelve to three against her – but the King commanded that she should be admitted and treated with the deepest respect. Professor Thiersch, the president of the club, had shown Sulivan this document, signed by the King.

> The number of people thrown into prison for one, two and even three months for having affronted Lola, or for not having taken their hats off when she passed, is extraordinary. The nobility is disgusted, the burghers are angry, and even the protestant party, who hope to profit by the present state of things, agree that the King of Bavaria has 'lost his senses'.[22]

Ludwig had not quite given up all his old friends. He was still visiting Constanze Dahn, but her continual sniping at Lola displeased him. When he stopped his visits she wrote complaining about his treatment of her, and as a result Ludwig proposed to banish her to Italy for six months. If on her return she held her tongue, there would be a substantial gratuity and, better still, he might actually visit her again. As with Nüssbammer and his first exile, she was pardoned before the expulsion actually took place. Nüssbammer himself was back in Munich by Christmas and took the opportunity to visit Lola. She did not, when the opportunity arose, tell Ludwig of his visit but Dr Ludwig Curtius helpfully did so.

One thing Lola could not stand was being lorgnetted (a practice of raising a pair of lorgnettes and deliberately and rudely ogling the victim) in the theatre – unless, of course, it was Ludwig doing the lorgnetting – and it could be an expensive pastime for those of whom she complained. On 26 December Lieutenant von Hörmann, the son of the government president and a sworn enemy of Lola, received three days' house arrest for the crime. Ludwig wrote on the signat (order) to him, 'I will hope, and quite earnestly, that father and son will behave obediently. The King is not joking.'[23]

There is no doubt that those under Lola's patronage also suffered at the hands of the general public. The files are full of letters to the King saying how the sender and his family have been ostracised. On 31 December Dr Curtius, one of the shadowy men around Ludwig's court, wrote to the King, 'I am losing all my patients; only Graf

Degenfeld is loyal to me – can you put me on a salary?' At the end of January the confectioner Gregor Mayrhofer complained that his friendship with Lola had cost him much of his Christmas trade; in consequence his fidelity was rewarded with the title of Court Chocolatier.

On New Year's Eve Maltzahn wrote to Ludwig. Things had not worked out. Any thoughts he had entertained of exercising control over Lola had evaporated. He no longer wanted the appointment as Flügeladjutant. So far as the King was concerned his life was his to command, but not his honour. People were saying it was he who had brought Lola to Munich and had been pimping for her. Would Ludwig be kind enough to see him? 'The situation here is completely different from what I thought; unfortunately during my absence Lolita has insulted all classes of society, offended everyone, and the city and the nation are so up in arms that with the best will it is too late, impossible, to improve her position. At least I am too feeble to manage it.'[24]

And so at the beginning of 1847 hostility to Lola was mounting on all sides: at a low level from such as Constanze Dahn; at a higher level from Ludwig's ministers, the police and the clergy; and at the highest level from his sister Karoline Auguste, who wrote reproaching her brother for his association with Lola. On New Year's Day 1847 Maltzahn's request was granted and he had his audience with the King. He also saw Lola. Ludwig was unmoveable in his defence of his mistress – and Lola was equally unmoveable, even though Maltzahn reportedly offered her 50,000 florins a year for life if she would leave Ludwig and go to Italy. Another version of the story has it that Ludwig's sister made the offer. The more they tried, the more they were doomed to failure. Ludwig was far too besotted and far too stubborn to listen.

Meanwhile he was busy writing poems for Lola and showing them to whomsoever he could persuade to read them. As a result they went into general circulation, attracting more ridicule. Now the elderly Heinrich von der Tann wrote as near an admonishment as he dared. 'I cannot suppress my conviction that such matters belong to the sacred realms of love and not to a public which passes judgment upon the poems so unworthily.'[25]

Lola had now become a major celebrity and a target for the scorn of the street urchins of Munich. When she went out, crowds would follow her, and the boys would whistle, yell, and sometimes toss horse manure from the street. Things became so bad that Ludwig assigned gendarmes to guard her at all times, and now she rarely ventured out on foot. A carriage had been purchased for her in Paris, a brown brougham; and with two superb black horses which the King had given her from the royal stables, she and her mounted gendarmes made an impressive parade. Up to 200 people would gather at the Goldener Hirsch to watch her descend to her carriage and ride off. In one incident a countess from one of the most conservative noble families was mistaken for Lola while shopping, and in a few minutes more than a hundred gawkers had gathered around the poor woman.

On a night early in January the windows of Lola's bedroom had been broken by stones, reportedly thrown by a young man of good family. The gendarme watch on her apartments was tightened and a sentinel was assigned to her new house in the Barerstrasse, which was still being extensively remodelled. Now the burghers began referring to the city gendarmes as 'the Spanish guard'.

Poor Nüssbammer was being pulled about like a puppet. On 17 January he was once more commanded to leave Munich and ordered back the same day. He did not help himself, however, for on 19 January he was found by the King in Lola's rooms when Ludwig went for tea. Lola explained that she had allowed him to come because he was still in love with her and it would be cruel to exile him. And, once more, Ludwig swallowed the facile story.

A fortnight later, on the day that the Council of State held a meeting to discuss her citizenship, there was another incident. Lola was still at the Goldener Hirsch. When she and her friends – who included a number of Poles, Berta Thierry and Lola's English minder, a sailor called Clements – returned from dinner there was trouble. Her companions were not all of the highest type; one Pole had been a croupier at Baden-Baden. On 3 February a pre-Lent party was being held by Ambros Havard for his clients, to which she had been invited, accepted, and then declined. Now, although she herself hung back, her friends decided to join the dance. Almost immediately the one-time croupier began to cause a disturbance – one report says he was lorgnetting the other guests – and was asked to leave.

As was so often the case with Lola, things escalated in a matter of seconds. She told Havard that if he did not treat her guests better she would move out. The sooner the better, he replied, and she responded with a slap. Another of Havard's guests, Ignaz Riehle, a master tailor, told Lola she wasn't welcome. For his troubles, he had his glasses broken. Havard's son Philip joined in the mêleé and Lola's friends pulled her away. One might think Lola would leave things alone, but instead she sent a note to Ludwig which was given to him when he was woken at about 5 am. Amazingly, he was prepared to intervene and walked to the hotel where the police were still questioning the party-goers. Reports have it that on his arrival he began to cry, but for once he was not prepared to stop the investigation. Later he visited Lola twice during the day. One immediate result was that Havard refused to serve food or drink to Lola and she moved out to rooms at Theresienstrasse, where the occupants of number 8a were ordered to leave to make room for her.

Three days later there was yet another incident. Lola was shopping with Mathilde Thierry and Clements, who was again acting as a bodyguard. Along with them was Turk, a black dog often described as a bulldog but in reality rather nearer a bull mastiff, probably named after Heinrich LXXII's dog. Turk, who had the same irrational temper as his mistress, bit Georg Dachgeuber, a deliveryman, on the foot. The man took a piece of wood to beat the dog and Lola quickly slapped him a number of times. Dachgeuber now began to threaten Clements.

For once Lola did not stay to see things through. With a crowd beginning to gather and threaten them, she and the others walked through the Frauenplatz and took refuge in a silversmith's shop owned by Simon Hopfer. The crowd grew to several hundred and began to swarm outside. After an hour, under the cover of darkness, Lola and her party left Turk behind, climbed a ladder at the back of the shop and disappeared into the rear of the Weiss Lamm guesthouse, and on to safety.

Any thought that this latest incident might sour the King's feelings was soon dispelled. The next night he came to her loge during the third act of *Robert le Diable*. On the Monday he was again trying to force through her naturalisation. There were two reasons for this. First, it was what he wished; second, the inquiry into the fight at the Goldener Hirsch was concluding and he feared that charges might be brought against her. As a foreigner, Lola might be imprisoned awaiting trial and he could not allow this to happen. The council once more declined to grant her citizenship, using the excuse to thwart the King that she had no documents to support her application.

They were told to rehear the application immediately, but only the loyal Georg Ludwig von Maurer, the sole Protestant member of the council, voted in favour. Even then there was a price for Maurer's loyalty. He wanted his son made a professor of law at the university, and for himself a house and hereditary membership of the Reichsrat. Ludwig would give a post only to his son.

The King was fortunate. The council could only advise, not veto. Privately Maurer recommended that Ludwig sign the decree for her citizenship as soon as possible and so obviate any arrest warrant. So, on Monday 10 February 1847, Lola was granted Bavarian citizenship 'with retention of her current citizenship' – wherever that was. As for the fight at the hotel, the inquiry found that Ambros Havard had insulted Lola and he was given four days' arrest; his son Anton was found not guilty of insulting her; the tailor Riehle received two days for insulting Lola. In her turn she was sentenced to a day, and along with Ambros and Riehle, was ordered to pay costs.

The battle against Lola lost, Abel now told his colleagues that he would resign. They joined him in preparing a letter of mass resignation. With hindsight the document was ill thought through, designed to make a stubborn man even more stubborn – particularly as it impugned Lola's character. It spoke of the bitter tears of the Prince-Bishop of Breslau and the laughter and scorn of both high and low, warning that the loyalty of the army was in question. One of the more telling – and for Ludwig, unacceptable – paragraphs read: 'At the same time, national pride is deeply offended because Bavaria believes itself governed by a foreigner whom the public regards as a branded woman and any number of opposing facts could not slake this belief.'

Duly signed, the letter was handed in on 11 February to the King, who promptly gave Abel and his colleagues two days to reconsider.[26] They did not do so and the government was dissolved that day. Ludwig was triumphant, writing to Tann that he had shown whether he or the Jesuits ruled. The control of the ultramontanes had finally been broken. Not that Ludwig found it easy to replace Abel and his supporters. Men to whom he offered positions declined them, either to cause the King problems or because they feared that sooner or later they would clash with him over Lola. Finally, he chose as his key men Maurer to be the Minister of Justice and Foreign Affairs, while Baron Friedrich von Zu Rhein, who had consistently opposed Abel, was placed in charge of finance, religious affairs and education, and Johann Baptist Zenetti became the Minister of the Interior. For the moment the public gave Ludwig their guarded support.

On a happier and personal note, on 26 January Lola gave Ludwig a marble cast of her foot made by the sculptor Leeb. The King was enchanted by the gift and on a piece of paper decorated with a serenade he wrote:

Corazon di mi corazon, mia Lolita

You gave me great pleasure by the lovely surprise of sending me your foot in marble – your foot has no equal – it appears to be an antique ideal – when Leeb had left, I covered it with ardent kisses. Thanks to you. I want you to receive my lively thanks, which I will express to you at noon. Tu fiel Luis.[27]

Over the months the King would become besotted both with it and her feet in general, developing a fetish for them.

Public enthusiasm for the changes did not last. In the middle of February S. H. Sulivan wrote again to Palmerston updating him on the Lola situation:

The influence and power of Lola Montez over the mind of the King of Bavaria is so great that everyone is alarmed.

She has beauty, talent and so violent a character that the King, partly from love and partly from fear, is sunk into the position of a simple reg-

ister of the acts of his mistress . . . The exasperation of all classes is so
great that the idea of dethroning the King is daily gaining ground, and if
the Prince Royal [Maximilian] was in Munich, instead of being at
Palermo, some serious riots would have already taken place.

Sulivan thought it would be difficult to guess quite how far the soldiers would side with the people, but he was certain that most of the
officers in Munich could not be depended upon. He thought that the
Queen and all the royal family were distressed. The Queen and
Princess Alexandra had decided to visit the Duchess of Modena, and
the Princess Royal would have continued to Berlin had they not been
persuaded that their sudden departure would create a bad effect and
that Lola might be installed at the palace in their absence.

At this period of her career Lola not only had a bad temper, she was
also spiteful. Francis Bridgeman, a nephew of Lord John Russell, was
a captain in the 10th Hussars, curiously the same regiment as Lola's
former friend Leigh. It is not quite clear how he insulted her, but he
seems to have written to Nüssbammer advising against continuing his
relationship. The lieutenant showed the letter to Lola, who showed it
to the King. Bridgeman was ordered to leave Bavaria.[28]

Unsurprisingly the British ambassador, John Milbanke, kept a
close eye on things. And in that month, February 1847, he wrote (if
only to himself):

> But the nature of the King's character is so vacillating and uncertain as to
> render it impossible to count upon what he may do next and in myself
> for one it would hardly excite surprise to see his passion suddenly
> diverted to some other object and himself fall back into the hands of the
> very Party from the trammels of which he now seems to think himself
> once for all emancipated.[29]

On 22 February Maltzahn wrote to Ludwig from Nuremberg giving
details of a plot worthy of Dumas or Anthony Hope. He had been
offered upwards of 50,000 florins to lure Lola into a trap. Just after
Ludwig had left her one evening, Maltzahn was to send a message
requesting a secret rendezvous with Lola, telling her he would be
waiting at the beginning of Ludwigstrasse and she should follow the

messenger. His coachman, in on the plot, would drive to the English Garden[30] where masked conspirators would kidnap her and drive to a castle a day's journey from Munich. There she would be kept underground and never see the light of day again. There was a variant. Lola would be invited to a late-night supper party. There she would be told that Maltzahn would be bringing her one-time English lover. She would instead be given a sleeping draught or have a sack put over her head, and then it would be off to the castle. Maltzahn assured Ludwig of his devotion, but warned the plotters would do everything in their power to destroy Lola. Curiously, the next day Ludwig himself received a note saying Lola would be kidnapped and taken to Vienna. It was only one of a number of anonymous threats.[31]

Some years later Lola would write that the plot had indeed been hatched. She was to have been kidnapped at a party given by a Mr Somers, who lived near Munich, and to have been taken to Brno, to the Spielberg prison which housed the Italian writer and patriot Silvio Pellico, and, 'where I would have been immured to this day, lost and unheard of'. She had been warned of the plot by one of the conspirators 'to whom I had done a kind action on the morning of the very day'. She also complained that Jesuits had poisoned her with arsenic and had her twice shot at, as well as placing 'a fanatic upon my stairs at midnight, with a poignard in his coat'. She closed, 'These are truths and facts.'[32]

Four days later Ludwig received a letter of reproach from Peter Richarz, the Archbishop of Augsburg, telling him that all reports on Lola were that she was totally unworthy of him and that his relationship with her was shameful. Meanwhile the long-suffering Heideck was at the end of his tether trying to budget Lola's finances. Her latest extravagance had been to ignore the 500 florins set aside for the purchase of Bavarian porcelain. Only Parisian porcelain would do, at an extra 100 florins. There was another bill for 500 florins for mirrors, and another for 1,348 florins for closets. Finally, Maltzahn sent in a bill for another 11,000 florins, making a total of 33,000.

There was worse to come. On 1 March there was a riot outside Lola's home. This time the cause had been the dismissal of the fanatical but gifted Catholic professor of philosophy at the university, Peter

Ernst von Lasaulx, who had been meddling in politics and paid the price. He had proposed a motion at a session of state that ministers who resigned should be given a vote of thanks and honour for their service to the monarchy. This was in fact a homage to Abel. The motion was rejected but Ludwig immediately pensioned off the professor. As a parting gift he posted a violent attack on the student notice board. The students took to the streets, marching to his house to protest their solidarity.

The meeting dispersed but then fly posters were seen around Munich. There was to be a march to Lola's house in the afternoon to deliver a *pereat* (complaint) about the dismissal of Lasaulx. The students were followed by a crowd which grew until it numbered in the thousands. They arrived around 3.30 pm. Lola was waiting for them at an upstairs window with four friends, one of whom was Nüssbammer. Reports vary as to what she actually did to inflame the crowd. One version is that she mockingly toasted them in champagne and another that she bared her breasts to them. Certainly the students threw stones; another account has her throwing them back and yet another firing a pistol at the students. At one stage Nüssbammer tried to pull her away but in a display of ingratitude she turned on him and hit him. This resulted in the unfortunate man facing disciplinary charges.

Ludwig, seeing a larger than usual gathering in the streets, went to investigate, taking with him his new minister of the interior, Johann Zenetti. Now troops were trying to clear the streets, but Lola was standing her ground and in effect baiting the mob. Zenetti soon turned tail and left Ludwig, who bravely walked through the crowd calling 'Hats off before the King.' Many complied, shouting 'Vivat Ludwig' in reply. With troops threatening a bayonet charge, Ludwig made his way to the apartment, where Lola was still laughing and making gestures at the crowd.

It took two hours for the streets to be cleared. The mob moved down Ludwigstrasse and threw rocks at the windows of the royal palace. The King now went in pursuit of them, but they turned on him and he was hustled and jeered as he walked down the street named after him. By ten o'clock all was quiet and he was back in the palace playing cards with his wife.

The next day Theresienstrasse was blocked off by the army and the town was under street patrol. There was a demonstration by the students at the King's Residenz and the Riot Act was read, but on the whole the town remained quiet. Two days later Ludwig and Therese appeared at the theatre for a performance of Auber's *Des Teufels Anteil* and were loudly cheered. For the present the crisis seemed to be over. *The Times* commented on the situation:

> The proverbial propriety of Munich is sadly outraged, and the domestic politics of Southern Germany bid fair to be speedily revolutionised, by the unexpected ascendancy of a stranger. Lola Montez – the famous Spanish danseuse . . . bounded *per saltum* from the precarious shelter of provincial patronage into a Royal Palace and a King's favour. She reigns supreme at Munich, dispenses all dignities, and bestows all favours . . . She has just bespoken a countess's title . . . The good Bavarians, however they might tolerate the estrangement of the King's love, are sorely wounded at the alienation of his money.[33]

Ludwig had already received another letter of remonstrance from his sister and it seems this time he wrote back saying that his love for Lola was finished: 'The intoxication of my soul is over.' He may have believed it was. But, even given that the spirit was willing, the flesh was weak.[34]

CHAPTER SEVEN

Lola Triumphant

UNSURPRISINGLY WITH ALL THIS TRAUMA, on 9 March 1847 Ludwig broke out in skin eruptions diagnosed by his doctors as a chronic skin rash. There has been much speculation that Ludwig caught syphilis from Lola, or vice versa, and that the skin rash was the early sign. Other candidates for infecting her include Nüssbammer, but it could as easily have been Alexandre Dumas or a host of others. If the speculation is correct it would be no great surprise. 'Venereal disease', wrote Ronald Pearsall, 'was the Russian roulette of Victorian sex. To the pure it was something to be dreaded and spoken of in whispers. To the rake and the courtesan it was a chance to be taken, no more predictable than rain in an English summer.'[1] No one in the second category worried unduly about gonorrhoea – little worse than a cold in the nose, thought the eminent Dr Grandin. Syphilis was the real worry.

Although the nature of the illness was not announced at the time, Ludwig's chest, neck and face had roseola mottling which developed into a painful rash. He also suffered from bone pain and night-time headaches. All these could have been symptoms of syphilis. Australian author Michael Cannon thought the timing of the appearance of these symptoms would place the date of infection about mid-December 1846, a week or two after Ludwig had purchased Barerstrasse 7 for Lola.

On the other hand, Ludwig's biographer, Count Corti, wrote that this skin rash had occurred on other occasions; if this is correct it would not necessarily be symptomatic of syphilis.[2]

Whichever is the case, Ludwig remained in his quarters for the rest of March and nearly all of April. Count Corti wrote, 'The King was greatly disfigured, and being confined for some time to his room, had to interrupt his visits to Lola. This did not stop Lola visiting him daily.' And indeed she behaved extremely well during this period, sitting with him of an afternoon reading *Don Quixote* and missing only a few days in the six weeks. After the outbursts of January and February she seems to have quietened down a little. Perhaps she realised that, whatever the cause, if Ludwig's health worsened she would become more and more vulnerable. Rumours about the couple still persisted; it was spread about town that he was in the habit of kissing her feet. At this stage in their affair this was not quite correct. It was the marble cast he kissed and fondled every day.

There were still problems with her free spending on the rebuilding and furnishing of Barerstrasse. Heideck announced that in future he would not be responsible for the cost; all bills must be referred to Lola directly. This in turn brought another outburst. She had been trying to order more silver, and when she was told she would have to settle the bill she flew into another temper and smashed the glass door of a cabinet, cutting herself so badly that a doctor had to be called. When Heideck told the King of this latest outburst, Ludwig remarked simply that it served her right.

All in all, however, Lola's image was improving slightly. Her profile in the city was lower and it was generally thought better that she should call on the King rather than the reverse. She now started a press campaign to improve her standing, writing to *The Times* and *Le National* explaining that the change in the government had been made by Ludwig alone; if she had been working for the Jesuits they would no longer have merely St Ignatius Loyola but also a Ste Lola. Ludwig was amused by this but the Jesuits were not.

Then on 20 March the *Pictorial Times* published a cartoon of her with a whip, setting out the facts of her early life and marriage. Immediately she sent a new, improved and 'true' version of her parentage to the major European newspapers. She had been born in Seville in 1823:

> My father was a Spanish officer in the service of Don Carlos, my mother a lady of Irish extraction, born at the Havannah, and married for a second time to an Irish gentleman, which I suppose is the cause of my being called Irish and sometimes English, 'Betsy Watson, Mrs James, &, &'.
>
> I beg leave to say that my name is Maria Dolores Porris Montez and I have never changed that name.

And, by the way, she had never had the presumption to think she had the qualifications to adopt the stage as a profession 'which I have now renounced forever'. She had become a naturalised Bavarian and intended to make Munich her residence.[3] In May she wrote another letter, this time to the *Allgemeine Zeitung*, appealing for fair play and challenging anyone who was spreading stories about her to provide proof. 'I declare any person who dares to speak evil of me without being able to prove it to be a dishonourable slanderer.'[4] It was a tactic she employed regularly over the decades. Now she moved into Barerstrasse and Ludwig allowed her to select an Etruscan vase from the state collection.

In response to the letter to *The Times*, William Bennett had something to say about her disastrous appearance at the Haymarket. 'These cunning fellows who are equally acquainted with horse and woman and cannot be deceived by either.' He suggested that she had not written the letters to *The Times* and other papers but that these had been sent as a joke to discredit Bavaria.[5]

Finally, on 26 April, Ludwig left his apartments. The next day he reappeared at the theatre, where he was given a fine reception. Lola just could not help herself. She promptly undid much of the good work of the past six weeks by remaining seated.

That spring there was a groundswell of public opinion in Ludwig's favour. There had been genuine political reform and some of the measures of the new cabinet, such as the separation of the courts from the administrative apparatus and the reform of certain of the university regulations, had met with widespread public approval. As a sop to Lola, an inveterate smoker throughout her life, the King now permitted smoking in public.

The abatement of agitation against the 'Spanish Woman', as she was known, brought new seekers after the King's favour fluttering about Lola's flame. Among them were a minor official in the War Ministry, Johann von Mussinan, a gossip and intriguer, and his son Oscar, who had a job in the Topographical Office and who became a Lola devotee. A more substantial recruit to Lola's cause was Franz von Berks, the fifty-four-year-old director of the provincial government of Niederbayern. Ten years earlier Berks had been a valued aide to Wallerstein, the Prime Minister who had preceded Abel. Following the fall of Wallerstein's government in 1837 and the rise of the conservative Catholic regime, Berks had been relegated to the provincial government at Landshut. Interior Minister Zenetti had been one of his subordinates there and thought him at best a lightweight and an intriguer. For a time Berks and the Mussinans would be Lola's most loyal supporters.

On 1 May street patrols were still in force, but for Lola it was a relatively quiet month. True, there was further lorgnetting, and her maid Jeanette walked out on her following allegations over some missing jewellery, over which Lola backed down. On the positive side, she gave a party in her new house for Taglioni, who had come to dance *La Sylphide*.

The main trauma that month was the publication in Paris of the first of many so-called autobiographies. *Lola Montès: Aventures de la célèbre danseuse raconté par elle-même avec son portrait et un fac-simile de son écriture* was yet another rewrite of her family history. It began fairly modestly in a mixture of the first and third person: 'If I were a Stael or a George Sand I would write dozens of novels each of four volumes in which I was the heroine. Instead of the dagger she carried at her *jarretière* she would have a fine Toledo pen.' From there the story took off. People said she was a gypsy, from Bohemia, from France, but she was Spanish, baptised in Seville and the despair of the curé of Gétafe. In fact her father was Don Montez Gonzalez and her mother Dona Paquita Umbro Sos. They were rich entirely through their honest endeavours. Her father hated the Jesuits and had probably transmitted this hate with his blood. She maintained that at the age of two months she had been in her cradle when, on the curé's instructions, a farmer had set fire to the house. She had only been rescued by a miracle.

She also claimed that she had been asked to dance in her parents' absence by an old hidalgo who then tried to kiss her. Fortunately she hit him with her castanets. He turned out to be a Jesuit in disguise who was going to kidnap her.

Lola, or her librettists, claimed that it was in Paris that her troubles began with the Jesuits. She had apparently been secretly approached by members of the Society who wished her to help them convert a Russian nobleman, one of her intimate friends. Lola not only declined but also informed Guizot, the French Foreign Minister. As a result the Jesuits were briefly banned from France for their attempt to interfere in Franco-Russian affairs.[6] The Society of Jesus swore eternal vengeance on Lola and she heartily reciprocated their animosity. The latter part of the story is palpably untrue but there may be a grain or two of fact in some of the early chapters. And how much, if anything, had Lola at one time contributed? In any event, the book grandly predicted, 'Ils verront que Lola Montès Ubro Sos saura, tout en se vengeant, sauver peut-être l'humanité' ['They will see that Lola Montès Ubro Sos revenging herself to perhaps save humanity']. It is impossible to know who wrote this flagrantly anti-Jesuit tract but by the time of its publication Lola was well settled in Munich, where the German translation was promptly banned.

Another book to fall foul of the censors was *Mola oder Tanz und Weltgeschichte*, (Mola or Dance and World History) a satire written in March or April 1847 and circulated underground in Munich. The pseudonyms are easy to translate: Liszt becomes Twist, Ludwig is Chodwig, Abel is Babel, Lola of course is Mola and so on. The interest is that it contains a number of inventions, such as Lola fighting a duel at Baden-Baden and first seeing Ludwig in a religious procession, which were incorporated into her so-called memoirs of 1851. It was definitely not an autobiography, but whoever wrote it must have known some of Lola's circle in Paris. At the end of July it was reprinted in a German translation, after which it was promptly banned in Bavaria.

In the spring of 1847 there was also a satirical poem *Glorreiches Leven und Chaten der edelen Sennora Dolores* circulating. In it Zorro is von Maltzahn and the reference to a Russian count is probably to Meller. There is also a reference to Fürst P., who was almost certainly Potocki and Mr L. is Leigh. Clearly the writer knew Lola's background because it seems likely that she was on her way to Vienna when she stopped in Munich. This accords with the version of her memoirs published in Grimma.

Meanwhile the unfortunate Nüssbammer, charged with allowing Lola to strike him during the riots of 1 March, was acquitted on all counts. Generously, if a little late in the day, she wrote to him accepting that the whole thing was her fault. The day before Ludwig's reappearance he was given three months' leave.

The Queen had already announced that she was intending to take the waters that summer at Franzenbad. And so the way was clear for Ludwig to take a cure at Bad Brückenau, provided Lola went with him. On 9 June Sulivan reported to his uncle that the King was going to Bad Brückenau to spend the 'honeymoon' with Lola Montez and Sir John Murray, who 'is an intimate friend'. Just how intimate a friend is not clear. There are suggestions that he had been a friend of Lola's mother, but quite where he met her is difficult to say. And if he did know Lola's parentage, why as a would-be court chamberlain did he not unmask Lola at an early stage in her Munich career?

The preparations for the trip were arranged by the faithful Tann. They did not go smoothly at all. For a start Tann's son Rudolph, who in April had been appointed aide-de-camp to the King, begged his father not to force him and his brother to go to Brückenau. Nor were either of them happy about their father being dragged further into the Montez affair. Tann obtained permission for his sons to be absent, but there was no way he could avoid the meeting himself. He was given instructions on how to behave: 'You must treat her as a lady ... she has a good manner and thinks a great deal of her noble birth. She is certainly of Moorish origin.'[7]

On 15 June the Queen left for Franzenbad, and two days later Ludwig spent a whole night with Lola, it seems the one and only time he did so. Throughout their relationship Lola used sex as a whip, and it is a measure of her ability as well as Ludwig's infatuation and obsession with her that she was allowed to create so much carnage for so long in Bavaria. There is an American expression that a single pubic hair can pull a train, but it seems in Ludwig's case that it derailed a monarchy. It was a game expertly played by Lola. She strung him along with the myriad excuses that may be offered by a skilful player – fear of pregnancy, menstruation, illness – to avoid actual intercourse while still remaining in control of the lover. Some of the excuses may even have been genuine, for there is no doubt that during her time in Bavaria Lola suffered from bouts of high fever.

The next day, 18 June, was another landmark in Lola's career in Munich and, it can be said, a major one in her ultimate downfall. For the first time she met the handsome twenty-one-year-old Elias Peissner, known as Fritz and said by some to be Ludwig's illegitimate son. The university at Munich had, as did many other German universities, a series of semi-formal, quasi-military student fraternities, often based on the regions from which the students came. The tradition, begun in the thirteenth century, is something completely unknown in England but can be very loosely related to fraternities such as Phi Beta Kappa in America's Ivy League universities. Peissner, in fact the son of a minor government functionary, was the leader of the Palatia, and along with some other members he paid a call on Lola at her house on Barerstrasse. Another group saw them through the windows; they promptly accused Peissner and his friends of disloyalty and consorting with the Spanish Woman. Worse, they had seen Peissner put a Palatia cap on Lola's head. It was proposed they be expelled from the fraternity.

Before Ludwig set off for Bad Brückenau there was to be further humiliation in return for the luxury of his night with Lola. She took him to see Nüssbammer, who had received severe abdominal injuries in a riding accident. At least Ludwig knew where her priorities lay and set off on his own. Lola left only when Nüssbammer was out of danger, and in her absence he was given full use of her carriage.

Unfortunately there was another incident in Bamburg, on Lola's way to Bad Brückenau. The journey to Nuremberg had been a long seven hours but she had been well received there. It was a further two hours to Bamburg, and while she was resting on arrival she seems to have made a denigratory remark about the town which provoked a demonstration against her. Always keen to blame the Jesuits, she asked if there was a monastery in town. When she was told there were two, she remarked that she now knew the cause of the outburst. There was renewed hostility from the crowd; the Bamburger Hof, where she was putting up, had to barricade its doors. A carriage was provided and she drove through the night, first to Würzburg and then to Bad Brückenau. Glowing in the aftermath of sexual passion, Ludwig demanded that the citizens of Bamburg should send her an apology.

Nor were things much better in Bad Brückenau itself. Even there, the loyal Tann found it increasingly difficult to keep the peace. Crown Prince Maximilian refused to meet Lola, and it was Tann who had to entertain her during the first part of her visit. As a result, infuriated by what she correctly saw as a public boycott and slight, Lola became ever more demanding in private. If she were to be ennobled as Ludwig had promised, she could no longer be snubbed. Now, in Bad Brückenau, he was able to kiss her foot and suck her toes. In lieu of further sexual intercourse, she gave him pieces of flannel; she said she had worn them beneath her underwear and that he was to wear them next to his skin. Ludwig was ecstatic, but it was a mixture of sun and dark clouds all summer.

There was another unhappy scene on 20 July when Ludwig, infuriated by her demands and behaviour, walked out of her apartments. The loser was the unfortunate Tann, who witnessed the episode. Tann began to explain that Lola could not treat the King in this way. He was fortunate not to have been horsewhipped; her screams and shouts could be heard in the street. Ludwig immediately sent a note to Tann – to be shown or read to Lola – asking if she was all right and piteously saying that if she would like to see him, Tann should tell him. After all, Lola was different from everyone else. If only she would treat him as a friend and one who loved her, rather than as a servant – even so, he should not have said what he did. It was total capitulation and humiliation.

Perhaps not quite total capitulation, because Lola, playing her cards very coolly, did not reply to the note. Ludwig was left to sweat things out overnight; worse, in the morning he heard that she had packed her bags and was preparing to leave. Ludwig prostrated himself. Lola was adamant. She would stay, but not when she was surrounded by spies. Within twenty-four hours the promptly expelled Tann left for Aschaffenburg. Lola was at the King's table for luncheon and afterwards he himself drove her into the countryside. Parting is such sweet sorrow, but reconciliation and forgiveness are so much sweeter. Now, with the restraining Tann out of play, Lola could devote herself to her imminent elevation to the aristocracy.

Back in Munich, Stieler's second portrait – the one that survives – had gone on show. It, if not the subject matter, was much admired. Ludwig's fourth volume of McGonagall-style poetry was now in print, to be read if not appreciated. One poem was clearly directed against the Catholic conservatives, while another was dedicated to and in praise of Lola:

> To L***
>
> I believe thee, and when appearances deceive,
> Thou art faithful and ever true,
> The inner voice betrays me not,
> It says: Your loving feeling is right.
>
> .   .   .
>
> The iron hardens beneath the hammer's blows,
> It becomes the hardest steel.
> When they array themselves to tear thee from me,
> They simply chain me all the firmer to my choice.

Ludwig could hardly have set out his stall more clearly. And so the summer holiday progressed; Lola was struck down with some sort of fever and prescribed huge doses of quinine, while the elderly monarch wandered around his summer palace with the pieces of flannel erotically hidden in his underwear.

On 4 August Ludwig went to Aschaffenburg, where he was to meet with Therese. Lola was first to travel to Würzburg before returning to Munich. As he left he gave her the long-awaited news. On his birthday, 25 August, he would ennoble her. Until then she must keep it a secret. He wrote to Maurer that as far as he was concerned there were to be no objections. Ludwig was simply fulfilling a royal promise.

Now it was Maurer's turn to suffer. Those, such as Lola's friends Alois and Sidonie Spraul, who had given any form of support had been socially ostracised. Maurer pointed out that any member of the Landtag who called on her would suffer in a similar way. He would prepare the required document for her ennoblement but he wanted Ludwig to find some other minister to sign it. Otherwise he believed it would be said that Lola really ruled Bavaria and he thought it better in the circumstances that he resign.

It was also the turn of another unfortunate public official to suffer. The lesson about not allowing Lola to travel on her own had been absorbed, and she arrived in Würzburg with her dog Zampa in reasonable humour and Mussinan in tow. They were joined by Berks, and a local nobleman, Baron von Ziegler, had been persuaded to hold a dinner at his home on the Domplatz in her honour. So far so good – for twenty-four hours, that is. On 5 August, the day after she learned that Ludwig had finally arranged her ennoblement, Lola, Berks and a local lawyer, Karl von Günther, went to give Zampa a run out in the Court Garden, disregarding a notice saying that it was forbidden to take dogs in the garden, walk on the grass or smoke. After all, rules are not there to be observed by soon-to-be countesses. One of the men picked Zampa up to carry him, but the sentry persisted. No dogs meant no dogs. And now – as with the incident that led to Lola hiding in the silversmith's – accounts vary. Andreas Menzel, the twenty-three-year-old sentry, said he reached for the dog; Lola said he reached for her. Whichever is correct, she gave him a good slap across the face for his troubles. Menzel tried to retaliate; Günther held him back, and now the crowd of around 200 which had been strolling behind the party turned hostile. Lola and her friends pushed into the garden and while the sentry went for assistance it was thought prudent she should leave by another exit to return to her hotel.

Unfortunately things did not end there. When she later drove to the Baron's she was whistled and jeered at by the crowd, who continued to demonstrate during the dinner. A decoy carriage was sent to her hotel but the protest continued. Lola wrote to Ludwig complaining that some 5,000 people had been demonstrating, naturally blaming it on the Jesuits and in particular the Archbishop. For his pains, a week later he, poor man, received a public dressing-down from the King.

On her return to Munich Lola suffered again from an attack of fever. With Ludwig safely out of the city, she turned her gaze on Elias Peissner and his newly formed student fraternity, the Allemania. They were to have a specially designed cap in her colours of red, blue and gold. Better still, she promised them Ludwig's protection. Now she began a protracted seduction of the youth. Probably only five years older than he, she had light years more sophistication and experience. As with Ludwig and Nüssbammer, she was very much in control in the matters of sex and bidding. Meanwhile Ludwig continued to write to her on a daily basis, numbering his letters, posing her questions, ending them in terms of unquestioned devotion – 'to see you again will be a delirium for your faithful Luis' – and begging her to write to him. Unless she actually wanted something, she rarely did.

What she really wanted was her ennoblement, which she duly received on the King's birthday. The diploma was mounted in a blue velvet cover, with a blue and white braided cord that led to the round metal box containing the wax impression of the great seal of King Ludwig I. Opposite the page bearing the King's signature was a hand-painted representation of Lola's arms as the Countess of Landsfeld. The four quarters of the shield depicted a sword on a red field, a rampant crowned lion on a blue field, a silver dolphin on a blue field, and a pale red rose on a white field, and above it all the nine-pointed crown of a countess. Ludwig gave it to a courier to be delivered to Lola on the morning of his birthday and wrote a note to go with it, trying to explain both his position and hers:

Countess of Landsfeld, for me, my ever dear Lolitta, on my birthday I give myself the gift of giving you your diploma as a countess. I hope it has a good effect on your social situation, but it can't change the government. Lolitta can't love, much less esteem a king who doesn't himself govern, and your Luis wants to be loved by his Lolitta. Enemies, especially your female enemies, will be furious to see you a countess, and it will be that much more *necessary* for you to be modest and prudent and to avoid all occasions for tumult, to avoid places where there are a lot of people. It's possible enemies will try to cause disturbances in order to make attempts on your life. Be careful![8]

That day Lola held a large party at her home and went to church in thanksgiving. Whether Maurer had been deliberately delaying things is not clear. But, to her fury, Lola learned that, like a matador given his *alternativa*, which does not really count until it has been confirmed in either Madrid or Mexico City, her ennoblement was invalid until it had been published in the *Regierunsblatt*. Again it was Ludwig who was to feel the force of her temper. On 2 September she wrote bitterly complaining of betrayal and utter humiliation: 'if this title is not *announced officially* in the paper in accordance and in regularity with and conforming to the order of all your other acts, you should not be surprised if I for my part don't want to accept this *title* which you have given me as if you were ashamed of your own act . . .'[9]

A week later the *Regierunsblatt* published the required notice, which contained details of penalties to be imposed on those who failed to recognise Lola's position. A week after that, the influential politician Karl Friedrich Wilhelm von Leiningen wrote that he feared Lola left unchecked would bring Bavaria to the point of revolution.[10]

For the time being, however, life progressed relatively quietly. In August Nüssbammer was again in trouble. Lola had pushed a Conrad von Berg on the street, something he resented, and he seems to have threatened her. Nüssbammer intervened and challenged Berg to a duel, but Lola would not allow it and instead invited Berg to breakfast. His army colleagues resented this fraternisation and Berg was given three months' leave. In turn Nüssbammer was ostracised for his pains.

That autumn Lola was sued in Paris for some 2,500 francs for non-payment of clothes she had bought; the ladies of the court still declined to meet her and her calling cards were left unanswered. On the plus side there had been verdicts in the perjury trial of de Beauvallon and d'Ecquevilley; best of all, Ludwig increased her monthly allowance to 20,000 florins, a sum more befitting a countess. In all, during the first year of their love affair he had spent over 100,000 florins on his mistress. He still kissed her portrait last thing at night and first thing in the morning. Although he sent her a detailed account of his daily activities, he did not say whether it was before or after he brushed his teeth. The most Ludwig could learn of Lola was not by letter from his inamorata but from a report by Berks. Part of the reason for this period of quietude was that once more Lola had been ill with a chest infection. When she was out and about again it could be seen that her bodyguard had been increased to nine men. This did not include the Allemania, members of which escorted her around the town, driving with her to the country and holding court in Rottman's, a bar they had established as their unofficial headquarters.

There was still one honour to which she aspired, one indeed which, in later years, she awarded herself. It was the Order of Therese, the highest honour in Bavaria. Later she would tell how this had been personally presented to her by the Queen, but the truth was that Therese quite understandably would not see her. On 13 October, two days before her name day, the saint-like Queen wrote a very moving letter to Ludwig pointing out that the announcement in the *Gazette* was one she had never foreseen. There was no reproach to be made, only some words to avoid any future misunderstanding:

> I owe it to my honour as a woman – which is dearer to me than life itself – she whom you have raised in rank never – under any circumstances, to see face to face; should she seek to gain admission at court through a promise of yours, you can tell her as a fact – yes, from my mouth: the Queen, the mother of your children, would never receive her.

In this she was adamant, but she continued as if she had simply avoided a particularly heavy shower of rain:

> And now, not one more word written or spoken, of this difficult matter. You will find me as before, cheerful, grateful for every joy you give me, and ever watchfully endeavouring to maintain for you, my Ludwig, the untroubled tranquillity of our home.[11]

For the rest of her life Lola would maintain that the Queen had personally presented her with the coveted Order, but it was not so. She had put a toe in the water to see what effect the ennoblement would have on her social status and was horrified with the result. She sent a card to two dozen or more of the first families in Munich and most were returned with words to the effect, 'We know not this Countess'. It was said that in poor humour she had left Munich for Chemnitz in Saxony.[12] This was incorrect, but many wished it was so.

Now, aided by Berks, she appeared to take an even firmer hand in the day-to-day running of the government. Her followers received royal favours, and both she and Berks interceded with the King on royal appointments in the army and government. The appointments may not individually have made any great difference but added together they gave the impression that Lola was not a, but the, power behind the throne.

The appointments and favours were on the plus side; the down side were the humiliations she had heaped upon those who stood against her, or whom she thought did so. Zenetti, whom she now deemed to be in league with the Jesuits, was a particular target, and she repeatedly told the King that Maurer was an incompetent. The court physician, Dr Feder, also fell foul of her, with the result that he was transferred to be the senior staff officer in the army with a salary reduction of 1,700 florins. As for the foreign papers, they were keen to print any story of Lola, however wildly inaccurate:

> The chronicles of scandal announce positively that the King of Bavaria has become wearied of the famous Lola Montez and that he has already taken a Russian countess into favour in her place. But the bold Lola swears she will not be turned off and vows vengeance on the Majesty of Bavaria. The King, it is added, is so frightened that he runs from place to place to avoid her.[13]

Even though Lola did not make an appearance in America for some four years, the newspapers there followed her activities with enthusiasm, even publishing jokes about her. One ran that the King of Bavaria was said to have had a dream of three rats, one fat, one thin and one blind. He went to a gypsy to have the dream interpreted and was told the fat rat was Lola, the thin one his people and the blind one himself.[14]

During the autumn poor Nüssbammer had been replaced in Lola's affection – some unkindly said that because of his riding accident he was no longer able to rise adequately to her sexual requirements – and was banished to Bamburg. On 2 November the sycophantic John Murray was promoted chamberlain; various other appointments were made and incumbents dismissed. Lola was also taking a greater interest in meddling in politics. She had arranged for Archbishop

Reisach to be put under police surveillance and was intriguing against the increasingly ineffectual Maurer, urging Ludwig to replace him with Prince Wallerstein.

In late October a Frenchman who had fought for the Carlists, Count de Los Valles, now reduced to selling wine and hoping for Lola's patronage, arrived in Munich. Most importantly, Peissner returned at Mussinan's and Lola's request. Within days Lola finally seduced him.

In their, or rather his, budding romance, they had held hands and caressed each other while she told him that they must save themselves for marriage – the present incumbent Captain James and Ludwig being respectively long and temporarily forgotten. Ludwig was just a dear friend, she told the student; really a father to her. It was a lie she embellished when some years later she arrived in America. Then one day she decided she and Peissner did not need to wait. The twenty-two-year-old student was a virgin no more. Afterwards Lola and he knelt together to swear their lifelong fidelity.

But suddenly where once there were two, now there were three. The young handsome Polishman, the *soi-disant* Count Eustace Karwowski, arrived in Munich and her life, and Lola now began playing off her new lovers against each other. Karwowski was set at her right hand at table, a position expected by the impoverished Count Los Valles and hoped for by Peissner. Unbeknown to Lola, Ludwig was in possession of papers from Prince Paskievich to the effect that Karwowski should be returned to his Russian-controlled country in short order.

As winter approached, over the weeks a series of warnings were given both to her and Ludwig. Los Valles wrote a long letter warning her that her conduct with the Allemania was a public scandal. He was also worried that her lifestyle was damaging her health. Ludwig's nephew, the Duke of Leuchtenberg, in Munich on a visit, also pleaded with his uncle to break this increasingly dangerous relationship. An actress, Maria Denker, who for a time had the ear both of the King and Lola, spoke with her privately, urging her not to be seen so publicly with Karwowski.

The next crisis, albeit a relatively small one, took place on 29 November when a soirée of magic was presented by Monsieur Robin, the French magician whose great illusion was the simultaneous lighting of 200 candles with a single pistol shot.[15] The Countess was now using the Allemania as private spies and they hung around the theatre listening for anti-Lola gossip. Now some members heard the French comte de Richemont discussing Karwowski in unfavourable terms with two of the King's nieces. They duly reported back. Within a matter of minutes Karwowski appeared, with three others in support, at the comte's box and demanded an explanation. The comte denied he had made any such remarks, but high words were passed.

It was not the first duel to have been threatened by Karwowski since his arrival in Munich. A month earlier Albert von Witzleben had been placed under house arrest for planning one. What was not needed was another. To protect the comte, during that night an extraordinary and *ad hoc* change was made to social convention. The *jeunesse doré* ruled that anyone who had crossed the threshold of Lola's door was *ipso facto* dishonoured and was therefore incapable of giving satisfaction in a duel.

This was still not enough for the grown-ups. The French ambassador called on Prince Wallerstein, asking him to protect de Richemont. This presented Wallerstein with a particularly difficult personal problem. He himself had been at Lola's house, indeed he owed his appointment to her influence, and as a result was now at risk of social ostracism. First he appointed a guard for de Richemont, then he told the King that Karwowski had been using Ludwig's name as a social lever and, at the same time, had been running up gambling debts.

During the afternoon of 1 December Lola physically, if not emotionally, betrayed Peissner when she had sex with Ludwig. It was to be the last occasion she did so; it was not by any means the last occasion she would betray Peissner. Whether she agreed to sex with Ludwig that afternoon in an attempt to save Karwowski from expulsion or whether it was part of a plan for greater influence on the King, it did the Pole no good. Lola had again miscalculated. Believing she had succeeded in saving him, she very publicly lorgnetted the Russian ambassador, Count Severine, from her box at the Theatre Royal on 3 December. It may be that this piece of bad behaviour was taken into account, because at four o'clock the following morning Karwowski

Lola's portrait appeared in King Ludwig's 'Gallery of Beauties' in 1847.
This is the second, and only surviving, portrait by Joseph Karl Stieler.
akg-images/Jérome da Cûnha)

Grange, Co. Sligo, Ireland. Lola claimed a number of cities and countries as her birthplace – this is the most likely. *(Scott MacGregor)*

The first known picture of Lola before her debut at the Theatre Royal, Haymarket. Her evening ended in disaster and she only appeared once more on the London stage. *(The Pictorial Times, 1843)*

Lord Brougham – the womanising Lord Chancellor who may have been Lola's lover. The London theatre-going public certainly thought so.
(Michael Nicholson/CORBIS)

Lord Blessington – the cricket-playing thespian friend of Lola and Lord Brougham.

Portrait of Lola Montez by Nicolas Toussaint Charlet, 1844. *(Bridgeman Art Librar*

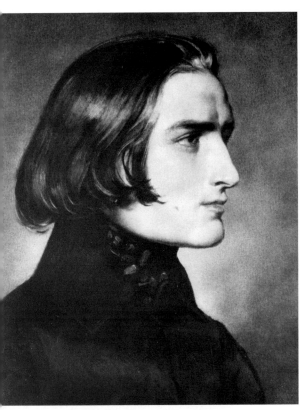

Lola's lover, the great pianist Franz Liszt. Lola set her cap at the composer on one of his tours. Painting by Amerling, 1838. *(akg-images)*

The great choreographer of *Swan Lake* Marius Petipa survived an encounter with Lola in Paris. *(Bridgeman Art Library)*

Alexandre Dumas Senior. A friend of Lola's lover Dujarrier, he was a pallbearer at his funeral, after Dujarrier was killed in a duel. *(Mary Evans Picture Library)*

Despite years of experience with women, King Ludwig I of Bavaria was quite unable to deal with Lola and her tempers. *(Mary Evans Picture Library)*

The French newspapers loved Lola and always kept an eye on her unhappy marriage to George Heald.
(Unattributed engraving)

Despite all the evidence to the contrary, Lola claimed all her life she was of noble Spanish birth and often appeared on stage in Spanish costume.
(Mary Evans Picture Library)

This caricature of Lola dancing in front of King Ludwig I of Bavaria dates from 1847.
(Bridgeman Art Library)

Nothing if not a leader of fashion, Lola openly smoked on the streets of Munich and must have been one of the first women to be photographed with a cigarette. This is a daguerreotype taken during her stay in America in the early 1850s.
(Bettmann/CORBIS)

was deported. He was not, however, returned to Poland but was sent to Salzburg and allowed to go to France to join the exiled Polish community. When it came to it, Karwowski was another of Lola's mountebanks. He was not a count but a tailor.

A hundred and sixty years later it is difficult to imagine the fear the King and his ministers had of Lola's temper and how they were cowed by it. The next question was who was to be the lucky man to tell her of the expulsion. Since he was her toady, Mussinan was given the task. It took him some hours before he was able to calm her down. But if they thought that was the end of the matter they soon found they were wrong. Next it was the turn of Berks to feel her wrath. After an hour and a half of ranting he thought the hurricane had blown itself out. He too was wrong. The actress Maria Denker was next in line to suffer an outburst when she was sent in to bat. The fact that Ernestine Opitz, who had come to show Lola some jewellery, was present did nothing to save her. Lola was raving and raging. She had created the ministers who were now all against her. Now, she would have them out. The actress retired in discomfort and sent a note to the King saying she was sorry she had failed in her mission – Lola was out of control.

Perhaps the King thought he himself would have a calming influence; perhaps he thought Lola had indeed calmed down as the day wore on; perhaps he just could not stay away from her; perhaps he had forgotten the summer quarrel with her which had resulted in Tann's dismissal. Perhaps all of those things. In any event he found himself sucked into a maelstrom when he went to her home that evening. It resulted in the unedifying spectacle of the King being chased into the street by his foul-mouthed mistress, explaining in terms what she thought of him and the situation as the guards pretended they could hear nothing.

And then the whirlwind had passed on. Perhaps Lola thought even she had stepped over the increasingly moveable line. When Mussinan arrived the next morning she was surrounded by her friends and it was two hours before he could speak with her privately. Either Lola had had a change of heart or someone had marked her card. She realised that Karwowski had indeed been an undesirable. Indeed, if he returned she would be among the first to seek his deportation. She even sent a rare note of apology to Ludwig: 'I beg you to forget what happened last night and to come at 5.30 this afternoon to your always faithful and devoted Lolitta.' And so that particular storm blew itself out, and sweetness and light and Ludwig reigned again until the next time.[16]

Over the next fortnight a great deal of time and effort was spent in an attempt to rehabilitate Lola. First, there was the question of her physical health – she had been steadily losing weight. Now Dr Martin, who had seen her in the summer, reported that she was suffering from periodic hysterical cramps and that while no medicine was required, she needed a careful diet and watching over the next few weeks.[17]

There was, perhaps more importantly, the question of her social health. The Allemania had to go; and it was thought that Lola as part of her rehabilitation could hold a weekly literary salon for the aristocracy. Both in theory were admirable ideas, it was the execution that would prove the problem. The unfortunate Count Hunolstein was deputed to attend her salon and resigned from the ministry in protest. It was next decided that Ludwig, in his role as King, should appear, setting an example.

The Allemania were still causing trouble. There had been a run-in with a nobleman at the theatre and a play, *Der bemooste Haupt*, at the Hoftheater, satirising them. Provoking general applause and laughter, it was promptly banned and the theatre director suspended. There were stories of drinking orgies at Lola's house on Barerstrasse at which the Allemania wore only their shirts. Even Ludwig was rumoured to have attended one. After the others left, Peissner regularly stayed behind.

Meanwhile, in December Ludwig struck a popular note when he granted the freedom of the press, silenced under the rule of the ultramontanes. It was something of which Lola disapproved, complaining he should have consulted her and that he had gone too far.

On Christmas Eve she held a party for the Allemania, leaving her curtains open to display her Christmas tree. Each was given a cap, a pipe, her portrait and a watch chain. The next day, in return, the Allemania planted a tree in Lola's garden.

On 30 December Ludwig was cheered when he went to the theatre.

The year ended very differently for his mistress. At a boisterous party on New Year's Eve the Allemania carried her around the room on their shoulders, allegedly once more in only their shirts. Unfortunately they carried her straight into a chandelier, cutting her head and knocking her unconscious. A doctor named Schlagintweit was sent for and, if they had been unclothed earlier, their trousers were back on by the time he arrived. Later Dr Martin appeared. Unfortunately Schlagintweit gossiped among his friends about the drunkenness he had seen and on 10 January he was questioned by the police about the incident. Now he assured them that when he had appeared everything had been as it should be. It was, however, more fuel to add to the bonfire of what little was left of Lola's reputation.

In a year that would see revolutions throughout Europe, January 1848 was a month of intriguing in Munich: Lola against Wallerstein; Wallerstein and Ludwig against the Allemania; the court and nobility against Lola. At the beginning of the month Ludwig learned that Peissner was seeing Lola at all hours of the day and night and there was another quarrel which, unsurprisingly, led to a further retreat by the King. By now Lola was regularly sleeping with Peissner and also with another Ludwig, this time a student named Leibinger. For the moment Leibinger was a relatively well-kept secret because the current gossip was that the King was planning to marry Lola off to Peissner. It was also said, probably more realistically, that Peissner was operating a quasi-employment agency, placing supplicants in governmental positions; the higher the degree of loyalty to Lola, the higher the position and salary.

Berks had by this time lost almost any semblance of operating independently from Lola, who appeared at his office daily with a fresh packet of demands. Another attempt was made to integrate her socially; this time it was Baron Hohenhausen, the Minister of War, who was asked by the King to join him for tea in Barerstrasse. The sweetener was a gift of the Knight's Cross of the order of Civil Service, the poison immediate social ostracism. Hohenhausen, loyal to the King and to his own honour, drank his tea and resigned the next day.

The army was another problem. Ludwig personally issued orders that there should be no complaints made about Lola by officers and that she must be greeted in the street with respect. Officers who failed to comply could expect a personal and public rebuke from him. Now he was specifically told that the men could not be guaranteed to come to Lola's aid.

Then there was the problem of the Allemania. They were being tormented both by members of the other fraternities, who saw their idol as a foreign whore, and even by outsiders at the university. If one of them deigned to turn up for a lecture, admittedly not necessarily a regular occurrence, then the other students would leave and the professor would decline to speak to an empty hall. The Allemania had to be reintegrated into student society.

The attempt to do so was short-lived. Lola provided money for a banquet for them to be held on 15 January at the Bayerischer Hof. Berks was invited to deliver the formal toast and a delegation arrived to invite Prince Wallerstein. He declined and wrote to the King explaining his fears over the event. He was right to do so. Berks's speech praising the Allemania for their manly virtue as a shining example to degenerate youth was calculated to upset the remaining 1,400 or so university students. Mussinan, the Allemania, some fifty other male guests and Lola, who made a token appearance on the balcony, may have applauded, but the rest of the university was outraged.

By the end of the month attacks on the Allemania had become so bad that Peissner drafted a petition for Lola to give to Ludwig asking for help. And if things could be made worse, Lola did what she could to help them along the way.

One of the most popular of lecturers, Joseph von Görres, who had defended German interests against Napoleon but who, as a conservative Catholic, was beyond Lola's pale, died on 29 January. The funeral took place two days later and Lola, not to be denied her usual lunchtime walk, encountered it as the procession made its way down Ludwigstrasse. It was incredibly crass behaviour. There were whistles and jeers and Lola flew into a temper, yelling at the mourners to get out of the way before the police were obliged to escort her home. This was an insult neither the students nor the burghers were prepared to forget. The persecution of the Allemania continued.

Things would only get worse in February. The literary afternoons did not achieve the required result. True, Hohenhausen's successor, General Heinrich von der Mark, was prevailed upon to take tea with Lola, but he was not a gracious guest, interpreting his invitation as an order. On 3 February the unhappy Wallerstein attended on Lola, who warned him that she would have him dismissed by the end of March. On 6 February she appeared at the theatre absolutely bedecked in diamonds. Whispers went round that Ludwig had paid some 60,000 florins for the jewels, but in fact they had been a bargain at 13,000. She gestured to the King in his box and compounded her insolence by insulting the unfortunate Hohenhausen.

The next day, 7 February, the Allemania were besieged by the other students. Extra police were on duty and Prince Wallerstein arrived to address them. There was, he said, no intention to interfere with their freedom of opinion and expression but law and order must be maintained. If they continued as they were doing then the King would lose patience with them and almost certainly the authorities would intervene. The students promised their good behaviour but the promise lasted a matter of minutes. There was fighting both that day and the next.

On 9 February a number of officers whom Lola disliked were dismissed by Ludwig. The same day there was a riot on the Odeonsplatz, during which one of the Allemania drew a dagger. He and his colleagues were chased into their headquarters at Rottmann's, from where they sent word to their patron. On her way there she met the King, who had left a formal luncheon when he heard the Allemania were trapped and that she might be with them. He took her back to Barerstrasse and made her promise not to leave the house.

Like the students' promise of two days earlier, hers lasted only a matter of minutes. Throughout her life it could never be said that Lola lacked physical courage. Dressed in a shawl and a blue bonnet – at least not in Allemania colours – she set off to relieve her troops and was promptly surrounded by the crowd. She drew her pistol and forced them back but the crowd rushed her, she was knocked to the ground – some accounts say she tripped – and as the crowd hesitated she was rescued by two apprentices and fled to refuge in the Theatriner Church. The crowd surged in after her, the priests there urging them to respect the traditional place of sanctuary. Yes, but she would soon have to leave, and they were there to make sure she would be dealt with when she did. Now, however, the police who had been at Rottmann's café on the other side of the square rode over and cleared the crowd outside the church doors. More police formed a wedge and she was escorted through the angry demonstrators down the Residenzstrasse to the gates of the palace, into the grounds and later to her home.[18]

The King was furious. The unfortunate Wallerstein was told to close the university immediately, an action he bitterly opposed. The order was promulgated the next day and the Prince resigned. In driving him from office, Lola had achieved her long publicly expressed wish. The students demonstrated and the police rode into the crowds to break them up. It was reported, wrongly, that one student had been killed; this only served to fan the flames.

A meeting at the town hall resulted in a decision to go to present a petition demanding that the university be reopened. Two thousand students marched to the palace, where Wallerstein told them he could do nothing because he was no longer in office. They waited for two hours while the King took dinner before his son, Prince Luitpold, agreed to see them. He went to see his father, who was also approached by his sister, the Duchess Auguste von Leuchtenberg, and the King eventually agreed to see the delegation. As might be expected from his character he took a hard line, asking whether it was usual to petition him with 2,000 men behind the spokesman. The university was going to stay closed and if the burghers did not like that he would move his capital. The crowd dispersed and Ludwig, who had intended to keep the university closed until the winter term, told Berks it could be reopened for the summer. But when Berks delivered the message to the town hall he was told it was insufficient. There were demonstrations outside the homes of both police captain Bauer and Lola, who stood on her balcony clapping her hands and calling out, 'Très bien, très bien' as the police mounted a bayonet charge into the demonstrators. The arrival of *cuirassiers* proved too much and the crowds moved on, overturning beer trucks and damaging ceramic ovens. After the streets became calm,

Burgomeister von Steinsdorf went to Berks to say that the King must order Lola to leave Munich.

The next day, another meeting at a full town hall sent a message via the Burgomeister. If the King did not concede their demands, they would go to Lola's house and smoke her out. Wallerstein reacted with considerable dignity. He would withdraw his resignation. In the face of probable further rioting it would be cowardly to do otherwise. There was talk of Ludwig's abdication and the accession of Crown Prince Maximilian if he would not expel Lola. Another attack on her house was almost certain. At 2 pm Lola sent Ludwig a message saying he must stand firm, but during the afternoon the situation deteriorated. Berks told him that a 6,000-strong citizens' army was gathering and the 2,000 men available to him – the most troops he could muster – would have difficulties even if they all proved loyal, which was by no means certain. Indeed, later Mark threatened to kill himself if he was ordered to use force to defend Lola. In the early evening the rector of the university handed in a detailed and documented list of Lola's felonies and the King's family and ministers begged him to take action against her. The saintly Therese went on her knees, not, she said, for her own sake but for that of the children.

The final demands were that Lola should leave Munich within the hour and Bavaria as soon as possible, the university must be reopened and police captain Bauer should be arrested. The King struck a compromise. Wallerstein announced at the town hall that the university would be reopened, not as a result of threats but because the burghers had appealed to the love and favour of their King. The crowd made their way to the palace, where Ludwig and Therese appeared on the balcony to resounding cheers. During that evening the King went to see the first act of Auber's *La Sirène*. Signing 'Yours ever faithful unto death', Lola wrote a note complaining of the conduct of Prince Luitpold and urging Ludwig to 'remain ever as *noble* and *great* as you are; it is your duty to demonstrate that now'.

By the next afternoon Lola must have realised her time in Munich was up. The crowd besieged her house, where she was sheltering with some of the Allemania who were pleading with her to leave. For a time she maintained she would stay and die. She even went into the garden to shout 'Kill me if you dare' at the mob. She was rewarded with a shower of stones. Her friends dragged her back into the house. A loyal supporter, Lieutenant Theodor Weber, whom she had had transferred back to Munich, helped her coachman George Humpelmeyer harness her horses and Lola was hustled into the carriage.

She must still have thought that if she could see the King person-ally she could change matters. Humpelmeyer drove to the palace by way of the English Garden, but it was locked and the crowd there was threatening. He turned around and drove to Grosshesselohe, some five miles away on the Isar. There Pfaner, a hotelier, and his family were prepared to put Lola, Weber and the coachman up. From there she wrote a note to Ludwig saying she was safe but begging him to stand firm against the crowd. Humpelmeyer was sent back to Munich in disguise to deliver it.

Back in the city the mob now stormed her house and began looting it. Again showing immense courage, the King walked there and spoke to the crowd personally, pointing out that it was his property they were looting and asking them to go home quietly. A military guard was posted. Although he was hit by a stone thrown from the crowd, the King then walked away to return to the palace. On the way he found one of Lola's friends, the chocolate maker Gregor Mayrhofer, who had been caught and beaten by the crowd. He took the man under his care and walked him home before returning to the palace, where there were cheers for him and Queen Therese.

Humpelmeyer seems to have been as indiscreet as his mistress. He delivered the message to a friend who would get it to the King and then, confident of his disguise as a farmer, joined the crowds in a tavern in the Barerstrasse. There he was recognised and given a sound beating before a passing patrol rescued him and took him into pro-tective custody.

With no word from George, Lola decided to return to Munich. It was not one of her better thought-through plans but she powdered her hair white, put on peasant clothing and persuaded Pfaner to drive her there, along with his seventeen-year-old daughter Caroline. In the city she failed to get past the sentries at the palace and was told by friends that the Allemania were camped out at a hunting lodge in

Blutenburg, to the west of Munich. The information was correct. When she arrived there she found about ten of them, including Peissner. She was still committed to returning to the city and begged Peissner to take her. When he refused, she berated and hit him, pointing out how his father owed to her his position as a ministry messenger. And, by the way, who had given him that handsome watch he was wearing? In operatic style Peissner ran into the courtyard, where he threatened to kill himself. Now it was her turn to plead with him. Eventually she persuaded him and they went to the landlord of the lodge, Joseph Schäfer, to get him to drive them. He refused. While the Allemania bedded down as best they could, she and Peissner went to an upstairs room where, he said later, she slept on the sofa and he on a chair.

It was a comedy of errors. Her note had reached Ludwig, who set off with Berks to Grosshesselohe. He had decided that she should travel to Lindau on Lake Constance and cross to Switzerland, where he would meet her in Lausanne. But, of course, there was no Lola in Grosshesselohe and the King returned to Munich. Meanwhile Schäfer had driven into Munich to make his report. At first Berks, back from his early morning drive, did not appear to take things seriously; nor did Wallerstein, whom he next met. The treacherous Schäfer then persuaded the commander of the *cuirassiers* at the Nymphenburg Palace to send cavalry to Blutenburg.

Meanwhile Berks had indeed taken steps. He sent police officers to Blutenburg to take Lola to Lindau. They found her in the lodge writing to Ludwig, urging him to move his court to Nuremberg as a punishment to the rebellious citizenry. She did not submit easily. First she scared off the police, shouting 'Raus, Raus', and followed up by threatening them with her pistol. Then, when Peissner, Leibinger and another member of the Allemania, Jacob Härteiss, tried to reason with her, she tore up the deportation order. It was Peissner who calmed her down. The six of them went by coach and then train to Lindau, arriving at ten in the evening. On the way she wrote to Ludwig complaining that she had no clothes and had to wear her pyjamas for the journey, and that her heart was broken. While she herself would be faithful unto death, he was not to trust Berks.[19]

Although the intention had been that she should immediately be put on a steamer to Switzerland, instead Lola took rooms at the Hôtel de la Couronne de la Poste and remained in Lindau for a fortnight. She was still betting each way, hoping she could persuade Ludwig she might return to the capital. Meanwhile there was considerable activity in Munich, where Ludwig was flexing both political and a little amorous muscle.

First Wallerstein wrote to him that the reason for the rioting was that the Bavarians, who loved their King, were convinced that Lola was deceiving him. He considered her completely unaccountable for her actions and as a result bore no personal grudge against her. Unfortunately, Lola had trained the King to see distrust where none existed. Anyone who was against Lola was automatically against him. When Count Arco-Valley distributed 5,000 guilden to the poor, as he had promised if Lola was expelled, in turn he was banned from the court. Now Ludwig believed his former mistress; it was all the work of the Jesuits. He wrote saying that Wallerstein would be dismissed the moment the students went on holiday. The British Foreign Office thought that the blame could only be laid in part upon them. It knew where the real blame lay:

> it has long been evident that the disregard of publick opinion shewn by the King & the arbitrary and illegal acts to which he had been made a party coupled with the extravagant and outrageous conduct of the obnoxious individual herself & those by whom she was surrounded had brought on a state of things intolerable to every body & which has eventually led to what I must term a signal degradation of the Royal dignity.[20]

Ludwig certainly intended to meet her in Switzerland, writing that while he had no objection to a proposed visit by her to Palermo, she must be at Lausanne for his arrival on 12 April. His health was good; he had spent much of the time weeping, but he was still kissing the marble cast of her foot. Maria Denker had been prevailed upon to forget the unpleasant incident over Karwowski's expulsion. She had agreed to travel with Lola. Lola was still doing what she could to manipulate the King. In turn she wrote claiming that her maid Augusta Masson, who had fled Munich with her and returned there on 16 February, had stolen a prayer book and cashmere shawl. She had spoken to the Count de Polinsky, who had told her his family had sacked the girl for theft. The police must search Augusta's house. The loyal young Oscar Mussinan, who would deliver the letter, was with Lola. Ludwig must believe in her and not the priests, who were not the sons of God but of the Devil. He must trust Mussinan and ignore the treacherous and lying courtier, Babette Shenker, as well as Princess Luitpold who was a great and dangerous intriguer. The whole thing was a test of their love for each other. She was confident that just as Josephine had remained with Napoleon, he would remain with his 'good star'.[21]

In principle Ludwig may not have been unhappy with the trip to Palermo, but he was adamant that Peissner and company should not travel with her. If they left Germany without his permission they would forfeit any hope of *Ausstellung* (Arts degree). He had meanwhile heard that she had slept with Peissner on the night of her escape to Blutenburg and was in despair. 'Your infidelities have deceived my heart but it forgives you and I repeat: the world isn't capable of making me break with you, you alone can do that.' Now she was a 'faithful friend but a faithless lover'. Her passport would be in the name of Mrs Bolton and Maria Denker would travel with her as Mme Baumann. Lola suggested that either Dr Martin or John Murray accompany her. But Ludwig thought there was no need for the former and he was not having the latter, whom people thought was one of her lovers. Mussinan reported that for the present, as required by Ludwig, the students were all sleeping in their own rooms. He had told them there was no question of accompanying her.

In fact Mussinan had only a matter of hours to last as a Lola favourite. In a letter to Berks she wrote that he had no intention of sending the students away and complained that he had been making false reports. She did not wish him to travel to Lausanne with her, while he, Mussinan, wanted a specific order in writing from the King. Meanwhile Maria Denker had been dispatched to Lindau, the King sending some orange blossoms with her. Mussinan reported that Lola was now paying more attention to Leibinger. The third student, Härteiss, told him that she had been doing this in Munich.[22]

Lola's response to Ludwig's letter was swift and to the point. How could her Luis think that she would demean herself and her love for him by sleeping with Peissner? He was not to believe the lies that were told about her.[23] And so for a little while the poor fool was happy again. The game went on and she continued to dangle him throughout the coming weeks.

Meanwhile some of her possessions were sent to her. Maria Denker was to have brought the mettlesome Turk the dog, who had run away during the rioting but had been found a few days later. Turk did not, however, arrive with the actress, and Lola wrote complaining bitterly both about that and the fact that Ludwig had not done anything about the thieving maid Augusta. Not only had the prayer book and shawl gone but so had a gold belt buckle studded with diamonds, two portraits and – something which should galvanise the flagging King – his portrait in a bracelet.[24] Given the time Ludwig spent kissing her marble foot, writing her letters, reading hers and generally running around doing her bidding, it is surprising he had any left for affairs of state.

On 22 February the students were finally despatched to Leipzig. She feared for their reception, for she believed the Jesuits had already started to influence the other students there against them. Lola was playing a deep game and it is interesting to note that at this stage she did not tell Ludwig of a letter from Robert Peel. The next day the spies Mussinan and Denker separately reported that Lola had been paying more and more attention to Leibinger. Denker thought she was actually in love with him, which must have been another dagger in Ludwig's heart. It was a nest of vipers: Lola then wrote to the King saying that Mussinan was angry with Denker. She, Lola, wouldn't give the actress a letter to Ludwig and that had upset her. The King should do nothing for her. Mussinan was also temporarily back in Lola's good books, but the new light in her life was the customs agent in Lindau, Count Anton Polinsky, who had been busying himself arranging her trip. Ludwig should think about an appointment in Munich for him. What Lola wanted from him was that he should spy for her on Wallerstein. She clearly still retained hopes of returning to Munich and power. That, or she would become a queen across the lake.[25]

On 24 February Lola finally left Lindau to travel to Switzerland. Polinsky went with her on the steamer *Ludwig* as far as Romankorn; she then took the post chaise to Zurich and Berne before, in theory, travelling to Lausanne. Before she went, there was one final quarrel with Maria Denker, whom she now believed had been another of Ludwig's mistresses. Denker had apparently pleaded with her not to cause a public scandal over her behaviour with Leibinger, who had been spending evenings alone with Lola in her room, and Lola hit her.

Back in England, Sir Jasper Nicolls, who liked her no better now than he had when she was a child, lovingly cut a piece from *The Times* about her deportation and pasted it into his journal, before writing: 'What a hold this miserable witch has obtained over this old, adulterous idiot Sovereign. Wretched country to be ruled by such a shameless rogue – but I must remember that Munich is the most abandoned capital in Europe.'[26]

At the end of it all, the author 'Q' remarked wryly: 'Some predicted this would break the heart of the old king. Monarchs' hearts are generally, however, rather tough, and it consequently bore the strain without cracking.'[27] For the moment that might have been so, but Lola had by no means finished with Ludwig.

CHAPTER EIGHT

Lola in Exile

O N 25 FEBRUARY LOLA REACHED Switzerland safely and travelled by
coach to Zurich. But she never reached Lausanne, for there to
pick up the pieces – or perhaps to debrief her – was the engaging,
moustachioed Robert Peel. All thoughts of her being too expensive for
him, if that was ever the case, were now gone. He had written her a
charming letter from Berne, assuring her that she would be able to
count on his assistance and goodwill: 'Having heard of your arrival at
Zuric, I write a line in haste to tell you what pleasure it would give me
in seeing you which might be arranged either by my going to Zuric or,
if it was not out of the way of your plans, by your coming here.'[1]

The anticipatory letter was waiting for her at the Hotel Bauer and
she was wise enough now to tell Ludwig she had received it. She also
took the opportunity to tell him how the Swiss were outraged at what
had happened in Munich and how popular he was. Moreover, she
bombarded him with advice. Berks was in her favour, Denker not so;
Wallerstein was a liar; the good Polinsky was in tears when he handed
her into the stage coach – he really must have that position in Munich.
And then came one of those splendid anti-clerical stories that circulated throughout Europe in the nineteenth century. The hotel proprietor had told her that soldiers found over twenty young girls, some as
young as thirteen or fourteen, who were kept in Jesuit convents for the

pleasure of the priests. The girls had spoken of the horrors and how they were never allowed to leave, because if they did the scandal would become public.[2]

Offers such as that from Peel are not to be refused lightly. Here was company, an introduction to diplomatic circles and probably some tin to go with it. So it was to Berne she went the next day. On her arrival there, Peel was said to have given her a public dinner and she was soon seen walking arm in arm with the handsome diplomat.[3] The Peel family certainly had a sense of humour. It cannot have been by chance that Robert Peel's uncle Sir Jonathan, brother of the former Prime Minister, named his bay filly Lola Montez (by Slane out of Hester). She was a more than halfway decent animal which ran in the 1,000 Guineas and The Oaks and on 9 October 1848 won a 50-sovereign sweepstake. She was later sold at Tattersalls for the good price of 350 guineas in a broodmare sale on 16 October 1854. *The Times*, with its tongue firmly wedged, wondered that she and her mother, who was in the same sale with other mares, had not been purchased for the royal stud.[4]

On 27 February, two days after Lola's arrival in Berne, Louis-Philippe became the first of the European monarchs to lose his throne in the revolutions of 1848 as the mob took to the Paris streets. As for Ludwig, he spent that day kissing Lola's portrait every time he went to his room, arranging that her friend Polinsky should have a better appointment, and avoiding a performance of Flotow's *Martha* at the opera house.

The news of the revolution in France reached Munich on 29 February and the people realised just how tenuous was Ludwig's grasp on power. They had shown only three weeks earlier that they could dictate affairs and now they saw themselves as being in a position to make a series of threatening demands. For a start, Berks must go.

During March European governments were anticipating the retreat of the gods into Valhalla. On 3 March Laszlo Kossuth, the Hungarian patriot who would later travel to America on the same boat as Lola, persuaded members of the Hungarian Diet to call on Austria to grant their own independent administration. The next day King Carlo Alberto of Italy granted constitutional charters to Sardinia, Piedmont and Savoy. A fortnight later the Papal States were granted the same. On 5 March liberal scholars gathered in Heidelberg to propose that all Germany should be represented in one National Assembly. On 13 March, to the total surprise of the seventy-five-year-old Prince Metternich and his secret police, crowds surged through the streets of Vienna. Metternich resigned and fled to England. Revolutions against Austria broke out in Bohemia, Croatia and Illyria. On 18 March Milan drove out its Austrian government and four days later Lombardy did the same. On 26 March a revolution in Spain was brutally crushed.

On 2 March barricades had been erected in Munich and the military was once again called out to maintain order. Rioting spread and the arsenal was stormed. Ludwig, for all his faults, loved his people and could not bring himself to countenance a civil war. Over the years he had shown he would not be seen to be pushed, but this time he was. Wallerstein advised that the Chambers be recalled, while Ludwig's brother Prince Karl announced at the town hall that the Stände was to reassemble on 16 March. On 5 March Ludwig wrote to the Crown Prince, then in Berlin, reporting that so far – shortly after luncheon – all was quiet, but Maximilian had already left for Munich. Count Bernstorff believed the King's position was fatally weak. He appeared to think only of being reunited with Lola and revenging himself on those who had forced her out of the country. Abdication was very much a proposition and Ludwig recognised it.

On 6 March the troops were called into the city, to the great indignation of the crowds. Ludwig still refused to grant their requests and was told that unless he accepted them by midday, there was every possibility the palace would be burned. He bowed to the inevitable and at eleven o'clock acknowleged every demand. For two days things were quiet in the city. Ludwig might have survived, at least as a titular monarch, until Lola put an end to any hope that he might have had of remaining on the throne.

Unhappy that she had not heard from Ludwig – his letters had been sent to Lausanne – and deluding herself that there was still a position for her in Munich and that, even if there was not, she could still win him back, she set off for Bavaria. On 8 March, this time disguised as a young man, she reappeared in the city, accompanied by the shadowy Baron Meller. About 8 pm that night the pair went to Weuzerstrasse 12, the house of Caroline Wegner and her father, on whom Lola could rely for support. Unfortunately Caroline did not immediately answer the bell. An officer who lived in the same building heard the ringing and, looking out, saw two figures wrapped in cloaks. The smaller clearly had a false beard and was speaking in French. He did not link them with Lola, but reported the matter because there had been rumours of an arson attack on the hay depot on the same street. When the police arrived the Wegners did their best, saying the visitors had left. The flat was searched and Lola was found hiding under a sofa.

She was taken to the police headquarters, where she demanded to see the King. After much discussion it was thought best that he be notified. Now the officials were in a dilemma. It was certainly not politically sensible for Ludwig to meet her again, but he was still on the throne. The officials feared severe repercussions if the King learned that she had been in the city and he had not been informed. He was therefore woken at one o'clock in the morning and, despite strong advice to the contrary from Heinrich von der Mark, demanded to see her. It was a fatal blunder. Until then Ludwig might still have saved his crown.

He was taken to the police headquarters where a scene worthy of the third act of any grand opera took place, Lola begging him to abdicate and go and live with her in Switzerland. She clearly had one eye on the financial clock, because they discussed the sale of her house and her maintenance. She also took the time to give him some political advice: Wallerstein was behind all the unrest, plotting to put the Crown Prince on the throne. He must go. Three hours later it was she who was taken away and put on a coach at dawn with Meller. Incredibly, no escort was sent with them and all trace of them ended in Landsburg.

Ludwig returned to the palace. Over the next few days he would write mooning letters to her: 'These three hours talking together with you were worth a year' . . . 'I picked out your vest to put on and in the presence of my servants couldn't resist giving it a kiss.'

Six years later, on 29 April 1854, he would write for the archives:

'When Lola Montez came to Munic, I met her at the police station. She wanted me to abdicate and live with her. When I told her it was impossible for her to live in Munic, she said it didn't matter to her where we lived. I couldn't agree. I didn't want to leave my wife. She wanted me to dismiss Prince Wallerstein.' Four years after that he added a note:

> Police Director Mark woke me. I didn't want to leave my wife. I gave no thought of giving up the crown. I began to wonder if she [Lola] were a tool of someone else, either conscious or unknowing. At the first light of day she left the city. Ultimately she got me to do a lot of things but not everything. I never did become a freemason no matter how often she asked. In the last months of her stay I was very unhappy.[5]

The passages seem to smack both of political revisionism and the police court and newspaper confession. Note the 'I didn't want to leave my wife' and 'Ultimately she got me to do a lot of things but not everything'. Either that or, unlikely as it might be, Ludwig was stringing Lola along in much the same way as she was him.

For some days the meeting remained secret. On 11 March Ludwig did what Lola wanted and dismissed Wallerstein. On 13 March he reviewed the *Landwehr*. After luncheon there was a serenade under the palace windows, and in the evening he and Therese drove through the city to tumultuous applause. Just as the students had done for Lola in Poland, now the students in Munich wanted to unhitch the horses and pull Ludwig and Therese themselves. Presciently, Ludwig remarked to the Queen, 'within the space of a few days Jesus Christ heard hosannas and then was crucified by the same people'.[6]

There was no real possibility that the news of the meeting with Lola could be kept secret for long. The story that she was still in Munich spread like wildfire, and following tip-offs houses were searched in an effort to find her – she was in the royal palace; she was at the palace at Fürstenreid; she was at the police headquarters, which were promptly attacked. In fact she was at none of these places.

Unfortunately for Caroline Wegner, in the past the King had been seen visiting her home. This led to the certainty that Lola was in the building. It was surrounded until the police could make a search, which included lighting a fire in case Lola was in the chimney and could be smoked out. Again the mob was disappointed. To quell anxiety it was announced that two days earlier Lola had been seen taking the train from Karlsruhe to Heidelberg.

Support and affection for Ludwig evaporated. In a desperate attempt to hold on to power he reluctantly announced that Lola had 'ceased to possess her Bavarian citizenship'. This somewhat Jesuitical phraseology would enable him to deny he had ever revoked it.

Once a house of cards begins to tumble the speed at which it is flattened is amazing. On 16 March Ludwig told Therese he was firmly against abdicating. The next day he wrote Lola a letter confirming this decision, but he was already bruiting the suggestion before his ministers. One proposition was that, in a way similar to the British system of monarchy, he should have limited powers and the country would be governed by a cabinet of ministers. On 18 March there was a proposal that he should appoint his son as co-regent. It garnered no support.

At one o'clock on Sunday 19 March he abdicated in front of his sons. He had sensibly negotiated himself a reasonable settlement. He would still be referred to as His Majesty, King Ludwig of Bavaria; he would retain his properties and he would have an annual income of 500,000 florins; there was no question that he would have to live outside Bavaria. He wrote his own simple and rather moving farewell speech:

> True to the constitution did I rule; to my people's welfare was my life dedicated; as conscientiously as a loyal civil servant did I handle the properties and money of the State. I can look every man in the eye. And my deeply felt thanks to all who were devoted to me. Even though descended from the throne, my heart beats ardently for Bavaria, for Germany!

He then wrote to Lola that he planned to come to Vevey in April to be with her for some time. 'God knows when I would have been able to see my Lolitta without this . . . I put down the crown, but Lola I could not leave.' She may not single-handedly have brought down a monarchy, but she was the single largest cause in Ludwig's fall.

->><-

Lola in Switzerland

S O WHERE WAS LOLA NOW that her true love was mourning the loss of his crown? Reports that she had been in Heidelberg, where she was recognised and jeered before moving on, were correct, if out of date. Regrettably, she was now in Berne, gambling with Robert Peel and Baron Meller and gambolling with 'Fritz' Peissner. It did not prevent her writing to Ludwig complaining that Maria Denker had taken her position in the King's affection. She was sure Denker – who, she claimed, had slept with a student as well as Berks and had caused Peissner's expulsion from the Allemania – had maligned both her and Peissner. There was no truth whatsoever in the suggestion that she and Peissner were lovers. Just as Ludwig, in the years when it suited, became a father to her, so currently Peissner was a brother: 'And believe me, Ludwig, that your Lolitta never saw in poor Peissner more than a man who had a pure love for her like the love for the Virgin Mary.'[1]

More like the Magdalen. Maria Denker also came in for a blast in another letter: 'I know all your vile intrigues with your lover, Herr Berks. His Majesty already knows everything and he won't believe anything you say to him.' Maria dutifully passed the letter on to the King. Lola wrote to Peissner asking him to join her.

Then came a series of congratulatory and begging letters.

Congratulations on the steps he had taken and requests for money: money to pay for the freight on her possessions, which were beginning to arrive; money to pay for the replacement of possessions smashed in transit; money to pay for the rent of the former home of the Empress Josephine, the Château de l'Imperatrice in Pregny with its boathouse on the lake. Peel seems to have been something of a restraining influence. He advised that rather than buy the chateau for what would be roughly £750,000 in today's money, she should lease it until Ludwig had the chance to see it. Very well then, money for repairs to and redecoration of the chateau; money for new carpets and curtains. Things were so black she had to give back her harp and discontinue her lessons. To the letters Ludwig replied that he would continue to pay her 20,000 florins a year but could no longer pick up the bills for her incidentals.

While the chateau was being redecorated she settled in the Hôtel de Bergues in Geneva. It was run by Alexandre Rufenacht, a former Napoleonic officer who would act as paymaster and during the summer would begin to spy on Lola and report her misdoings to the King.

But first there was Ludwig's visit in mid-April to look forward to. Peel wrote a neat, if ambiguous, little letter to Ludwig saying how Lola was always thinking of him, how grateful his father Sir Robert was for Ludwig's kind thoughts and how he, Peel, hoped the people of Bavaria would stand faithful to Ludwig, who had done so much for them and the country. And, of course, Lola 'looks forward to the accomplishment of all her wishes in your Majesty's anticipated journey to Switzerland'.[2]

Unfortunately, with his abdication Ludwig was having financial troubles. When it became known that he was planning to visit Lola, the burghers began threatening that if he did make the trip he could be placed in permanent exile and lose his annuity. Given the troubles throughout Europe, there was a real possibility that if he left there might be a revolution in Bavaria to go along with the others. Johann Mussinan, once Lola's faithful handservant, had changed sides within the month and now argued this was a real possibility. Maximilian begged his father not to go, saying he was never sure from night to night whether he would wake to find he had been deposed. Ludwig wrote that the trip must be postponed, but that he would ensure in his will that she had the interest on 400,000 florins; at five per cent this would guarantee her the annuity of 20,000 florins.

In fact it was just as well the King did not make the trip, because had he done so he would have found Peissner *in situ*. The youth arrived on 8 April to find that Lola had once again fallen out with Peel and Meller. Not only was she not willing to reimburse them for their expenses in the chateau hunt, she had also been losing heavily to them at cards and was unwilling to pay her debts. The initial amount was 2,000 francs, but as Ludwig paid more and more of her extras it was upped to 3,000. Lola now thought the Prime Minister's son to be a thief. What was more, she locked Meller in her hotel room and wanted Peissner to stab him. At least that is what Peissner later told Ludwig.

Ludwig had already heard that Peissner was on his way to Geneva and Lola was obliged to write another lying letter. Peissner was simply passing through on his way to Schleswig-Holstein and she had given him money for a sabre and helmet. She hoped that this would be the last of him and that Ludwig would arrive soon, so that she could give him some years of her life, because 'without you life is nothing'. She was always unhappy, and so depressed that she thought she might die.

Her life became a little better when Ludwig sent her an additional 1,000 florins. But this was soon eaten up, for she had returned to living in the grand style. She was running up credit by the day. There were unpaid bills for flowers, jewellery and horses, and the wages of her servants – now getting on for ten in number – had to be found. Peissner was behaving badly. He was now spending far too much time with one of Rufenacht's daughters and was gone by the end of the month, off to Giessen where he hoped he would be admitted to the university. Things moved at breakneck speed in Lola's life.

Ludwig wrote that he was prepared to make her a gift of the interest on 400,000 florins in a bank in Bavaria, or in Switzerland if she preferred. This would be irrespective of whether his state pension was withdrawn. Sensibly he was not prepared to advance her capital. Lola dithered. Her admirers suggest that this shows she was not a complete adventuress. She could have had the secured income at no cost to herself, but she was incapable of making such a decision. What she wanted was cash up front and she was going to do away with herself if she did not receive it: 'I don't know what I've done to deserve this terrible punishment from you that you refuse me a few thousand francs . . . if only you knew how hard it is to suffer for lack of money – if you don't help me I will kill myself and go mad . . . This is what I get for my sacrifices in Munich. I hope this letter will touch your heart.'[3]

And indeed it did, sufficiently to provide another cash infusion which kept her going for another few weeks.

Lola finally moved into the chateau on 24 May, on the advice of Rufenacht taking with her two ladies, Constance Petitpierre and Jenny More, to give some semblance of respectability to her household. This was just as well. Throughout the summer she surrounded herself with the male *jeunesse doré* of Geneva, who were allowed to stay overnight at the chateau and who took her for outings on the lake; she in a large boat she had purchased and her hangers-on, calling themselves Corsairs, rowing behind her. It was the Allemania all over again. She still owed Rufenacht rent but she hoped Ludwig would do her the small favour of paying it. Over the next week she fell ill with fevers and chills. At one time she was coughing blood. But when she was not it was out with the Corsairs on the lake.

But now there was another hanger-on, one far more sinister and who would last for some years, in one form or another, as a constant worry to Ludwig. It was the diminutive but handsome and charming Auguste Papon, who now wore the self-bestowed title the Marquis de Sarde. Aged about thirty, he was small, bronzed and spoke Spanish well. He must have appealed to Lola with her varied views of her own parentage. His father had been adjunct-principal of the Treasury of France and his mother came from one of the foremost families in Provence. Well, perhaps not quite. His grandfather had been a waiter in Geneva while his father, a confidence trickster, had run off with an actress to the south of France. Educated for the priesthood, Papon followed his father's line of business. He set himself up as an attorney in Marseilles and, after running up a series of debts, was struck off before he returned to Switzerland. Rufenacht, to add to Ludwig's woes, thought Papon missed no chance to be amiable, but he did not believe

the Marquis had a heart. Most surprising of all, he was a Jesuit. Immediately Lola had met him she was charmed, although Rufenacht did
not know what Lola saw in him. Rufenacht thought that despite her
initial reluctance to meet Papon she had known him somewhere in
the past, possibly in Paris. Later he would write to Ludwig that he
thought she was in fear of him and that he had some hold on her.[4]
Papon also introduced her to yet another dilettante; this was Oscar
Hurt-Binet, who lived nearby and with whom she discussed the possibility of publishing her memoirs.

Lola first encountered Papon in Switzerland that spring at the
Hôtel de Bergues, which he had been using as his headquarters since
the summer of 1847. He invited her to meet his family, and the Corsairs dutifully rowed her to Nyort where she lunched with them and
the local curé. By the end of June Papon had moved into the chateau.
Lola's letters, never as frequent as Ludwig's, dried to a trickle.

Was Ludwig getting anything for the money he was lavishing on his
feckless and unfaithful Lola? Not very much was the answer, but Lola
was skilful enough to ensure the promise was there. When they met
would she *besar* (fuck) him, he asked in one letter? How could he
doubt it? It was the one thing above everything else that she wanted.
For the moment he contented himself with thoughts of sucking her
unwashed feet.[5]

And throughout the summer Rufenacht continued to act as Lola's
rapporteur and financier – a sort of replacement for Heideck. It was
probably the latter position which caused her to fall out with him.

At the beginning of July Ludwig was again making plans to meet
with Lola. First, he paid out twice for furniture for her. Then he paid
out for two members of the Allemania who visited her. In future there
would be no extra payments unless he had previously authorised the
expenditure – until the next time. Ludwig wanted to come to Pregny
but thought that a short stay near the Tirolean border was more sensible. Politically things were extremely difficult and he believed that
no prince of a reigning house could travel outside his country, certainly not for long. They should meet in Malans in eastern Switzerland, halfway between Geneva and Innsbruck. Rufenacht did the
mathematics. For her to travel there would take at least eight days and

four horses, with 80 Swiss francs per day when on the road, 20 francs for rest days and a further 15 for her personal expenses. And what about buying her some property?

Back in England Lola made her first appearance in the legitimate theatre. Well, actually Mrs L. S. Buckingham appeared as Lola in the enormously popular one-act farce by J. S. Coyne, *Lola Montez or Countess for an Hour*. Originally it was licensed by the Lord Chancellor but it was then banned, possibly at the request of Peel's father, after playing for three days at the Haymarket in April; 'though a mere trifle serves to create laughter for half an hour or so', thought the *Weekly Dispatch*.

It soon reappeared, entitled *Pas de Fascination*, with William Harries Tilbury as Muffenpuff, the Russian Governor of Neveraskwhere. Other characters had their roles spelled out for them in fine comic tradition: Kyboshki, Stiffenbach (a gentleman usher), and so on. The Lola character, now renamed Jolijambe and played by Mrs Clifford, has struck an officer and flees to a clean starcher, played by Mrs Keeley, changing clothes with her. She appears at court and shocks everyone by her vulgarity but fascinates a prince. The Keeleys 'drew roars of laughter ... the caricature of real personages has been effected in a proper spirit and with pointed humour', wrote the *Weekly Dispatch*.[6]

It was Coyne's most popular play and on the back of Lola's name and reputation it played for years around the world. Even before she came to America *Lola Montez*, its American title, was a long-running staple of the theatre, played by such stalwarts as Mary Gannon, then at her height, and the Irish-born George Holland as the comic hero. In true pantomime tradition, there was of course plenty of opportunity for ad-libbing and topical jokes. For example, when the piece played in California some years later, at a time when Lola had a number of such animals, the hero Michael, in despair, uttered the line, 'I'll return home and slaughter myself and my four innocent bears.'

Ludwig was becoming increasingly excited by the prospect of seeing Lola again. He would travel to Innsbruck and then arrive in Malans on 16 August, where he expected to find Lola – unless it was her period, in which case what about 2 September? He had to be back home by the middle of the month. There must be the utmost secrecy about his visit. But somehow secrecy and Lola were not synonymous. On 29 July *The Satirist* suggested that she was 'expecting the visit of an illustrious personage'.

Meanwhile Sir Jasper Nicolls was keeping track of his former ward, writing in his diary: 'Lola Montez is in London driven in a Brougham and dressed in an extravagant manner with an immense bouquet of flowers. Her mother was said to be in Jersey just now and has refused two offers of marriage.'[7]

The meeting was postponed until September and now Ludwig wanted her to arrive on the first. No dogs and certainly no men unless it was Rufenacht, currently deemed to be no threat by Ludwig. There were continuing money troubles. Ludwig sent 3,633 Swiss francs to the hotelier, but somehow Lola got there first and so he sent another 600. There would be no more money sent – that was until the next begging letter. Meanwhile, back in Munich, her debts amounted to some 14,400 florins and there were difficulties in trying to sell her house. Lola's female companions were also cutting up rough over the behaviour of the Corsairs and Papon and on 31 July left the chateau. 'Please', begged Rufenacht, 'don't ask me what's going on at the villa – I'm no diplomat or courtier, and I could only speak as an old soldier.' What was going on was that Papon had moved into the room next to Lola. Rufenacht thought Lola expected to receive a million francs from Ludwig; Papon was looking forward to getting his hands on the money and also a genuine title of some sort.[8]

And so throughout that year a game of musical chairs was played on the shores of the lake. If Peel was in favour, Murray was out; if Murray was out then Meller was in; or it was Papon or one or more of the Corsairs. If Lola wrote warning Ludwig about Murray, so then did Murray warn the King about her. No one was in favour throughout the whole summer. Few lasted more than a few weeks at a time.

The proposed meeting with Ludwig was a fiasco. Lola left for Malans on 25 August and arrived in the town on 2 September, but the next day there was no Ludwig in sight. Instead there was a valet with a welcome 2,000 francs, some poems by Ludwig and an unwelcome letter explaining the ex-monarch's absence. If it was found – and how could it not be – that he had left the country to visit Lola, there would have been immediate and severe financial and other repercussions. He had not been prepared to risk it.

Now Ludwig wrote a further letter explaining the situation. His birthday had been a miserable one. It was the anniversary of his ennoblement of Lola and also the first birthday which had not been a public holiday. There was still unrest in the town and stories were going the rounds that he had stolen the state diamonds and given them to Lola, 'but don't love me the less. It is not my fault.' If things quietened down he should be able to see her in October. Therese was going to Bolzano with her daughter, who was expecting a child. When he went to visit the baby he could stop at Innsbruck and then make a side trip to Malans. He was enchanted with the drawing of her lips in the margin of a letter and had mistaken it for a representation of her *cuno*. He kept kissing it, which was sufficient to keep his *jarajo* erect in anticipation – and to keep the cash coming.[9]

As for Lola, Rufenacht was distinctly out of favour. She was warning Ludwig about trusting him. Ludwig had had answers to his questions about Papon from Rufenacht, but now he wanted some from Lola. Was he an old or a new acquaintance? Handsome? How old? Where was he sleeping? She was starting to hedge her bets about the faux Marquis. He seemed distinguished, but who could tell nowadays. He was studying politics, neither young nor handsome – Luis did not need to worry – most interestingly he was a great ultramontane. And please could Ludwig send the case with her diamonds. Oh, and also money to Rufenacht. In a rather ungentlemanly manner, the innkeeper had made her sign a receipt for his last advance. Meanwhile, although she did not tell Ludwig, Peissner was back staying with her.

On 13 September, Ludwig wrote finally giving up all hope of seeing Lola that year. She had been thinking of staying at the King's villa in Rome, but so far as Ludwig was concerned there was no question of that. For once in his love life he put his foot down. Now Papon wrote to Ludwig suggesting that Lola should avoid Geneva, where there were creditors – one summons had already been taken out – and Rufenacht was storing up trouble for her. She had pawned part of her silver and the doctors feared for her health. He, Papon, thought she should go straight to Italy for the winter.

As the autumn wore on Lola began to press for a deposit in the Bank of England. She was convinced a tempest was hanging over not only Ludwig and his son but all the crowned heads of Germany. He must act to protect her before it was too late. Efforts to sell her home in Munich were progressing slowly, but the proceeds would be eaten up paying her debts. Rufenacht reported to Ludwig on Papon. Children were jeering at him and Lola in the street. He was known to be a bad lot, but nothing could be proved. He had an illegitimate son.

And then Ludwig received a surprise visit from the Marquis himself, carrying a letter from Lola. In substance all her misfortunes were Rufenacht's work. She was facing a disgrace worse than death and she begged Ludwig to receive Papon, who surprisingly, since he was an ultramontane, was also a freemason. It all seems to have been part of another extended confidence trick, for Papon's mother now wrote to the ex-King saying that Lola once more had had a fever. All her money had been seized and she must leave for Italy at once. Lola's bills for jewellery bought in Geneva were sent to Ludwig for settlement and still the ex-King kept paying. He did make vain efforts to stem the tide: he would send 10,000 francs against the sale of her house, but he must have some form of mortgage. That idea came and went and he sent 20,000 francs before receiving any documents. Meanwhile Papon was insinuating himself into Ludwig's favour. The ex-King regarded him as 'a man of spirit' and kindly gave him another 400 francs for his expenses. Rufenacht reported that Lola had moved to a smaller, rented house, protecting her furniture against her creditors by selling it to a Monsieur Darier, the father of the friend who had gone with her to Malans. She was saying Papon would collect a million from the ex-King and she would be off to Rome where Ludwig had provided her with a palace. Certainly, throughout October Papon was negotiating with Ludwig for Lola to go to Rome, where the ex-King would join her.[10]

In fact, in mid-October Lola did finally move out of the chateau, taking in Papon's parents to live with her at her smaller villa. They all drank Ludwig's health every night at dinner – as well they might, since he was their principal provider of sustenance. Meanwhile the Marquis had superseded Rufenacht as the principal provider of information about Lola. There had been an incident at the theatre and on the way home she feared she was going to be attacked by armed men. She fell and hurt her elbow. She was being cared for by the best doctor in Geneva, along with Papon's devoted family. The injury prevented her from writing herself. Indeed, ninety-nine out of a hundred people would have been killed on the spot. She was definitely wanting to go to Rome, and now Ludwig was happy for her to arrive there after he left Munich and take a villa near his. More money – this time another 20,000 francs – exchanged hands for the proposed trip. 'The dear patient must be carefully spared every emotion', wrote Ludwig. In turn Papon was keeping all troubles from her. It was snowing and Rome would be good for Lola's physical and moral health. He even admiringly quoted Ludwig's own poem 'Tivoli' to him. Papon had taken over negotiations for the deposit of a capital sum by the ex-monarch. It has all the hallmarks of an expertly carried out long-term confidence trick, but quite who was working it is not wholly clear. Lola now wrote that she so wanted to kiss Ludwig's mouth again; Ludwig that he wished to kiss her feet. Less romantically, he worked out that in addition to the payments to the Allemania and other of Lola's friends, he had paid out over 57,000 florins to her that year to go with the 100,000 in 1846–7. It just could not go on, he wrote.[11]

And then it appeared to all go bang. Papon wrote a neat little letter saying he and his family had been obliged to leave Lola's house. If Ludwig wanted to know why, he would explain as delicately as possible. Lola wrote that she had discovered the Marquis had previously been convicted of fraud in Marseilles. He and his mother had been telling *le tout* Geneva of an impending marriage to Lola. She had been obliged to give him 1,000 francs, which had broken her purse. Now she learned that the Marquis preferred men. He had been ordered to leave Geneva and had sworn vengeance against her. Peel and Meller were back in favour and advising her.

There was one last surprise from Lola that year. The very hand-some, very rich and very young Julius, Count of Schleissen, had been paying court to her. She had resisted this one and only temptation to her fidelity to Ludwig, and Peel and the Baron were supporting her in this brave decision although the Count had been visiting her every

day with tears and protestations. Most other women would have succumbed by now, but her fidelity to Luis was such that although she
had nothing in her own name she was still faithful. There was also in
the background a Count Barney of Milan but he was forty. Her Luis
surely could not leave her without 'very promptly guaranteeing my
independence for life and putting the money in *English* funds'.

The truth was rather different. It is more likely that Lola was in hot
pursuit of the young Count and this was the reason for the banish-
ment of Papon and his family. She had seen him while at the theatre
with Meller, himself more or less last heard of in Lola's bedroom
awaiting a stabbing from Peissner. Meller had effected the introduction and the Countess was out of the traps in what was to be a dress
rehearsal for her adventure the following year with George Heald.
Lola would meet Count Julius at her new home; if the ungracious
Papon was there, she would borrow the Baron's rooms at the Hôtel de
Bergues.

Lola believed that Julius would propose to her. Indeed he may have
done, but he was whisked away by his fearful family to Chambéry in
France, with Lola in hot pursuit. She retrieved him easily enough, but
the police were asked to intervene over possible undue influence exer-
cised by the Countess. Fearful that she would lose the right to call
herself the Countess of Landsfeld, she had failed to take Rufenacht's
advice and apply for Swiss citizenship. Now she had no defence when
the authorities decided she should take an extended trip and expelled
her. She opted for London rather than Rome.

So on 27 November 1848, much to Ludwig's annoyance, Lola set off
via Basle, Mainz, Cologne and Ostend to England, travelling with
Meller and a servant apiece. There was no need for her faithful Luis to
worry about his faithful Lolitta. The Baron was old and ugly – perhaps
only two years older and uglier than when she had been cavorting
with him around the spas in Germany in the summer of 1846, but still
old and ugly. Before she went, Lola was able to tell Ludwig that Papon
had been found in a compromising position with a young man in the
park. And please don't forget to send her money. Why London? asked
Ludwig peevishly. London was an expensive city. And second, why
make two journeys? The steaks and porter there were good for her

health, was the answer to the first. As for the second, she had been able to rent a house at 6 Queen Street on the fringes of Covent Garden in the name of Mrs Bolton at a modest four guineas a week. She finally arrived in England on 28 December and very quickly moved to Half Moon Street, where she had lived as Eva James on her first stay six years earlier.

By the end of 1848 Ludwig had managed to get most of the truth out of Peissner, with whom he was now in correspondence. When and where had sex taken place between him and the Countess, Ludwig wanted to know. And what about Leibinger and the other Allemania? Had she favoured them also? And what had she said about the King? 'Pure truth, the whole truth is what I want.' Peissner, seeing the opportunity of money and favours if he confessed, did just that.

When Peissner first met Lola on 18 June 1847 he had been full of respect for her, in fact in awe of her. He had not seen her again until 8 August. She had clearly been making subtle advances, because 'I kept moving back as much as I could so that my knee wouldn't brush her dress.' As he left she had said, 'Don't forget me.' He had then heard from her at the end of October. She had spoken of the King as 'noble', 'my good old man', and referred to him as 'her dear father'. She had told Peissner that she would marry him. 'Here is my heart, never ask for my body before our marriage.' He had moved into her house and after that saw her frequently. By the time she left Munich she was dallying with Leibinger, but this had ended when she left Lindau. She still continued to write to Peissner, suggesting she was alone, unhappy and abandoned. He then accepted her invitation to Switzerland, where he met Peel and Meller, along with John Murray. He found the relationship now changed and so, to Lola's annoyance, began to whisper in the ear of Rufenacht's daughter. He returned in August and there found 'a disreputable lawyer as her chevalier', along with the Corsairs. He stayed to have his linen washed and left after a few days.

In return for this breast-beating, Peissner hoped for some help in his proposed travel to America. Ludwig was pleased and the correspondence continued in the New Year. In the meantime he wrote that he would provide 600 guilden for the student that summer term. Along with being a foot fetishist and masochist, there must have been something of the voyeur in Ludwig, because he demanded further and better particulars of Peissner's seduction and that of Leibinger. But it was news to him that Lola had actually spoken to Peissner about marriage. This gives the lie to the story that it was Ludwig who was planning to marry her off to the youth.

Now, at the King's insistence, Peissner told all the sordid or romantic details. The seduction had taken place in the Countess's bedroom in November when after prolonged heavy petting she asked: '"What do you want? You are so red . . ." She then touched me and cleared the way for me to enjoy her and then – to put it briefly – I felt what I had never felt before.'

They then knelt by the bed and swore fidelity to each other. As for Leibinger, he was sure that sex was taking place at Lindau and thought it very probable that it had begun during Lola's final days in Munich. And, now that he had been so forthcoming, might he mention that his parents had been driven from their home and that his father had ruined the family? In short, could he have his name added to Ludwig's lengthening support list?[12]

The pre-Christmas period had begun nicely for Ludwig with a letter from Papon, who wrote to him explaining of the sacrifices he had made on the King's and Lola's behalf. If his ex-Majesty could graciously pay him 10,000 francs as compensation, then he need not write and publish his memoirs as his friends were suggesting he should do.[13] Sometimes Ludwig must have wondered how on earth he had become so entangled with Lola, but he would persevere for some time yet.

CHAPTER TEN

London: Lola Remarried

Settled in London at the beginning of 1849, for a time Lola main-tained a relatively low and, she claimed to Ludwig, a lonely profile. For the moment she must have forgotten that Baron Meller was still in attendance. She was now considering publishing her own memoirs and was in idle discussion with both the author George Augustus Sala, who had a sideline in pornography, and a most curious man, David Wemyss Jobson. Writing some years later, Sala thought they had first met that year in a little cigar shop in Norreys Street off Regent Street. He seemed to think Lola had once been the wife of a solicitor. According to Sala's memoirs she suggested he should start her life, beginning with the assumption that she was the daughter of Montez the bullfighter.[1]

Jobson was a wholly different kettle of fish. Regularly described as a charlatan, he published a book on dentistry and also claimed to have written one on the French Revolution. Certainly he visited Lola when she was living in Half Moon Street that year and holding her evening salons. Jobson had stood for the borough of Montrose in the April 1842 parliamentary election but no one would nominate him. All the other candidates had stood down in favour of the sitting member, Joseph Hume, who years earlier had been a lone voice on behalf of Jane Digby in her divorce case, and was a persistent questioner of the desirability of Lord Cardigan as Commander in Chief of the Light

Brigade.[2] By the time he met Lola, Jobson seems to have become a jobbing journalist. Nothing came of the memoirs, but some years later they met again in New York in one of Lola's more entertaining court battles.

Lola continued to meet people in high places, among them Lords Bessborough and Brougham. It is easy to see how the bachelor Bessborough would have attracted her. A barrister by training if not by inclination, he had recently inherited the title and was a great cricketer, once scoring nine runs – all run – off a single ball. He also had a keen interest in theatricals and amateur dramatics and founded the Old Stagers, the oldest amateur theatrical company in the world.

There has been a great deal of speculation over Lola's relationship with the Lord Chancellor, Henry Brougham. She was clearly close to him, or at least the public thought so. Commenting on her departure from Munich, *The Satirist* wrote: 'Lola Montez, more fortunate than many ladies who leave Bavaria on their travels, can with her money, come to this country and actually do what others in the song advise, "Buy a Brougham".'[3]

The next month, when their names were linked together with Sardanopolous and a big feather bed in a music-hall patter song performed by the hugely popular Charles Mathews, the audience roared its appreciation.[4] *The Times* also noted that they were both in the audience for the opening of Auber's *Ambassadrice* on 26 January 1849 – Lola would claim to Ludwig that on the two occasions she had been to the theatre she had been in a curtained box so no one would recognise her. On 1 November that year a report in the *New York Mirror* from its London correspondent described her as 'Lord Brougham's fair and fiery friend Lola Montez', adding 'or Peg Waters or Mrs James or the Countess of Landsfeldt'. When a list of 'powers' was compiled for the *Brooklyn Daily Eagle*, there were Lola and Brougham:

A power of Evil – that's Russia.
A power of Misery – that's Ireland.
A power of Ignorance – that's Austria.
A power of Mischief – that's Lola Montez.
A power of Fun – that's Lord Brougham.[5]

The rather ungainly Brougham – described as 'the ugliest man of the present century next to Liston and Lord Carlyle'[6] – had already been through the mill with Harriette Wilson, perhaps the best-known adventuress of a previous generation. That courtesan had attempted to blackmail him at the rate of £40 a year (the first year to be payable in advance) to omit him from her memoirs. On 16 December 1827 she wrote to him from Calais where she was camped out at the time:

> If [the answer] does not arrive at no 14 rue du Colysée à Paris Faubourg St. Honoré I shall apply to *Mrs* Brougham directly sending her a copy of this letter. Should that lady *not object to the publication* of her husband's adultery – B—lting etc, [then why] should I?[7]

She thoughtfully added a postscript:

> If you will make no sacrifice to spare Mrs Brougham's feeling *why should I*? You certainly must be expected to sacrifice more for the mother of your children, the wife you have chosen than *I* who never saw her.

Even when Brougham held the office of Lord Chancellor his behaviour was strange. One evening, as a guest of the Duchess of Bedford, he 'romped so familiarly with the ladies that, to be revenged on him they stole the Great Seal and hid it in a tea chest'.[8] The free-thinking author and lecturer Harriet Martineau had no time for him at all. 'He wears a black stock or collar and it is so wide that you see a dirty coloured handkerchief under, tied tight round his neck.' She thought of him as 'vain, selfish, low in morals and unrestrained in temper'.[9] In *Punch* cartoons he was regularly depicted as a crow or Othello.

It has already been suggested that Brougham perhaps met Lola at Fanny Kelly's theatrical academy; such places were frequented by young and not so young men around town. He certainly acted for Fanny in the action brought by her landlord. Later Lola claimed that Brougham had obtained a divorce for her, but she soon abandoned that line of defence. There is a story that he took her to the House of Lords, putting her in the Peeresses' Gallery one evening to watch some of the debate. Even if he did, can Lola really have thought that night that a special divorce bill had been passed on her behalf? Very likely she wanted to think so; and for Lola the wish often became the reality.

There is no mention of Lola in Brougham's papers. Some com-
mentators argue that this shows her relationship with him was rather
less than she claimed, but the absence is not surprising. What was he
to write? 'I had an affair with the notorious courtesan Lola Montez',
giving time and place so that his children could read he had learned
nothing from Harriette Wilson? Some writers also suggest Brougham
was happily married. If he was, it was in the same style that Ludwig
was happily married to Queen Therese.

Back in Munich, Ludwig may have been desolated by the revelations of Lola's infidelity made by Peissner, but the bogus Papon was
causing more serious trouble. He announced the publication of his
book *Lola Montes, Memoirs Together with Intimate Letters from His
Majesty, Louis, King of Bavaria (the most recent of 4 October 1848).*

On 13 January 1849 Rufenacht wrote to Ludwig enclosing a pamphlet by a group calling itself Une Société d'Hommes de Marins d'Eau
Douce, announcing that it would publish a retaliatory pamphlet entitled *Lola Montès and her Monkey Papon*. A summary of the chapters
survives but sadly there is no detail. It follows the acknowledged facts
of Papon's early life, but also offers titillating mention of his double-
crossing his father over his grandfather's will, an affair over a
diamond, the seduction of a young person in Geneva, the renewal of
his acquaintance with Lola, the disappearance of a valuable brooch
and his subsequent dismissal by her.

There was also a letter from Lola, who was incensed and making all
sorts of empty threats and boasts in a letter to Rufenacht of what
would happen to the erring Marquis: 'I have friends here, powerful
friends, who have long arms and who will not allow an old man to be
insulted, who cannot defend himself . . . The newspapers are all at my
service here if I want . . .' Ludwig immediately wrote to Lola asking
whether Papon had taken any of his letters or had merely made
copies. And what about French translations of the poems Ludwig had
sent? In turn Lola wrote to Ludwig:

I've heard Senor Papon, who's nothing more than a tool of the Jesuits
who they introduced as a spy into my house to do me harm and separate
me from you . . . if you were no more, I hope to die – there's nothing for

me in this vile, infamous world – without you this is my constant prayer
and desire – adios, my ever beloved Louis. I am for life and until death
your faithful and tender Lolitta.

The last sentence may have been what Ludwig wished to hear, but he
cannot have been encouraged by a letter from Rufenacht confirming
that what Papon wanted was simply money. Rufenacht was trying to
retrieve the letters and was putting pressure on the printer. To add to
the problems, Oscar Hurt-Binet sent a letter to the *Journal de Genève*
saying that Lola had reneged on an agreement with him to write her
memoirs. 'It is as impossible to know where she was born as where she
will die.'[10] Meanwhile Lola confirmed that all Ludwig's letters were in
her hands. Nor could Papon have obtained copies, because they had
been locked in her writing desk which had a tamper-proof English
patent lock. She would be happy if Papon published the three letters
she had written to him, because they contained nothing but praise for
Ludwig, as well as begging him to get Ludwig to pay her debts in
Geneva. Ludwig was not convinced some letters were not missing. He
wrote to Papon saying that while he did not know why he should be
asked to pay, he would send him 10,000 francs for the return of all
letters. Amazingly, and foolishly, he signed it 'Your affectionate
Ludwig'. Now the two-faced Murray joined in proceedings. He would
do what he could to save Ludwig money. If only Ludwig had listened
to him the previous May this would never had happened. And did
Ludwig know that Lola was living at a rate of £10,000 a year in
London? If Ludwig didn't pay then Murray was afraid she would
follow Papon's example. And for once Murray was right.[11]

The first instalment of Papon's memoirs came out on 1 February.
They began, 'This book is not a scurrilous pamphlet; it is not a satire.
Written without hatred, without passion, it is quite simply an
account.'[12] In fact the book was a splendid mish-mash of gossip and
half-truths, some of which he must have had from Lola:

Driven from Munich, this girl has been seen in many different countries,
parading the delusive luxury of a courtesan, multiplying around her
scandals and profligacy, to exhibit the sad spectacle of folly, vice and
vanity.

While she continued this life of shame, of noise, and of misery, Louis
to whom the revolution had taught no lesson, still remained for her an
unwearied treasurer, both of love and money.

Papon claimed that she had wanted him to write her autobiography.
She had told him she had been born in Spain and at another time in
Ireland, of Catholic parents who had died when she was young. She
was to have married Sir Archibald Turnbull, who took her to Calcutta
to the court of the Governor whose niece she was. Papon had no high
opinion of her knowledge of literature or art, claiming that Lola confused Byron and Cervantes, thought Henri IV was the son of Henri III
and that Jeanne d'Arc was a Roman woman. She had, he said, a litho-
graph, *Love Passing Away Time in a Shallop*.

Later in the memoirs, Papon recounts Lola's meeting with the
young count Julius. She spent all her time with Meller on the fourth
floor of the Hôtel des Bergues, where she met with the young man,
and in the company of the Rufenachts. He also claimed that Lola
spoke of Meller as a rogue, a swindler and a spy. He had some information on her in England, claiming that she had been beaten by two
lionesses in London who called on her late one night and that she had
sold herself to a titled Englishman for a box at the Italian opera. He
also had a story that she had tried to sell her paste diamonds as real,
and when discovered had sold some of the real stones to Mortimer of
London. The rest of the real ones had gone to Meunier in Paris. Lola
was bound to end in Botany Bay, he believed.

A good deal of this could have been obtained from the newspapers,
but there was undoubtedly some additional material which could
have been true. According to Papon – and this at least is correct –
Lola's extravagances knew no bounds. He gave one account of going
shopping with her when she had bought monkeys and Amazon
parrots and, had he not intervened, would even have purchased a rhi-
noceros. He effectively dragged her away from the menagerie store;
from there they went to Liodet the jewellers, where she bought some
rings. Over 1,000 francs went in this two-hour shopping spree. Papon
claimed he took the rings back, later piously writing to Ludwig that he
had saved him 500 francs by so doing.

When it came to it the memoirs contained little in the way of hard facts, and indeed years later Lola borrowed some sentences for her autobiography. Nor did they have a wide circulation in any language. There was, however, a German translation in which the publisher thoughtfully added a story of an affair in Poland and another with a Spanish-speaking count in Nuremberg.

Also included in the first instalment was a wonderful piece of hypocritical hyperbole directed solely at Ludwig. Papon had, so he said, been to the Gallery of Beauties; there, next to a portrait of the King's daughter Princess Alexandra, was one of Lola. Papon almost burst with indignation: 'After having so long soiled the conjugal bed, the throne, he dared to scourge with this impure contact the spotless beauty of a girl who weeps on her mother's bosom over the eternal disorders of her father! Is then nothing sacred for this man?'

The Geneva bookseller Joel Cherbuliez, acting very much in concert with Rufenacht, had tried to stop the publication. His reward was that Papon published his correspondence. Rufenacht had by now clearly established himself as the King's agent for dealings with Lola and those surrounding her. He reported that Papon had been paid 40,000 francs by Ludwig's sister the Archduchess Sophie and that his agent was Dr Charles Peschier. Would the King please appoint someone to stand up to the Jesuits? He clearly fancied himself for that task.

By the middle of February Papon was threatening to publish part two of the memoirs and was now seeking 100,000 francs to restrain himself. In turn the King wanted everything that Papon had written to Lola, while Rufenacht suggested there should be a reply published. For the moment Ludwig stood firm against efforts to extract more money from him. Rufenacht now approached a Russian, Prince Babouchkine, an officer for the Czar who had apparently known Lola in Paris, as the man most able to publish a reply to Papon's book. Rufenacht was planning a trip to Marseilles in connection with the publication and naturally Ludwig was expected to finance it.

By March Ludwig was accusing Lola of sleeping with Peissner; in turn she denied that she had had sex in Munich with anyone except her dearest. Now Meller had fallen out of favour. He was, she believed, in league with Papon. Rufenacht produced a draft of the first chapter of the riposte to Papon, who had now produced the second part of his own work. On 23 March Peschier wrote to Ludwig demanding money to suppress the remaining proposed eight instalments, which he threatened would make 'your royal heart bleed'. Rufenacht thought 20,000 francs would be sufficient to settle the claim of 100,000. Ludwig was very tempted but finally decided that, as much of the damage had been done, 10,000 was the maximum he would pay.

Now Babouchkine joined the farce. He thought he was to receive 10,000 francs for the cost of editing and publishing, but since Ludwig had decided not to go ahead he was out of pocket. He did not expect to get the full amount but he wanted to be paid for his time. And, by the way, he had some of Papon's letters and poems to Lola. Finally, in lieu of payment he seems to have kept a poem from Papon to Lola. But Ludwig remained staunch in his refusal to pay and Rufenacht bemoaned his own fate. He had had to pay 500 francs himself to get rid of Papon, who was now said not to have enough money to publish the third instalment; this, it was rumoured, would contain an obscene drawing.

The Swiss authorities now took a hand. In the middle of May Papon and his family were expelled and for the moment the curtain was rung down on him – if not on Peschier, who wrote to Ludwig to say he had several hundred copies of instalments one and two, letters from the King to Papon and one from the King to Lola, along with seven poems. This was the last time he was going to ask for money. If none was forthcoming he would publish Ludwig's 'idyllic writings'; 15,000 francs would be sufficient to suppress them. It seems that Ludwig paid Rufenacht to conclude the transaction, for the innkeeper turned man of affairs sent Ludwig his letter to Papon. He did not pay enough, because at the end of June Papon sold six letters and four poems in Paris for a total of 6,500 francs. The purchaser, apparently a comte de Mélano, had bought the letters and poems for a very reasonable sum and now, acting in concert with Papon, wanted 11,000 francs.[13]

A *Response to the Memoirs* was eventually published, exposing

Papon as the cheat and fraud he was and attributed to a Johnson Richardson. It began:

> A certain marquis, Auguste Papon, a quondam pander to the natural desires and affections which are common to the whole human race . . . disappointed in his expectation of the reward he looked for, not in gratitude, but gold, for having sold himself as the slave of the woman whom he now affects to despise and overwhelm with the world's obloquy, has published and circulated throughout Europe a volume which stamps his own infamy, as we shall have occasion to show in the course of this reply, in far more ineffaceable characters than that of those, whom, in his vindictiveness, he gloatingly sought to destroy.

In fact it only raked over old material and said nothing new at all. Probably it did as much harm as the memoirs themselves and certainly it lasted longer. In a letter to the *New York Herald* Lola repudiated the pamphlet, but it was still on sale in Cincinnati in 1853 when she appeared in that city.

In London during the first months of 1849 Lola's financial ill-health continued. As Ludwig had warned, the city was far more expensive than Lola had thought. For example, seats at the opera were the equivalent of a week's rent. But, she told Luis, Lord Brougham had kindly given her a box for Konradin Kreutzer's popular *The Night Camp of Granada*.[14] Could Luis help with a little more money? He could indeed.

Then in March, when it was announced that she was likely to be making an extended tour of the Far East, Lola put up 'the property of a foreign lady leaving England' for auction at Phillips. Sold were suites of damask, linen, porcelain, Bohemian glass, which 'evinced in their selection the most refined and ladylike taste'. On many of the articles were emblazoned the royal arms of Bavaria.

There was also a portrait of the Countess herself by Stieler. 'A portrait of a Lady in Spanish costume' attracted some 'spirited bidding' and went for 12 guineas. Her carriage horses fetched 80 guineas and her 'elegant brougham' made eighty-five. Apparently all this was to finance her tour of Alexandria, Turkey, Constantinople, Cairo and Egypt.[15]

Privately she was now telling Ludwig that she wanted to go to Spain, to see her country again, as she plaintively put it. Her health was poor – she had an infected left lung – and she wrote once more to Ludwig for help; a certificate from Dr Thomas Watson, Lord Bessborough's physician, was enclosed, saying that southern Spain in the spring was just the cure. Ludwig thought she should go but declined to increase his allowance. He also thought it would be a good idea for her to go to Seville, where she would be able to obtain a copy of her birth certificate and family records and have them legally certified so they could be used if necessary in court. This would of course provide a serious problem for Lola. She backtracked on the proposed visit.[16]

She was now hoist with her own petard. To the world she was Spanish. She could not bring herself to admit that such was not the case and apply for an English passport, to which she was perfectly entitled. She worked her way around this by saying she had lost her Spanish rights when she became a naturalised Bavarian. Now she no longer had Bavarian citizenship and Ludwig must help her. But for once he refused. Nothing came of the proposed trip and by the summer she thought she might simply go abroad, possibly to Nice. There was nothing for her in London and, moreover, she was afraid of the prevalent cholera epidemic. She seems to have forgotten her passport troubles.

Her fear of cholera was a continual theme in her letters to Ludwig. The epidemic, which ran for decades, had broken out on the Ganges in 1817, making its way to Bombay the next year. From there it spread through India and Peking before arriving in Moscow in 1831. It broke out again in Calais the same year and swept through Paris in the spring of 1832, when in a single month over 18,000 died. Although it was never as dangerous again, there were repeated outbreaks in Europe over the following decades. In fact Lola was by no means the only one who feared the disease. On 30 March 1849 the Princess Lieven wrote to her friend Lady Holland that cholera had reached London, and their correspondence is peppered with references to the illness.[17]

Meanwhile Ludwig had rekindled his religious streak and spent Easter at the church of Santa Maria de los Dolores: 'I'm not Jesuit but

Catholic. Lolitta, how much it is to be wished that you repent and confess your sins with the firm resolution to sin no more. Believe me, reconciliation with God is sweet; the peace of the soul is worth more than all the world. Believe me. Don't lose yourself for eternity.'[18]

According to one letter that summer, Lola was also looking after a young girl named Nina. Just who was this child has never become clear. There have been suggestions that she was Dujarier's daughter, born in the months when Lola was gambolling on the Rhine. This is just possible but is most unlikely. Can the child have been a figment of her imagination? Again, possibly, but Ludwig was keeping tabs on Lola and would surely have received a report. Whoever she was, Nina was soon abandoned when Lola's next lover rode into view. In one of the plaintive letters he wrote around that time, Ludwig asked what was to happen to the child if Lola did marry a new suitor. But there was no answer and there does not seem to have been any further reference to her. Most likely Lola was amusing herself with the child of a neighbour or a serving girl. As was often the case with prostitutes, Lola was undoubtedly fond of children and animals. But when she decided to move on and they became an impediment they were soon forgotten or, in the case of animals, given away or sold off with impunity.

Nor was she very good with her servants. The coachman George Humpelmeyer, who had managed to get her out of Munich, was, she maintained, behaving badly and in the spring she sent him back to Bavaria. Her other male servant, Samuel, had already been packed off to Switzerland. Now her letters to Ludwig became prosaic. Queen Victoria was due to give birth in June; she was jealous of Prince Albert – delicately Lola did not mention the assassination attempt on 19 May – Metternich and his wife were still in Brighton – cholera was prevalent in Paris and Ireland – why didn't the King of Prussia want to be the German Emperor?[19] There were occasional lures cast on Bavarian waters: 'Everyone thinks it would be better if you came to London than stay in Munich – you can't believe how enthusiastic they are for you – you'd do well, believe me dear Louis, to come here and live on the Isle of Wight, the garden of England it's very beautiful and quiet.'[20]

When he replied there was no responsive bite from Ludwig on that subject, but Lola's dogs were still causing problems in Munich – one had bitten the paper-boy. Ludwig wanted an account of Lola's daily movements. Not content with bits of her underwear and the slippers she had given him, which he wore every morning, now he also wanted the black velvet dress she had been wearing when she auditioned for the ballet in Munich. She had promised it to him when she no longer wore it.[21] He had also been reading a biography of Harriette Wilson, she who had caused Lord Brougham and a number of others so much trouble with her memoirs. Had Lola met her? What was she like? Ludwig must have been thinking by now that Lola and Harriette were kindred spirits. It was one of dozens of questions to which Lola never bothered to reply. In fact it is most unlikely that Lola ever met Mrs Q, as Harriette was known. She had almost certainly died on 10 March 1845, by which time she was described as 'a pious widow' – a long way removed from Lola's short and rackety career on the London stage.

In June Lola wrote that her health was still poor and she had a persistent cough, but that she hoped to go to the Isle of Wight for the bathing. Things turned for the better in July when finally, through an unnamed woman she knew, she obtained a false French passport in the name of Mlle Marie Marie. She was now off to Seville, taking the cheap route via Southampton and Cadiz. Please would her very dearest Luis send her some money – three months' advance, in addition to the August and September drafts she had already received; if possible to a London banker who could give her letters of credit. It was far too dangerous to carry gold and money in Andalusia. She had, she said, profited by the example of Henriette Sontag, who had lost all her money and had returned to the stage to clear her husband's debts.[22] Then, in a matter of four days, Lola's life changed irrevocably.

-+->-<+-

CHAPTER ELEVEN

Lola in Trouble

SUDDENLY THERE WAS TO BE no trip to Seville. On her evening walks in the parks, Lola had been followed at a respectful distance in his carriage by a 'tall young man of juvenile figure and aspect with straight hair and small light downy mustachios and whiskers. The nose being turned up gives him an air of great simplicity'.[1] The handsome if somewhat effete young man with a 'very pretty dog' (a Newfoundland) in his carriage was twenty-one-year-old George Trafford Heald, a cornet in the 2nd Life Guards with an income variously described as between £3,000 and £14,000 per annum.[2] Most likely it was somewhere around £6,000, but everyone agreed he had 'fine expectancies'.

Heald was born in London on 7 January 1828, the son of a barrister, George Heald, who originally came from Wakefield in Yorkshire. After his father's death Heald was brought up by his spinster aunt Susanna Heald in Horncastle, Lincolnshire.[3] He had been educated at Eton and Corpus Christi, Oxford before purchasing a commission in the army.

In one of the numerous varying accounts of how they met, a Mr X approached Lola and pointed out that Heald was an aspiring suitor, conveying the message back that an approach would not be rejected: 'On the following day the very pretty dog was at the residence of the fair Lola and then – but you know the rest . . .'[4]

The rest was that 'A soft lad with a large fortune was as sure a prey to so experienced a hand as a hungry pike to Walton. Mr Heald, booted, spurred and cuirassed with something like £12,000, was hooked at the very first cast and the victorious lady gaily dragged her unresisting prize into the meshes of matrimony.'[5] If that figure is correct, his income was serious money indeed. Some fifteen years later the celebrated and highly successful courtesan 'Skittles' Walters was content to run off with Aubrey de Vere Beauclerk, whose fortune ran to around a mere £4,500.[6]

In no way was Lola a desirable match for a young officer; the courtship was necessarily a whirlwind one. Time was of the essence so far as Lola was concerned. Although Heald was now twenty-one and could not be made a ward of court, there is no doubt that extreme pressure would have been brought to bear by his relatives had they heard of the infatuation, and that was the last thing she needed. She had learned how tiresome relatives could be from her experience the previous November with Count Julius. For the moment, however, her new young man was firmly in her clutches.

On a rainy Thursday, 19 July 1849, she bigamously married the handsome and wealthy young man, not once but twice. To make sure that the marriage was recognised – apart from the bigamy, that is – the ceremony at St George's, Hanover Square was preceded by one at the Chapel of St Louis, Carton Street, Marylebone, a small mews near Baker Street. There was going to be no question that the marriage might be annulled on the grounds it had been conducted in a Catholic church. At St George's she described herself as a widow and gave her address as Piccadilly. She named her father as Juan Porris and his occupation as colonel in the army. Her own name was now Maria de los Dolores de Landsfeld. Later that month Benjamin Disraeli, late Lord Beaconsfield, wrote to his sister:

Lola Montes' marriage makes a sensation. I believe he has only 3,000 l. per annum not 13,000 l. It was an affair of a few days. She sent to ask the refusal of his dog, which she understood was for sale. Of course, it wasn't, being very beautiful, but he sent it as a present; she rejoined, he called, and they were married in a week. He is only 21 and wished to be distinguished. Their dinner invitations are already out I am told. She quite convinced him previously that she was not Mrs James, and as for the King of Bavaria (who, by the bye, allows her 1,500 l. a year and to whom she really writes every day) that was only a *malheureuse passion* . . .[7]

It is extremely doubtful that she would have made a conquest of Heald's eight bachelor uncles and maiden aunts, however much charm she had exerted. But she made no effort at all, refusing to see or receive them. What the infatuated Heald's relatives had to do now was to wean him from Lola before she weaned him from his inheritance. And so his aunt and guardian, Susanna Heald, began work. When he learned of the alliance, Heald's commanding officer, the Marquis of Londonderry, had already required him to resign his commission immediately.[8]

What was Lola thinking of in marrying Heald and so in all probability forfeiting her pension from Ludwig? She must have known she would never be accepted in hypocritical London society. As in Paris, mistresses were one thing, wives quite another. The only explanation must be that she thought she could manage to keep both Ludwig's pension and Heald's money. And, for a time, she succeeded. During their honeymoon, partly spent in reclusion in Half Moon Street, she wrote to Ludwig, trying with complete success to hold him to his promise to pay the pension and saying that she felt nothing for Heald. Which was a good start to the marriage.

Meanwhile the unhappy pair went to Dublin – to which Queen Victoria was paying a visit – for another part of the honeymoon. Back in England at the beginning of August, they intended to go to Greenwich to spend a night at the Trafalgar. Indeed they reached the hotel and Heald ordered private rooms. While he was waiting he saw a copy of the Sunday edition of the *Weekly Chronicle* for 5 August. It carried a piece claiming the gossip of the London clubs was that a youngish, recently married woman of Hibernian-Spanish ancestry was likely to face a charge for bigamy. Indeed the only reason the warrant had not been executed was because of her absence in Dublin. The rooms were cancelled and the pair left immediately for Half Moon Street, where a carriage was ordered for 9 am the following morning to take them to a port.

Sloth undid them. They were half an hour too late. At 8.30 am, there on the doorstep were Inspector John Whall and Sergeant Gray with a warrant, accompanied by Miss Heald and a solicitor. Lola was flabbergasted, as might be expected. The first thing she said was 'What will the King say?', following it up even more pertinently with 'Lord Brougham has divorced me. He obtained an Act of Parliament for divorce for me.' She became furious, threatening to do away with herself if she was molested. Over the years it was a manoeuvre she repeated whenever necessary, and with some success.

Unlike many officers in many countries Whall stood his ground. During the morning she calmed down and was taken to Vine Street, where she apologised and offered the station sergeant a cigar. He declined, pointing out that smoking was forbidden on the premises, but undaunted she 'smoked herself into good humour'.[9]

Lola appeared at Marlborough Street Police Court that afternoon, *The Times* reporting that while she was reputed to be twenty-four she looked thirty. A trifle plump, she was dressed in a close-fitting black velvet jacket and a straw bonnet trimmed in blue, with a blue veil. She was allowed to sit with Heald throughout the hearing before the bar of the court. He held her hand between both his and at suitable moments pressed it to his lips while looking at her.

A charge of bigamy was triable only at assizes, and so the hearing was in the nature of committal proceedings to determine if Lola had a *prima facie* case to answer. Captain Charles Ingram, who had brought her back to England on the *Larkins* and given evidence in the divorce proceedings, was now living in Blackheath and he was wheeled out to identify her. It was not, however, wholly plain sailing for the prosecution. The magistrate, Peregrine Bingham, wanted strict proof that James was alive at the date of the Heald marriage. Anything could have happened to him in the Indian climate. It was quite possible she had received a letter informing her of his death. Heald's own solicitors, the rather fashionable firm of Davies Son & Campbell, who acted for the Land Commissioners, instructed Sir William Bodkin; he now made what, at least with hindsight, was a grave error. Instead of asking for the case to be dismissed there and then – something to which the magistrate might well have agreed –

Bodkin consented to an adjournment for further proof to be obtained from India.

Lola was bailed in her own recognisance of £1,000 and two sureties of £500 until 10 September and was allowed to remain in the court, billing and cooing with Heald, until the crowd had been dispersed. The pair then left on their slightly delayed trip to Europe. In the meantime the lawyers were left to try to arrange a compromise with Miss Heald. This had been recommended by the magazine *The Satirist*, which thought Heald's aunt to be indiscreet:

> It may be that she is sincere enough in all she has said and done; but age seems to have somewhat soured the ancient spinster's disposition. She should have reflected, that it is not precisely in accordance with good taste to rake up family matters, and expose them before a scandalising world unnecessarily. It looks ungracious, bitter and paltry and, moreover, unChristian.

It went on to counsel the old lady:

> who is in pursuit of difficulties, to give up the hunt and forgive and forget. Young hearts and legs will always circumvent and outrun age in a 'love chase'; the wings of Cupid are as rapid as the pulsation of crabbed senility is slow.

As for Heald, the paper thought he would have to challenge the Marquis of Londonderry, for whom it had no time, to a duel. Another officer, a Lieutenant Battier, whom the Marquis had upset had called him out:

> How can he do less if he wishes to protect his dear Lola Montez – she of the large blue eyes and black lashes? Perhaps if he does not challenge Londonderry the Countess will inflict on Heald *lashes* of a less agreeable description.

It also warned the lovelorn young man:

> But Mr Heald should not allow himself to lose sight of the awkward fact, that Lola is fickle and that *he* may eventually share the common lot of Lola Montez' lovers – from the King of Bavaria to Queen Victoria's

subjects. In the midst of all these serio-comic occurrences, however, it cannot be denied that – Lola's the girl for bewitching 'em![10]

Over the next weeks the couple could be found in Paris, Capua and then Naples, where they stayed in Room 10 on the *piano nobile* at the Vittoria Hotel in the rooms recently occupied by Mme Tadolini.[11] How appropriate that a *grande danseuse* should follow a *grande diva*, thought Rushton Green, who sent the story back to England. They were not there for long. Heald received a telegram at his bankers' and it was a question of *sauve qui peut*. Or at least save the bail money. The negotiations had clearly broken down and they had to return home. There were no boats scheduled to go to Marseilles and so Heald paid £400 for a special charter. By now he must have begun to realise that Lola was an expensive luxury.

The pair turned up back in London two days before the hearing, but their rooms in Half Moon Street were not ready and they stayed in a hotel. It was a *cause célèbre* to rival the current committal proceedings of the Mannings, accused of a particularly savage murder,[12] and the court was packed to see Lola's reappearance at the hearing on the Monday before John Hardwick, the magistrate. But there was neither Lola nor lawyer. A helpful solicitor said that while he did not act for her, he thought an adjournment had been arranged until Wednesday. Clarkson, appearing for Miss Heald, was less than pleased. He would not have minded a two-day adjournment if someone had been considerate enough to ask him first. He was, he said, in a position to produce new and damning evidence. It was all very gentlemanly. If the Countess cared to appear on the Wednesday, Clarkson would say nothing more about forfeiting her bail.

But on Wednesday it was raining heavily and the Countess did not care to appear. It was nothing to do with the downpour, however. Accurately smelling the way the wind was blowing, she jumped her bail; on the Monday night, with her Newfoundland dog Turk, she had headed for Folkestone and the Boulogne packet. Her sureties, provided by the lawyers Daniel Davies and his son Henry, were ordered to be forfeited, but for some time they put up a spirited argument to protect the money and that part of the case dragged through the sessions over the next nine months. Now *The Times* reported that the crowd had been much less than on Monday, possibly because of the pelting rain.[13] The *Weekly Chronicle* glowed, 'Mrs Heald thought an old lady could be bought up as a spare steamer; but she was in error ... The military idlers who have some faint recollections of Bessy Watson and stronger reminiscences of the frail Mrs James and could tell you good mess-room stories of her liveliness will stand quite aghast as the daring flight of a King's ex-mistress.'

The 2nd Life Guards seems to have been in some amorous confusion at the time. Another officer had run off with the 'lady frail' of a brother officer who had been her protector for some months and, having settled a sum of £1,500 a year on the faithless girl, had compounded his bad behaviour by marrying her in Brighton.[14]

Should Lola have stood her ground? Certainly the barrister Sergeant Ballantine, who had been a guest at one of her salon evenings, thought so. Describing her as 'with much dash of manner and an extremely outré style of dress', his impression was that the charge 'could not have been sustained'.[15] And indeed, without James actually coming to England it might have been extremely difficult.

Lola could now be found, tucked safely away from the jurisdiction of the English courts, at the Hôtel de Londres in Boulogne, a town which had long been the home of the Englishman escaping from his creditors. Some years before Lola's appearance, the leader of society had been Brooke Richmond, said to be to Boulogne what Brummel was to Calais. In an earlier life in England, he had once ridden a cow down St James's for a bet. Another local worthy was Sackville Cresswell, who was accustomed to his comforts, of which a pack of hounds was one and a racecourse another. He established the latter at Hardelot; his inability to keep his new French creditors at bay had him retired from the turf to the Hôtel d'Angleterre, as the local gaol was known.

Lola was joined by Heald on the evening of 15 September. From there she wrote to her 'very dearest Luis' mounting assorted defences to her latest misconduct. The letter was something of a masterpiece and one wonders just how many drafts went into the wastepaper basket before she was satisfied. The whole thing had been the result of a vendetta by Heald's aunt: 'It seems the aunt of Senor Heald committed this infamy not to avenge herself on me but on her nephew – It seems the father of Senor Heald hadn't spoken to this person for fourteen years and even on his death bed he refused to see her.'[16]

His aunt, she wrote, had wanted a cash settlement in addition to a £600 annuity Heald had settled on her; and, not receiving it, had begun the proceedings. In fact there may have been a grain of truth in this. *The Satirist* was by no means sure that this 'straight-laced old spinster' might not have had an eye on her nephew's fortune. The paper had no time for her at all. 'She ought rather to be called his grandmother.'[17]

Finally, since Lola now took the view that she had been baptised a Catholic, her first marriage was not a legal one and her conscience was clear. Lords Lyndhurst and Brougham 'and the most honourable people are indignant at all the persecution of which I am a victim'. Indeed that, she thought, was the general opinion of all classes of society. She would not speak of her health but she managed to add, 'it's very bad'. Her greatest happiness was to receive *querido* Luis' letters, but would he send half of what he used to give her:

> And this only for the time I have yet to live on earth – what I ask is little, it's easy for you to give it to me – and if it happens (may God forbid) that before mine, your precious life is taken by God, you will have the consciousness of having done your duty that I will not die of hunger – and who knows when that might happen . . .[18]

At least one part of her account was true: some of the newspapers thought the divorce laws extremely unfair. Ludwig continued to send his drafts, but he was far from happy. In the meantime the Healds took the sea breeze and went for donkey rides in the countryside; she sitting on a sheepskin and he leading her. Perhaps it should have been the other way about.[19] Later she would say of the gallant officer: 'He was quite unsuited to my character . . . instead of finding myself a quiet, domestic happiness I found myself the wife of a dissipated and impoverished English spendthrift.'[20]

There would have been an interesting legal wrinkle if Lola had been committed for trial. As a Spaniard, she would have been entitled to a jury composed half of foreigners. It would have been particularly interesting to see who, such as Lord Ranelagh, might have come forward to denounce her and deprive her of this right.

And so Lola once more disappeared from the newspapers and from sight. It was a temporary disappearance, for she resurfaced within the month. The pair had been to Ostend and had then travelled to Barcelona via Perpignan. Lola's thoughts on the tendency of travel to kill romance are well documented, and they had been quarrelling. Indeed, so Heald told the Barcelona consul on 7 October, she had stabbed him, producing a bloodstained waistcoat as evidence. Would the consul advise him to leave her? The consul, who wondered why Heald had not been to the police, very sensibly would not give that advice but he did visé his passport. On the 16th Heald was issued with a fresh one and promptly disappeared over the border into France. Two days later Lola received an anonymous letter in English, 'Use discretion or you are lost'. The adviser thought that if she rejoined Heald in Perpignan she would be able to win him round. She feared that it might be a trap and that if she crossed the border she might be arrested and extradited. The *Weekly Chronicle* advised that it could not guarantee the story was genuine but, given her history, it seemed quite probably correct. In substance it was.[21]

Lola now inserted notices in the Spanish newspapers requesting that if anyone found her husband would they kindly return him to her. In fact Heald could not stay away from her and was back within the week, piteously whining that his friends had effectively kidnapped him. Three times he had tried to escape, but too good a watch had been kept over him. At Mataro he had refused to go any further and with the help of a Frenchman Lola had retrieved him. On his return Heald wrote a note, 'If you have ever to complain of me show me this letter and it will be your talisman.' The *Illustrated London News*, which had the story from the Barcelona newspaper *Formento*, was highly amused. 'Lola has been able to catch her faithless husband and has brought him back to the conjugal roof.'[22] Not that relations were much improved. There was a story that when they went gaming Lola lost a good deal of money. When Heald refused to advance more she hit him about the face, saying that those who had the great fortune to be allowed to accompany her must bend to her wishes.[23]

There were other stories in the newspapers that one of Heald's uncles had offered 300,000 francs to any girl who would lure his nephew back to England. Lola was quoted as saying her lawyers could keep the case running for a decade. Reports which have her and Heald at the opera in Paris in November are a total invention. She was in Spain at the time, where according to the Barcelona papers she was practising pistol shooting daily, and shooting well.[24]

Reunited again with Heald, Lola took the opportunity to write another despairing letter to Ludwig. And she put her heart into it:

> What a pity you aren't near to me to see for yourself the eternal punish-ment I've brought upon myself – This man not only is without spirit, foolish, brutal but he is without heart, and he insults me before the whole world . . . How after knowing you, can I give my love to another, and this other man is without spirit, ignorant, a quasi-lunatic who is incapable of taking a step by himself.

She said that she and Heald were going to Cadiz for a fortnight and she would write to Luis the moment she arrived. In the meantime:

> My soul is yours forever and ever – I can love no other but you – believe my words they are written in affliction far from you – if I have one wish, it is to see you again mi querido Louis – once more I beg you to write to me – it is my consolation – I love you more in my unhappiness than when I was happy – Goodbye dear Louis, I am still the same Lolitta of heart and soul, loving you more than ever – Your Lolitta, yours unto death.[25]

The reconciliation with Heald did not last long. On the morning of Christmas Day he and his servant left the Hotel Ismenez in Cadiz with Turk, ostensibly to go for a walk. Instead they headed for England via Gibraltar, where he boarded the *Pacha*, taking everything but 500 francs with him. Lola thought a letter from Ludwig might bring him to his senses. 'He wrote a letter saying he has nothing against me but it's his idea and impulse.'[26] She took a steamer down the coast to Alge-ciras in the hope of intercepting him, but the *Pacha* had already sailed.

Once back in England he went to stay in Cork Street off Piccadilly. Meanwhile Ludwig turned up trumps again, sending Lola her allowance for January, February and March, but saying that there could be no more money until April. Curiously the split had been anticipated by the press, even if they had it back to front:

[Lola] has shaken herself free from young Heald having first secured on her for her life as Miss Lola, £3,000 a year which, with economy, will probably keep her in bull dogs, cigars and horsewhips. Heald is inconsolable but his strapping inamorata having vowed she would welt him if he came within the reach of her arm, he confesses at last that he has put his foot in it and walks off on his bootless errand to his maiden aunt.[27]

Lola left Cadiz at the beginning of February. The newspapers thought she might be sailing for England, but instead it was back to Boulogne and the Hôtel Folkestone. From there, on 25 February, she wrote once more to Ludwig, reproaching him for what she saw as his abandonment of her in her ill-health. She also told him that she had sent to London for the package of his letters. She would like to send them to him personally, but now how could she? She could not afford a personal courier. Would Ludwig send someone? The letters were certainly not safe with her; Heald could steal them and would surely publish them. Lola was hoping Ludwig would write to Brougham, who would confirm her troubles.[28] And so began what amounted to a long-term attempt at blackmail.

Initially Ludwig responded to the bait. As soon as the letters were in his hands he would send her drafts for April, May and June. But Lola was not pleased at the tone. On 8 March she wrote complaining of the cruel words in his letters – 'you have a very capricious heart and you forget easily' – and to say she was leaving incognito for England that night. She was going to get Heald to pay her and return her things. Ludwig could continue to write to her at the usual address.

The proposed visit was another attempt to retrieve Heald himself. This time, much to the despair of his relations and his lawyers, Lola was successful. Whether she went to England herself is doubtful. A letter from his lawyers six months later indicates that instead of going to England herself, Lola sent men after her husband.[29] What is certain is that her mission paid off. By the end of March 1850 all was once more sweetness and light for the reconciled pair. They were back in Paris, where *Le Siècle*, its tongue firmly wedged, wrote, 'Paris is in a great uproar. The excitement is terrible. Lola Montez is back again in Paris.' At first she stayed, accompanied only by a major domo and chambermaid, at the Hôtel du Rhin in the place Vendôme before moving to the Hôtel Beaujois on rue de Poithieu. Then on Good Friday she was joined by Heald with a large number of servants and five carriages.

Where many people had two horses, Lola drove in the Champs-Elysées with four magnificent white animals. When she went to the Cirque she was accompanied by powdered footmen dressed in crimson velvet, and it was there at the beginning of May that her flunkies narrowly averted a disaster. While they were waiting for her a hostile crowd gathered, complaining that the coachmen by their livery insulted the poverty of the people and demanding to know to whom the carriage belonged. The men had the wit to answer that it belonged to Eugène Sue. The coach went undamaged.

When she went to the Champs de Mars for the races that month she was dressed as a Madrilena in a black satin dress, Spanish veil of black lace, a red camellia and a black comb. It was now that she executed one of the classic con tricks, circulating the rumour that she had deposited $80,000 with an American banker. Her intention, she let it be known, was to buy a hotel in the Champs-Elysées. The *New York Herald*, happy to give its readers every possible morsel of gossip, had at that time an ambivalent attitude towards her. 'Not having the power of a lady of "quality" she wishes to have the peculiarity of being a lady of quantity.'[30]

Indeed, however she may have wrapped up the marriage in her mind, Lola was a courtesan during the time she was with Heald and she behaved as one. The more money lavished on her, the more she spent. In *Grandes Horizontales*, Virginia Rounding suggests that 'It was often her [the courtesan's] part of the bargain to spend, rather than save, the money given by a wealthy protector, for the conventions of the age demanded that the mistress of a man of the world would be an ostentatious status symbol, not someone to be hidden away in a secluded apartment.'[31]

Lola played the part admirably. When Louis Napoleon went to open the railway at St Quentin, Lola was present and 'her rich livery, her astonishing toilettes were the *point de mire* of all beholders'. There were also thoughts that she might be making a play for Louis Napoleon but that she would not succeed, that sceptre being firmly in the grasp of a Mrs H. of Baltimore. Then came a story that she had fought with the owner and niece of her hotel over the removal of some wine. Had Lola's maid not been on hand to help her mistress, Lola might have come off worst.[32] Back in England, in May that year at Middlesex Sessions, Daniel and Henry Davies gave up their struggle to avoid forfeiting the bail money. They wanted it made clear, however, that they had been acting for Heald and not Lola.

With Lola back in funds there was no question of her handing over the letters to Ludwig. She told him they were deposited with Brougham, forgetting that in a previous letter she wrote that Heald had them. There were constant reproaches for the poor man, whom she deemed was treating her badly. In June that year Ludwig made his final allowance payment and then dug in his heels. There would be no further payment if the letters were not in his hands. He was still, however, besotted. Just as he had used Rufenacht as a spy, now he wrote to his ambassador in Paris, August von Wendland, asking him to find out whether Lola was with Heald or had a lover. On 15 June Wendland reported back that she was with her husband, adding that the workmen seemed to have been paid at once and that there was quite a household. Except for appearing at the races and driving in the Champs-Elysées, she did not appear much in public.

Lola was still playing a game of bluff. On 26 June she wrote to Ludwig once more, pleading poverty and suggesting he write to the solicitor Henry Davies for confirmation. She still had pre-Munich debts. And for just about the first time came a serious hint about her memoirs. Indeed, her letter might have been modelled on Harriette Wilson's to Brougham. It read:

In your last letter to me you say nothing to my question whether if I send your letters to me back, you'll give me security with the little pension you swore to give me all my life . . . Your letters are at my house and well locked up. A great many people would like to see them, but I've shown them to no one. Believe me its much better *for you* as well as for me to conclude this thing and to give me a sum of money – once and for all, I'll renounce the pension you gave me.

Nothing I have written here on the subject of your letters or the pension is my own idea, it's the advice of friends who want to manage the whole thing without scandal and in a manner to satisfy you.[33]

By July 1850 Heald had been in Lola's clutches for almost exactly a year. His relations, along with Davies, were now making another serious effort to extricate him and what was left of his rapidly diminishing fortune. Quite why the Scots-born builder-cum-developer George Duncan was sent to Paris by Davies to facilitate Heald's return is not apparent, but, in a series of notes and letters sent to his wife back in London, he gives a clear picture of the final break-up and Lola's desperate efforts to retain a hold on Heald.[34]

George Duncan liked neither the French nor Paris, and he certainly did not like Lola. On 28 July he was not at all pleased with the way things were going. He was staying with her and Heald at 3 rue Beaujon. The crossing from Dover to Calais had been rough – he was the only one not seasick – and the weather was poor in Paris. Duncan was particularly lamenting over the vacillations of the young man: 'I have only to say that I am quite well but have a great deal of trouble about the business I came to settle, for the principal party concerned is so destitute of firmness that no dependence can be put upon his promise so he is continually upsetting all my arrangements as soon as they are made.'

He was a little brighter the next day, 'everything is going on pleasantly', and he had sent for Davies to join him and his two companions, Kellow and Reeves. But by 2 August things had gone off the boil again. Letters were to be sent to him at the Hôtel des Colonies at 4 rue d'Amsterdam near the Gare St Lazare.

It was clear that hatches were being battened down against the Countess. That same day Davies wrote a sharp letter to Heald about his finances, telling him that the coachman and the four horses had arrived safely. They would be given a few days' rest and then put up for sale. He hoped that the carriages could be returned to the makers. He went on to explain to Heald that he must return to England for a short time to clear things up: 'I mention this now because when you came over here last two persons were sent after you by the Countess who hastened your return home before any arrangements could be made, and I think it better to anticipate these questions in order that no discussion may arise on such subjects when I have the pleasure of seeing you.'[35] This seems to indicate that Lola never made the trip to England after Heald left her in Cadiz the previous Christmas.

Duncan's first long letter, on 3 August, was written to his wife when Heald and Lola were away playing billiards – like a number of other actresses, she was regarded as a fine player. Duncan was sorry about the scraps he had previously written:

> But on account of the suspicious disposition of the Countess and from a shrewd guess she has that I am not here for her interest, I have been continually watched and as I do not wish to do anything that might prevent me settling the business I came about, it was considered by me most advisable to keep on good terms with her.

He had found the French law very difficult, and whatever arrangements he had made before leaving, they had come to a temporary halt:

> I hope things are in a proper train now and that they will be settled to the satisfaction of all Parties. The Business has been so ticklish and difficult that I scarcely think of undertaking the like again excepting the prospect of compensation is very good.

Lola was sticking to him

> like wax and will not allow Mr Heald and me to be together ourselves for a minute she always insists upon me accompanying her in the carriage – along with Mr Heald – I do not like it much and would rather decline the *honour* but my old maxim of holding the candle to the devil prevents me from saying anything.

He was staying in the house with the pair and taking his meals with them. Fortunately, he had provided his own food sent from London. There were obviously other guests, because the 'French people are quite astonished at the talents of Scotch bakers'. The climate was treacherous. Kellow had developed rheumatic fever and was returning to London, but the good news was that Davies was expected imminently. Clearly Lola had made a move on Duncan, because:

> To use the words of Mr Davies I never knew the value of a good wife until I saw Mrs Lola – she is a dirty, beastly, ugly, blagard strumpet – Destitute of every accomplishment and talent and only carried sway over weak minded fools by bullying and threatening – she tryed the same upon me but I told her it was quite thrown away and she might as well talk Greek – and that I had certain duties to perform and all attempts to alter my determination and plans were useless – so she has given it up and now talks calmly enough but I am always on my guard.

She had taken Heald and Duncan to the circus, where:

> Would you believe it among all the Company there – I did not see one good looking Lady all the stories about French beauty is mere humbug – I would rather have one peep at you and my dear little boys than at that can be seen in Paris.

But for all his protestations of affection, his wife was not going to get a present on the canny Scot's return:

> Do not expect that I will bring anything from Paris for Englishmen can buy cheaper in London for here the tradesmen think it their duty to impose upon strangers.

On 11 August Duncan was both pleased with himself and a bit homesick: 'I never knew how much I liked you all until now and am not likely to forget it after my return.' They were not to worry; the only danger he was in was from being likely to figure in the newspapers. Things had definitely progressed:

> The great talk in Paris just now among the scandal-mongers is the way I have done Loli – she has been outwitted and for the first time in her life – numbers of people congratulate me upon having done so – Perhaps you will have learned before this that Mr Heald has arrived in London – and what is more wonderful he went with Loli's consent – when Mr Davies arrived here on Tuesday afternoon I had everything ready for him

– now I am busy all day in breaking up the establishment and settling
with the Thieves of Tradesmen which is really a most difficult matter on
account of the strict and peculiar laws of France.

There was still a major problem to overcome:

> Another great obstacle is that I have not yet succeeded in getting Loli out
> of the house but hope to do so tomorrow then I will be off for London
> and leave them to fight and squabble as much as they choose – I have
> power to call in the Police and turn out every person by force but do not
> wish to exercise it on account of the scandal it might cause and which Mr
> Heald dreads very much.

Once Heald had left the house so did Duncan:

> and have only gone there since along with other people on account of the
> character of Lola who is such a bad one she might get up to all sorts of
> stories against me through revenge so it is my intention to put the chance
> out of her power.

And the temptation out of his way? Meanwhile:

> Paris is not the place for me to feel comfortable in were even you and the
> little ones in my company it would be the same . . . Cookery especially is
> so disgusting to me that I am almost starved and have got so thin you will
> scarcely know me.

It seems there had been some sort of domestic trouble between
Duncan and his wife before he left, but in future everything would be
sweetness and light:

> The journey here has certainly done me good my head feels clearer than
> it has felt since February last and again my estimation of you and my little
> darling boys has increased wonderfully.

But things were still not going smoothly. Duncan had written the
letter on Friday night in the hope of posting it on Saturday. Then he
found there was no post and, worse, Lola *furiosa:*

> On Saturday morning Loli would not go out and remained blagarding
> every one in the house Mr Davies called and she promised to leave in

order that I might settle everything as quick as possible and with little sacrifice – no sooner had he gone than she turned round and went on as usual delaying everything and on account of the strict verbal injunctions of Mr Heald it was considered best to let her do as she please.

Suddenly things were taken out of everyone's hands:

All at once the Court yard was filled with Creditors who began a perfect revolution cursing and swearing and threatening all kinds of vengeance to Loli and those connected with her for that they had been swindled and robbed Loli got dreadfully alarmed for with all her ill temper and fury she is a complete coward when a struggle begins so off she bolted after giving instructions to her maid to seize what ever could be got away then what a scene began such plundering and thieving while I was enjoying the fun exceedingly from one of the windows – things went on that way until about six o'clock when I heard the Police were to be put into possession on behalf of the Landlord and Creditors.

Cowardice was contagious that day:

My Lawyer recommended me to bolt or I might be put in prison so I followed the example of Loli and am now hiding in a back street up five flights of stairs – not that I am in any danger or at all alarmed but if the Creditors found out they would annoy me – and I wish to examine their accounts at my leisure before settling with them . . . Loli is hiding in a small room along with her maid under false names – I took a case of Letters to her which she places a very high value upon they being written by the late King of Bavaria to her – she thought they had been lost in the scramble but all the papers were 'boned' by me at the commencement of the outbreak as you may imagine she was highly pleased – at my forethought – I never in my life have had such a troublesome matter in hand it has been necessary to be continually prepared for changes and trickery yet I flatter myself I have succeeded in a manner no one anticipated.

And finally a few more words directed at the Countess:

The loss to Mr Heald will be enormous but that was expected and even intended in order that he would feel as well as see the disgraceful position he occupied from his connexion with a low dirty strumpet.

Duncan went to see her, saying that it was best he did not return for fear of being followed and Lola found and arrested. It seems as though the Countess did not quite understand what had happened. 'Her eyes are not opened yet.'

The newspapers had a version of this or another, earlier flight from the creditors. When they called she told them her husband had indeed sent the money, but that she had lost the key to her cashbox. Would they kindly wait while she went for a locksmith? They would, and so she escaped in a carriage which was waiting for her in the avenue de Châteaubriand near the barrière de l'Etoile.

Duncan next saw her in Boulogne on Sunday 25 August, 'in a dirty Public House – pretending to be very ill and broken-hearted – I scarcely know what to make of her – she is either insane or a deep rogue – I am inclined to think her head is really affected.' Apparently she received him in a most friendly manner and told him she was travelling on to London, 'but I know she is too great a coward to do so'.

For some reason, although seemingly he had completed his business, Duncan was not going straight back to England. It is possible he may have been still trying to negotiate a reduced annuity of £50 to be paid by Heald. Duncan concluded his letter that he was staying in Boulogne for a day or so and then could be contacted back in Paris. As for Lola, Paris was the direction in which she too travelled. There were reported sightings, if not of her, of her maid, who was said to be making regular visits to the Monte-de-Piété and to be busy there pawning jewels and lace.[36]

As for Heald, it was not a lucky time for him. Even when he managed to get his possessions away from Lola he had trouble getting them home. One packing case was damaged at Dunkirk and was sent to a warehouse in London, where it was ruined in a fire. Heald sued the shipping agents. Although he won at first instance, the Court of Appeal rather scathingly quashed the verdict, saying the agent had done the best he could and Heald had a case 'neither in law nor in good sense'. Heald was ordered to pay costs, the matter dragging on when he challenged the need for the defendant to have had three counsel in court for him for which Heald, as the loser, was liable to pay.[37]

→>—<←

CHAPTER TWELVE

Lola Resurgent

ALL THIS WAS, OF COURSE, only a temporary setback. There were still plenty of wealthy men on whose shoulder Lola could lean and it did not take her more than a few days to recover herself. With the sticky heat coming to an end it was indeed back to Paris. Briefly, the *New York Herald* had been ironically worried about her: 'It appears that the *adventurière* has been unfortunate in her attempt to make the *volage mari* return to her feet, and that she is here in a very destitute condition, knowing not what to do. No doubt she will soon find a solution to her critical position. She is not a woman to lose her head for so little.'[1]

One creditor who had gone to court was the artist Jacquand, who had agreed to paint Lola and Heald in one of the flushes of their romance. Heald was to be depicted in his guard's uniform and Lola seated on a sofa receiving a present of jewellery. When Jacquand learned that Heald was about to flee Paris, he went to the courts to sue for 15,000 francs, the price of the painting. Heald's adviser, if not the former officer himself, was made of stern stuff and contested the claim. The celebrated painter Ingres was invited to examine the work and he thought 10,000 francs to be a fair price. On 15 February 1851 the court ruled that Heald should pay 8,000 francs and that costs should be shared by the parties.[2] It was still a huge sum. Heald had better luck obtaining the return of his billiard table in another action.

In fact, Lola's short-term solution was probably the consolatory arms of the Nepalese ambassador, Jung Bahadur – another of those credited from time to time with giving her syphilis – who on 24 August had arrived with a twelve-strong retinue and an English interpreter and, staying at the Hôtel Sinet, was said to be cutting a swathe through the opera girls that season:

> The famed mermaid who is always somewhat interested with princes of all nations has been, during the stay of Jung Bahadoor, very intimate with the educated barbarian. Having resided for some time in the great Indies, and speaking the language of the Bramas, she was the pet of the Nepaul Ambassador who regretted her very much when he left Paris.[3]

Born in 1817, Jung Bahadur was himself very much a princeling, formerly the heir apparent of the prime ministership and Commander in Chief of Nepal. Guided by the Queen and her lover, he assassinated his maternal uncle Matbar Singh in 1845, shooting him in the head and chest. As a reward he became Prime Minister the following year. When Frederick Leveson-Gower, the writer and son of the Earl of Granville, met him in India, he described him as dressed in a most theatrical fashion: 'a green velvet coat, black satin breeches and white boots with gold trimmings and spurs, all brand new. He was very cordial, free and easy, entirely emptying my cigar case, sticking its contents in his belt.'[4]

In 1850 it was decided it was politically safe for Jung to visit England to pay the respects of the King and assure Britain of Nepal's friendship. He left Kathmandu on 15 January, landing for his state visit on 25 May and staying in Richmond. There was still plenty of time for socialising: he rode, wrestled at Crystal Palace and went to Epsom races. Despite the fact that he spoke no English, he was a huge success. More importantly, he saw the beautiful golden-haired Irish actress and courtesan Laura Bell – a very much more successful version of Lola, whose career paralleled hers – when she was working at Jay's General Mourning House in Regent Street and promptly set her up in a house in Wilton Place. In the three months she was with him before his urgent recall home, she relieved him of £250,000.[5]

Quite apart from his wealth, he was a man who would appeal to

Lola, but she did not have a long time to work on him. He arrived in Paris about the same time as Lola was in Boulogne, and left at the end of September. One complication was that Laura may well have been with him for part of the time, when he attended a review of French troops at Satory near Versailles. It may be that in a matter of days Laura had moved onwards and upwards, because she remained in Paris, living in the avenue Friedland under the protection of Napoleon III. In 1851 she was sentenced to imprisonment there for not paying a bill of exchange she had used to buy jewellery in London. She was only saved when an admirer, Guy de la Tour-du-Pin, paid the debt.[6]

During his stay in Paris Jung was said to have sent Lola precious jewels and an Indian shawl covered with gold and diamonds. He also had his portrait painted by Jacquand, paying him 10,000 francs. He, and possibly Lola – or perhaps Laura – had a great escape at the Opéra when he went to see the ballet *Violon de Diable*. The Baron d'Ardennes, who led a gang of cut-throats in Belleville, had tried to take a nearby box to rob him and his guests of their jewellery during the performance, but it had already been let to the royal princes. After Jung left on 1 October for Marseilles to take a steamer back to Calcutta Lola was reportedly distraught, but in short order there was the *soi-disant* comte de Corail to take over duties.[7]

How was Lola living? Ludwig continually demanded answers from his ambassador, Wendland. In style but with some difficulty, was the reply. She was, it seems, in an apartment in rue St Honoré rented for her by Michael de Corail. Wendland thought that de Corail was her lover and businessman – whatever that latter might imply. There was, however, no danger of another fiasco along the Heald lines. Nothing was in her name. The rent had apparently been paid six months in advance by a woman named Buisson and the furniture had been paid for in cash at various sales.

Over the following weeks Ludwig peppered Wendland with questions. How much was her pension? For how long? Was it irrevocable? What was Heald paying her? What about a gold dress given by an Indian prince? Who was supporting her? Ludwig had no intention of reading her proposed memoirs in *Le Pays* but he was anxious to know how he was treated in them. But what was she making from them? What sort of newspaper was *Le Pays*? Were the memoirs likely to be widely read?

The answers were probably a trifle unsatisfactory. Heald was a nothing and no one knew anything about him. Lola undoubtedly had received presents from the Indian but Wendland could not say anything definite about a gold dress. There were reports that James was still alive. Heald's family were thinking of trying to have the marriage annulled and he had possibly stopped paying her the £1,000 annual maintenance (other information was that it was £700. Yet another that he was paying nothing). One of her creditors had gone to the police and so obtained payment. Others were not too worried because a representative had been to England and obtained assurances that all debts before 1 July would be paid; genuine creditors should make claims to Discon et Maugham at 12 rue de la Concorde. Lola was going through a religious period but at the same time was spending her days smoking large cigars and beating the servants. There had been one particular incident when, on 10 December, she had given her chambermaid a frightful thrashing; when the girl's husband had intervened she had threatened him with a knife. Wendland was sure proceedings would follow.

There was worse news for Ludwig. Lola was now in love with an artist and they had been closeted three days and nights with food being sent in. A friend of the comte de Corail was helping with the memoirs based on notes Lola was sending him.[8] Lola was thinking of moving to a larger apartment. She had given several well-attended soirées and had been visited by Messieurs de Belleyme and de Laborde among others. It is not clear to which de Belleyme Wendland was referring: the father, Louis-Marie, was the prefect of police and later the president of the tribunal of first instance; his son Charles-Louis was a judge on the tribunal de la Seine and a second son, Adolphe, sat in the Chamber of Deputies. Whichever was her visitor, Lola had friends in reasonably high places.[9]

At least the report of the soirées was accurate. The first had been on 3 December and the *New York Herald* correspondent had been promised an invitation for the second. 'How curious to meet a woman who possesses the most refined education in a parlour who that morning had been fighting with her milk furnisher', thought the journalist. He believed that much of the money for the evening's entertainment had come from the King of Bavaria.

Whoever financed the soirée, the *New York Herald* was impressed both with it and the hostess: 'Lola dispensed the honors of the new home with a gracefulness, an elegance and a natural naiveté which gave much astonishment to those who had formed an opinion of her, from the fame which the public has given her.' Her hair was adorned with a simple gold chain and a natural camellia. She wore a white watered-silk robe, 'upon which she had placed the grand cordon of the Order of St Thérèse which had been given to her by the King of Bavaria with the title of *Pairette*'.[10] The concert was thought to be exquisite and a 'splendid *souper* followed at half past one and was much appreciated for the deliciousness of the comestibles which had been furnished by Chevet, the famed restaurateur of the National Palace'.[11]

It would seem that de Corail lasted no more than a few weeks, for another of her lovers at the time was the fair-haired, blond-bearded Savile Morton, described in the *Dictionary of National Biography* as a journalist and philanderer. Morton, born in Cavan, went to Cambridge and read for the Bar but never qualified. For a time this friend of Thackeray and Tennyson lived in Rome. In 1846, with the former's help, he became the *Daily News* correspondent in Constantinople and later moved to Paris. With his genial good countenance he was attractive to women, and the attraction was mutual. He was, however, completely incapable of fidelity and would seem to have been a man to suit Lola admirably.

In fact their relationship was, as with almost all of Lola's affairs, short-lived. On 10 December Morton wrote to his friend R. M. Milnes: 'I have done with Lola – not broken but I visit her rarely. We cannot help quarrelling before people which is scandalous and odious. The fault is I believe mine – I am insolent and she is susceptible as [unreadable].'[12]

From necessity there could only be the shortest of gaps between lovers. A fortnight before Christmas that year Lola wrote to an unnamed admirer:

Caro amigo

Have you forgotten me? If so, you will disappoint two of the prettiest women in Paris who expect to be admired this evening at the Opera and, above all I who expect to meet *you* there.

Then forget me not – M De Landsfeld.[13]

Yet another of Lola's friends was the Paris dandy and minor novelist Roger de Beauvoir, with whom Dujarier had quarrelled at the Trois Frères dinner. But Lola did not hold this against him. She thought him a great ladies' man and admired the way in which he, just as she did, eluded his creditors. Once he had thrown the contents of his bath tub over his creditor, and on another occasion heaped hot ashes over a bunch who were standing in the courtyard outside his apartment.

Sometime in December 1850, Savile Morton challenged de Beauvoir to a duel over 'coarse' remarks made at one of Lola's parties. This time the matter was settled, principally because no one would act as his second. But on a subsequent occasion Morton was reported to have thrown a man named Forbes Campbell down the stairs of her apartment and fought an inconclusive duel as a result. Campbell seems to have continued to slander Morton, who wanted to fight a second time but was advised by his friends that enough was enough.[14] The novelist Thackeray wrote of his friend: 'Morton has a genius for scrapes such as no man out of Ireland can hope for – and the wonder is that he has lasted up to forty years of age with a whole skin – why he is always in some feminine mischief.'[15]

For the purposes of her autobiography and her lectures Lola painted a picture of her house as 'the resort of the most gifted literary geniuses of Paris and there she had the honour and happiness of entertaining many literary gentlemen from America, who were temporarily sojourning in the French capital'.[16] The full truth was rather different. It was now very much the second division; gone were the likes of Dumas from the Dujarier days. Lola was mixing with a louche literary set. She still knew and associated with the literati, such as François Méry, who co-wrote the libretto for *Don Carlos*. But in addition to his love of opera Méry also loved gambling, casinos and German baths.

It was clearly the duelling season. On 8 June 1851 Lola's long-standing friend Pier-Angelo Fiorentino fought a duel with the duc d'Amédée Archaud over an actress. Archaud was hit in the lung and when it was thought he would die Fiorentino fled to London. On Archaud's recovery Fiorentino returned to Paris where he was, as expected, acquitted.

Lola also greatly admired Samson, the actor and teacher of the great tragedienne, Rachel, whom she thought far too committed to money for anyone to be committed to her. Unsurprisingly she did not like Jules Janin, the caustic critic of *Journal des Débats*, whom Samson called 'the guillotinist of artists' and at whose hands Lola, and many others, suffered. She was definitely enamoured of Eugène Sue: 'His courage in avowing his opinions in the face of whatever opposition, and even threats, marks him as one of the great heroes of the age. He was an honest, sincere, truth-loving man; and it will be long before Paris can fill the place which death has made vacant.'[17]

This was rather contrary to general opinion of Sue. He had been a ship's surgeon before beginning to write seafaring novels, but with the increasing success of his novels of the Paris underworld, for which he relied heavily on the experiences of the criminal turned detective Vidocq, he was regarded as deeply unpleasant.

Although, once she arrived in America, Lola would claim to have been an intimate of George Sand, generally her set included a ragbag of minor aristocrats such as the Prince of Montlear, father-in-law of the King of Piedmont, General Prince Soltikoff and the Count of Sussy. There was also a rich American, William Tudor, famed for the fêtes he gave, and the very dubious American Henry Wikoff, said to be 'the one time Chevalier of Fanny Elssler'[18] and who in 1850 does seem to have been employed as a spy by Palmerston. Later he had a child by the ballerina and possibly cheated her out of her money.[19]

Another old friend who was in Paris at the time was Benjamin Lumley of Her Majesty's Theatre, but he had not been prospering in Lola's absence. The new opera house in Covent Garden had opened and Lumley had suffered severe financial losses trying to compete. Now he was in Paris managing the Théâtre Italiens. Although there were rumours that she might dance for him, he does not appear to have been invited to her table, nor did he suggest she appear on the stage at his theatre.[20]

On 2 January 1851 Wendland reported that Lola was thought to have an income of 15,000 francs. She hoped to receive 90,000 francs for the proposed memoirs, in which there would be a good deal about life in Munich society. He had been to see both the foreign and justice ministers. As a result, the editor of *Le Pays* had been called in and told that any offence to a friendly government would result in an immediate arrest.

If Ludwig and Wendland thought they could suppress publication they were swiftly disabused. The editor rather thumbed his nose; this was the problem with a free press, thought the ambassador. As for public interest, well, he reported, Paris was really quite excited in advance of the proposed starting date of 15 January for the serialisation. On 7 January Wendland received a letter from the secretary to the editor saying Lola had written to Ludwig several times but had received no reply. Perhaps the memoirs and the letters were lost? The galley proofs to the foreword would be sent via the embassy. There was no question of Lola withdrawing her memoirs; but, as a sop, if she returned Ludwig's letters and refrained from using them in the memoirs she would be looking for a pension of 25,000 francs. Wendland asked that publication be delayed until after Ludwig had the opportunity to look them over, but the first instalment appeared the next day.

Meanwhile Ludwig was dithering over the removal of the dedication in his name and Wendland decided not to seek a delay. In turn Lola appears to have been dithering. Wendland reported that a life pension of £1,200 was on offer from Heald if she gave up all claims against him but that she could not make up her mind. For the time being he was still financing her. By 18 January there was a marked lack of interest in the memoirs and Lola, who had been speaking well of Ludwig, had now turned against him. Wendland thought she had fallen into the hands of low speculators.

On 7 February Wendland wrote again. The memoirs were doing badly and they had not appeared for a week. No one believed them anyway. Lola had been trying to contact him in an effort to try to persuade the King to pay to keep his name out of them. He had told her that the only possibility for redemption in Ludwig's eyes was that the letters should be returned.

One of the reasons that the memoirs were doing badly was that in the past weeks *Le Pays* had been taken over and the staunch Republican politician Alphonse Prat de Lamartine was now in charge. Born in Mâcon in 1790, he divided his career between politics and literature. In 1848, as a member of the provisional government, he was for a few weeks the true leader of France, but in the December election of 1848 he received rather less than 8,000 votes. Broken in politics, he had now returned to literature and publishing. Memoirs such as Lola's were anathema to him and they were quickly spiked. Sometimes Lola would claim the friendship of Lamartine, at others that they only met on business. The latter is more likely, as he seems to have done nothing but impede her.[21]

Ludwig was now intending to go to Rome at the beginning of April. The last thing he wished, or at least said he wished, was that Lola should present herself there. Wendland was to make sure she never found out, for he was sure she would follow him. 'It is better if nothing makes her think of me. Let sleeping cats lie.'[22]

Then, at the end of March, came the letter Ludwig wanted in his heart to receive. It was from a very penitent and humble Lola: 'It is in supplication and the greatest humility that I write you these lines, Louis, to you who once loved me so much and who without fault of mine has completely abandoned me . . .'

His poor Lolitta was cold and hungry. Heald was ruined; his creditors had seized everything. As for her, she did not have money for carpets for the floor and had nothing but a sofa on which to sleep. She had no money to buy clothes for the cold. He must not listen to the lies of her enemies. She had had fever – originally caught in Bad Brückenau – and been in bed for four weeks. Disregard the memoirs. There would be nothing of Munich. And by the way, there was no one else in her life, although there could have been: 'money ill come by is always evil – I'd prefer to live as I do than possess luxury in evil'.[23] Clearly Lola was still playing with a stacked deck of cards held very closely to her famous bosom.

If her Luis ever replied, there is no answering letter from Lola. There was, however, another surprise for Ludwig, this time in the form of a new admirer of Lola's. The Irishman Patrick O'Brien in effect simply appeared on the doorstep to deliver her letters to the ex-King.

O'Brien was another of the curious, louche young men to whom Lola was attracted. He had been employed by *The Times* in Constantinople and then in Greece. In 1850 he was reprimanded by Mowbray Morris, the manager, for accepting a decoration from King Otto.[24] O'Brien did not learn and on 25 July Morris wrote again, pointing out: 'The matter unfortunately has not escaped notice from our contemporaries who have mentioned it in a very disagreeable way'.

O'Brien kept a dignified silence and was rewarded with the sack. There were

> private and public letters which make it appear beyond a doubt that you are entirely in the hands of the Athenian Court – these circumstances leave us no alternative but to dismiss you from the service of *The Times*.
>
> After the advice I gave you in my last with reference to the independence of your correspondence, I did not anticipate that you would enter upon a tour of Greece in a royal yacht placed at your disposal by the King expressly for that purpose.

The letters by O'Brien 'written from on board the yacht will be considered as unwritten'. O'Brien then travelled to Paris to stay with his friend and fellow rogue Savile Morton, while his brother entered the service of the Greek court as a paid hack.

Ludwig declined to see O'Brien and the transaction was undertaken by Graf Franz von Poci. O'Brien had appeared with the open package and in passing had mentioned that Lola had pawn tickets amounting to 2,000 francs. Poci gave his oath to the King that he had not read a word of the letters.

Once they had been handed over, O'Brien started to plead Lola's cause. Lola's defects were of the head and not the heart; Ludwig had been her best and truest friend; he had seen her 'a prey to the most heart-breaking grief at the thought of having lost Your Majesty's friendship'. The pawn tickets he had mentioned actually amounted to 2,900 francs.

Ludwig sent only 2,000 francs and in return received a well-couched letter appealing to his goodheartedness. It was all O'Brien's fault that he had mentioned the figure of 2,000 francs in the first place. Lola should not be blamed. Nor should Ludwig think that O'Brien had any relationship with Lola other than that 'she is a weak and friendless woman steeped to the chin in sorrow and distress'. In fact Lola could not have done better herself. One might think she had been at O'Brien's elbow dictating the letters. In a foretaste of some of her later religious outpouring, she had written: 'Tell the King that his poor Lola is now morally dead and will never trouble him any more. She will hide the pangs of her breaking heart from all the world and will try to end her days in peace with God and men.'

Ludwig was still sniffing at the bait, but not convinced. Now he wanted to know that Heald could pay nothing more. O'Brien was meanwhile showering the King with praise: 'God is my witness that I would go tomorrow to the farthest end of the earth to please Your Majesty not only because of the great kindnesses you have shown me although that in itself is sufficient but also because Your Majesty is the father of King Otto, whom I love with my whole heart and soul.'[25]

Lola had been wanting, and O'Brien angling for, a return to the monthly allowance. But both were to be disappointed. On 1 June, the day Lola went to the premiere of Dumas' *Pauline* at the Théâtre Historique, Ludwig sent an *ex gratia* 3,000 francs. That was the last money she ever received from him. The old man had finally had enough, both emotionally and financially. At the end of June Wendland wrote that she was receiving 1,033 francs a month from Heald. There was nothing wrong with Lola's health. O'Brien was in love with her and she had pretended to pawn her silver. The whole thing was a trick.

Meanwhile O'Brien, who was staying with Lola's man-about-town Savile Morton at 29 boulevard des Capucines, tried once more, suggesting 1,000 francs would help while the annuity was sorted out. But Lola had misplayed her cards yet again. With accounts of her duplicity coming in from Wendland and the letters safely back in his possession, Ludwig was finally putting some steel into his backbone. After all, the letters had been returned unconditionally and she had collected 5,000 francs in total. He still wanted an eye kept on her friends, finances and lovers. Meanwhile she seems to have double-crossed O'Brien, for he wrote to Poci saying he had never heard of the payment of 3,000 francs and that Lola had spread a rumour that he was trying to make money out of the letters. 'I am grieved to say that I have been most bitterly deceived.' He had not seen her again and had returned to Ireland. And so, on his way went yet another lover.[26]

As requested, Wendland reported on her throughout the summer. Privately Ludwig learned that she was still getting a pension from Heald. After the last day of the races at the Champs de Mars, there had been a fight with another woman at the Rond Point, at the bottom of the Champs Elysées. The other woman had been the stronger but Lola had grabbed her hair and pulled her from her carriage. She was supposedly seeing an Englishman. From the newspapers he would have learned that Lola was leaving Paris, and the Jockey Club was going to give her a farewell dinner at which she would be the only woman. She was taking dancing lessons with a view to taking up the stage again, going to Lumley in London. The reports were, in one way or another, more or less accurate. But on what or with whom she was living, nothing was said.

There was also a suggestion that she was going to America with P. T. Barnum, the celebrated impresario. From the 1840s onwards it was realised that there was enormous money to be made in America by European artists. The first star to go was the dancer Fanny Elssler, whose tour was organised by Stephen Price, with the curious Henry Wikoff as her manager and current lover. Elssler opened to a standing ovation when she made her debut on stage at the Park Theatre, New York on 14 May 1849, while the house grossed over a thousand dollars a night in Boston – she was paid $500 a night. In addition there were Elssler shoes, stockings, garters, fans, cigars, shaving soap, bootjacks, even bread.

When Jenny Lind, the Swedish Nightingale, turned her back on opera with a final performance of *Robert Le Diable* on 10 May 1848 – as well as on her engagement to the Englishman Claudius Harris, whose family had wanted an undertaking she would never again appear on a stage – she was courted by P. T. Barnum. Now Jenny would bring in $10,000 in a single night for Barnum.

One of the great showmen of his and many another generation, Barnum had made his money with Joice Heth, allegedly the 161-year-old former nurse of George Washington. Heth, a wizened old black woman, had been well schooled in her role and poured out anecdotes of young Georgie. When her attraction began to pall Barnum planted a story that she was in fact an automaton constructed from 'whalebone, india rubber and numberless springs'. From such beginnings are empires made.

Jenny Lind split with Barnum in June 1851, paying a $32,000 penalty. One cause of disagreement was that much of her time was spent in other Barnum attractions, such as reviewing the parade of his Great Asiatic Caravan – ten elephants who marched up Broadway pulling a chariot. There was certainly space for a Lola promotion. She probably would not have objected to reviewing parades of dwarves, wild animals and acrobats, and there is no doubt that if Barnum could have harnessed Lola's temperament they would have done very well for each other. 'Lola Montez had nowhere near the talent of Elssler, but she had "an electric, dynamic quality that injected color and excitement in an era when temperament could draw as much as talent".'[27]

The suggestion was that, in turn, Barnum would promote Lola; she was to be paid $800,000, some $200,000 more than Jenny Lind. 'Absurd,' thought the *Courrier de l'Europe*, 'even in America you need talent.' Nevertheless 'a number of gentlemen and well-known lions were thinking how they could catch the same boat'.

Barnum denied the story and wrote that, while he had received an approach, he had declined it. His agent, Le Grand Smith, who Lola said had made the approach, was now travelling throughout Scotland with the highly successful if repellent Bateman children, who made a speciality of playing Shakespearean tragedy in piping voices. Cudgels were taken up on Lola's behalf by James Gordon Bennett of the *New York Herald*, who had been duped more than once over Joice Heth.

Lola had told Bennett she was 'humbug enough herself without uniting her forces with the Prince of Humbugs'. She probably thought that Barnum and Lola Montez – two of the greatest humbugs of the age – would be too great a quantity for the generous people of the United States to accept in a single dose. Bennett reported Lola's claim that she had received letters from London saying that if she went to America without Barnum, the impresario would use his influence to bring the newspapers and magazines out against her. Bravely, she had replied that she had met kings, politicians and poets, and had upset them all. 'Barnum may expect a challenge to mortal combat with any weapons he chooses. She comes here "on her own hook".'[28] Barnum later shifted his stance. Lola had indeed received an approach from Smith, but he had been acting independently and without authority. Barnum is quoted as saying, 'Lola, if rightly managed will draw immensely but I am not the man for her.' According to the *Herald*, there was yet another marriage in the offing for her, this time in Haiti where King Faustin I was said to be looking for a new wife, 'divorcing his black Josephine'.[29]

Although later it thawed in its attitude towards her, the *New York Times* was then by no means her greatest admirer:

> We shall be sadly disappointed if this creature has any degree of success in the United States. She has no special reputation as a dancer. She is known to the world only as an abandoned woman. If such a reputation shall prove attractive in this country we have greatly mistaken its character. We predict that her visit to the United States will prove a failure.[30]

What Lola could not do, at the time, and almost to her death, was keep her hands off attractive young men, and it may be that the Englishman Wendland reported her to be seeing was in fact an American. In the spring she had been introduced to the black sheep Edward Payson Willis, who came from a literary family. His brother, the rake Nathaniel Parker Willis, described as 'an anticipation of Oscar Wilde', wrote short stories with surprise endings and co-edited the *New York Mirror*, engaging Edgar Allan Poe as literary critic. His sister Sara wrote satire and melodrama as Fanny Fern and was a columnist for the *New York Ledger*. Whether Ned Willis suggested that there was money to be made from following Fanny Elssler and Jenny Lind across the Atlantic, or whether Lola realised that she and Paris were once more done with each other, is difficult to say. Whichever is the case, she appointed him to be her agent for a forthcoming tour.

It was certainly correct that she was taking lessons. This time it was from the celebrated dancer Mabille, who with his father had a louche dance hall in the Allée des Veuves by 33 Champs-Elysées. The street was famed for its cloisters, which provided ideal cover for many an illicit rendezvous; one of its most celebrated performers was the courtesan Mlle Pomaré. Part of the repertoire of six dances Mabille taught Lola was a tarantella, which over the months metamorphosed into her famous Spider Dance.

The Spider Dance took a variety of forms and what was performed depended upon both the quality or otherwise of the audience, and Lola's mood each night. In Australia, it depended on what money was thrown on the stage. The governor and his lady undoubtedly did not experience as enhanced a performance as the miners in Ballarat. There were two parts to the simple version of the dance: in the first part she was the spider spinning its web and in the second the increasingly enmeshed female. The spider strikes and the poison envelopes the young girl, who collapses to the ground. She recovers and searches for the spider in her petticoats. On discovering it she stamps on it. In its more extreme versions there were a number of spiders to be dislodged, with the consequently inevitable artistic display of ankles, legs and possibly even thighs. One account has her crawling round the stage, but this has been dismissed by her admirers.

After years off the stage, and despite her ill-health, Lola trained hard. By September she thought she was in a position to make her first appearance on the stage for five years. On 12 September she appeared at Le Jardin Mabille before an invited audience of friends and some members of the press. The night before her reappearance she wrote a little poem in French:

> Free daughter of the air; I have refound my wings
> As you, in springtime, light swallows
> I shall fly to the scene where tomorrow
> Will I have friends who will hold my hand?[31]

She need not have worried about the reception she received – there was punch, cigarettes and ice creams for the guests to while away the two hours they were kept waiting for her reappearance, and they did not mind – but the reaction of the press was seriously worrying. She danced three national dances. *The Sunday Times* thought one was a Polonaise, while the *Courrier de l'Europe* thought it to be Hungarian. The latter thought the dances were not badly choreographed but that the music was dreadful. Everyone agreed that her costumes were ravishing and that her dancing was well applauded, particularly after she pulled the ribbons from her ballet shoes and tossed them into the orchestra. After the performance she produced a guitar and a half-empty bottle of champagne and began singing lewd songs. After each couplet she took another drink. 'Today the poor woman, abandoned by youth, lets herself be exhibited as a curiosity.'[32]

It may be her impulsiveness that made her a girl who could not say no, but there were clearly going to be contractual problems. On 26 August she had already signed up with the theatrical managers Roux et cie for a half-year tour which would bring most people to their knees – France, America, Cuba, Brazil, Mexico, Chile, Peru and Africa. She was to dance at least six performances a week in every city selected by Roux. She would pay for all the costumes and music, while he was to take twenty-five per cent of her gross earnings. In return he would accompany her, make the bookings, prepare and get up soirées, be the advance man and stay behind where necessary.

Now, a month short of five years since her retirement, she began to tour again. First stop was for two nights at the Salle de Monsigny in Boulogne on 16 September, where there was a predominantly English audience. On the first night she was received so well that she was booked for a third. She received a good notice in the *Revue et Gazette*: 'The travels of the famous Lola Montez have begun and already the echo of the applause she has won has reached us . . . Lola Montez' dance is poetry in motion, sometimes fantastic, often lascivious, always engaging.'[33] The third night, however, went poorly. Most of the audience came in for free and the receipts totalled 34 francs.

Then it was the hundred miles or so on to Arras, where things were even worse. She had a poor reception from the audience and would not continue until a large bouquet was presented to her. She was childishly delighted when told the flowers came from the wife of the Prefect, but in fact they came from the Prefect himself. In the wings she demanded a carafe of cognac, drank five glasses, smoked two cigarettes and reappeared to silence. Later she was defiant, saying she had more money than all of them and that she had diamonds from a king. The reporter noted that she insisted on being addressed as Countess.[34]

Ludwig had still not quite shaken off her shadow. Was she still living in Paris as the Countess? and what had happened to that dog Turk, which had caused more than unpleasantness in Munich?[35]

Meanwhile, on the road things went from bad to worse, in a pattern which would be repeated for the rest of her stage career. A stunning opening night was followed by a fiasco the next. The *Journal de la Belgique* was really rather pleased: 'We have a compliment to make to the Belgian public. Lola Montez has had a more complete fiasco than it is possible to imagine. The world was there the first night and nobody the second. She didn't even have the same *success de scandale* of Fieschi's mistress Nina Lassave [sic].'[36]

This was really handing it to Lola. Corsican-born Joseph Fieschi had devised a *machine infernale*, a primitive sort of machine gun, firing it at a review by Louis-Philippe of the National Guard on 28 July 1835 as it passed his house in the boulevard du Temple, not far from what is now place de la République. The King and his sons escaped unharmed but eighteen others, including a twelve-year-old girl and Maréchal Mortier, duc de Treviso, were killed. Nina Lasalle was the daughter of a woman named Petit; both were mistresses of Fieschi and both in turn became prosecution witnesses. As a child Lasalle had a scrofulus illness which left her with a paralysed hand and only one eye. This did not in any way seem to detract from her drawing power. The day after the trial she was engaged to appear in a café before she was sent on tour.[37]

This time the reporter thought that while Lola had never had any talent, she had now lost her looks. When the few spectators began to whistle, Lola turned on them, denouncing them as vengeful Jesuits.[38] There was, however, a third night, which produced takings of a mere 300 francs – still, it was better than Boulogne.

One offer she angrily turned down. While she was again staying in the Hôtel de Suède in Brussels, the director Arnaud offered her 3,000 francs for six performances at the Hippodrome, during which she would simply ride around the ring two or three times. She was furious: 'Do you know I am Grand Cross of the Order of Maria Theresa, that I am Countess of Landsfeld, that I have an entrée at the court of Bavaria, that I married a man belonging to one of the best families in England!'

In full flow, she was looking for a knife when Mabille arrived and tried to calm her. She then turned on him, but her final thrust was at Arnaud's representative: 'Sir, if my friends or my husband were here, you should wipe away this insult with your blood.'[39]

And so it went on. On 19 October, when she appeared in Ghent to dance at the Théâtre Minard, there was hissing, ironical applause, cock-crowing and yelling. The audience had come to see a woman of ill-fame, not a dancer. 'We might say it was a contest between the audience and the danseuse on the stage. Lola Montez sustained the fight most firmly . . . As to her talents we may safely assert she never possessed any. That or they had been exchanged for a title.'[40]

Political connotations, however, still attached to her. In Antwerp she was fêted, if not necessarily for her dancing. Arriving on the day the Liberal party received its first majority in history, she was applauded in the theatre by Liberals and whistled by the Royalists, who were eventually driven out. She was encored and cheered to the doors of her hotel. There were reports that the King of Holland had sent an envoy to inform her she could not cross the border. At Aix-la-Chapelle the cavalry had to disperse ticket seekers, despite doubled prices, and after her performance the town's students escorted her to her lodgings. On the reverse of the coin, appearances in Cologne, Koblenz, Düsseldorf, Mainz and Frankfurt were all cancelled. The Minister of the Interior announced that she would not be allowed to dance in Germany again.

It was an arduous tour, even by standards of a hundred years later. Lola then moved down south, and it was much better when she appeared in one-night stands – Bordeaux, Montpellier, Lyons and back to Boulogne – before returning to Paris on 6 November.

Throughout the tour the manager, Roux, was selling a purported biography at the theatres; he had thereby badly upset Lola, something which admittedly was not difficult. The pamphlet was the usual mixture of gossip and invention. In it he suggested she had lived for several years in China and Persia as well as in Hindustan. He was, however, correct when he mentioned her relationship with Jung Bahadur.

Financially the tour seems to have been a success, but now she was besieged on a number of fronts. For a start, she was locked in battle with Louis-Désiré Véron, once director of the Opéra. Véron, a former doctor who had made a fortune exploiting a patent medicine, had then founded the *Revue de Paris*. He was now the editor of *Le Constitutionnel*, which he had turned into a great success by publishing novels in daily instalments. *Le Constitutionnel* had been critical of Lola's tour and so she wrote a letter, published by the Lyons paper *Saint Public*, complaining about supposed slights and correcting an inaccuracy, saying that she could in fact swim. In a play on the nature of his comments and his previous occupation, her letter also challenged Véron to a duel in which each would swallow a pill; one would be poisonous: 'You will not be able to refuse a duel with arms that are so familiar to you.' Véron did not rise to the bait.

Lola had thought of the poison challenge when she was in Munich. The playwright Johann von Plotz had been invited to tea. When he had drunk a cup he noticed hers had not been filled. She told him 'Sir, you have taken liberties with my character, and as a Spaniard I must have revenge. Pain is your cup. Sir, you are a dead man.' The journalist fled to a chemist for an antidote before realising he had been duped.[41] It was a tactic she would repeat during her stay in California.

Second, so far as she was concerned she was going to sail with Ned Willis to America. So, on 10 November, Roux duly presented her with a legal demand that she fulfil the remaining four and a half months of her contract. She declined the next day. Roux sued and obtained an attachment order against her furniture, jewels and costumes. On 18 November she had the order discharged.

The full hearing of Roux's claim was the following day, when she set out her grievances against him. He had been supposed to travel with her but had not; nor had he looked after her interests. He had made her dance several times a day and the travelling had begun at 4 am. She had been accustomed to receive visits in her dressing room after performances, but Roux would introduce her as an 'enfant terrible' and tell ridiculous stories. The supposed biography was abusive.

Lola may not have been a good actress on the stage, but in the smaller confines of the court she was a most effective witness. She had intended to dance in Paris but Roux had found her nothing. The next day the Tribunal Civile for the Seine decided in her favour, finding that Roux had no serious agreement with any Paris theatre except perhaps the National; but as he had not notified Lola, she was not bound by it.[42]

So, with all that seemingly over, Lola was free to sail with Willis and her German maid, Anna Behr, for the home of the brave and the land of the free. They departed on the *Humboldt*, sailing from Le Havre on 20 November. Also on board was the Hungarian patriot Laszlo Kossuth, who suffered from seasickness the whole of what was a very rough crossing. He kept to his cabin for most of the voyage, whereas she kept the gentlemen passengers thoroughly entertained.

Before they sailed, Willis had booked her into the refurbished Montgomery Hotel, once Kimball's Old Museum. The *New York Times* thought she should have it to herself. It had learned that a pamphlet would soon be published in reply to the one by Marquis Poposi.[43]

When they arrived in New York on 5 December, Lola was somewhat annoyed to find much of the attention being paid to Kossuth and insufficient to herself. She did however give a very early version of a press conference: she had indeed been political adviser to Ludwig; she would marry tomorrow if she met the right man; no, Roux was not her agent; Edward Willis was her agent but E. A. Marshall, the lessee of a number of theatres, including the National in Washington where Lola later appeared, was not standing behind him as her manager; she had been born in Seville and was a direct descendant of Francisco Montes; she did not carry a gun in her purse, nor did she have a chest filled with gold and jewels.

By the time she arrived, the story of the Jockey Club farewell dinner had circulated. It was said that before she left Paris she had participated in a mass orgy with fifty men who had deposited the equivalent of $10,000 in her account. True? Not at all. 'If I was a woman of that description which I am represented, would I be compelled to go on the stage to earn a livelihood?' Had she turned down an offer to dance naked? Indeed she had not even considered the proposition.[44]

Meanwhile, however, the court decision in Paris was not a judgement Roux was prepared to accept. He brought his action against her to New York, and he and his friends were expected to try to disrupt her performance. Having arrived on the *America*, he camped out in the lobby of her hotel trying to serve a summons on her. She moved in the middle of the night to White Street; when the landlady complained about the stream of late-night gentleman callers she moved again, this time to Waverley Place. The owner of White Street now sued to collect three months' rent in advance and the lawyers Howe and Treadwell published the Roux contract. The litigation fizzled out, but it was all good publicity – as was a later story about two boys from New Haven who had got out of college late at night, taken a train to New York and been granted an audience. A mezzotint of her titled *A Belle of the Boulevards*, flashing eyes, chamois-gauntleted, holding a riding crop and wearing a black hat with a white plume, sold well and the *Herald* published a short series, 'Three Evenings with Lola Montez'.[45] For the moment, Lola was indeed the Belle of New York.

CHAPTER THIRTEEN

Lola on the Boards

WILLIS LASTED AS HER manager in New York for only a matter of days. Privately Lola was furious that she had been booked on the same steamer as Kossuth, who was bound, at least temporarily, to be a bigger attraction. Now a wrangle began over the money Willis had received and spent. Naturally, the *Herald* knew what was going on. Once Kossuth was out of New York, Lola would reappear 'lacking only the sanctification of the Church and a pair of wings'. The stage manager of the Broadway Theatre, Thomas Barry, announced he had reserved a box for her to see *Ingomar the Barbarian* and shortly afterwards, on Christmas Day, came the eagerly awaited news. Lola would appear at that theatre in *Betley the Tyrolean*.

The reason for Lola's delayed appearance was that the theatrical management realised audiences would not pay premium prices to see her dance a few short pieces. She had to appear in a full-length ballet, and that was the problem. There was no point whatsoever in expecting Lola even to try to dance Giselle or a similar role. A ballet must be devised for her that would show off her personality while limiting the exposure of her technical deficiencies. The lucky man chosen for this task was George Washington Smith, and he was equal to it.

Described as 'a nose with a little man on the end of it', Smith was by no means an inconsiderable artist. He first appeared in 1838, and in

1849 joined Fanny Elssler when she toured America, beginning as a clog dancer and ending as her leading man. He was still dancing in 1883 and taught until his death in 1899. During his career he was thought of as America's premier danseur, appearing as Albrecht in *Giselle* with Mary Ann Lee; the pair, along with Augusta Maywood, were regarded as the three great dancers America produced in the nineteenth century.[1] He later danced for Marius Petipa in Russia. Now, after the retirement of Mary Ann Lee, he was recruited to deal with Mme Lola's problems.

First he devised *Betley the Tyrolean*, based on the comic opera *Le Chalet* by Adolphe Adam, with adaptations to the music. Smith gave himself a character role while Gaetano Neri, the ballerina Giovanna Ciocca's former partner, danced the hero. And, give or take a few wobbles, it was a great success. On 29 December Lola made her debut at the Broadway Theatre before a house of some 3,000. Dress circle seats for the first night were $1.

In the first scene she descended a staircase representing a mountain path; this went well. On her appearance at the top she received a tremendous burst of applause, and another when she reached the stage. After that she danced a Tyrolienne, which was well enough received; but the next item, a *pas de deux* with Neri, saw her stumble and draw a hiss from the audience while he garnered the applause. The corps then performed the Mountaineer Dance, and for a time it seemed as though she would not reappear, which brought more hissing. When she did, it was in quasi-Hungarian military uniform; when she led a company of soldiers off the stage to a military tread, she was enthusiastically applauded. Smith had earned his slippers.

Generally the newspapers were not impressed. Even the *New York Herald*'s critic admitted she seemed fatigued and out of breath. Nor did she have 'the requisite strength or muscular development for great dancing'. The *Albion* was much more scathing:

> The crowd, almost exclusively of the masculine gender, was immense; and they had a merry time of it, for the failure of the great attraction was so complete that one could scarcely forbear laughing at the thought of all the excitement got up for the occasion. Never was quotation more appro-

priate than the one already applied. *Parturiant Montes, nascitur ridiculus mus.*

There was faint praise for the Hungarian dance, but 'we have only to add that she does not in the least resemble any engraved portraits of her which we have seen – they do not do her justice'.[2]

Initially there had only been a handful of women in the audience, which was 'a credit to our people', thought the *Brooklyn Eagle*. But now the crowds, women included, came. And so Smith had to do it all over again and devise another piece. On 5 January Lola appeared in *Un Jour de Carneval à Seville*, in which she danced as Donna Inez – later the name of her part was changed to Marguerita. Smith was Marco and Neri was replaced by a Mr Schmidt. It was suggested at the time that Lola was jealous of the applause Neri had garnered; she could dispose of him but not Smith. In fact, Neri was a seriously ill man, dying of cancer the same year in Philadelphia.

Now the troubles with Ned Willis began in earnest. She first complained about irregularities in the accounts, and later about his conduct in general. The *New York Herald*, in pro-Lola mood, was very pleased: 'It seems his accounts were not suitable to the noble countess and she with the generous assistance of a fire eater from the South dismissed him at one fell swoop.' It expected there might be a police case and hoped that, with revelations about both Willis's brother and P. T. Barnum, there might be some entertainment. As for the Countess, she was thinking of moving from Waverley Place to a hotel on Fifth Avenue and would be seen more in company, à la Kossuth or à la Forrest – a reference to the celebrated actor, then undergoing a very messy divorce.

Willis replied immediately. He had never been Lola's business agent and had 'never, as shown to the satisfaction of her umpire, received a penny from her that I did not expend for her business interests. I would state moreover I have labored to secure her a successful reception in America through evil report and good report.' He thought he was deserving of some other return than the attack which had been made on his character. The *Washington Union* thought Willis had made a poor fist of his defence and the *New York Herald* wondered, if E. P. Willis was not the agent of Lola Montez, what was he? 'What does he call "laboring for ten months to secure her a favourable reception"? What does the chap mean? Give us the facts or romance or something. Give us the letters, the negotiations – the fun, all the fun with the Home Page.'

Into the fray jumped Count F. M. Bobo, who had been appointed umpire over the accounts. He would give the lie to Willis's version. Certainly most of the money had been accounted for, but not all. Lola then confused things. Bobo had cleared the accounts and she would abide by it but, by the way, he was wrong to have done so. She now gave the story of how she and Willis had met in Paris. He had represented his brother as the editor of the *Home Journal*, 'The *Times* of America', which not only made public opinion but controlled it. As a result she had turned down Le Grand Smith and Barnum. Not only that, she had picked Willis out of his wretched garret, refurbished his scanty wardrobe and redeemed his watch from his 'uncle'. What had happened to the 400 francs she had given him to hand to an American lady in some temporary financial embarrassment in Paris? To cap it all, he had tried to enter her bedchamber.

Willis was not completely finished. He wrote an entertainingly satirical letter to the *Herald*, first raising the story of how Lola felt impelled to bring an old and respectable lady in Munich 'who had offended [Lola], to a mock trial in presence of the King and his courtiers – convict her – very much to her surprise – of having destroyed her illegitimate offspring and actually burn her in effigy in her own presence'.

He then recounted how they had met around March in Paris, but would not disclose the circumstances, 'as we have each of us expressed a different opinion on the subject. Sufficient to say that I found you surrounded by all that is valuable in French society and your salons filled nightly with the *plus-beaux esprits de Paris* with the purest of the cream of cream of art.' He suggested that she should pose for a statue, to be placed on the top of the Capitol, of her just having stamped on a tarantula.

Under any sort of attack Lola always fought back, and Willis was a goat to her tiger. She wrote to Bennett of the *Herald* another of her biographical letters giving her current version of her life, calculated to obtain the maximum sympathy per phrase. This was Lola in denial-penitent mode. She had been forced to marry her first husband at the age of thirteen. Because of his unloving behaviour she was divorced in the East Indies. 'No one ever accused me of falsehood to my vows of fidelity to him . . . Friendless', she became a dancer. 'My enemies made enemies because I was a proud woman – a self-willed woman – an ambitious woman if you will, but an honourable woman, who would not become their instrument of wickedness . . .' She had been forced to endure the attentions of licentious men. She had indeed been 'wild and wayward' but 'never wicked'. And now for a little Christian charity. 'The sweetest revenge I can take of all my enemies is to forgive them.' As for her relationship with Ludwig, she still corresponded with him and she loved him 'as she would a father'. Then she turned her attentions to the Jesuits and Austrians who, having pursued her throughout Europe and to America, were trying to deprive her of such little property as she had acquired over the years from her own hard work and Ludwig's kindness. She appealed to 'high-souled free, liberal and honourable Americans' to accept her 'simple story, told in my poor way'. And one final plea: 'Can I ask of my own sex to speak a gentle word for me, and be refused?' As Bennett wrote some years later, 'Most managers seem to have fallen in love with her or robbed her or both.'[3]

The patriot Kossuth, who was having a hard time rallying troops to, and funds for, the Hungarian cause, would have done well to take lessons from her – or possibly from former Senator Wescott of Florida, the firebrand from the South, who was suspected of having composed the letter for her. The one person she did not convince, however, was Arpin, the editor of the French-language paper *Courrier des Etats Unis*, whose comments on her were uniformly hostile.

The *Herald* was now firmly on her side, pointing out her triumphs in comparison with Kossuth's failures. It was not because of her large expressive eyes or her 'lively piquant and sparkling conversation and manners – not because she had been the prime minister to the good old King of Bavaria . . .' but because she is 'sound, sound as a roach on the Intervention question'. Lola was thinking that there would eventually be a president for each of the North and South. She commended the views of the late pro-slavery congressman John Caldwell Calhoun, saying she was sending a copy to Eugène Sue to be translated into French.[4]

Goodbye Willis – or rather *au revoir*, for in April, despite her former comments on his character, there was a temporary rapprochement. It lasted a very short time, and he became another of those involved with Lola who died prematurely when he succumbed to pleurisy in Boston within a year.[5] It is possible that her return to Willis caused her to lose favour with James Gordon Bennett and the *New York Herald*, which for much of the spring and early summer turned against her.

Meanwhile, for the time being, Lola was prospering. She had a new manager, another who might be described as a character, the 'Reverend' Joseph C. Scoville. There is no doubt from where she obtained her advice on the slavery question, because Scoville had once been the private secretary to Calhoun. Far from being ordained, he had earned his soubriquet, given to him by James Gordon Bennett, by once standing in for a Swedenborg pastor, R. C. Craillé, when he was detained at work. Scoville had rather enjoyed himself: 'we went to church, read the prayers, the hymns to the sermon, much to the astonishment of some of the "first" and fairest girls in Washington who had never dreamed that we were "gifted" in that way before, or that we were in "that line".'[6]

Now a reformed alcoholic, Scoville had until a few days before his appointment as Lola's manager been 'Mr Pick' of the *New York Picayune*. The *New York Herald* welcomed the appointment, albeit with a reservation: 'The Reverend gentleman possesses talents and honesty and as long as he sticks to the pledge he will manage her affairs with unrivalled skill and undoubted honour.'[7]

Since joining the *New York Picayune* in March 1851 Scoville had written more or less the whole of the newspaper with the exception of the 'Negro Sermons'. It had been started as an advertising sheet for Hutchings Bitters, but he developed it to a point where it had a circulation of 33,600 copies by October that year. He left the paper in some acrimony and started his own, *The Pick*.[8] For the moment he would try the dangerous combination of editorship with managing Lola. And since he was at least temporarily in Lola's corner, the *Herald* was in his, describing him as 'a young man of a great deal of talent and some eccentricity. He has every prospect of succeeding wonderfully in his new journal called the *Pick*.'[9]

Scoville, the sensible newsman, ensured Lola kept a low profile to avoid clashing with Kossuth-mania – and to counter some of the stories circulating that there had been alcoholic orgies at Waverley Place and that her bed, canopied in purple and gold, could and did hold three people. No, Lola only seldom drank, but she smoked. Up to 500 a day, said one report; even for her, that must have been going it a bit.

Back on the stage itself, Smith also created *Diana and her Nymphs*. It was a *succès de scandale*:

> When a certain piece first presented a partly unclothed woman to the gaze of a crowded auditory she was met with a gasp of astonishment at the effrontery which dared so much. Men grew pale at the boldness of the thing; young girls hung their heads; a death-like silence fell over the house. But it passed; and in view of the fact that these women were French ballet-dancers, they were tolerated.[10]

Smith also devised a *Pas de Matelot* which had her dancing a merry dance, caught in a storm, a rush to the rescue of those in peril and the safe return to land with the ship's Flag of Liberty. Finally he converted the Spider Dance into a *pas de deux* for himself and Lola. One of his (and others') complaints was her complete lack of rhythm, and orders were given that, as with a circus horse, the band should follow her rather than she the band. 'When you play to the Countess, follow her precisely. When she stops, you also stop, no matter whether or not the music is finished.'[11]

Meanwhile, according to some accounts, Lola was doing well in the Broadway Theatre:

> Her share was an enormous $3,400 and she has made a second engagement equally profitable. Contrary to all expectations, though not a great artist, she is the most modest danseuse that ever appeared on the stage.

Ladies are now going to see her perform as rapidly as they did Fanny Elssler. She is going to Philadelphia, Baltimore and Washington and we pity the poor M.C.s in the latter place when she gets there. She will kick up as great a dust as Kossuth, but of a kind altogether different and diverse. What a funny world this is.[12]

According to the *Herald*, her last night at the Broadway was a triumphant benefit for the Firemen's Fund. Amid a shower of bouquets she made a delicate little speech: 'Ladies and Gentlemen – My heart is so full, I cannot speak more than my grateful thanks for your kindnesses. Gallant friends, God bless you and your noble institutions. Farewell. God Bless You!' There were, however, stories that – benefits apart – things had gone less than well. The *Courrier des Etats Unis* thought her dancing was hopeless. The sale of tickets at auction had gone badly and she was barely covering her weekly fee of $200. 'It's worse than a fiasco. It's total indifference.'[13]

Inevitably with Lola, behind the scenes there were problems. On 13 January 1852 Thomas Barry, the manager of the Broadway, wrote, 'The movements of Lola Montez are becoming more mysterious.' She had closed at the Broadway and was due to open in Philadelphia. 'But this is somewhat doubtful. If she please she will keep her engagement, but if she does not please the Devil can't make her. I shall be thankful to get rid of her.'[14] There were also problems about her lodgings. She had been asked to leave her hotel in Waverley Place and the police had been called. Now she was in private accommodation in Chambers Street. She blamed Willis for her removal, saying the scandal he had caused by entering her bedroom had been the reason for the move.

She did deign to go to Philadelphia, where the *Daily Pennsylvanian* thought of this 'distinguished and world renowned lady' that 'in point of graceful action, she has never had her superior on stage. There is something irresistibly fascinating in her manner which wins all her auditors in her favor.'[15]

While she was in Philadelphia she went to the gallery of M. A. Root; there she was photographed with her hand on the arm of the Native American Chief Light in the Cloud, whom she met quite by chance at the studio. The *New York Herald* promptly wrote up the meeting, suggesting that the chiefs had admitted her to their tribe and made her their queen. Some days later a letter was published correcting much of the article. Lola was not made a queen, a word unknown in the Indian language. When asked if he would take her as a wife, one of the chiefs had replied that while he would not object to possessing her, he would not have her as a wife as she would neither be able to cook for him nor make him a buffalo robe.[16] There is no doubt whatever that once more Lola had defied convention by merely touching a Native American, let alone being photographed doing so.

For the moment the newspapers could not have enough of her. Even if there was no true gossip to peddle, some connection with Lola could be invented. It was her umpire in the dispute with Willis who next featured:

> We understand that he is the son and heir of the famous Prince Bobo, the grand chamberlain to his Imperial Majesty Faustin I, the Emperor of Hayti [sic]. Prince Bobo the Younger came to New York to induce Lola Montez to make a visit to Hayti, and grace the court circles there. He is a splendid looking Negro six feet high and well proportioned, and is as black as the ace of spades. He would make a capital presidential candidate for the abolitionists at the next election and would run better than W. H. Seward, the white man.[17]

Along the East Coast she was picking up good audiences, but they were still mostly 'black' houses, so called because there were few women and the men wore dark suits. In early February Lola and Smith moved on to Washington, where she created a sensation on and off the stage. First there was something of a scandal. Lola was seen driving in the Avenue with Major William Hawkins Polk, brother of the former President, and she was at her most wilful about whom she would and would not receive: 'There are from 50 to 75 callers at the Irving House daily to see her. They are mostly Senators and Representatives, with the exception of two or three persons who bought tickets of introduction. Governor Houston called twice but failed to gain admission. Most of the Foreign Ministers and Chargés, with their ladies are going to her debut tonight.'[18]

In fact a levee with Lola could be something of a strain. Edwin De

Leon, one-time diplomatic agent and consul-general, attended one such at midday in New York, which she held wearing 'a coquettish garment, a compromise between a nightdress and a dressing gown ... She was a very restless woman in perpetual motion and every movement she made beneath the covers disturbed my nerves and inspired the fear that she would jump out and give us further surprises.' He thought she had the most wonderful eyes he ever saw and that she spoke most eloquently with them when her lips were silent.[19]

Lilian Moore's article in *Dance Index* claimed that in Philadelphia the diminutive Smith spanked her in front of the whole company. 'The gay and gallant lady was too astonished to do anything but submit like a spoiled child.' If the story is true, she seems to have shown no immediate resentment and they continued together. But, however skilful and undemanding Smith's choreography might be, her limitations were cruelly and nightly exposed. 'To speak seriously of her as a dancer could but be regarded as a joke ...'[20]

So the tour progressed, with Lola fêted almost everywhere she went. In Richmond the Armory brass band serenaded her with 'God Save the King' – the news that Victoria was now on the throne does not seem to have percolated, or perhaps it was a sly reference to Ludwig. In Virginia William F. Ritchie, who edited the leading Democratic paper, 'seems in danger of going beside himself'.[21] In Baltimore she went to see the captivating actress Catherine Sinclair, the other half of the Forrest divorce case, at Brougham's Lyceum. In Georgetown she was invited to the ball of the Young Men's Dramatic Association. A week later, on 26 February, Lola was taken ill while dancing, but she reappeared the next night.

Generally she was well received, but then came another incident which entered the Montez annals. She decided to smoke on a train to Buffalo. One of the conductors approached her, saying 'Madame, you can't smoke here.' Withdrawing the cigarette from her 'pretty mouth', she replied, 'But you see I can', and 'puffed forth a volume of smoke into the very face of the mystified and abashed conductor'. Match to Lola. The conductor withdrew and she finished her cigarette in peace.[22]

There are various versions of this story. One of them is that when two women complained about her smoking she went to the baggage car and sat on the luggage, scattering ash. When the dangers of fire were pointed out to her, she said it was her luggage on which she was sitting and she would stand any loss: 'Better with ze baggage than wiz ze boors.' Another is that she told Superintendent Collamore, who tried to make her put out the cigarette, that she had whipped larger men than he.[23]

In Boston, however, through no fault of her own for once, she found herself in the midst of a political storm. The appearances had gone well, particularly when at a curtain call she waved a miniature American flag. As the days went by more and more women ventured to see her. She held court at the Tremont House, entertaining 'some fifty or sixty white liveried fools', all of whom were there to be able to say they had spoken with the Countess. She was invited to pronounce on issues such as the Maine Liquor Law, which she thought 'no great pumpkins', and the Forrest divorce, on which she tactfully remained more or less silent. Then on 25 March she was taken by Frederick Emerson of the Grammar School Board and Robert E. Hudson of the Merchants' Exchange to visit three schools. And this was when all hell broke loose.

The visits themselves went well. The boys at the English High School recited a declamation. She spoke in French to some boys and in Latin to others. But the next day came an outburst. Why on earth were these innocents being subjected to Lola's corrupting morals? She could rely on the support of some newspapers, but the *Boston Daily Evening Transcript*, edited by the Puritan Epes Sargeant, was not one of them. Sargeant had not approved of her coming to America at all and he certainly did not approve of the school visit: 'It is to be hoped that the individual who has inflicted so deep a stain upon our schools will have all the dishonour and shame of so infamous an outrage.'[24]

In turn Emerson felt the wrath of another member of the Grammar School Committee when it met on 30 March. Committee member Felt raised the matter and Emerson interrupted him:

Does the gentleman wish what he is saying reported and spread among the children of our schools?

Felt: The children know more about it than we are aware of. Ninety-nine out of a hundred of the Misses of the school visited know more than we do about the character of the woman in question.

At first the *New York Times* thought it quite amusing:

We cannot help feeling a little curious to know how the fathers and mothers of Boston will sustain the catechism they are quite certain to have propounded to them when their rising hopes come home. 'Oh, mamma, such a nice lady as we had at our school today! So very handsome – with such large black eyes and such splendid rings, mamma! Where did she get her rings, mamma? Did somebody give them to her? What did they give them to her for? . . . What has she done? Whose wife is she? Is she very pious, or a Queen . . . I do wish you would tell me all about her, mamma.'

Then it began to thunder:

One thing is certain – if Lola Montez had come to this country without bringing the reputation of a prostitute with her she would never have been paraded through the schools of Boston as a lady of distinction.[25]

Back in Boston battle lines were forming. Nathan Hale of the *Advertiser* was warned off supporting her. The same day an Edward Everett wrote to him:

If the controversy relative to Lola Montez continues, I would not, if I were you, commit the *Advertiser* in her defence. She is better known in Europe than here and is there regarded as a very low person. I cannot but think her introduction to our public schools a most unfortunate step for the good name of our city. And but too well adapted to confound all ideas of right and wrong in the minds of our children.[26]

Naturally, Lola took the opportunity to mount a defence on her own behalf. It was time for another attack on the Jesuits who had invented all these lies about her. The lies included suggestions that she had 'tamed wild horses, horsewhipped gendarmes, knocked flies with a pistol ball off the bald heads of aldermen'. Nor had she fought duels or thrown people overboard for the sake of saving them from drowning. The Jesuits had been trying to 'unsex her and deny her that protection normally accorded women'. She defied 'ANY MAN LIVING TO PROVE' these allegations.[27]

Sargeant for one was unwilling to try. As the *New York Times* pointed out, he was probably unable to do so. 'And probably nine out of ten of the professional wantons of this City could make the same defiance with equal impunity.' Instead, he simply wrote that Satan had arrived in the form of a 'charming danseuse' who had 'crazed the descendants of the sober Puritans'. He regretted that the 'good days of witch-burning were past'.[28]

Apart from anything else it was extremely good box office. On 1 April the *Boston Daily Mail* noted that in the audience at the previous night's performance were 'several gentlemen who bore the strongest likeness to some of the straightest sect of our school committee'. The immediate storm blew over quickly enough. There was even some approval when two days later, in company with an archbishop, she visited the House of Correction 'but did not remain there', asking intelligently about the treatment and employment of the inmates.[29] Amazingly the row continued until the middle of November, when the committee to investigate Lola's visit reported that it had not been made by the invitation of the Board and that no particular honour was intended by her introduction to these seminaries.[30]

The *New York Times* and *Tribune*, as well as the *Courrier des Etats Unis*, were down on Boston for giving her such a press. She was said to be suing each paper for $30,000. They had been variously calling her Aspasia, a cast-off mistress, a rake and a Lorette as well as a bigamist 'without any positive evidence of the charges within their reach, and on the mere newspaper rumour of other countries'. Naturally the *Herald* leaped to her defence.[31]

She did a quick tour of the eastern seaboard before she was back in Boston at the Howard Atheneum for another benefit, in aid of the victims of a fire at the Tremont Temple. Unfortunately she took the opportunity to become involved in one of the backstage quarrels that punctuated her career. This time it was a prompter, Mr Parsons, who suffered at her hands. According to one report the cause of the quarrel was Lola's old acquaintance Mme Julia de Marguerittes, who intervened on his behalf. Lola claimed to have lost a gold pin and, accompanied by half a dozen supporters, went searching in the Green Room and then the property room. Parsons tried to get her to leave; instead he was expelled 'vi et armus, pull nosibus et scratch-faceibus'. Lola then stalked off cursing the world in general and Mme de Marguerittes in particular. One writer thought that the words she used settled questions over her nationality. They were all good old Anglo-Saxon ones.[32]

She did not go down well in Hartford. The local critic thought:

> [She] does not even exercise good taste in selecting the 'spider dance' as one of her performances; for that makes her appear disgusting as well as a miserable danseuse. In it she flounces about like a stuck pig, and clenches her short clothes, raising them nearly to her waist, while with a thin, scrawny leg, she keeps up a constant thumping upon the stage, as if she was in a slight spasm.[33]

And just to compound stories of her increasingly unsettled behaviour, Lola met a New Haven medium. It was the era of great frauds by so-called mediums. The craze had begun in 1848 with the Fox sisters, Margaretta and Kate. They claimed their house in Hydesville, New York was haunted by a murdered pedlar and their fame spread. The knockings with which he replied to their questions were simulated by Margaretta's ability to crack her big toe in a manner that suggested a knock on wood. The sisters were the first of many.

A number of men called to see the New Haven manifestations, but as was often the case a connection was impossible until 'uncongenial minds' had left the room; after this there were rappings. It was possibly the first instance of Lola's attraction to 'spiritualism', which lasted for several years.

Whether it was the temporary revival of her interest in Ned Willis or her slapping of Parsons, suddenly so far as the *Herald* was concerned the Lola bubble had burst. Apparently, to end the affair, she had given Count Bobo $10 for kicking Willis (brother of Namby Pamby Willis, as the *Herald* referred to Nathaniel) downstairs and Willis $100 for being kicked down. Now she was reconciled with him. Bostonians were beginning to think they had been 'sucked'. The paper suggested that she should pack her carpet bag and head for California, where even if dust was thrown in her face it would be $16 an ounce worth of dust.[34]

So the *Herald* now took to printing unfavourable comments from other papers such as the *New Orleans Bee*, which in turn was attacking both those who lauded and vilified her. What about the fools who pulled Fanny Elssler's carriage around Baltimore? Everyone knew that ninety-nine out of a hundred members of the corps de ballet 'are notoriously women of impure and depraved character'. The *Herald* now thought the praise for her in New York had been out of 'pure pity, jocular compassion'.[35]

About this time Lola signed a new contract with E. G. Marshall and also obtained the services of a private chaplain. The Reverend Olmstead was to be her new 'man of business, legal adviser, religious confessor, prime minister and grand vizier'. The *Herald* thought she had cleared $10,000 in the Atlantic cities; if she could keep her temper long enough she might take another $50,000 before she returned to New York in the late autumn.[36] It suggested that perhaps Lola might have failed as a dancer because the Jesuits had found a way to smuggle one into each pit to put the music out and spoil her steps. Lola was not alone. Kossuth was also suffering as the press turned against him.[37]

Now ironic article after ironic article appeared. 'She has on every occasion put her foot on the Jesuits and prevented them from making any head in the interior of the country.' Lola had got rid of 'all her princes, counts, barons, and other vagabonds. When she does not dance she goes to the theatre or some lecture or prayer meeting or any public place that is open . . . If any of the princes persist in annoying her she has engaged an immense strapping fellow in Albany to lick them out of the place she is in . . .'[38]

Back in New York at the beginning of May there was much applause for *Un Jour de Carneval*, but unfortunately most of it went to two young ladies who danced a *grand pas de deux* 'with much taste and artistic ability'.[39] On 30 April Forrest had enjoyed a triumphant benefit night at the Broadway, but the next night Lola pulled in an even bigger audience. She was triumphant over the Jesuits but not over the excellent corps de ballet. 'And then going through the pantomimic display of wiping imaginary tears from her eye the Countess retired.'[40]

From New York it was to Albany, from where she wrote to a friend, 'I will never stop at a Temperance House again. It contains nothing but bedbugs and Bibles.'[41] She then moved on to Buffalo. Theatres in America at the time had a low life expectancy. Fires were constantly breaking out and on 11 May the Eagle Theatre there went up in flames. The fire solved a problem for Lola. She had not been pleased with the reception she received for *Un Jour de Carneval* and had refused to appear the following night. She demanded her money and took all her wardrobe with her; she and the troupe were on the walkway near the theatre when the fire broke out. 'The night was clear and moderately warm. Just right for firemen, who worked with common spirit.'

Next day once again Lola showed her generous side. She announced she would give a benefit for those who had lost their wardrobes in the fire. There was some doubt about the depth of her reception, but when it came to it she was welcomed with 'a perfect torrent of applause' and her *pas de deux* with Smith was 'most rapturously encored'. She was such a success she stayed for a second benefit performance.[42]

Now Lola was about to change direction and appear on the legitimate stage at the Broadway Theatre. The piece was to be a biographical five-act drama, *Lola Montez in Bavaria*, and was probably written by a man called Charles Pace. It roughly followed her life in the capital, with a very favourable tilt, and each act represented an 'era' – The Danseuse, The Politician, The Countess, The Revolutionist and finally The Fugitive. The setting of the fourth act was 'a correct view of the Lola Montez Palace in Munich'. Naturally Lola was the heroine. Her Broadway stage manager Thomas Barry played the King, with H. J. Conway as the villain d'Abel. There were two comic characters, Baron von Poppenheim and Ludwig von Shootenbottom, who fought a duel. At the end, when she escaped from Bavaria disguised as a mute, the cast of thirty-four leaped backwards and forwards across the stage, somewhat curiously to the sound of the Marseillaise.

As with all things Lola, critics and audiences were divided over the merits of the play and her acting. In general the New York papers were favourable. Some thought she should give up dancing and take up the straight theatre. The *Herald*, which for the moment was in anti-Lola mode, wrote 'The play possesses no plot whatsoever.' It did concede that she had made a 'successful hit in exchanging the ballet for the drama'. However, it thought with the gift of foresight, albeit with its tongue in its cheek, that the lecture circuit – 'Lola in Paris', 'Lola in London' – was really her métier.[43] Some weeks later it ironically suggested that a new piece, *Lola Montes in New York*, featuring Kossuth, the editor Horace Greeley and a number of others, was in preparation.[44]

In Philadelphia the *Sunday Dispatch* thought the play was a lying 'acted autobiography', the production 'destitute of all merit' and the various characters 'devoid of interest or originality'. When the piece later played in Sydney the correspondent for the Melbourne *Argus* was devastating: 'Her voice is, if not bad, deficient altogether in flexibility and sweetness.' But his most damning comments were for the play itself: 'The piece she played in . . . is about the greatest piece of trash and humbug ever introduced before an English audience. There is no indecency in the acting but the whole tenor of it, socially, politically and religiously is profligate and immoral in the extreme.'[45]

Lola polarised critics. In Boston, as a general rule, they liked her. Philadelphian critics did not. When *Charlotte Corday*, which Lola claimed to have written, was played on 14 October that year both she and the play received a coating. It was all a great deal of historical nonsense in which Charlotte rather reflected Lola's appetite for men. Hitherto unrevealed by history, Charlotte had a number of admirers and lovers – Henri de Franqueville, who loved her to distraction, the young artist Adam Lux, Nero Wax, a humble cobbler, a lawyer named Chevaux Legard who became a Girondist for her, at least five other potentials and Marat, who seems to have strayed in thought if not deed. She was also the protectress of a young girl, Julie, from the approaches of the loathsome Herbert. It was the greatest nonsense. Marat was buried by a priest; Jacobins rushed up and down to be confounded by the sound of the Marseillaise, to which Lola was clearly partial; in the execution scene a canvas bag depicting Lola/Charlotte's head was raised as the curtain fell. Lola did not receive a good notice from the *Sunday Dispatch* of Philadelphia:

The result has not been such as will advance her claims to histrionic honours. Her style of elocution is very unnatural. She emphasises every third or fourth word with energy and slides over those which are intermediate with scarcely fair enunciation. This gives to her delivery a singsong monotony which is unnatural and affected. There is no spirit about her delineation.[46]

Off stage Lola had remained in fighting trim, three bouts coming inside two months. On 28 April there was a fight in her rooms at the Howard Hotel. She had been entertaining a motley group that included Count Wallowski, an emigré Polish pianist, his father, and Count Kazinski, another emigré. Also present were the Prince of Como, who had known Lola in Paris and was described as her *cavalière-servente*, and a Mr Davis of Boston who apparently was her current house guest. Naturally champagne circulated; the quarrel arose over a discussion of the unfavourable treatment of Edwin Forrest, who had been found guilty of adultery and ordered to pay substantial alimony to his wife, Catherine Sinclair. Part of the problem was the thought that Como had turned his affections to Mrs Forrest, thereafter dividing his time between her and Lola. Unfortunately Como's loyalties were still divided and he took Mrs Forrest's part. Lola took his moustaches and began to pull them. He hit her and, as the expression goes, fighting broke out. Como was evicted from the suite and retreated to the bar, from where he sent a card challenging Kazinski to a duel. Lola forbade the Pole to leave her apartment and Como, together with another Italian, then tried to break back into the apartment. The Italian boarding party was repelled and thrown down the stairs by the Poles, aided by Lola, her maid, her manager Joe Scoville – who had by now arrived – and, it seems, her poodle, Flora. Lola was invited to vacate her rooms.[47]

In the middle of May, there was the slapping of a Rochester man who had apparently insulted her. Then, on 18 June 1852 the balletmaster George Smith once more offended her. This time he felt the weight of her fists. She was appearing at the Holliday Theatre in Baltimore on her own benefit night when, just before she went out to dance, a row broke out in the wings over the terms of his engagement.

Since Smith was only four feet ten inches tall, Lola had height and possible weight advantage:

> 'You 'ave traduce my character,' said Lola with the emphasis of justly excited indignation.
> Mamsell!!
> Silence sare, you talk about me – you traduce my reputation – you say I no keep my professionale agreemenz.
> Deprecatingly and with a due regard for the gauzy sylph-like impersonation of ariel gracefulness did George reply, until in a hasty moment he uttered a repartee in reply and bang came the right hand of the danseuse in retort upon his face. Stars innumerable of course tingled up before the astonished optics of the *maitre du danse*, and again a blow was aimed at his proboscis, when intervention came in the person of the prompter and other gentlemen and the emeute was quelled by bearing the pretty Countess away from the object of her indignation. Ten minutes afterwards the bell tinkled, uprose the curtain and radiant with angelic smiles, flashing eyes, wavy motion she bounded on the stage in the bewitching pas La Zapateado – 'Vive la bagatelle!'[48]

This little spat seems to have ended their association. Her last performance, scheduled for the next day, was cancelled. Ten days later she was back in New York opening the Bowery Theatre's season on 28 June as *Lola Montez in Bavaria*. Now there were ironic suggestions that for the opening at the theatre a 'Requiem to Broadway' was being composed by a Charles Ware and would be sung by Lola.[49]

The Bowery Theatre, which could hold 2,000 spectators, was a very different proposition from the Broadway. It had opened in 1826 on the corner of Canal Street and, as with many theatres in New York, suffered from a series of fires. For a time some of the Broadway stars – Junius Brutus Booth, the father of Edwin and his infamous brother John Wilkes Booth, Edwin Forrest and Edmund Kean – all played in the Bowery, but over the years the management gave up the pretence of catering even for the partially educated. As the poet Walt Whitman said, 'A while after 1840 the character of the Bowery . . . completely changed. Cheap prices and vulgar programmes came in.'[50]

By the time Lola appeared, the Bowery Theatre had gone through a series of spectacles such as *Ben Hur* and *The Earthquake*. The latter grossed $8,000 in its first week at a time when a good lodging and board for a single person was around $15 a week. Melodramas such as the old stalwart *Ten Nights in a Bar-Room* and *Ambition, or the Throne, the Scaffold* were now the order of the day. *Lola Montez in Bavaria* was wholly suitable.

A Bowery audience was markedly different from a Broadway one. There were backless, uncushioned benches in the pit, or 'the parquet' as the cheap seats were known. If they became bored, members of the almost exclusively male audience would throw peanut shells at each other and at the actors. Younger boys sat in the even cheaper gods, the boots of those in the front row dangling over the balconies, throwing pennies on to the stage. Families gnawed bones and tossed them over the sides. One thing in Lola's favour was her repartee and ability to charm a house. These were the days when actors broke up their speeches with asides to the audience and queries such as 'Isn't that so?'[51]

Things went so well that on 8 July she received a benefit performance. This would, said an advertisement on the previous day, be the first benefit she had received in America. All the so-called previous benefits under the management of E. A. Marshall, from whom she had split in April, were humbugs and she had received nothing.

On 16 July she wrote another long defensive letter to the *New York Times* complaining about an editorial. Now, possibly with the intervention of Scoville, or just to strike at its rival, the *Herald* switched again to backing her and attacking Kossuth and her critics:

> If there is anything mean, venal or more cowardly than a monkey in breeches, it is the exhibition of one pretending to be a man, assailing a woman under any circumstances, or under any provocation. Whatever Lola Montes may be, her male slanderers are utterly beneath contempt, and only deserve to be trotted through Broadway in the carts of the dirt collectors and sold for dog's meat out of town.[52]

Back in Europe Ludwig still could not get her out of his system. To him she was like a dose of ringworm. Just when he thought he was

clear of it something reminded him. In June he had written to Wendland, thanking him for sending him clippings and commenting sadly:

> Let me know anything you hear . . . Not the art of her dancing but the
> memory of her stay in Bavaria brings her so much income, but I'm afraid
> that unfortunately she won't be bringing much of it back across the sea
> with her, which would be, however, much to be desired since she must
> invest her profits well. Gold doesn't stay with her and where she is there
> must be luxury . . .[53]

Then, out of the blue, came a letter in early August from Auguste
Papon. Writing from the Dominican monastery at Flavigne sur
Ozerain, he claimed he was now Frère Antoine and begged
Ludwig's forgiveness. The remainder of Ludwig's letters to Lola
could be collected from an address in Batignolles. 'Do you hear
anything of Lola Montez? Are the newspapers silent about her?'
Ludwig wrote to Wendland. Later Papon wrote that he was burning
all the remaining copies of his book. The old fraud had, it seems,
temporarily got religion. 'I have given everything to God and I do
not regret it.'

In the summer Lola went to the Catskill Mountains but she was
back in New York by the end of August. She, or at least Scoville, was
back in favour with the *Herald*, because the paper gave only a slightly
ironic account of a Pick Club reunion in the Yonkers attended by
Horace Greeley and P. T. Barnum. Lola presented the club with an
illuminated banner and made a slightly tearful speech, swearing 'by
the soul of my mother that I will ever possess the most grateful
remembrances of all their kindness to a poor and friendless artiste'.
Then, 'overcome by emotion she signalled Pick to bring her poodle to
her'. The outing ended with a march behind a brass band to the
steamer to take them back to the city. Greeley took her arm and
Barnum carried 'The Queen of Bavaria's' no doubt tired poodle.[54]

On 6 September she danced the Sailor's Dance at the Castle Garden
during a charity performance of *The Merchant of Venice* to celebrate
100 years of drama in America. She was obviously in a good humour
that day; when she put her hat on a chair and one of the actresses
inquired in less than kindly terms as to who had deposited it on her

seat, Lola merely smiled and chatted pleasantly with her. At least that is how Scoville put the meeting.[55]

In the early autumn Lola expanded her repertory, appearing to good notices in Boston and Philadelphia. Theatres of the time maintained full rosters of actors who worked a given line of business. If an actor knew the standard roles in his line, then any number of plays could be put on at short notice. For example, in his first full season in the Philadelphia Theatre, Lincoln's future assassin, John Wilkes Booth, performed in eighty-three of the 153 plays staged.[56] There was the leading man and lady, the supporting man and lady, the servant, the villain, the old man or woman – something in which Mrs Judah, who played with Lola in San Francisco, specialised, even as a young girl – first and second walking gentleman, and so forth.

Then it was back to New York for a benefit. By the end of October Lola was preparing a southern tour to Charleston, Mobile and on to New Orleans, where she arrived on 30 December and stayed in the Verandah Hotel. Scoville, who was said to have been bullied by Lola, stayed behind looking after his paper. The next year she engaged a series of wholly unsuitable managers, mostly young.

Indeed, life in 1853 in the Crescent City and California would prove much more exciting. By the end of that year there would be another two court cases, a faked suicide attempt, a shooting, a possible involvement in a revolution, definitely another marriage and possibly another divorce.

CHAPTER FOURTEEN

Lola in New Orleans, San Francisco and Sacramento

THE YEAR 1853 was one of the more exciting and difficult in what was generally an exciting and difficult life for Lola. It began with a contract to appear at Thomas Placide's Varieties Theatre on Gravier Street in New Orleans. As was becoming routine, she would open in *Lola Montez in Bavaria*, which she played for four nights before adding the Spider Dance. Things did not get off to a great start. True, showers of bouquets were thrown by ladies, but people were talking in boxes during the performance on 4 January (the second night) and she came to the front of the stage to say, 'Ladies and gentlemen, I am truly delighted to appear before you; but if there is a cabal against me I shall retire.' This was 'an annihilator', thought one spectator.[1]

On 22 January she appeared in *The School for Scandal*, of which the *New Orleans Daily Picayune* thought, 'It was not such a Lady Teazle as we have seen but it was nevertheless very commendable.' This was hardly surprising, since during the closet scene in which Lady Teazle hides, Lola took the opportunity to have a quick cigarette.

On 14 January the *New York Daily Times* had reported that the mails were behind because of a big storm, the Royal Mail steamship bound for New York had put into Halifax for refuelling, there was 'some interesting news of Queen Victoria' but nothing more on that subject, and – at the end of the paragraph – that the death by drowning had occurred at Lisbon of Mr Heald, the husband of Lola Montez, by the upsetting of his yacht.

In fact the story had already appeared in *The Times* before Christmas. Heald had apparently been with a friend and two young women aboard the *Sparrow Hawk* in poor weather. The *Inflexible* had put to in an effort to save Heald and his companions and fourteen hands had been lost. The story was denied on 4 January. No hands had been lost on the *Inflexible*, mainly because it had never attempted a rescue.

On 22 January came the news Heald was alive, and on 25 January much of the story came out:

> Lola Montez need not put on mourning yet . . . Subsequent intelligence stated that, although Mr Heald's yachting cruise had been perilous, it had happily not proved fatal. He had succeeded in crossing the bar of Lisbon and reached Cadiz in safety in the *Sparrow Hawk*, on board of which, by the way, were, not one, but two young and beautiful ladies, who would of course have shared his watery grave, had such been his destiny. I trust that Lola Montez will bear the disappointment with creditable fortitude; for I perceive in one paper that Mr Heald had left a will by which Lola was to receive the interest of £30,000 for the rest of her life, after which it was to be paid to another old 'flame' of the testator and afterwards revert to the family. Supposing the bequest to be correct, which is more than I believe, it amounts to nothing, since Mr Heald is, after all, not drowned, and should he have made a will, may yet live to alter it.[2]

In fact Heald had a number of years yet to live.

The contract with the Varieties having ended, Lola stayed in New Orleans to play at the Theatre d'Orleans, opening on 2 February. Then began the first of her court cases in the Crescent City, when on 9 February her maid sued her. Lola had been out of sorts and in poor humour for some time, possibly because of the news of the loss of Heald and possibly because of the news that he was not lost after all. In any event the maid had, it was reported, put up with her temper without grumbling but now was losing patience. She had, said the *New Orleans Delta*, 'set up a bill of rights, among which a privilege to grumble was specially insisted upon'. On 22 February a quarrel blew up:

The maid demanded payment for her work and dismissal from her service and argued the demand with so much democratic daring, that the Countess grew furious and, forgetting the aristocratic distinctions of rank, 'pitched into her' vulgarly so speaking, and gave her what a comical Irishman said to be named Paddy once gave a drum.[3]

Off went the maid to take out a summons from the recorder, and then came the problem of who was to have the dubious privilege of serving it. News of Lola's attitude to officialdom and others who displeased her was well known. But this time, instead of simply hitting the officers she drew a dagger, declaring she would defend her own liberty and honour. One man distracted her while the other seized the dagger. Now she bit them and kicked one in the breadbasket. Friends entered the room, persuading her to calm down and having the officers release her. Lola promptly took the opportunity to seize a small phial appropriately labelled 'Poison'. She swallowed it, exclaiming 'Now I shall be free from all further indignity,' and then passed out. According to the *New Orleans Delta*, various helpers and officials stood around in a variety of poses, looking at the stricken Lola while a chemist supplied antidotes. One had even started composing a few lines for a poem, 'Early Stricken Flowers'. Fortunately the chemist was able to revive her, to the extent that she managed to smoke two cigars before fainting again. With the signs of her impending recovery, her friends persuaded the officers to leave in exchange for an undertaking to bring her to court. She withdrew to her bed, took the night off and cancelled an appearance for a benefit concert. When it came to it, however, good sense prevailed and the matter was settled.

Another paper, the pro-Lola *Courrier de la Louisiane*, took a much less mocking and more sympathetic line. The maid had not wanted to stay in New Orleans; Lola, while willing to pay her wages, was not prepared to pay her fare back to New York. The police had been brutal with the Countess and the marks on her arms still showed.[4] In any event, within a short time she had sailed for Cincinnati where she was engaged to appear at the National, taking rooms at the Broadway. Everything, for the moment at least, was to be sweetness and light.

'It is seldom our pride and pleasure to herald the appearance of a bright and particular star of such sweet beauty and soft effulgence', wrote the *Daily Cincinnati Commercial* on 28 February 1853. And after her performance, 'The criticisms we had seen in the Eastern papers of her style of acting had not prepared us for the exhibition on her part of so much artistic excellence as she certainly displayed', thought the *Cincinnati Daily Gazette* on 2 March. From there it was a short sail to St Louis, for her if not for others in the troupe; the Fields, who were putting on the season, took twelve days to travel from New Orleans. Their thirteen-year-old daughter, Kate, was entranced by Lola: 'The theatre was crowded from parquette to doors. She has the most beautiful eyes I ever saw. I like her very much. But she performed a young girl, so I cannot say what she may do in speaking characters or as a danseuse.' Lola may have charmed young Kate but things were not going so well with Mr Field. 'She is trying to trouble father as much as possible.'[5]

The troubles included having to put up the prices from 75c to $1 to meet Lola's demands. Field took a defensive attitude, pointing out that it was done 'at the imperative demand of that lady'.[6] There was worse to come. She quarrelled with her new manager and tried to whip him. She was also credited with breaking the nose of her then agent with a brass candlestick. From there it was on to Louisville with her newest agent, Jonathan Henning. Lola certainly did pick them; probably more for their youth and virility than their managerial acumen. Before she discovered him, twenty-five-year-old Henning had been working in the telegraph office in Louisville.[7] Now it was announced she would leave with him for Havana, Vera Cruz and California. Before her departure from Louisville one of the local charmers called on her at the Galt House, where she was staying, but she declined to see him. 'Lola Montez exhibits as much independence of character and as much discretion too as anybody else. Hurra for Lola!'[8]

The troupe arrived back in New Orleans on 7 April and the next day there was another incident. Lola and Henning attacked the prompter at the Varieties Theatre, seventy-year-old George T. Rowe, who brought a charge of assault. In an early show of what is now a standard litigatory defence and counter-attack, she claimed that back in January he had indecently assaulted her.[9]

It seems that events had unfolded as follows. Lola had wished to appear at a benefit evening and the manager Thomas Placide had declined her services. Nevertheless she gained entrance to the theatre and went to the wings to watch the French dancer Ducy Barre perform. Although this was standard practice among artistes, it was not permitted by Placide; Rowe told her to stop and ordered her out. This was, of course, a red rag: 'Her blood was up and there she stood, uncorking the phials of her inextinguishable wrath.'[10] Lola gave Rowe a smacking and, so he claimed, called for help from Henning, who strangled the poor man with his cravat.

Rowe, probably egged on inadvisedly by Thomas Placide, took out summonses for assault against both Lola and Henning. In her lifetime Lola must have had nearly thirty court cases as defendant, witness and very occasionally as aggrieved party. When she deigned to appear – which was not always the case – she always played both the *grande dame* and to the spectators. Her first appearance before Recorder Winter was no exception: 'The Countess on Saturday a.m. appeared in Court, accompanied by her suite, and after some extra flourishes declaring that she was entitled to be addressed as the Countess of Landsfelt etc. etc. made a counter affidavit charging Rowe with an assault, battery on her, and so on.'[11]

There was even more fun to be had when she and Henning appeared at the preliminary hearing on 14 April. In fact, given the aplomb with which she handled her many court appearances, she would probably have done well as a theatrical director. First, she did not appear. Henning was in court with her counsel to say she was too ill to attend and there must be an adjournment. Colonel A. P. Field for Rowe objected and Recorder Winter would have nothing to do with the application: no medical certificate; no adjournment. Court officers were dispatched to retrieve her. If she was in a state of nerves or had a stomach upset she quelled it by smoking two Havana cigars on the way. Just as she had smoked herself into good humour when she was arrested over the bigamy charge, she had done so again by the time she arrived at court.

By this time the original crowd of 'sturdy yeomen and perfumed beaux, fiery gallants that love the smell of muslin, attorneys and counsellors, and liquorish old gentlemen with standing shirt collars and double chin' had grown in number and now the anticipation was overpowering:

> All were agog and looking toward the door and along the passage way leading to the Hall of Justice anxious to catch the first glimpse of that delightful human effulgence that, like an Aurora, dawned on the menial vision, and who, like Helen, was bringing a much shedding of ink upon this, our hitherto quiescent metropolis.[12]

And they were not disappointed:

> At last she came, and escorted by her gentleman of business, tripped into the Court room, light as a young gazelle, pale with agitation at the unusual scene and with eyes flashing out of the wild illumination of a poetic and tropical soul.

Lola had taken the time to dress neatly and tastefully for the occasion. She wore

> a skirt of straw-coloured China glass linen, a black mantilla of Canton crepe, a Tuscan bonnet smothered in the richest lace, and a white lace veil, star-besprent, that waved at her slightest breath, and like the mist of her own dear Cyreness but half concealed while it adorned her finely chiselled and classic head.

Perhaps she slightly spoiled the effect by loudly remarking, on seeing the crowded room, that the court had made a great mistake in not charging $2 a head admission. Now she applied for an adjournment because her witnesses were not in court. No, they could have been subpoenaed, said the Registrar. 'I to suffer when ignorant of my rights and the laws of the country?' she asked, quite forgetting the thoroughly useful legal maxim, 'Ignorance of the law is no excuse'.

'Your agent knew the laws, and it was his place to protect your interests,' replied the recorder. Lola responded, 'Mr Henning is my agent but not my protector. I would have you know, sir, that I am my protector.'

The statement deservedly brought a burst of applause. And after the prelude, the first act began, with Rowe as the first witness. That night he had been performing his duties; he was about to ring up the curtain for Ducy Barre when Lola had

> pressed up in the prompt side, thereby violating the rules of the house and interfering with me. I told her she could not stop there, when she indignantly drew back and asked me what I meant, damned my soul, struck at me and kicked me. She then called her agent, Mr Henning, and told him I had insulted her, whereat he jumped at me, seized me by the throat, and with his knuckles against my neck almost choked me. He behaved very violently, and for a time there was great confusion and noise in the green room.

There can be advantages in appearing for oneself. The court has to grant a certain amount of leeway to the unrepresented and when asked if she wanted to ask Rowe questions, she took the opportunity to make a statement. She had, she said, agreed after much solicitation to play this insignificant engagement at the Varieties; on the second week the witness had made a very foolish, dishonourable and indelicate statement which caused her to threaten to break off the engagement. She had lectured him, saying that a man of his age should be ashamed of himself. He had then pretended it was a joke and had begged, 'At any rate, don't tell the old woman' (Much laughter in court.) As for the incident when Ducy Barre was dancing, she had gone to the wings to give her encouragement and Rowe had kicked her. She had called him a Jesuit for the spite he had shown her. But as for questions to Rowe? 'I, sir? Not I indeed, I'll ask him no questions.'

Then came the manager Thomas Placide, who had been called to the disturbance. He had found her repeating to herself, 'Lola Montez! Lola Montez! to be turned out by a common actor!' He told her to go; she said she would not; he said he would call an officer: 'She then swore she would not go and called me a damned scoundrel and a damned liar and a damned thief.' To which Lola added, 'And so you are.'

There were questions for Placide: 'Didn't you come behind the scenes in your shirt tail when I was playing your theatre in a very immodest manner? And you know, Mr Placide, you're far from being a handsome man.' But the answer was lost in the laughter and applause for the question.

> Lola: Didn't I offer to dance for that poor little Ducy Barre and you would not permit of so generous an act?
> Placide: I thought you would be no benefit to the house.
> Lola: You know very well that I always draw good houses and in proof I appeal to the audience now present. [Loud and long continuous applause].
> Lola: Don't you owe me a few dollars, Mr Placide for treating the French artists to liquors, who were playing for the benefit on that night?
> Placide: I had nothing to do with the house that night, the benefit was for the Dramatic Fund Association. Instead of being a witness, I'm beginning to think I'm on trial here.

Which was, of course, just what Lola intended. Placide was saved from further embarrassment by Recorder Winter, who told Lola the questions were irrelevant and had another witness called. As the day progressed, witnesses were called to say they saw Lola and Henning attack Rowe, while an English actor who appeared on the bill, Sir William Don, said it was quite normal for actors to stand in the wings although Placide did not permit it. Don gave some support to Lola:[13]

> Don: You said he had insulted you.
> Lola: Well, there are but two or three ways in which a woman can get insulted. Your Honour knows the most probable one. [Laughter].

And there was time for a Madame X, presumably one of the French actresses playing that night, to give evidence that Lola had told her Rowe had kicked her, and had shown her a mark the size of a Mexican dollar on her calf which looked as though it had been made by the heel of a boot. Lola wanted an adjournment so more witnesses could be called, but Winter had had enough. There was a case for both her and Henning to answer. Despite their protests he committed them for trial at the First District Court. Bail was set at $500. And so the free spectacle for the day concluded. Lola drove home in a carriage and four. The recorder had, the newspapers remarked, been unable to stop himself grinning at some of the sallies, while Lola had the sympathy of the larger portion of the audience.[14]

In fact it might indeed have been better had Lola danced for poor little Ducy Barre, who appeared in the divertissement. The *Picayune* thought it had been spoiled by the 'awkwardness and ungainliness of a novice who didn't know enough to walk across the stage'.[15]

Those who hoped for something more than a dress rehearsal and were waiting for the first night proper were, however, disappointed. Very sensibly Rowe and Placide did not want to go through a second humiliation. The Countess was due to be on her way and on 20 April 1853 it was announced that the matter had been settled. That day the *Courrier de la Louisiane* printed a thank-you letter from the stock-holders of the Varieties Theatre to Lola wishing her well: 'In leaving us to fulfil other and we trust still more brilliant, profitable and satisfactory engagements, permit us to say, that you will go with a growing popularity as an artist and a lady and that you will carry with you the highest regards and esteem of your friends and obedient servants.'

Now Lola was effectively played out in the East and South. The first actors to move West to take advantage of the Gold Rush were the stock actors who could play the leads denied them in the East. By the 1850s there were no stars and no audiences as the jaded public stayed away from the theatres. The stars began the trek.

At that time in California there was nearly an equal number of very young men and women, but for three men in their twenties there was only one woman, and for a woman in her thirties there were more than four men. What better place for Lola to revive her flagging theatrical career and find another wealthy husband? But again she came up short on both counts.

A week later, at 8 am on 22 April, she and Henning, along with Lola's maid, left Jackson Square Wharf on the *Philadelphia* for what is now Colón but was then Aspinwall, Panama on the first stage of their journey to Caifornia. They arrived on 1 May and began the fifty-mile trek across the isthmus to catch the *Northerner*, which was waiting to sail for San Francisco.

Lola, along with other passengers, later put a thank-you note in the *Panama Star* to say that the crossing of the isthmus had gone well, but in fact it had been the usual hell of a journey. In 1849 Mary Jane Megquier, probably the first woman to cross the isthmus, wrote that in twenty-four miles there had been fifty-two dead horses. Originally the whole journey took between eighteen and twenty-one days but as the boats became faster the time was reduced by up to ten days.[16] Even so, it must have been preferable to the overland stage from New Orleans to San Francisco. This was drawn by six mules, except for the crossing of the 100-mile Colorado desert which was done on mule-back. There was an armed escort through Indian country.[17]

Now the rainy season had begun. For the thirty-hour journey the Gorgona road was impassable so travellers had use the Cruces road. At Barbacoas the passengers had to be poled up the river to Gorgona, where what passed for hotels charged extortionate prices.

When Lola demanded a cot for her dog she was told all had been taken and the animal would have to sleep on the floor. She pointed out that the dog had slept in palaces and so a cot was found for it. When, the next morning, the manager tried to charge $5 she threatened to shoot him.[18] Now mules took her and the others to Panama, where she stayed at the Cocoa Grove Hotel, and here another Lola legend sprang up. She had been talking late at night with a group of men on the porch when in the darkness the voice of a fellow passenger was heard, calling out that someone was trying to shoot him. There were also a number of clicks which sounded like the pulling of a trigger. Lola asked a man for a light and led the way to the rescue. The attacker headed for the jungle, while Lola advised the shaken Californian that he should have grabbed the man's hair and yelled for help.

Another story, which in later life Lola spent a good deal of effort refuting during her lectures, was put about by Mary Seacole, the black nurse who went to the Crimea. She claimed that she had seen Lola slashing a man with a crop after he had touched the tails of her riding habit on a stop at Las Cruces. It was a story to which she took great exception and, given the number of stories about her which were patently false, it is interesting to wonder why this one riled her so much. But rile her it did. One explanation is that when she began giving lectures in 1857 Lola was in revisionist mode. A possible implication of wearing riding habit was that Lola might have lesbian tendencies, and she was keen to refute any such thought. She specifically pointed out that, with the exception of her return to Bavaria in disguise, she had never worn men's clothing off stage.

In fact Lola was said to have had various female admirers, including the noted swordswoman, Madame Leoni. They met on Washington's birthday at a dance at Niblo's, a one-time circus and racehorse training establishment on Broadway and Prince, later transformed into a pleasure garden and regarded as the most elegant of all such establishments. Leoni, who at the time was with a man, was instantly smitten. When Lola did not wish to dance she sat with her, and the same happened when Lola declined the buffet. The man retired hurt.

It was later suggested that Lola was in love with another minx, Miriam Follin, way over and above any remorse she felt over involvement in the death of her brother on the way back from Australia. On another occasion Lola said herself, 'I never behold a beautiful woman but I fall in love with her myself and wish I were a man that I might marry her.'[19]

After the adventures in Panama the journey on the *Northerner*, lasting fifteen days with stops in Acapulco and San Diego, was a quiet one. Only one passenger died, noted Colonel Thomas Ely Buchanan in a letter to his wife. Lola had by no means the best cabin on the voyage. She had contrived a meeting with Buchanan, who had a state-room, and asked to be allowed to use it as it was cooler than her cabin. Once landed at San Francisco, Buchanan wrote to his wife:

> Whilst coming to the steamer in a small boat from the beach she got into an argument with the Captain and drew her dirk on him. She is a fast woman, and altogether a very remarkable one.
>
> I found her to be highly cultivated, and full of information; without being beautiful, she is a woman of striking appearance, and possesses a face that one could not easily forget.[20]

The arrival of a vessel was signalled by giant markers on the San Francisco harbour and it was reported that when the *Northerner* docked at 6 am on 21 May 1853 some 5,000 cheering enthusiasts were on hand to meet Lola. More likely many of the men on the quayside were there for the mail being carried by the vessel. The 275 mailbags were the most to have yet been brought through the Golden Gate. Lola was, of course, recognised, and gave some suitably modest answers to questions put to her. The next day the *Golden Era* remarked on the arrival of the 'world-renowned Lola Montez', while the San Francisco *Whig* thought, 'She comes in a quiet, unobtrusive manner and will doubtless succeed in this new field of her enterprise'. That latter bit of adulation was not surprising since on the boat she had met with Patrick Hull, part-owner of the paper.

She had survived travelling with Henning but neither he nor Hull lasted long in her life. In fact, Henning lasted a bare twenty-four hours longer. During a furious quarrel he resigned his post. She told him he could not resign because he had been sacked, gave him a beating and, for good measure, tore up $200 to show that money meant nothing to her. It made for good copy and better box office.

There had been no question of her being booked in advance for a theatre; the time of arrival of a boat was far too unpredictable for that. Lola put up at the Russ, then on the corner of Montgomery and Pine, and now she was courted by the owners of the principal two theatres.

San Francisco and its theatres had come a long way in a very short time. As for the city itself, the Mission De Los Dolores de Nuestro Padre San Francisco de Asis had been founded on 9 October 1776 at what is now 16th Street and Mission. Fifty years later there were only some 500 Indians, along with 5,000 head of cattle, around the mission but things looked up considerably when Sam Brannan brought a party of Mormons to the area on 8 July 1846. By January 1847 the 300 Americans had a weekly newspaper, Brannan's *Californian Star*. In 1849 gold was found and the rush began.

When the Protestant missionary Henry B. Sheldon arrived the year before Lola, initially he spent a Sabbath at the mission. It had been used for bear and bull fights but these entertainments had recently been banned. Now there was worse. On Sundays there were horse races and even worse than that: 'The horses are frequently ridden by courtesans of whom there are in this city alone, nearly one thousand and there are no villages of any size in the country where they are not to be found – They are the aristocracy.'

The women rode in the 'most splendid carriages and on the most showy studs'. Sheldon reported that of an evening all the saloons 'had prostitutes lined up at the bar in plain view of innocent promenaders such as myself. If a virtuous woman could be found her price would be far above rubies.' The ratio of harlots to honest women was so great that the latter class of women had to 'conduct themselves with the strictest propriety or be cast from the pale of good society'.[21] Welcome to San Francisco, Mme Montez.

'California was the last frontier, a land of milk, honey, gold and endless possibilities . . . If it was Utopia then San Francisco was the capital of Paradise. If people went home it was only to sleep. They acted their lives in public. The City was full of characters who delighted in eccentricity. To be noticed was to be famous.'[22] It was something that would appeal to Lola.

The first public entertainment had been a circus in early 1849. Then, on 22 May that year, the enterprising Englishman Stephen Massett, who appeared as Jeemes Pipes, gave a concert in which he sang, played the piano, imitated two German ladies competing for a place in the church choir and recited poems. It netted him £500. The front seats were reserved for ladies but there were only four in the audience.[23]

Between 1850 and 1859 there were 1,105 productions, of which 907 were plays, forty-eight operas in five different languages, eighty-four extravaganzas or pantomimes and sixty-six minstrel shows. The first theatrical performance proper had been a double bill in 1850 of *The Wife* and *Charles the Second* in Washington Hall, a flimsy board structure on Portsmouth Square. The building later became an elegant brothel. In April 1850 a French vaudeville company appeared in a new building in Washington Square near Montgomery.

In September that year the illiterate gambler and sportsman Tom Maguire opened his own Jenny Lind Theatre – in tribute to, rather than because of an appearance by, the Swedish Nightingale. Like so many wooden theatres and other buildings of the era, it burned down within a few months. Maguire replaced it with a stone theatre which was later bought by the authorities and used as the city hall.[24]

Maguire's rival for Lola's theatrical hand was Lewis Baker of the elegant American Theater. He and his actress wife Alexina Fisher Baker had arrived in the city the previous year. Baker, a very short man with what was described as an 'ugly ultra-aquiline nose', was an esteemed minor performer and a conscientious manager who introduced new measures of discipline among his casts. It was he who secured Lola's services – perhaps she was influenced by the facilities; there were sixty feet of private dressing rooms, a green room and a stage – but he may have lived to regret his bargain. Discipline and Lola were not automatic bedfellows. She smoked during rehearsals and was abusive to Lam Beattie, who became another in the line of men she threatened to horsewhip – he was due to play the King of Bavaria and had asked what the 'old duffer' was like.

Green-room troubles apart, at first Baker must have thought he had the better of Maguire when the Countess was still a novelty on the coast:

> As all the world and the rest of mankind have either seen or heard tell of this extraordinary woman we will not speak of her as her notoriety might seem to demand. Suffice it to say that Lola Montez, the artiste, the politician, the noblesse, and the 'fair shoulder-striker' is among us and that her name has attracted to the American Theatre the most brilliant and overflowing audience witnessed in this city and who have given her talents an unequivocal endorsement by the cordial manner in which she has been greeted. We can't say we admire Lola's acting, but we do think her dancing is – 'heavenly'. Success to the Countess of Landsfeldt. She will appear again at the American tomorrow night.[25]

What was not really Lola's fault was that she immediately upset the local favourite, the English-born Caroline Chapman. Caroline and William B. Chapman, known as 'Uncle Billy', were a sister-and-brother act – in fact she was probably his illegitimate daughter. Her purported father (probably grandfather), William Chapman, had managed the Theatre Royal, Covent Garden, for thirty years before going to America where he ran Chapman's Floating Palace, a showboat on the Mississippi. This rather gawky girl, popularly known as 'Our Caroline' and who played in New York from 1848 to 1852, was well able to convince an audience as a touching Juliet. Then, like so many, she and her 'brother' moved West, where she played Ophelia in Edwin Booth's first performance of *Hamlet*.

It was common practice for theatre companies of the time to retain actors who would complement a touring star figure. Lola's repertoire was limited and it was desirable to put her into a production that could easily be assembled. She knew the part of Lady Teazle in *The School for Scandal* but unfortunately it was one that Caroline Chapman had made her own. In fact she had played the role at the San Francisco Theatre on 22 May, four days before Lola first appeared at the American. Caroline was understandably put out. It may not have been the whole reason behind the merciless mickey-taking to which she and Uncle Billy subjected the Countess, but it was a major contributing factor.

Lola was a huge sensation. There were a great number of Europeans in the town and tickets were auctioned for between seven and twenty dollars. It was a great box-office success with a take of $4,500. The take was more rewarding than the critical acclaim. The *Golden Era*, a paper generally very favourable towards Lola, thought that 'our good citizens are coming to their senses again and that the days of "premium" humbuggery are past in California'.

The rival *Daily Alta California* liked her, however. 'The world-renowned Lola made her first appearance last evening . . . Her appearance more than justified general expectation.' She began nervously but then 'warmed into life' and 'presented Lady Teazle with a truthfulness to nature that might have served as a warning to all Sir Peters to beware how they link themselves to young and high-spirited lasses'.[26]

And next day it was on to the races at the newly opened Pioneer track, when the mare Lola Montes ran in a four-horse $700 two-mile race. The Countess was there to see her namesake, running in all white, readily defeat the favourite, The Senator. From the beginning of the second circuit she had been 'coquettishly playing with *The Senator*'. The race, however, might not have been all it seemed. Both Lola Montes and The Senator were in the same ownership and 'the jockey of *Anna* engaged in some very singular operations with a syringe applied to her mouth'. In no way did that hamper the

Countess. She threw a rug over the horse and, never one to miss an opportunity, said she would be prepared to ride the mare in a ladies' challenge race.[27]

That night Lola appeared in *Yelva*, which she claimed to have translated from the French, supported by two other local favourites, Henry Coad and the very dependable Mrs Judah. After the performance the paper was able to confirm, 'Lola is sure to have a fine success with us – this is a fact.'[28] John Phoenix, another critic in love with Lola, wrote: 'Madame la Comtesse delighted the audience with her artistic delineation of the character of an artless and affectionate dumb girl'.[29]

It was only a matter of days before she introduced the Spider Dance:

> After that first night she interpolated her spider dance in almost every program. Then came the signal for a kind of high jinks in which the entire audience joined. As the dancer unfolded her pantomime, trying to shake the spider from her clothes denizens of the gallery and pit would shout derisive advice. Perhaps on both sides there was some misunderstanding. Did these rough miners know Lola was addicted to footlight tirades? Did the danseuse know that California audiences thought nothing of taking part in theatricals when they were so moved? In any case she would stop the show, come forward and berate them; they in turn would retaliate with such exclamations as 'She's mad!' 'Don't you see the blood in her eyes?' until shouts and laughter put an end to the exchange of repartee.[30]

On 31 May 1853 Mary Jane Megquier, the wife of a doctor from Winthrop, Maine who came in search of riches, leaving behind their children, wrote back home:

> Lola is making quite a stir here now but many say that her playing is of that character that it is not proper for respectable ladies to attend but I do want to see her very much. Mr Clark said in dancing the spider dance, a favorite play of hers where she performs the antics of one with a tarantula up on their person, some thought she was obliged to look rather higher than was proper in so public a place.[31]

Lola appeared in two benefits during her first weeks in San Francisco. One for the Hebrew Society raised over $3,000 and there was a similar sum for the Fire Brigade. For the latter there was an all-star turnout, including Caroline Chapman and her brother, Mr and Mrs Lewis Baker and Lola's tame violinist Miska Hauser, who had followed her from New Orleans. It was a huge success, but the real plaudits were for Caroline Chapman: 'for pure, fresh, natural acting, ever-graceful, sparkling and all-pretty as she appeared, she certainly could not be excelled ...' As for Lola, 'she performed with inimitable grace and elasticity and very much to the satisfaction of the audience, if I may judge by the roars that rent the air as she appeared before the curtain in response to their call'.[32]

But as was almost invariably the case, promising starts soon led to disappointment. One of the reasons was the Chapmans, along with 'Doctor' Tom Robinson, whose speciality was patter songs which could run to dozens of verses and were performed during scene changes. One began:

> A Baker once, as I am told
> Became so fond of shining gold
> That he at public auction sold
> The Countess of Bavaria. [and so on]

And then, more or less without warning, Lola married for the third time. Now the unlucky man was thirty-three-year-old Patrick Purdy Hull, described as good-looking, although not elegant: 'Tall, ruddy, likeable enough in a rough fashion.' He had been on the Committee of Vigilance of 1851 which had dealt with a group of Australian criminals known as the Sydney Ducks. Having landed in San Francisco, they had terrorised the waterfront as well as starting a number of fires and looting the damaged buildings. Another of Lola's friends, Sam Brannan, was also a leading member of the Vigilance Committee who had summarily hanged them.

Word of the marriage had been in the air for a few days, or certainly in the papers. A little note appeared to the effect that she was likely soon to be led to the altar by a 'gallant gentleman from San Francisco on whom she smiled'.[33]

One unsupported story is that Sam Brannan had sailed with Hull and Lola on the *Northerner*; while she played footsie with Hull, she had left her cabin door open for Brannan. However, his name does not appear on the passenger list for the ship, unless he was one of the 250 passengers in steerage. Given his wealth, this seems unlikely. Of course, passenger lists in those days were not wholly reliable.[34]

Why on earth had she agreed to marry Hull? Was she tired of the ridicule from the Chapmans and Doc Robinson? Did she see marriage as a new challenge? Were her legs simply getting stiff? Youth was in his favour, as well as intellect – although some said he lacked brains, perhaps evidenced by his marriage to Lola – and he possessed undoubtedly a measure of Irish wit. He could tell racy stories that delighted his bride. She married him, she said, because he was the best story-teller she had ever known.[35]

A likely reason for the marriage was that it provided her with a respectable withdrawal from the San Francisco stage, where she was being increasingly overshadowed by Caroline Chapman. While Lola played three parts in *Maritana*, Caroline Chapman played seven in *An Actress of All Work*. Caroline also appeared in *Who's Got the Countess?*, in which she played Mola, a tempestuous actress who never knew her lines. It featured the 'Spy Dear' dance, a travesty of Lola's. There was some criticism of her and Uncle Billy, but Caroline was born and bred in the theatre. To her Lola must have been a parvenu, and so fair game.

A third explanation for the marriage is certainly the most entertaining, if the most improbable. Lola was approached to become the Empress of California if a revolution, said to have been organised by Herballa Castillino and John Crawford Haywood, took place. The transfer from Mexico had never been wholly accepted and Castillino could count on Spanish support. Who better as Empress than a Spanish grandee? According to this account, on her arrival on the docks she was approached by Castillino and Haywood with the proposal. The plot was thwarted by the derring-do of a young journalist from the *Sacramento Union*, Joseph Carlton Hardy. The scenario even provides an explanation for her marriage to Patrick Hull. He apparently knew a dreadful secret of Lola's, so she was persuaded to entice him into her bed. So entranced was he that he married her.[36]

How fanciful is that story? Well, there were certainly a number of plots in California's early years to set up an empire. In vague support of the story is a letter, dated 3 November 1853, from Washington DC and said to have been found in an old trunk in 1914 by a Mrs F. Rountree who had worked for Lola:

> My dear Lola
>
> Since our last meeting in S.F., I have been most actively engaged in securing aid from wealthy southern gentlemen in our project. I am fully convinced that there are sufficient powerful men in California, to at once start the project and revolution.
>
> Have T— call at once on you and tell him of my actions. The Spanish inhabitants of California are so bitter they can be depended upon to enlist themselves in our cause. C— is attending to that end.
>
> Do you remember meeting that wealthy Spanish gentleman of Los Angeles? He called at your room one evening after your performance. He had nothing but contempt and hatred for the Americans as he called them 'Yankees'.
>
> Let the conflict begin in San Francisco, Los Angeles, and Stockton, I will remain here. We will win.
>
> Trust none but the chosen leaders. When we succeed and succeed we will, remember you are to be the Empress of California. Have sent by Steamer $5,000 to 'T'.
>
> Be careful and prudent,
>
> Faithfully, J.C.[37]

The actor Walter Leman recalled that while there may have been rumours, the actual details of the wedding were kept secret. It was only at midnight that a friend who was to be a witness told him of the impending nuptials at dawn on 2 July 1853 at the Mission Dolores. Certainly the marriage took place at the odd time of six in the morning. One story is that shortly before the marriage Lola received an emissary from Ludwig to ask if she would return to Paris. It crops up regularly but it seems to be without support. Was Ludwig keeping tabs on her still? He appears to have been doing so, but now only in a fairly desultory way. He had his letters back and by now he had realised just how thoroughly he had been duped by her.

There was never any question from the start who wore the trousers in Lola's latest marriage:

At sunrise near the Old Mission Church some fifteen or twenty persons were walking listlessly around as if waiting for something; among them was Governor W and his wife, the only lady beside the bride who was present at the wedding.

Presently the carriage containing Lola and Hull drove up. Lola turned and on entering the church waved her hand to close the front door but some forty spectators in all had already got inside.

Lola carried in her hand two vases containing artificial white roses, and presented them to the officiating clergyman at the altar. From the church the party went into an ante-room where was a spread of cake, wine, cigars and cigarettes. Gov. W. giving Mrs C. a significant wink approaching Lola kissed her, and C, 'to make the occasion memorable' as he said did the same. Lola made no objection, remarking 'such is the custom of my country', She received the congratulations of all who were present and had a pleasant word for all; she then inquired, 'where can we get a good breakfast?' Hull replied 'at the Bull's Head;' Lola said she had rather go to the Tivoli; and to the Tivoli they went.[38]

The priest was Father Flavel Fontaine, who shortly afterwards fled to avoid a prosecution for embezzlement.[39]

Immediately the *San Francisco Evening Journal* had doubts about the longevity of the union. 'We have not heard whether the gentle Lola "cowhided" her lord and master after the ceremony . . . all we have to say is the captain's a bold man.' Back East the *New York Daily Times* thoroughly enjoyed hearing of the marriage:

The announcement in the California papers of the marriage of Lola Montez has caused some amusement among her old admirers in this country, who begin to wonder how many husbands the fair Lola is destined ultimately to have. She was avowedly a widow before she bestowed her hand (rather a heavy one, as several gentlemen will know) on Mr Heald. At that time, however, she was charged with doing a little business in the way of bigamy; and Mr Heald, after brief connubial experiment, was manifestly pleased to be rid of his bargain. Her experiences in the New World are better known to you than ourselves. It is to be hoped, however, that her new *caro sposo* Mr Hull, late of the *San Francisco Whig*, will find her a more traducable wife than his predecessors.[40]

The *Shasta Courier*, never a champion of Lola, was even more disrespectful, calling her 'the celebrated actress of unblemished virtue'. It was rather like the joke which had appeared some time earlier in the *Boston Bee*: '"Lola Montez is pure nonsense." "That's right, she's pure in no sense."'[41]

On the afternoon of their marriage they sailed up river on the appropriately named *New World* to Sacramento. They were accompanied by Hull's friend Louis Lull and Miska Hauser, who along with two other musicians would play with Lola in the theatre.

Life was rough in Sacramento. Single guests in the best hotel were expected to sleep in dormitories, bed and breakfast was the then equivalent of £150 a week and board consisted of boiled leg of grizzly bear, donkey steak and jackrabbit. The artistic competition was tough as well, ranging from Edwin Booth, the Norwegian violinist Ole Bull, who brought tears down the cheeks of the miners as he played 'Home Sweet Home', and the improbable Zoyara the Hermaphrodite, who had a riding act as well as a 'certificate of genuineness as to her equestrian skill and her virtues of a lady, from H.M. the King of Sardinia'. Nevertheless Zoyara later married another of the ladies in the circus. There is no record as to whether it was a lasting, or even happy, union.[42]

Nor was Lola's stay in Sacramento altogether a happy one. It started well enough; in fact very well indeed. The *Golden Era* pointed out that there was no question of who had the Countess now and there was a saccharine piece in the *Shasta Courier* about the ceremony conducted by Father Flavel Fontaine. 'It is confidently asserted that Mr and Mrs Hull intend making the State their permanent residence, which announcement . . . we are frank to confess, fills our soul with emotions of sublime pleasure.' And it does not even seem as though the paper's tongue was wedged in its cheek. The next day she was serenaded by two companies of firemen in full dress uniform. In return she volunteered a benefit performance. At the Swiss rifle club that afternoon she received an honorary salute from the club's cannon and made a pretty little toast to 'The Land of Tell'.

Unfortunately all her tomorrows were nearly yesterday. She was to appear only as a dancer – the logistical and financial problems of shifting scenery and a large company were too great. The first night she performed El Olle, a hornpipe, a Swiss dance from *William Tell* and, naturally, the Spider Dance. Her band now comprised Hauser, Charles Chenal – who had accompanied Catherine Hayes, 'the Sweet Swan of Erin', in her 1852 tour – on the piano *russe* and Charles Eigenschenk, who had studied at the Paris Conservatoire. It proceeded well enough and Hauser was particularly well received.

The second night was, however, a very different story. Almost as soon as Lola began to dance the audience broke out into convulsive laughter. Normally she could be relied on to quell a disturbance by coming to the front of the stage and making a short but telling speech. She duly did so, but she chose her words badly and for once she had misjudged the mood of the spectators. Some years later Miska Hauser recalled the evening. His memoirs have been criticised as unreliable, but he has her speech pattern correct. Lola regularly referred to herself in the third person:

> 'Ladies and Gentlemen, Lola Montez has too much respect for the people of California not to perceive that this stupid laughter comes from a few silly puppies.' There was more laughter but she continued. 'I will speak. Come up here. Give me your men's trousers and take in their place my women's skirts; you are not worthy to be called men.' Tremendous laughter. 'Lola Montez is proud to be what she is, but you haven't the courage to fight with her – yes, this woman who has no fear of you all, who despises you.' She wished to go on, but the uproar had reached its culmination point; decayed apples and eggs shot through the air and the bombardment lasted so long that this female opponent was constrained to take a better view of the male sex and with strategic backward movement withdrew herself from the firing line.

The theatre manager then asked Hauser to go on stage and try to divert the audience from what was turning into a full-scale riot. '[His] distress and the $100 which he in his misery offered me for the service touched my heart', and on he went. To Hauser's astonishment the booing and jeering died away and the audience quietened. He played 'Der Vögel auf dem Baume' and everything seemed all right when the manager was called for. He appeared and was told by someone in the

Not all American audiences appreciated Lola's sometimes amateurish efforts.
(Bettmann/CORBIS)

From the time of her arrival in Munich, the Bavarian papers were thoroughly hostile to Lola and delighted in publishing cartoons to her detriment.
(Mary Evans Picture Library)

'Uncle' Billy and Caroline Chapman. Caroline was a far better actress than Lol
and the pair tormented her whilst she was in San Francisco.
(Chapman, William, POR 1 and Chapman, Caroline, POR 1. Courtesy of the Bancroft Library,
University of California, Berkeley)

The San Francisco Mission where Lola married Patrick Hull – her second bigamous marriage. *(Dock Bateson)*

Lola's house in Grass Valley, California, where she was perhaps at her happiest.

On a good evening Lo[l]
would be showered
with roses – and some-
times gold.

Pas de Fascination: This is
the only drawing of Lola's
unfortunate lover Noel Follin,
who feared he would not
survive her Australian tour.

One of a number of sketches of Lola taken during her successful stay in Adelaide.
(Image courtesy of the State Library of South Australia)

A sketch of Lola doing her famous 'spider dance', taken during her trip to Adelaide.
(Image courtesy of the State Library of South Australia)

Ballarat, Victoria: the gold-mining town where Lola horse-whipped the editor of the local newspaper. *(Courtesy of Ballarat Fine Art Gallery)*

Lola's memoirs sold worldwide, but since there were a number of pirated editions available she only received a fraction of the money due to her. *(Montez, Lola, POR 4. Courtesy of the Bancroft Library, University of California, Berkeley)*

VICTORIA THEATRE,
BALLARAT.

This New and Elegant Theatre WILL OPEN

On SATURDAY, Feb. 16,

1856, under the Management of

MR. JAMES CROSBY,

Late Manager of the Victoria Theatre, Sydney,

On which occasion that world-renowned Artist, MADAME

LOLA
MONTES

And Troupe, will have the honor of making their first appearance, supported by the

Best Company ever assembled on Ballarat!

Aided by New Scenery, Dresses, and Appointments.

A theatre bill advertising Lola's first performance at the Victoria Theatre in Sydney in 1856, promoted by Crosby. Lola had switched management and affection from Follin to Crosby, as a result of which Mrs Crosby took a whip to her. *(Courtesy of the Hans Tasiemka Archives)*

Mrs Frank Leslie, once Minnie Montez – Lola's so-called sister (*Carrie Chapman Catt Collection, Bryn Mawr College Library*)

Martine Carol, one of the best on-screen Lolas, as seen here in Max Ophüls' underrated film. Anton Walbrook starred as Ludwig and Peter Ustinov played her admirer. *(akg-images)*

parterre that they didn't wish to see Lola again; Hauser was the man for them. At this she reappeared and the attack on her recommenced with cries that the audience wanted their money back. Hauser started to play again, this time variations on 'Yankee Doodle Dandy' and that old Paganini warhorse *Carnival in Venice*. Once again Lola demonstrated that she lacked nothing in courage. On she came for a third time. This time she managed to get through the Spider Dance. She had to be protected on her way back to the Orleans Hotel, where she was treated to a serenade of banging on kettles, drums and broken pots. Even then she was not finished. Out she came to speak on the balcony. 'You cowards, low blackguards, cringing dogs. And lazy fellows! I would not despise a dirty dog so much as I do you.' This brought a round of applause and the crowd was broken up. The *Sacramento Union* suggested the firemen would do well to cancel their proposed benefit performance.

The next night things had changed once more. It was a contrite and clever, very clever, Lola who appeared. It was reconciliation time and she went before the curtain to make another speech. It was appealing – she had been ill since she had been in California and her behaviour the previous night had stemmed from it. It was patriotic – she was sure that the harassment had not come from Americans but from her enemies in Europe. And it gave the audience a choice – 'Ladies and Gentlemen, if you wish me to go on with my dance you have only to say the word.' And of course they did. The evening ended with curtsies and five curtain speeches. Now the *Sacramento Union* ate its words: 'Altogether, so rare a night's entertainment has never been experienced in Sacramento.' Later she told Hauser, 'Believe me, dear H., last evening was worth more to me than $1,000. I was delightfully amused and I have added another to my list of adventures.'

Only the *Daily Californian* cast a jaundiced eye over the audience: 'in looking it over we could distinguish only a few of our citizens present. To strangers, impelled by mere curiosity, and to free use of free tickets, is she indebted for an audience.' Lola had papered the house.

So came another challenge. On 9 July the *Daily Alta California* printed what was said to be a copy of the letter thoughtfully sent to them in which she invited the editor of the *Daily Californian* to a duel by pistols; he should wear petticoats, which she would lend him. If, given her known skill, he did not care for that, then it would be by selection of pills from a box. 'One shall be poisoned and the other not.' Sensibly he ignored the challenge, but it was all good publicity.[43]

The rest of her stay was an unmitigated triumph. There were curtain calls, the firemen marched to the Orleans Hotel after her final performance, a band played, Lola appeared on the balcony, threw a flag to the firemen, there were more speeches. Best of all, the hitherto retiring Pat Hull appeared to make a short speech, ending with an invitation for the men to go to the bar and drink at his expense. Just the sort of thing husbands are there to do. Had he lived long enough, with that sort of attitude a successful political career would have been almost guaranteed.

-+->-<+-

CHAPTER FIFTEEN

Lola at Pasture

ON 15 JULY LOLA and the troupe left for Marysville, but all was not well in the camp. For a start, travelling between towns in California was, at the time, never a particularly enjoyable experience:

> A stage ride from Marysville to Nevada (City) presents little attraction under the most favorable circumstances, but for those unfortunates whose business compels them to be constantly on the move . . . it can only be regarded as a necessary evil . . . We travelled over a decidedly undulating road not gravelly, but rocky and the many unexpected concussions we received led us to deplore the negligence and want of enterprise . . . in not having the plank road finished that has been so long talked of but still remains in 'status quo'.[1]

The next day there was another fiasco; the dancing was not well received and Miska Hauser, possibly unable to weather another of Lola's tempers or possibly because his romantic involvement with her was over, returned to San Francisco to continue as a soloist. Chenal and Eigenschenk took over playing for her in the miners' camps. An appearance in Nevada City went rather better: 'The Houses have been crowded with an enthusiastic audience at double the usual prices. The lady had exhibited herself in here in her most gracious mood . . . She has reversed many prejudices against her in the public view.'[2]

But another low soon followed. When she returned from Nevada City to the Alta Theatre in Grass Valley there were not enough in the audience and she refused to appear. Instead, it is said, she 'took the rag off the bush' and danced for a private audience. 'All that was seen on the occasion has not been divulged.'[3] The story has been dismissed on the grounds that Lola simply did not behave in this way, but set against this there is the letter to Ludwig which said that in her early days that was just how she earned her money. Then there was her behaviour in the German spas.

By the middle of the month the San Francisco and Sacramento papers were hinting at a marital breakdown. One story was that Lola had pitched poor Patrick's clothes from the window, a second that she had narrowly avoided another arrest.[4] She and Hull now made their way to Grass Valley, where Lola settled for the longest period of her life and from where on 22 July Alonso Delano, 'Old Block', reported in the *Union*:

> Despite all the ugly stories your papers have published about a 'Marysville fight', the smiles of the bridegroom are still upon the husband's face and happiness and good nature pervade the countenance of the heroine and her liege lord. From this place they go to Nevada and Downieville, more to enjoy the mountain air and unrivalled scenery, than for the worship of mammon.

The Grass Valley settlement, which took its name from the abundant vegetation in the region, began in 1849 when a number of saw mills were built. These were regularly attacked by Native Americans; eventually the miners of Deer Creek summoned the cavalry from the Far West military post and drove them back into the mountains.

The first log cabin was built on what is now Main Street, and as late as January 1851 there were only three or four in the whole of Grass Valley. After gold was found there in September 1850 expansion was exponential. A rich vein was discovered in November 1851 and during the winter $20,000 of gold was mined. The Gold Hill Co. opened its first mine in early 1851, followed by one built by Judge Walsh. The Empire Mine began operations in 1850 and was still going strong into the twentieth century. At its height it employed 500 miners in an around-the-clock operation extracting gold-bearing quartz, and the roar of its stamp mill was part of Grass Valley life. The mine's 400 miles of tunnels honeycombed the entire area and reached a depth of 11,000 feet.[5] The actor Edward P. Hingston wrote:

> Grass Valley is a town and one of considerable size and importance. It takes first class rank among the quartz-mining towns of California. In it are more than twenty quartz crushing mills, constantly employed crushing ore, which yields a return of from five to twenty-five pounds a ton, and sometimes as high as seventy-five or eighty pounds sterling.[6]

There was something of a slump in 1852, but business had picked up by the following year when Lola decided to settle there, taking a single-storey white cottage on Main Street.[7] Now, 'pedlars travelling through the mining community if they could afford mule driven wagons carried an amazing assortment of velvet, laces, broadcloth coats, sealing wax and yellow backed novels – none of them necessities. The dirty collars of two years earlier had been replaced with clean ones.'[8]

What on earth was this most sophisticated woman doing burying herself away in what, in European terms, was the back of beyond? Forty miles by road from Sacramento, itself not the centre of the universe, Grass Valley was then the sixth largest town in California with a population of around 1,400, of which all but 200 were men. The nearest town of any size was Nevada City. Its streets were still unpaved and it was noisy day and night because of the stamp mills used in quartz mining. But the countryside around was beautiful, even though the once lush oak groves had been cleared away for lumber and the valley itself had been ravaged by the mining operations. The town had a theatre on the second storey of the Alta saloon, a school, a church and hotels, lodges, clubs, societies including the Grass Valley Literary Society, and a sewing circle. It was usual for miners' diggings to be named after famous women and there was a Lola Montez Hill even before she arrived.

However bravely Delano wrote, the marriage was clearly wrong from the start. As early as 5 August a man named Gil Meredith was said to be the envy of the whole town, 'but he deserves his success with the fair for he possesses a noble heart and winning ways. A lucky dog is he to have a live Countess at his bachelor box.'[9] It was from Meredith she purchased the house. It had originally been the office of Meredith's Gold Hill Mining Company and had also been used as the first schoolhouse. Now she planted what was the first cactus garden from cuttings and plants she had found on her rides through the countryside.

Six weeks later there was a suggestion that one of her closest friends was a Colonel Robert H. Taylor. The *Golden Era* thought she was showing 'a decided distaste for the Hull, believing that the Colonel (kernel) is somewhat more digestible'.[10] The word back East was that Hull was jealous of 'a violinist from whom she had received some polite attentions'. 'Serve him right!' said the paper.[11]

In fact the marriage had only a matter of days to run. Quite what was the final act is the subject of a variety of stories. One is that Hull shot Lola's pet bear and as a result was expelled from Grass Valley.[12] Another, more probable – since the general consensus of opinion is that the bear, or even bears, did not arrive until after he left – is that she thought he was sponging off her and she was not having it. The date of his final departure can be fixed as 14 September, for the next day she wrote to a friend, 'Bien cher Paco', complaining that she hadn't heard from him for four days and saying that 'Mr Hull est parti hier matin pour San Francisco, pourvu qu'il ne me trouble plus'[13] ('Mr Hull left yesterday morning for San Francisco. Hopefully he won't bother me anymore').

By the middle of September there were reports that she had filed for divorce and in early October the *Nevada (City) Journal* joked that she had applied to be divorced from the bands of 'Hully' wedlock.[14] The reasons were never made quite clear. There were suggestions that he suffered from body odour or flatulence or both. If so, why had she married him in the first place? She must have known of his hygiene problems already. There is also a suggestion that he too had contracted syphilis. No papers exist to show that either of them filed a divorce petition, but yet another story is that she did file and the personal complaints she made about him destroyed him. In fact she may well never even have bothered to file divorce papers. After all, to coin a word, the marriage was trigamous.

By November 1853 Lola had settled well in Grass Valley. There were reports that she was making friends and tending her garden. She was said to have bought an interest in a quartz mine for $20,000. The papers reported that Hull had definitely been sacked and told to make a living on his own. She was not going to give him any more money.[15]

> She has money and is one of the shrewdest women in matters of business and one of the best informed on general subjects whom I ever saw. She is perfectly well-bred and her manners are entirely unpretending. She is very popular with the miners as a class; and, in short, is a remarkable woman. Her failings are a high temper, and *some obtuseness on moral questions*; but she pays well those whom she employs, and that, in a Californian's eye, 'covers a multitude of sins'.[16]

The editor of the *Grass Valley Telegraph*, Henry Shipley, was one more who can be added to the list of unfortunates who went to an early grave after encountering Lola. It was another story of which there exist a variety of versions. Both Shipley and Lola gave sharply contrasting accounts of what had happened, each naturally assuming the more favourable position.

Lola had taken against the hard-drinking, Amherst-educated Shipley, thinking he was both arrogant and pretentious. Whether this was dislike at first sight or whether he was an invitee to Main Street with whom she fell out, or there had been an even closer relationship, is not wholly clear. Given that her home was something of an open house for those who could spell their names, it is likely that at one time he had been a guest.

What is certain is that she later heard he intended to savage the performance of three singers who came to Grass Valley. She begged him to 'reflect' and he promised to give a balanced view. Instead he published a review suggesting the troupe had joined forces 'for the purpose of inflicting misery upon all who will place themselves within hearing distance'. Lola leaped to their defence and Shipley, perhaps unwisely, called on her while she was ill. There is no doubt that she then threatened him with a revolver – to defend herself after he threatened to cut her throat, she said. Nonsense, he maintained: he retreated gracefully in the face of an outraged and rampant Lola.

Given her temper and his tendency to alcohol, as is often the case the truth probably lies somewhere in the middle.

The following week Shipley published an editorial attacking the literary efforts of Queen Christina of Spain. 'There is such a Lola Montez-like insolence and barefaced hypocrisy in her lines that the ex-King of Bavaria might be delightfully mystified with them.' Lola boiled over; bonnet on head and horsewhip in hand, she was off down Main Street to find Shipley having a morning drink in the Golden Gate saloon.

Shipley's account was that Lola, 'using language which our devil says he will not set up', struck out at him but he caught the whip while she raked him with her nails. None of those in the saloon would move an inch to help her, nor would they take up the challenge when he invited a champion to step forward and fight him. He then left the saloon 'in disgust and regret that a woman could so far forget her position. Sic transit gloria mundi.'

Inaccurate, thought Lola, who laid out her side of the story to the *Nevada Gazette* four miles away. She had, she said, recalled the Women's Rights Convention and, emulating Miss Lucy Stone's principle that a whip was to be used only on a horse but 'this time was to be disgraced by falling on the back of an ass', gave the seated Shipley four cuts about the head and shoulders. Shipley stood and squared up to her 'on the most approved Yankee Sullivan principles' and tried to hit her in the eye. In turn she followed the spirit of her 'Irish, Spanish and Scotch ancestors' and 'on the most approved Tom Hyer principles' hit him about the eye with her ringed hand. 'As usual this would-be shoulder striker ended the combat with certain abuse, of which, to do him justice, he is perfect master. Sic transit gloria Shipley. Alas! Poor Yorick.'[17]

Shipley left Grass Valley a few weeks later to work for the *Nevada Democrat*. Some have suggested it was from the shame of being whipped by Lola. On the other hand, Lola remained a firm fixture in Grass Valley for the next fifteen months.[18]

It is impossible to determine accurately the number of lovers she had while she was at Grass Valley. John Southwick, who acted as host at her home and probably provided the funds to purchase the cottage, is certainly a likely candidate and Gil Meredith was another probability. Nor should the fact that they failed to record an association in their memoirs be regarded as absolute proof that they did not have one. There is a reference in a letter to his sister by Gil Meredith to 'a crazy German who followed her [Lola] all over the country'. The German is said to be a Kirke Adler and to have been her lover, or possibly even to have married her. Apart from this brief mention by Meredith, which gives some credence to the story, Adler seems to have first surfaced in an article in *Europa, Chronik der Gebildeten*; since this is a premature obituary for Lola, it may not have been all that accurate. The German accounts do not name him but say he was 'ein Arzt von Adel' (doctor from the aristocracy), which may have been corrupted to Adler in translation. The suggestion is that he died in a shooting accident while out riding and so can have his name added to the Valhalla of Lola's unfortunate acquaintances.

In October Lola was on board when the *Alta California* collided with the *Antelope* on the Sacramento river. All the passengers were rescued. She then began a theatrical tour of the mining camps.

Grass Valley for a time provided some peace and quiet. She had something of a menagerie, including a pet bear named Major which she took for walks:

> Lola Montez had her beautiful little hand severely bitten by her pet grizzly at her residence in Grass Valley a few days hence. She was feeding him with sugar at the time. Enviable Bruin! How many hombres would have faced all manner of danger for the privilege of even kissing those sweet little digits to say nothing about biting them! It is unbearable to think about, that such a happiness was reserved for a miserable cub.[19]

Another story is that the bear was put on trial for attempted murder and given counsel for its defence after it nearly crushed her ribs. It was ruled that 'the temptation to hug Lola always is excessive' and the bear was acquitted.[20]

The bear, or bears, featured in a number of stories. The most fanciful was that Lola agreed to give a tress of her hair to a John Hull Pennville, a man with a hair fetish who apparently was in the habit of playing the violin for her, if he wrestled the animal. When he succeeded in downing the bear he put a strand of her hair in his violin bow.[21]

Others thought rather differently of Lola and the animal. Miner Edwin Morse, who claimed he knew Lola well and that she had nicknamed him 'The Greyhound', recalled years later:

> In reality she was mortally afraid of the brute and used to stand at a good safe distance when she fed him throwing his meat within reach, although the bear was only a cub and anything but fierce.[22]

Nor was Morse sure she was paying close attention to her cleanliness:

> When carefully dressed and gotten up she was still very handsome, but ordinarily she was such a slattern that to me she was frankly disgusting. When attired in a low necked gown as was her usual custom, even her liberal use of powder failed to conceal the fact that she stood much in need of a good application of soap and water.

Lola still made some stage appearances. On 22 December 1853 she played *An Actress of All Work* at the nearby hamlet of Rough and Ready. Two days later she threw a Christmas party for the children in Grass Valley. Even a fleeting glimpse of her was news: 'On Tuesday Lola Montez paid us a visit in a sleigh and a span of horses decorated with impromptu cowbells. She flashed like a meteor through the snowflakes and wanton snowballs and then disappeared in the direction of Grass Valley.'[23]

Another lover was John E. 'Johnny' Southwick, part owner and director of Empire Mine. He certainly lived with her in Grass Valley, for there is a reference by Stephen Massett to his visit: 'She and Johnny S. received me very hospitably.'[24] In Southwick's absence he told her to use his friend Conrad K. Hotalling as a banker. Some time during the year she borrowed $60 from him to settle 'the most pressing need'. Southwick was injured when thrown from his horse in March 1855; he was to witness one of the contracts on 28 May for Lola's later visit to Australia and was also given her will for safe custody. He returned to New York in 1872 after being a mental patient for some time. He is probably the man obliquely referred to here as having been ruined by Lola:

A rich quartz miner fell in love with her. Lola, Countess of Landsfeldt, from having been the favourite of a Bavarian monarch, became the mistress of a Californian gold miner. He was rich but not strong minded. In a few years she succeeded in reducing him to poverty and lunacy. I visited the little cottage where they had resided, and asked the landlord if he knew anything about the fate of the miner who loved not wisely but too well. 'He was a muggins,' was the reply; 'he did what all muggins do. When he'd lost all his gold, he took a lead pill out of a steel box'.[25]

There was even a wholly unsubstantiated story that, after Hull's departure, Lola had a brief affair with the bandit Joaquim Murietta, the Californian equivalent of Robin Hood.[26] This may have been difficult because the bandit's head had apparently been exhibited a few weeks before she came to Grass Valley, although that in itself was perhaps not a complete disqualification; by all accounts there were at least six heads in circulation over the next fifty years.

Generally she had a good press from people in Grass Valley. She liked being called Madame Lola and there are numerous stories of her helping injured miners and riding over the hills to be with sick children whose parents could not afford a nurse. The theory goes that if she had been as bad as her reputation, the miners' respectable wives would not have allowed their children to go anywhere near her. On the other hand, there were stories that she was ignored by the wives in the miners' camps as 'unchaste'; something that would anyway apply to a woman who smoked cigarettes. Certainly respectable pioneer women could be very sniffy indeed. In 1849 Lucinda Brown crossed the isthmus in the company of 'seven females'. In her diary she deliberately did not write 'ladies', 'for all do not deserve the name'.[27]

The camps and theatres were always on the lookout for novelties, and child prodigies were always welcome. Anna Maria Quinn played Hamlet for one act of the tragedy in 1854 when she was not quite seven. Other children had more enduring careers; one of these was the red-headed Lotta Crabtree. The child lived literally two doors away from Lola on Mill Road; a Grass Valley story has it that Lola taught Lotta Crabtree to sing and dance, as well as instructing Susan

Robinson, 'The Fairy Star'. In fact Susan's father had a theatrical school, and it is much more probable that she learned her trade there.

At the other end of the social scale, Lola entertained numerous men friends, very often on a Wednesday, offering fine brandy and cigars to an intimate circle as well as to passing players. They included Ole Bull, whom the composer Robert Schumann regarded as the equal of Paganini, and the journalist and writer Alonso Delano. Guests had to sing for their supper, performing party pieces, making up monologues, singing songs. Occasionally Lola would dance. Gil Meredith was a regular caller; he wrote to his sister that what he really liked was her piano player, which had a roll of selections from Donizetti. Years later W. M. Stewart, the senator for Nevada, recalled how he counted the days to the next of Lola's Wednesday soirées, which were said to be attended by Victor Hugo's sons.[28]

Nearly twenty years after Lola's death, the theatrical agent Charles Warwick remembered her in Grass Valley when she showed him around the town:

> She was bareheaded, sunburnt almost to the color of a Mexican, and with her hair hanging in rich profusion over her graceful shoulders . . . I was prepared to find a blasée woman of the world, an artful speculative adventuress . . . I can only aver that as I found her she was a generous, charitable whole-souled woman.

He was certainly her champion:

> Let the proud, self-righteous and would-be godly turn up their noses and sweep their stainless crinolines aside, if such as Lola pass near. Let such 'lost ones' survive even their contempt and perhaps find within their hearts a reliance and a hope which their self-constituted censors never dream of.[29]

He goes on to say that while she was showing him around, a mob tried to drag a horse thief from the local jail with the local law officer, Judge Sowers, powerless to stop them. Lola, 'with a tone and gesture worthy of Joan of Arc or a Queen of the Amazons', threw herself between the crowd and the man, ordering them back. 'In my whole stage experience I never saw a finer tableau.' Unfortunately this part of the story is probably not true. There are no other accounts in contemporary newspapers and other recollections and Lola never appears to have mentioned it. Surely someone would have done.

As the years went by there were more and more varied recollections of her time in Grass Valley, reliable in equally varying degrees – she had a lion; she had a rugged bear; she had two bears, one of which bit Hull and was shot by him; she had a panther; there were three or four black maids; she had $14,000 credit at two banks. And of her life in the theatre as well – she bullied her managers; she received in bed; she liked to be referred to as Madame la Comtesse; she carried her money with her in a box of which she kept the only key.[30]

It is not clear why Lola now decided to make another stage tour, this time to Australia. She may have become bored with the domesticity of Grass Valley, but there is also the likelihood that she was having another financial crisis. San Francisco was in something of a slump. There was a great deal of political chicanery and in February 1855 the banking firm of Page, Bacon and Company failed, setting off a run on the other banks. Wells Fargo could meet the run, but in Grass Valley Adams Express also failed. Nor did a series of floods and fires help. Just as eastern actors had moved to the West Coast in the early 1850s, now, with the uncertainty of the Californian economy, they began travelling to Australia.

Lola was not the first to go. In 1854 English-born Laura Keene had toured Australia with D. C. 'Dave' Anderson and Edwin Booth, John Wilkes Booth's actor-manager brother. There was already some bad feeling between Keene and Booth; she thought him at that stage of his career to be a poor actor. Inevitably the tour had not been a success and the trio had split up. In fact the blame should not have been wholly placed on Edwin's shoulders. Laura Keene had married a criminal who had been transported and the whole tour was devised by her to try to find him and obtain a divorce.[31] On the other hand, a tour made by James Stark and his family, not exactly household names, had netted around $100,000.

Whatever the reason, it was time for Lola to move on again. Despite her protests to the contrary, she must have loved travelling. She had thought about a tour of the mining towns, but nothing had come of it. Now she planned an ambitious worldwide tour – Australia, the Far East, India, Constantinople and back to Europe.

In June 1855 she signed an agreement to tour Australia. She also had a new love interest. In the company was Augustus Noel Follin, who acted as Frank Folland. The son of Charles, a dissolute but handsome businessman who had ruined a New Orleans heiress, Follin had left his wife and two children in Cincinnati to seek his fortune out West. He had worked in the box office of a San Francisco theatre and met Lola when he appeared in Grass Valley.[32] He had also appeared in Nevada City in *The Lady of Lyons* on 30 July. He had been instantly smitten. On 16 March 1855 he wrote to his half-sister Miriam that

> Madam the Countess of Landsfeldt thinks your daguerrotype the most beautiful she ever saw. She says 'una cara tan *intelegente* tan *linda*'. She is in love with you, and actually kept it for two days. She lives in Grass Valley . . . with a pet . . . a dozen dogs: birds, a summer house filled with the rarest flowers, all sorts of musical instruments . . . there is all the remnants of a lovely woman about her, her nose appears chisseled [sic] out of marble and her conversational powers are fascinating to a degree: I talked with her in English, French and Spanish. She speaks German, Italian, Portuguese and Russian in addition.[33]

The tour to Australia was said to have been financed by the sale of her jewels to a madam for $20,000. The cast was second rate, with the possible exception of Josephine Fiddes, who at least later understudied the actress and poetess Adah Isaacs Menken of *Mazeppa* fame.[34] Also in the troupe were Fiddes' sister and her mother, who as Harriet Cawse had appeared in opera in San Francisco with no great success. That did not stop the *Placer Times* cooing that it was 'a very respectable troupe, comprising more than ordinary dramatic talent'.[35] At least the musical side was in better order. The long-serving conservatoire-educated Charles Eigenschenk was to be the leader of the orchestra.

The players were to get between £40 and £60 a week, beginning after the first professional performance and lasting for a tour of China and the East Indies, with £20 a week when travelling. Lola would pay travel from port to port and bed and board on land or sea. She would also pay the return passage to San Francisco. Benjamin Napthali Jones was hired as a 'walking gentleman' and for 'other useful business as, in theatrical engagements in such cases, is made and provided'. George Daniels had a similar contract. James Simmonds was to be 'First Low Comedy and Stage Manager'. He received £60 a week and was to be given a benefit after the third night. Freeborough Jones was to be an 'agent', a position Follin thought was his.

Financial hopes were high. Three days before he left for Australia, Follin wrote another letter to his sister and mother asking them to tell his wife he was off: 'I shall be gone for two years or more. I go with the Countess of Lansfeldt, Lola Montes, as agent – if successful I shall make twenty-five thousand dollars. I have nothing to lose and all to gain . . . I dare not trust myself to say more. I should die if I did. God bless you, I love you. Noel.'

The actor Walter Leman, who had been at Lola's wedding to Hull, recalled that he and Laura Keene went to see her at the International Hotel the night before she sailed for Australia. Lola was in the highest of spirits. Leman thought that even as early as that time 'she had begun to abate something of the imperious and reckless manner for which she was so notorious'.[36] He was wrong.

Lola, Follin and the rest of the troupe sailed on the *Fanny Major* at 5.30 pm on 6 June. It was generally agreed there was a good crowd to see them off, but as usual she divided the press. The various correspondents were not sure whether 'several faint attempts were made to get up three cheers for Lola but except for an occasional enthusiastic yell, the multitude only laughed or remained silent',[37] or 'the God Speeds that followed her from a large concourse yesterday bespoke a good feeling from a large class of people in the State. Among them we noticed a number who had left their mining precincts to bid farewell to one who as they felt and had reason to feel was a tried and good friend . . . Success attend her!'[38] Lola remained on deck, pink ribbons and green parasol fluttering in the breeze, as the ship sailed through the Golden Gate.

The New York papers kept track of Lola on their readers' behalf: 'Lola Montez has quitted California for Australia. She has had her sorrows, we hear, in the loss of her favorite poodle – lost, stolen or strayed. She is, however, of the same high spirit as ever, and has taken with her a necessary supply of canes, whips and revolvers.'

'E puribus sausageibus', the *Golden Era* had rather unkindly said a month earlier, referring to the dog's disappearance.[39]

There were ominous signs on the voyage that all might not be well. A steward kicked Lola's dog and she drew a knife on him, threatening to kill him if he did it again.[40] One report suggests that when the rest of the troupe failed to back her she left the saloon area and went into steerage, where she spent the rest of the stiflingly hot voyage.

-+->-<-+-

CHAPTER SIXTEEN

Lola Down Under

THE *FANNY MAJOR* DOCKED at Sydney on 16 August in weather conditions that foreshadowed what was to come in the following weeks. There was rain, a strong wind, dark cloud and then showers.

Playing in the Australian cities at the time could be rough and ready. Miska Hauser recalled a performance in Sydney of *Lucia di Lammermoor* where the impresario was a German masquerading as English gentry and the soprano Miss Waverley, an African-American, was 'as dark as a crow'. The tenor was German, the baritone Italian and the bass French. Everyone else sang in English. The gas lights went out during the mad scene and the shock cured Lucia's madness. Miss Waverley let out a piercing scream. The baritone fell over and cracked his head; uninvited, the tenor ran on yelling in German and four nobles appeared in their shirt sleeves to carry the baritone away. The audience was laughing and swearing. It appeared that the impresario had failed to pay the gas bill.[1]

Lola's ragbag American company did not last a month. The tour opened on 23 August at the Royal Victoria Theatre, Sydney, the oldest and most popular theatre in the city, which held between 2,500 and 3,000 spectators. Lola appeared as herself in *Lola Montez in Bavaria*, of which the *Sydney Empire* thought, 'Many of the characters introduced into this interesting Drama were very creditably sustained.' As for the possible effect on public morals, 'it is only due to the author and to Madame Montez herself, to state that there is not a single passage in the play against which the slightest objection could be urged by the most fastidious'.

Six days later, on 29 August 1855, she failed to appear. Although it was said there would be refunds, like Lola they failed to materialise. Tickets had been sold at a high price. As a letter writer to the *Empire* said, it was 'rather more than sharp'.

The pattern she followed throughout her tour relied on her notoriety to bring in the punters for the first night of the thoroughly dull *Lola in Bavaria*. And when that did not catch on, rougher but more entertaining fare was offered. Houses were reasonably good, but they dwindled as the company ran through its repertory – *Yelva*, *The Jacobite*, *Morning Call*, *Maidens Beware*, *Antony and Cleopatra Married and Settled*, *Follies of a Night*. On 29 August she was billed to appear in the last scheduled performance of *Morning Call* but she was ill. A refund was announced and almost immediately withdrawn. Then, on 4 September, out came the trump card. 'For this night only,' the Spider Dance, 'performed 200 consecutive nights in New York'. But this one night turned into another, and the one after and the one after that as well.

'It is most amusing,' said the Melbourne *Argus* stringer in Sydney, 'to find parties who were always yelling against the FitzRoys for their doings, or supposed doings, in the privacy of Government House, coolly seated in the parquette, or in a well-chosen place in the boxes, gloating over the Spider Dance.'[2]

At the time of Lola's arrival, Catherine Hayes, 'The Sweet Swan of Erin', was playing Bellini's *Norma* in the Prince of Wales Theatre, where she had been for a fortnight.[3] There had been both parallels and rivalry between the pair. Both had been born in Ireland, both had made their London debuts under Benjamin Lumley's management at the Theatre Royal, Haymarket and both had married at St George's, Hanover Square. Now the diva and the danseuse took it in turn to try to upstage each other. First, Miss Hayes was taken ill and then the Countess was indisposed; Catherine then recovered and so did Lola.

The author Frank Fowler recalled watching Lola and speaking to her after a performance. He 'found her to be – much to my surprise – a very simple-mannered, well behaved cigar-loving person. Her general conduct in the colony, however, was very outré.' She had developed a good line in repartee with audiences: 'A practice with Lola during her stay in Sydney was, whenever she was unfavourably criticised in the papers, to step forward to the footlights on the following evening, and throwing her pretty white glove on the stage, challenge her accuser to come and pick it up.'[4]

Meanwhile Follin, to his chagrin, had been temporarily replaced as her manager and possibly lover. James Crosby, with a 'long, thin, white black-bearded face' like Mephistopheles, now organised a claque, handing round wilted bouquets to be thrown, and hammering with a stick on the back of the box when his employer came on. There were almost no women in the audience; when Catherine Hayes attended she went cloaked because she would have lost her female following had she been seen. Anyone who complained about the production was liable to be roughly handled by Crosby's stooges.[5]

The critic of the *Sydney Morning Herald*, invited to Lola's lodgings one Sunday evening, found an interesting and very mixed bohemian collection of people. It included a small 'Hindoo boy in a white robe and turban', as well as an artist who had taken part in the miners' uprising at the Eureka stockade in Ballarat dressed in a fez and smoking a hookah, along with his wife, who had been a 'Bloomer lecturess'. Also present were Follin, generously described as 'a recently imported star from North and South American theatres, large-eyed and long-limbed, Lola's "sheep dog", a French danseuse and a southern States lady who "loved Lola as much as she detested that 'she-Judas' Mrs Beecher Stowe"' as well as local and visiting Californian actors and actresses.[6]

Between seven in the evening and 2 am when the levee broke up, Lola smoked some two dozen cigarettes in what she called the Spanish fashion. She would inhale and open her mouth but no smoke would come out. She then took a drink of water and again opened her mouth, this time emitting a cloud of smoke. Lola was still in her table-rapping mode, because during the evening she and the other

Americans produced 'taps' from the middle of telescope tables and made claw tables stand on one toe.

A little over a week later, *Bell's Life in Sydney* reported that things were going well; huge crowds, enthusiastic audiences, both she and Follin acting well. He had a benefit.[7] But there were already worms in the rosy apple, or at least serious discontent in the green room. Lola was about to jump ship – or rather take one and leave most of the troupe behind. On 8 September, the day Bell thought things were going well, accordingly writs totalling £12,000 went in. This was the company's version, published in the *Sydney Morning Herald*:

> Sir: Will you allow me, through the medium of your widely circulated journal, to say a few words to the theatre-going public of Sydney respecting the desertion of Lola Montez in this city from her company.
>
> About four months ago, Lola Montez conceived the idea of making a theatrical tour through Australia, China, and India, in furtherance of which object she engaged a small company of comedians then playing in San Francisco to accompany her for one year, binding herself to pay the return passages of said Company to the port of San Francisco at the termination of said engagements.
>
> On arriving at Sydney, she was informed by competent judges, that the tour through China and India would not prove profitable to her, she therefore at once abandoned the idea, and as the company were not sufficiently needed by her in these colonies . . . she discharges them, little caring what the consequences may be. This is the *good hearted* Lola Montez, so widely eulogised throughout Sydney . . .
>
> ONE OF THE LOLA MONTEZ COMPANY[8]

Not so, replied Lola's solicitors Levy and Michael. The company was composed of 'very inferior actors' engaged at enormous expense and paid large advances before they left America. They had 'loaded her with insult' and refused to perform their allotted parts.

Lola had told her agent, Freeborough Jones, she could not and would not take him and the others to Melbourne with her and the statement that they might all go to hell applied equally to him. In his affidavit supporting the action, James Simmonds claimed she had told him she was a married woman, something which would have been a defence to the claim because her husband would have been liable – 'which I verily believe to be untrue'.

On 8 September, Lola, with Follin – by now almost certainly her lover – and the violinist Charles Eigenschenk, who remained loyal, sailed for Melbourne on the SS *Waratah*. She had still not learned the necessity of a quick exit left. The one-time opera singer Mrs Fiddes had an attachment warrant issued and the corpulent bailiff Thomas Brown was on deck to serve it. What Lola had learned, however, was that Sydney bailiffs were not made of the same stuff as London policemen. The story goes that when Brown knocked on her cabin door she called out that she was naked and had no intention of dressing; if he wished, he could arrest her in the flesh. Discretion was the better part of valour and he declined. Wrong, he said in a letter to the newspapers. He had thrown the summons on the bed. Lola had made what is colonially termed a 'bolt' of it.

In the same edition, an unnamed officer on the vessel wrote that Lola had remained fully clothed in the stateroom and the whole thing was Brown's fault. Her solicitor, also on board, had been prepared to lodge £500 against the one writ for £100 but Brown claimed £7,000 was due and would not accept it.[9] Despite his protestations, poor Brown never recovered from the humiliation of the incident and took to drink, another in the long list of men who, one way or another, suffered at Lola's hands.

At 10 am on 11 September the *Waratah* docked off Port Phillips Head. Melbourne was then a very youthful city compared with Sydney. Many roads which twenty-five years later had become main thoroughfares were still uncleared and tree stumps remained in the streets. At what became the railway station at Prince's Bridge, newly arrived immigrants had erected a tented village before they went on to Bendigo and Ballarat. Canton's Bull and Mouth bar in Bourke Street was regarded as the real hive of democracy. The English writer Richard Horne, who at one time commanded a gold escort and at another administered Melbourne's water supply, thought that 'the scenes that are witnessed even during the day half way up Bourke

Street actually surpass anything in St Giles or Covent Garden.' It was not that there were more prostitutes – perhaps around 500 – than in, say, Hamburg, which had a similar overall population, it was just that their drunkenness and bad behaviour were more extreme.

Curiously, supposedly backward Melbourne's first theatre pre-dated that of Sydney and was established almost a decade before that of San Francisco. The first performance had been *The Widow's Victim* on 21 February 1842, and within a matter of months a rash of theatres had arisen, one of which was George Coppin's Queen's at the corner of the street of that name and Little Collins. He then developed the Olympic Theatre, known as the Iron Pot.

Lola's first Australian impresario was John Black. He too was afflicted by her evil eye. Within a matter of weeks after her appearance the bailiffs were in and he went bankrupt, taking to drink. He died in 1866 when returning from England on the SS *London*, which foundered in the Bay of Biscay. Lola opened in *Lola Montez in Bavaria* at the Royal Victorian Theatre two days after her arrival. It was a handsome place, built to seat 3,000 people and with accommodation for a further 500 on benches. There were six bars, varying from thirty to 150 feet in length, they included one known as the Saddling Paddock where the barmaids wore tights and which was populated by girls 'in pink bonnets and cheeks to match'. Richard Horne wrote:

> Between every act it is the custom of the audience to rush out to the bars for a nobbler of brandy or other drinks. They all think they need it what-ever the weather may be. The only exceptions are the occupants of the dress circle. More especially on those public occasions when the Gover-nor is present as patron. As the dress circle has never more than a sprin-kling on ordinary nights the house is nearly emptied at the close of every act and not very quickly refilled after the curtain has risen again.[10]

Horne may have met Lola when he was travelling in Germany, and he believed she had been instrumental in having his play *Judas Iscariot* staged in Munich. He called on her when she was staying at the Impe-rial Hotel, Collins Street, and remembered that her eyes were of 'deep blue but gave the effect of an extraordinary kind of blackness because of the jet black eyebrows'.[11]

He wrote a burletta, a musical farce, titled *The Fair Chameleon* for her, but it was never produced. He wrote on the manuscript, '[It] may as well be burnt. Nobody but Lola Montez would be able to play it.' Later he lent her a copy of Mrs Crowe's *The Night Side of Nature*, noting in his diary that he would 'never see *that* again'.[12] It was a book which heavily influenced her towards her subsequent plunge to religion.

Lola Montez in Bavaria was slated by the critic of the Melbourne *Age*:

> We do not quarrel with her version of those Bavarian events which cul-
> minated in the 'Affair' of March 1848 . . . Lola is a lady and therefore her
> veracity is unimpeachable. That is a *pun d'onore*, as they say in the penin-
> sula. All we complain of is that the drama entitled 'Lola Montez in
> Bavaria' is utterly destitute of either plot, incident or situation; that the
> dialogue is made up of stilted and clap-trap appeals *ad populum*, stale
> witticisms and exploded jokes. The jokes were indeed so bad, that the
> audience last night, laughed at them contemptuously, the clap-trap was
> so palpable, that the most democratic individual present 'sniggered' at it
> derisively.[13]

He was fortunate not to be horsewhipped.

The repertory was once more a version of her standard fare. There was the comedietta *Morning Call*, a farce, *Eton Boy*, with Lola as both Tom and Fanny Curry, and *Anthony and Cleopatra, Married and Settled*. Crosby was still maintaining his strong-arm tactics to deal with recalcitrant spectators. In Melbourne one man hissed on 14 September and was told that if he continued he would be thrown into the pit.[14] Lola rather approved the tactics. It was in Melbourne that she was an early victim of a stalker when a miner, a 'frightful-looking' old man named Thomas O'Callaghan, leaped on the stage and pursued her waving a pistol which, he said, would 'make an impression on her heart'. He received a modest three days' imprisonment.[15]

On 19 September, a benefit for the actress Mrs Brougham had been cancelled when Lola declined to appear. This was unusual behaviour for her. Normally she was generous in her support of other artistes. The next day she performed her celebrated Spider Dance and on

21 September an attempt was made by a Dr John Milton, once of the local mission, to have her arrested for indecency. He had spent much of the previous week trying to take out a summons and had been turned down on each occasion. Then, when he stood in the pit to protest against the performance, this 'little old gentleman in his rusty black suit, long grey beard, black "nail-can" hat and generally woebegone appearance' had been summarily evicted.

Now he appeared just as the magistrates, the Mayor and Mr Sturt, were about to rise, and lodged his complaint for what amounted to an injunction to prevent further performances. Sturt ruled that the complaint was based on hearsay and refused a warrant, while the Mayor suggested that the proper course of action was a private application for a private summons. Milton tried that course, but Sturt refused to issue one. There was a story that Milton might go to see Lola and beg her in the interests of propriety to desist. There is no account of him having done so, but in any case it would not have benefited him. Lola had already published a letter that the Spider Dance was a national Spanish dance, beloved by everyone from Queen to peasant.[16]

The English-born George Coppin, owner of the Olympic Theatre, was another comedian who mocked Lola and, while Lola was in trouble with Milton, he produced a Spider Dance of his own at the theatre. He galumphed across the stage in a very short skirt, producing from underneath it as a climax 'an enormous animal resembling a spider'. In his act as Billy Barlow, Coppin also sang a song:

> When famed Lola Montez for spiders did look
> I took a leaf out of her very blue book
> The first night she danced she something did show
> Not at all like the spider of Billy Barlow.[17]

Coppin promoted the act with mock posters headed 'Against Vice and Immorality'. Whatever her temper, however, Lola could take a good deal of ribbing. She and Coppin became friends and even appeared together.

Lola in Bavaria had played two more nights before it gave way to *Anthony and Cleopatra* and *Follies of a Night* on 17 September. *Follies of a Night* was an appropriate offering. At 3 am there was an earthquake. According to the former Paris courtesan Mogador, who had married and was in the city with her husband, Lola ran into the street in her night attire. 'She still has her adorable figure and eccentric character.'

Lola sailed for Geelong on 25 September. On her arrival she was taken ill with pains in her head and eyes. She had not been well during her stay in Melbourne, and this time she stayed in her room for a fortnight. The headaches would recur throughout the remainder of her life. When she was well enough to appear the critics were ecstatic.

In Melbourne there was another old friend, the violinist Miska Hauser, who was touring Australia at the time. According to a letter, he saw Lola some days before 4 August 1855. She invited him to her rooms. He was a trifle reluctant because they had parted on poor terms in California, but he went, to find her stretched on a white ottoman smoking cigars and just as beautiful as ever. 'She is still the same, adventurous unrestrained creature, untamed, indiscreet, flighty, pleasure-loving to excess, witty to the point of rudeness and passionate to madness.'[18] However, the dates do not coincide; and either the story is an invention or he was behind with the news.

Lola's detractors had begun to suggest that her looks were fading, but Australian socialite and writer Isobel Massary, who met her by chance, thought otherwise. She recalled: 'Her beauty was startling, her eyes especially were so remarkable I forgot almost to notice the other features of her handsome face.'[19] In Melbourne Lola had been heckled on one occasion and had turned upon the man, whipping up the audience to such an extent that he was roughly handled and thrown out of the theatre. Massey wondered what would have been the result if that had happened in Ballarat.

Because of Lola's illness, some performances had to be cancelled when she reached Geelong as she took to her bed. Generally, though, she was well received there. The critic for the local paper raved about her performance in *Maidens Beware*, which 'drew many a tear'. He even liked the Spider Dance. 'Applause rained on her.'[20]

Lola sailed down the coast, appearing in Adelaide on 13 December 1855. There, in the presence of the state governor and his wife, Sir

Richard and Lady MacDonnell, and a turnout of the Free and
Accepted Masons of South Australia, she played in a benefit for the
widows and orphans of men killed at Sebastopol. Any doubts in the
city of her respectability vanished with it. She always knew how to
please an audience when she wanted, saying on this occasion that it
was 'a constant wish that your charming little city shall experience
increased and continued prosperity, and that no evil shall befall you'.[21]

Now it was time for Lola to go up country. Travel from Melbourne
to Ballarat was by coach. Cobb & Co., founded by the American
Freeman Cobb and his partners, began services from Melbourne to
the Victorian goldfields soon afterwards. Their coaches, stronger than
English ones, were made of American hickory, with leather suspen-
sion that took some of the jolt out of the bumps on the tracks but
could lead to coach sickness. The drivers were Americans who had
worked for companies such as Wells Fargo and were able to control
the horses as they crossed the ruts. Nevertheless, travel in Australia
was hard. William Kelly recalled one of his first experiences in a coach:

> My friend and I tried the inside, but even while motionless the position
> was barely endurable, for the close proximity of the seats brought the
> knees or shins of the passenger unavoidably in contact with the sharp
> edges of that in front, and how it can be borne while bouncing over rocks
> and crab-holes is a mystery scarcely reconcilable even with the Christian
> toleration of the most veteran pilgrims. We therefore selected the hind-
> ermost seat, where we were placed with our backs to the horses and our
> feet supported by a swinging-tray, delighted besides in having it to
> ourselves.
>
> However our gratification was doomed to a speedy dissolution, for as
> the Post-office clock struck and the horses jumped madly off to the wild
> Indian 'Heigh!' of the driver, we very soon found that it required all the
> muscular powers of our arms to retain our places. The violent oscillation
> of these oblong vehicles in rounding corners or avoiding unexpected
> obstacles, the fearful way in which they plunge and dip in uneven
> ground, and the heart-heaving bounds they cause in clearing blind
> drains and broken tree-limbs, require the most liberal exercise of imagi-
> nation to conceive . . .[22]

Nor did he much enjoy the stops for meals. He accepted that coach-breakfasts had never been very ceremonious meals, even in the best-regulated countries, and acknowledged that it would be a 'swap-and-cram affair':

> but I certainly thought that the scramble would be conducted in the true British principles of fair play, where everyone would get a fair start and the devil take the hindmost.

He was sadly disappointed:

> Everything desirable was appropriated *in transitu*. Potatoes were grabbed from the dish on its passage, while chops, steaks and fried bacon were harpooned in like manner before they reached the table.[23]

Gold had been discovered in the area in 1851. Lieutenant-Governor La Trobe, afraid of the influx of fortune hunters and the threat to what was perceived as the colony's social fabric, ordered diggers to pay a licence fee of 30 shillings a month – a sum which those heading for Buninyong, later Ballarrat (sic), could not afford. The diggers refused to pay. When La Trobe's successor tried to force the tax through, the diggers made a stand under the flag of the Southern Cross. On 3 December 1854, redcoated soldiers attacked the stockade at Eureka, Bakery Hill. Twenty-four miners were killed, as were five soldiers. None of those later charged with treason was found guilty. The editor of the *Ballarat Times*, Henry Erle Seekamp, took the miners' part. When the police came to his office the next morning he was found to be typesetting his editorial to end, 'This foul and bloody murder calls to High Heaven for vengeance, terrible and immediate.' He was promptly arrested and charged with sedition. He was given the opportunity to recant, but when he had not done so by the middle of March 1855 the Chief Justice, Sir William à Beckett, sentenced him to six months' imprisonment.[24]

Lola's friend Stephen Massett toured Australia in the autumn of 1856 as a one-man show, giving readings and recitals of such stalwarts as *The Lady of Lyons*, *The Charge of the Light Brigade* and *The Lament of the Irish Emigrant*. Massett was less than impressed with the conditions. He wrote of pouring rain and fearful heat. The mining town of

Ballarat was intensely cold, even in the middle of summer. Stage conditions were primitive. The Drinking and Concert Hall of the Shamrock Hotel was 75 feet by 50 feet, at the end of which was a stage or raised platform upon which stood one of Erard's grand pianos. There was no entrance fee and the profits came from the liquor and cigars consumed. Receipts were immense; the performance could net between £200 and £300 a night. The orchestra conductor received £30 a week:

> The jingling of glasses and clattering of pots, the dense clouds of smoke from the fumes of tobacco and cigars and *not* the choicest brands at that, mixed in with some of the richest colonial Billingsgate that ever came from the mouth of a costermonger, rendered the resort particularly attractive to the refined, the philosophical or intellectual listener.[25]

The Victoria Theatre on Main Road in Ballarat was modelled on Coppin's Olympic, with a 'pit and gallery on the most commodious and improved principles'.[26] Lola made her first appearance there on Saturday 16 February 1856 in *Morning Call* and *Anthony and Cleopatra Married*. The programme itself lasted from 7 pm until 10 pm, after which the seats were removed and dancing commenced. The auditorium held 2,500 and there were two bars, one in the dress circle and the other in the stalls. When Lola obliquely hinted that the miners might show their appreciation in nuggets, she was well rewarded.

    Both her time in Ballarat and the reception she received from her performance were mixed. On 18 February, Henry Seekamp criticised the poor taste of her performance. The next day Lola literally struck back. Naturally, accounts vary as to who landed how many blows, but there is no doubt that their fight took place at the United States Hotel on Old Main Road, where she was staying. That afternoon she had attended a charity lottery at the Star Concert Hall and had won a riding whip. She let it be known that Seekamp was just the man on whom to break it in. When word came to him, he took his own whip and went to the hotel, where he ordered a drink at the bar. Lola had been on the balcony watching the street. Told the little man with glasses was the editor, she went in pursuit, striking first and then rhetorically demanding, 'How dare you attack me in your paper? Will you abuse me again?'

He struck back with whip and fist, before spectators took hold of both combatants. Unfortunately they did not hold them for long enough. When he was released, Seekamp charged at her and they began pulling each other's hair before they were again separated.

Follin now appeared. Seeing Seekamp produce something from his coat, he drew a gun on him, but it turned out that the editor only had a cosh. The crowd now began to pelt him. He made various mooning gestures at them as he retreated to the Charles Napier, while Lola, in triumph, took up her position in the window of the United States Hotel waving her whip in his direction. That night she told her audience, 'I will make Seekamp decamp.' After her performance Lola held a celebratory dinner in her hotel, providing champagne and hand-rolled cigarettes for her guests.[27]

The Melbourne *Punch* saw the match as a draw and made up a twenty-eight-verse quatrain, one verse of which ran:

> Erle Seekamp's face wore a bloody trace
> Of Lola Montez' lash
> Her shoulder fair if it was bare
> Would show a crimson gash.

In fact the whipping of Seekamp was not as heroic as it may seem. He had taken his imprisonment very badly and now, drinking heavily, he was in poor health. Seekamp duly reported the incident and added his own little recollection: 'You say that I ate with you and drank with you and I wonder you did not go further but perhaps you could not call on Mr Crosby [her manager] to prove it.'

She swore out a warrant for criminal libel. In turn he sued her for assault, but both charges were dismissed, the magistrate telling Seekamp: 'You have insulted a woman in a cowardly manner on hearsay, without having met her and with the intention of harming her livelihood. She took revenge openly, in the presence of hundreds of your friends. There is no need for the court to intervene.' Charles Eberlé thought Lola to have been fortunate and considered the magistrate to have been politically biased.[28]

Seekamp may not have admired Lola's performance but the paying customers, the miners, still smarting from their defeat at the Eureka

Stockade, adored her, paying a steep ten shillings to see her and throwing more gold nuggets on to the stage. First, she was Irish rather than English; second, she was still most handsome; and third, as they were to find, she was game enough to go down a mineshaft holding a glass of champagne.

Within months of the whipping Seekamp had not only sold a minority share in the *Ballarat Times* to lawyer Henry Cuthbert but gave up sole proprietorship on 23 October 1856. He died on 19 January 1864 in Queensland, his health ruined by excessive drinking. His widow Clara said of him, 'If he sinned, it was with single-minded aim of bettering the people.'

There were, however, other troubles. Lola might have outwhipped Seekamp but she was no match for the formidable Mrs Crosby. Lola was on a percentage but, despite good houses, her share of the gate seemed suspiciously low, and she thought she had been cheated out of some £80.[29] On 1 March, when an argument broke out between Lola and Crosby in his wife's presence, out came Lola's whip. The stronger Mrs Crosby gave her such a beating with her own weapon that it soon broke; undeterred, she continued with her fists. Lola, so bruised that she could not appear at the evening house, took another beating the next day and temporarily retreated to Melbourne.

That evening James Crosby produced a medical certificate from a Dr Mount to say Lola was unfit to appear. Crosby then introduced his wife on to the stage as the 'whipperess of the whipperess of whippers'. The audience was not amused. They demanded to see Lola, and after a man leaped on the stage and read out the terms of the medical certificate, the spectators demanded their money back.

Curiously, Seekamp seems to have been reasonably fair towards Lola over the whipping she received from Mrs Crosby:

> It appears that Mrs Crosby had not had enough of glory for during the whole of yesterday forenoon she had kept up a sort of hen-crow, and actually made another whipping assault on Lola Montez, using at the time, language the most disgusting that could grace the mouth of a man, much more of a woman. Lola is very severely hurt in several places and it is likely she will not appear again on the stage in Ballarat.[30]

He was quite correct: Lola never again played the town. Instead, on 8 March she appeared at Coppin's Royal Amphitheatre in Melbourne, making the most of her defeat at the hands of Mrs Crosby:

> In direct opposition to the advice of her Medical Attendants, MADAME LOLA MONTEZ (who is still suffering from her injuries received at Ballarat) has been prevailed upon to remain in Melbourne FOR SIX NIGHTS, previous to her engagement at Bendigo, after which she leaves immediately for California, and will make her first appearance before the public since the late outrageous attacks (both Moral and Physical) upon her.

She was given a tremendous reception, told the audience she was 'sure that her enemies would find that they had injured themselves more than they had hurt her' and played to full houses during the week.[31]

On 1 April 1856 she made her first appearance in Bendigo in *The Little Devil*, immediately endearing herself to the miners. That night there was a thunderstorm and the stage was struck by lightning, leaving a three-foot hole in the eaves and injuring two of the cast. Undaunted, she came to the front of the stage to remark, 'I have played the Devil scores of times, but this is the first occasion on which I have been favoured with real thunder and lightning.' If it continued, she said, they wouldn't need 'any sham affair –only a little brandy'.[32]

William Kelly remembered her in the town filling the theatre – with tickets at five shillings – night after night. Whenever she did not feel in the mood to perform the Spider Dance, she would appear before the drop scene like Charles Mathews in *The Critic* and tell a story, or make some excuse which was received with uproarious satisfaction. On her benefit night, when everyone was expecting to see the Spider Dance with all its variations, she failed to appear, but the audience could hear her laughing behind the scenery:

> Then the laughing stopped and one miner called out 'Come on, Lola, damn it, come on ole girl, afore the moon goes down.' She eventually appeared holding her stomach and the miner called out asking if she took the water neat. No, she said, 'Never eat any of your preserved Bendigo lobster; I tried some after the play, and only that I had the good luck of having a stiff spider within reach, I was a gone coon.'

This produced roars of laughter. A spider was an American drink of brandy and lemonade. 'I cannot give you the Spider Dance tonight (spasms) but go all of you and drink honest spiders to my health and I will do the same towards yours.' Shouts of approval. She made to leave the stage and then returned to say, 'To be sure and put the brandy in first.' In fact she rarely let a performance go without an aside or interpolation.

On another occasion there was a call from a miner by way of an oblique proposal: '"Oh but you're a darlint Loly! 'Tis pity yez aren't some dacent man's wife." This produces peals of laughter in which the ex-Queen herself heartily joins.'[33]

There had been suggestions in the *Argus* that she was drinking before the performances, which had led to excessive indelicacy in the Spider Dance. Before her appearance Follin now took to going in front of the curtain to say that Madame never, well only rarely, touched alcohol.

Away from the theatre she would take her turn in buying drinks and charmed the diggers by going down the mineshafts. When invited to christen the great Victoria Reef, she was provided with an armchair gorgeously rigged out for her comfort. Instead she put her foot in the noose and, a glass of champagne in her hand, went down the shaft to wild applause.[34]

In Bendigo William Craig wrote:

> In a few minutes the primitive edifice is so crowded that barely standing room can be obtained . . . The admission is five shillings a head and the packed houses every night demonstrate that the enterprise of the owner or lessee is justified . . . There is no mistaking the leading 'star' when she makes her appearance. She has evidently inherited the best points of her aristocratic father and her handsome Creole mother. One has only to look at her magnificent dark flashing eyes, her willowy form, the traces of former beauty, and her lithe active movements to see that one is in the presence of a very remarkable woman.

Enchanted with her he might have been, but even he noticed the voice of the prompter 'distinctly audible in every part of the building'.[35]

It was not always plain sailing. Lola was getting tired, and there was an unfortunate incident when she played Castlemaine town, which like

Melbourne still had tree stumps in the main road. When she appeared there on 10 April she told the miners she was too tired to perform the Spider Dance, and was promptly hissed and jeered with shouts of 'coward'. As usual she turned on her audience, telling them she was worth £70,000 and did not care a pin for them. The miners replied that they had paid ten shillings of good money. She refused again three nights later, dismissing the town with the words that for a small town it had too many churches. She then told one hisser he should go back to school and learn not to hiss what he did not understand. She had held five million lives in her hands in Bavaria and because she did not sacrifice them, as a result she was now appearing here.[36]

She was back in Bendigo at the end of April, where she earned another £1,500 and was presented with a silver snuffbox by Henry Coleman. With the money he made from her he was able to lease the Lyceum in Queen Street, Melbourne, as well as the 'elegant drawing-room' Victoria theatre in St Kilda.[37]

The American newspapers kept tabs on Lola in her absence. On 26 April 1856 the *New York Daily Times* reported that a California correspondent of the *Mobile Advertiser* had written:

> Near where I am writing is the 'cottage' formerly the residence of the renowned Lola Montez. Since her departure for Australia, the place seems neglected and going to decay and, like its mistress, its attractions are rapidly fading away. Her large and costly green-house of exotics is going to ruin, its glass broken and her vases and flower pots are broken and scattered, and her flower garden surrounding her residence and planted and nourished by her at great cost and care, has gone to waste – 'sic transit gloria mundi'.

It went on to say that the tour had not been a success and she was returning to Grass Valley

> to spend the rest of her chequered life. She finds the charm that attached to her earlier life departed, and though she still seems determined to preserve her name notorious, if not immortal, she now finds few so poor as to do her reverence.[38]

In its vision of the future the paper was only partly correct.

· CHAPTER SEVENTEEN ·

→>-<←

Lola Changes Jobs

On 28 June 1856 Lola's problems with the English courts finally came to an end when George Trafford Heald died at the Pavilion Hotel, Folkestone, at the age of twenty-eight. He had been suffering from phthisis for some three or four years. He also had ulceration of the bowels. Unsurprisingly there was no legacy for her in his will, dated 6 May 1855. He left his aunt some pictures, minor gifts including £200 to his groom, and the rest to the Hon. Caroline Sambley of Maidstone for life, with the residue to her children.[1]

On 19 May 1856, five weeks before Heald's death, Lola Montez and Follin arrived in Newcastle, New South Wales and boarded the *Jane A. Falkenberg* for America. The *Falkenberg* was perhaps not a lucky ship. In January its owner, Captain Charles Falkenberg, had died in a carriage-driving accident on Folsom Street, San Francisco. The horse became unruly and backed the carriage off the wharf, killing the captain and slightly injuring his wife.

Hardly had her bags been unpacked when Lola went on shore, and with a posse of Yankee skippers and other passengers went to view the Pacific. The next day they sailed from Sydney for San Francisco via Tahiti and Honolulu. It was a spirited if not altogether happy voyage. There were strong eastern breezes to Tahiti and on to Honolulu. On 4 July, Second Officer William N. Rumsville blew off his hand when lighting the holiday fireworks and three days later the ship put in to Honolulu to land him. Lola took the opportunity to spend some time on shore. Time was beginning to tell on her. 'The expression on her countenance was pleasing, but seems to show a careworn look. We should judge her to be about forty.'[2] That, or things were not going well with Follin. There had been troubles between them in Melbourne; the writer Richard Horne had intervened when Lola attempted to stab Follin with a pair of scissors at a dinner party at the Imperial Hotel. There were also stories that Lola had upset Follin by having a brief affair with Major-General Charles Wellesley, the younger brother of the 2nd Duke of Wellington. There had been further troubles in Bendigo when, after a spat, he had refused to appear on stage. Lola came before the curtain to denounce him, saying that she had never allowed personal quarrels to stop her appearance.[3] Any lingering thoughts of a tour of Asia had long disappeared.

The *Falkenberg* sailed again on the evening of 7 July. Sometime during the next night, not long out of Honolulu, Follin went overboard. Naturally there were a number of versions of how he came to drown; the least favourable to Lola was that she pushed him. Another version is that he committed suicide after a quarrel, jumping overboard with the tour takings in his pocket. John H. McCabe in his diary has it that Follin was sleeping on deck.[4]

The semi-official version is one of a tragic accident: '[Follin] was drowned on the anniversary of his birth, which was being celebrated with a supper. He stepped on deck to empty a glass, and being somewhat under the influence of champagne, a sudden lurch of the vessel pitched him overboard.'[5] His headstone at Woodlawn Cemetery reads 'And the sea shall give up its dead'. The *Golden Era*, which generally supported Lola, wrote:

The admirers of the 'Divine Lola' will be pained to hear that the death of Folland, her 'agent' has nearly unseated her reason. Ever since the event she has mourned and refused to be comforted. She says he was the first and only man she ever loved – which is quite complimentary to her two husbands – and will henceforth cast aside the foolish vanities of life, and

gather jewels which rust not and gold which never perisheth . . . For
several days Lola seemed almost distracted, a demonstration of grief
which at length gave place to a settled gloom and indifference to everything. One of the best evidences that her anguish is real is that she no
longer uses narcotics and stimulants. She has lost her taste for cigarettes
and cobblers. May she recover and live to break a thousand hearts.[6]

There is only very circumstantial evidence to support the theory that
Follin was pushed rather than that he jumped or slipped. It is based
principally on the story that when Lola met Follin's mother she threw
herself on the woman's feet, saying she had killed her son.[7] This may
rather have been the great actress conning another part. But there is
no doubt she did feel responsible for Follin's death. From then on her
behaviour gradually began to change, many would say for the better.

Nor were things good for the theatre in San Francisco when Lola
landed. That year the city was in the grip of a struggle by the Second
Committee of Vigilance to combat the growing and corrupt influence
of the politician David C. Broderick, who had purchased Tom
Maguire's Jenny Lind Theatre for $200,000 to use as the City Hall. In
1855 two-thirds of the 489 murders in California had taken place in the
city, while not a single murderer there had been punished. On 14 May
James P. Casey shot James King of William near the corner of Montgomery and Washington Streets. King of William (who adopted that
name because he was the fourteenth James King working on Washington) had accused Broderick of importing Casey, a ballot stuffer,
from New York where he had been in prison in Sing Sing. The next day
the Second Committee of Vigilance was formed. Justice was swift. On
22 May, before an estimated crowd of 20,000, Casey was hanged along
with gambler and brothel owner Charles Cora, convicted of shooting
General W. H. Richardson, United States Marshal for the Northern
District of California. Richardson's wife had complained that Cora's
prostitute girlfriend Arabella Ryan had been in the audience at the
American Theatre to watch *Nicodemus or the Unfortunate Fisherman*.

Nine days later the prize-fighter Yankee Sullivan, another alleged
ballot-stuffer, either committed suicide in his cell at the vigilante
headquarters or, more likely, was murdered by the vigilantes them-

selves. On 3 June Governor Johnson declared that San Francisco was in a state of insurrection. By 18 August order had been restored, and the committee was voluntarily disbanded after a march by some 6,000 to 8,000 armed men. Broderick continued his corrupt ways unhindered until, on 11 September 1859, he was shot in a duel with his former friend and helpmate Judge David S. Terry, of the California Supreme Court, over comments that he had made that Terry was corrupt. The duel ensured Broderick's martyrdom and, after his acquittal in Marin County on a charge of murder, Terry's ostracism.[8]

Once Lola landed in San Francisco she announced she would put her entire collection of jewellery up for auction, the proceeds to go to support Follin's children. She also made a will leaving her estate to Mrs Susan Follin in trust for his children. Now Lola took a small iron house in the city, 'and hung it with gay cages with many coloured birds about the rooms and walked around the streets with a magnificent white cockatoo perched on her shoulder and a pack of dogs at her heels'.[9]

With Lola still at sea the managers had partially rallied. A new eastern star, Julia Dean Hayne, had appeared at the Metropolitan to reopen what was to be an insecure season for the legitimate theatre. On stage Lola was in the hands of the Chapmans, who were now managing the American. On 7 August she appeared there as Mrs Chillington in *The Morning Call* opposite Uncle Billy, before switching the next night to *Lola in Bavaria*. After running through the repertory, out came the Spider Dance. She may have played with the Chapmans, but on a spare night they burlesqued her in *The Trip to Australia: Lola Montez on the Fanny Major*. Uncle Billy Chapman gave a male spider dance, but Lola seems to have taken it in good part. Perhaps, because of Follin, her horsewhipping days were over; perhaps it was because she was in the Chapmans' power. They compounded their bad behaviour when, on the eve of the jewellery sale, they played the piece again. This time the San Francisco papers were united in Lola's defence. Perhaps the Chapmans thought the sale was just another publicity stunt; unrepentant, they continued to play the piece on a regular basis with a good deal of success.[10]

In October Lola appeared as the Duchess of Chartres in *Follies of a*

Night at the Metropolitan, with Junius Brutus Booth Jr., and then in *Anthony and Cleopatra*. The second night she played Asmodeus and gave the Spider Dance. *Charlotte Corday* and the Italian Tarantella made up the third night and the fourth was *Pas de Matelot* and another Spider Dance. The fifth and final night saw her once more as *Yelva* – the limit of her repertoire, and presented as something new.

On her return one paper thought she had actually improved.[11] The *Daily Evening Bulletin* thought otherwise. 'It is vain to oppose nature. It is very plain however, to all but herself that . . . her dancing days are over.'[12] Unfortunately, although she was initially well received it was the same old story. Nevertheless she had a reasonably good two weeks at the American.[13]

In contrast, the auction conducted by Duncan & Company on 8 September 1856, of eighty-nine lots of 'jewellery comprising chains, medallions, Australian goldwork, a diamond set, and watches' – including a ruby and diamond ring which, she told the auctioneer, had been given to her by Louis Napoleon[14] – was not a great success; the items fetched less than $10,000.[15] The outcome might have been better had she been at the auction to present the jewels to the successful bidder, but by then she had travelled to Sacramento to play *Follies of a Night* at the Forrest Theatre.

After Sacramento Lola returned to Grass Valley. Times were changing. She may have avoided the financial depression of 1855 but from then on there were signs of social change. The miners were moving towards middle-class respectability. Conduct became more decorous as bonds of correct behaviour began to tighten.[16] Lola sold her house, 'which Southwick had deeded her, over his head, and departed from Grass Valley never to return'.[17] According to some reports, she continued her efforts to lure Lotta Crabtree away to the stage, Lotta's mother becoming so concerned that Lola was going to kidnap her daughter that she hid her away until the Countess had left the area.[18]

Nor, that year, were things going well for her legitimate husband. Thomas James had survived the life-threatening illness he suffered in 1852. Now, promoted major, he was still in India. On 12 November it was discovered that nearly 1,000 rupees was missing from the Kotah contingent and he was being blamed. It was another scrape from which he extricated himself without too much loss of face and certainly none of rank.[19]

Now on 20 November, Thanksgiving Day, Lola boarded the *Orizaba* to sail to the East Coast where she intended to provide for Follin's children. That evening her protégée, Lotta Crabtree, made her first appearance on the legitimate stage at the American. The next night she was replaced by the other child prodigy from Grass Valley; the ill-fated Susan Robinson was billed for the first time as 'The Fairy Star'.[20]

Unsurprisingly Lola was not well received by Follin's estranged widow. But now she turned her attention to his mother, Susan Follin, and his half-sister, the wild Miriam. The mother was impressed by Lola's demonstration of grief, while the astute Miriam realised that here was a ready-made entry through the stage door.

Like Lola at the same age, Miriam had already racked up a few social black marks. Principally, at the age of seventeen she had fallen in love with – or at least had allowed herself to be seduced by – a jewellery store clerk, David Peacock. Mrs Follin, displaying far more skill than Mrs Gilbert, had dealt with the situation admirably. She had Peacock arrested and forced him to marry Miriam on the understanding that he would not be required to live with her. Once the wedding had taken place the charges were dropped and both went their separate ways.[21]

Lola, in her declining years, was now completely overwhelmed by the girl, whom she saw as a younger sister. Miriam's training was as brief as that Lola had herself undertaken; but, in almost every way, Miriam had far more talent than her mentor.

On 23 January 1857 the *New York Times* reported that Lola was living quietly but in some style at 13 Stuyvesant Place, owned by Miriam and Noel's father, Charles Follin, and was preparing to bring the sixteen-year-old to the stage. Lola had netted $23,000 from *Lola Montez in Bavaria* in California alone. A lecture tour of England was also said to be on the cards, after which she would write her memoirs.[22]

On 2 February 1857 Miriam, billed as Lola's sister Minnie Montez, appeared at the Green Theatre, Albany, opening in the old faithful *The*

Eton Boy and *Follies of a Night*. There was no questioning where this teenage sibling had suddenly sprung from. Two days later they shared the billing in *The Cabin Boy*, a two-act melodrama by Edward Stirling. Minnie played the part of 'Jenny from Dominique', whose 'whole life has been a strange mystery'. It was pretty standard abolitionist fare. Declared to be the daughter of a Frenchman and a slave, Minnie was auctioned off at the block, only to be saved from a life of degradation by Lola as the heroine. Even though Minnie's acting ability at the time seems to have been confined to a great deal of hand-wringing and piteous looks, it was a huge success. Later in the week they appeared together in *Lola Montez in Bavaria* and *Maidens Beware*. On 7 February Lola performed the Spider Dance.[23]

Their greatest success, however, came at the end of the week when they were due to travel to Providence for their next engagement. It was a hard winter and on 20 January there was a major snowstorm in New York City. In Albany it had rained heavily during the week and the icy Hudson burst its banks, drowning cattle, bringing down houses and stores and flooding the basement of the theatre. Instead of acting sensibly and going to Troy (now New York State), Lola embarked on another publicity stunt. On 9 February she offered $100 for anyone who would row her and Minnie across the river and through its floating ice:

> The indomitable Lola Montez, (and her sister) who had been playing a theatrical engagement at Albany, desired for some purpose known to herself to cross the river, and nothing daunted at the fearful danger before her, challenged some boatmen to take her across, and after a perilous voyage she was safely landed being the first person after the storm who accomplished this feat. The men in coming back became exhausted and were carried with the floating ice below the city.[24]

In the event the men managed to make the shore but on the way over, much of the sisters' baggage was lost. Nevertheless it was tremendous publicity for Lola and Minnie. Their reward was the paragraph in *Frank Leslie's Weekly News* and sold-out houses. The first night at Forbes' Theatre drew an audience of 2,000. From there it was on to Pittsburgh.

The fortnight was a great success but their association ended, possibly because Minnie developed her abilities so quickly that she became a challenge to her mentor. Or perhaps she resented playing second fiddle. It is also possible that Lola, now moving into her religious and moral phase, took exception to Miriam's sexual adventures.

Not everyone accepted that Minnie was Lola's sister and there were constant rumours about her lineage. When in June 1857 Minnie returned to Albany to play at the Green Street Theatre in *Plot and Passion*, a three-act drama, she ignored the comment that 'a young debutante is being palmed off as a sister of the famous Lola'.[25] Two months later the jig was finally up. Minnie Montez was definitely revealed as Follin's sister. 'Lola Montez has a kind heart with all her faults', thought the *Golden Era*.[26]

On 28 February 1857 Lola had a benefit in Pittsburgh. It was a great success; not even standing room was available. She still had not learned to follow the music, however, and that night she quarrelled publicly with M. Zittebart, the violinist leading the orchestra, complaining he was playing too fast. When he replied she turned back to the audience: 'Ladies and gentlemen – this is unpleasant. You are treated to more than you were promised. But you cannot complain – it is so cheap.' They started over again, but the audience would not let her leave without an encore. Another spider was killed, to tremendous applause and three cheers for Lola.[27]

Her often triumphant tour in the spring of that year was marred by tempers and illness. Her appearances in Louisville ended suddenly after she complained about a carpet and refused to appear unless it was replaced. On 10 April a full house waited until the manager, George Mellus, conceded; flushed with that triumph, she refused to appear at all. The *Louisville Daily Democrat* thought she had insulted the crowds who had turned out in bad weather for her benefit. Her contract was terminated the next day and on 12 April she left for Cincinnati, standing on the wharf waiting for the boat and displaying complete indifference towards those who had come to stare at her. Her bad behaviour did her next engagement no harm at all. 'Cincinnatians are a curious people. They are fond of notoriety and hence the reason the Countess of Landsfeld draws such houses,' thought a local paper.[28]

She was reported to have been taken seriously ill in St Louis in May.[29] Undoubtedly she was slowing down. The level of fitness required to perform the Spider Dance was gone, her body wasted by cigars, travel, consumption and possibly syphilis. It is a measure of her spirit and courage that she continued as long as she did.

Lola's career on the stage was coming to an end that summer. On 17 July 1857 she appeared at the Royal Lyceum, Toronto, where she gave her last performance of the Spider Dance. Three days later she cancelled her appearance. On 21 July she appeared in *Lola in Bavaria*, on the 23rd as *Charlotte Corday* and on the 24th in *Margot the Poultry Dealer* and *Betsy*. It was her last recorded performance as a dancer.

With her dancing career over, Lola looked about for suitable alternative employment. And she found it – as have so many when their activities on the playing field come to a close – on the lecture circuit. For the first months she combined it with a few more stage appearances. The series of lectures were organised by the Rev. Chauncey Burr and his father Heman, whom she had met the previous year in New York and into whose clutches she fell when she employed Chauncey as her agent in July 1857.[30]

They were a curious pair and over the next three years they almost literally worked her to death. Heman Merrick Burr was born in England and married in Leicester in 1813. His son Charles was said in his youth to be one of the most handsome of men. At one time a Universalist minister and influential Democrat, he edited *Odd Fellows Magazine* and numerous other publications. He believed that the Negro had never been destined by nature 'for a man and a brother', that he belonged to an inferior race and was therefore destined for slavery.[31] An anti-abolitionist and pro-secessionist, Burr was a curious religious and political bedfellow for Lola. Some years later an article appeared in the Chicago *Daily News* in which the writer said he had met Burr and Lola:

> Burr was an extraordinary person . . . He was a man of great force of character, such character as he possessed. Like his notorious namesake Aaron Burr, he had apparently great power not only over women but also over men . . . How Burr got interested in Lola Montez I have no means of

knowing. Accordingly he 'worked the oracle' as long as the venture proved profitable. My impression at the time was that the lectures Lola delivered were by Burr.[32]

Others were not even so charitable in their views:

> Burr, a dissolute whale of a New York bay remarkable for suction, spout and tallow, declared that the cowardice of the Democratic party had ruined the country. Mr Burr may be one of the 'unterrified' but we are not aware of his having exposed his person to danger except by acting as private secretary to Lola Montez and other less notorious females ... Like most Burrs he cares very little whether he sticks to a black sheep or a white one.[33]

Burr was undoubtedly in the mould of Lola's collection of hangers-on. The *Illustrated News of the World* thought that after Burr had failed as a newspaperman and Lola's stage career was coming to an end, 'the moral-lecture dodge was decided on and the Rev. C.C.B. produced to order this very pretty hash of dull common-places, plagiarisms, cuttings, stale anecdotes, cribs, fudges and parodies'.[34]

That may be so – although certainly as time went on Lola took more and more of a hand in writing the lectures – but they were highly successful. On 27 July, dressed modestly and beginning to eliminate the last traces of her Spanish accent – although throughout her mother remained Spanish – she commenced her new career at the Mechanic's Hall in Hamilton, Ontario. 'Beautiful Women' was her lecture about celebrated beauties of the past, the differences in what one nation perceived as beauty compared with another, with the addition of some hints on health and hygiene. No alcohol, but every woman should ensure her home had a bath. There was also a daring reference to a harem in Constantinople which Lola had visited through the assistance of Sir Stratford Canning – which, since she had never been near Turkey, was a hitherto unrecorded episode in her career. It all went down well enough and there was a repeat performance four nights later in Buffalo. Then came 'The Origin and Power of Rome', her latest attack on Catholicism. Right enough in the Dark Ages but a backward step since the Renaissance; it was Protestantism which had delivered the 'four greatest facts of modern times – steam-boats, railroads, telegraphs and the American republic'. Then it was on to Burlington and Rochester. And as her delivery improved, so the crowds increased and the papers wrote more and more favourably of her performances. No band to have to try to follow, nothing to learn, no expensive costumes to be transported, no more talented actors and dancers with whom to compete, just Lola in a modest dress and wearing no jewellery, reading for an hour; rather shorter than the usual lecture of the time.

Sensibly she did not give her lecture on Rome in Montreal, which she visited at the end of August, but it did not save her from a lashing in the newspapers. The *Witness* began the attack: 'The notorious Lola Montez is about to lecture in this city. It is to be hoped that respectable people will not degrade themselves by forming part of her audience.'

Off went a letter to the rival newspaper the *Pilot*, in which she maintained she was earning her money as honestly as the editor of the *Witness*. She pitied and forgave him. If he practised the precept of the Master he would never throw stones at her or anyone else again. And, cowed into silence, he did not – at least in her direction. Instead *La Minerve* took up the challenge: 'What mother who has gone to hear this could return to her family and expect esteem and authority?'[35]

The answer was hundreds – and fathers as well. Lola's lectures, including the new 'Wits and Women of Paris', were sold out. This was Lola back among the literati – Dumas, Victor Hugo, her old friend Roger de Beauvoir,[36] George Sand. There was a touch of spice in the story of Dumas' marriage, a touch of religion and morality. Perhaps Lola was speaking of herself when she repeated the story told her by George Sand of seeing

a beautiful girl who, asked by a student where she was going, replied 'nowhere'. 'Then', said the student, 'as we are bound for the same place, we will both go together.'

How many of those girls that go 'nowhere' would have been types of noble, industrious, frugal women, are fallen down and run over by the waysides of life, without one good Samaritan to lift them up again, and to tell that we have all to live to go – somewhere.[37]

Throughout the autumn, when 'Gallantry' and 'Heroines of History and Strong-minded Women' were added to the repertory, Lola plied her new trade up and down the eastern seaboard from Boston to Washington. King Ludwig was given a fine encomium in the former lecture. Not only was he 'one of the cleverest men of genius in all Europe', he was 'one of the most refined and high-toned gentlemen of the old school of manners'. Perhaps it was fortunate Lola took no questions at the end of her lectures. As for 'Heroines', they included Cleopatra and Catherine the Great as well as, by implication, herself. She did not help her standing with the burgeoning feminist movement:

> One woman going forth in the independence and power of self-reliant strength to assert her own individuality, and to defend, with whatever means God has given her, her right to a just portion of the earth's privileges, will do more than a million of convention-women to make herself known and felt in the world.

And the ending of her talk would certainly not have appealed to the Claflin sisters or Lucy Stone – or, for that matter, to more modern feminists:

> But she is still far the happiest, and, ordinarily the most useful woman, who has no ambition beyond the sphere that completes the duties of a happy and virtuous home.[38]

In theory, Lola's lecture tours were coming to an end. The *Philadelphia Press* noted rather coyly:

> We have to state with much gratification, that this is the close of Madame Lola Montez's career as a public lecturer. We break no confidence and do not intrude on the secrecy of private life by mentioning that this fair and gifted woman is on the eve of a very brilliant matrimonial alliance. She proposes in ten days from this time to be en route to Paris. Her return to this country for a short visit may be expected in the spring.[39]

What was this then and who was to be the lucky bridegroom? It was another of the extraordinary incidents in her life. She was either duped, or deceived herself into believing, that Prince Ludwig Johann

Sulkowski, a forty-three-year-old Austrian whom she had met in Berlin thirteen years earlier, and of whom there is no record that she had contact over the years, was going to marry her in Paris. Sulkowski had left Austria after the 1848 revolutions across Europe. He first travelled to Switzerland and then on to the United States, where he had settled in upstate New York as a farmer and married. Now he had five children. The theory was that he was, at last, to be allowed to return to his homeland and reclaim his estates.

In fact Lola was still not in a position to marry. Heald was dead but James was still very much alive and, assuming there had been no Californian divorce, so for that matter was Patrick Hull. Although she must by now have known the law, this was not a serious consideration for her. On 12 December 1857 she sailed on the *Fulton* to Le Havre to meet her fiancé.[40]

Unsurprisingly the Prince was not there to meet her on Christmas Day. The next day, also unsurprisingly in a very bad temper, she boxed the ears of a man who accidentally trod on her skirt near the rue de la Vieille Comédie. A week later, on 2 January, she sailed from Liverpool on the *America* to Boston. On her return it was reported that she had married Sulkowski, and indeed over the weeks she still maintained she would soon marry. But as time went by she explained that she had broken off the engagement because the Prince was travelling with a well-known singer as man and wife.

Later, in her lectures, she named Sulkowski as a one-time fiancé and partially explained:

> It is one of the romances of life that after so many years he should, in this far-off Republican land seek and obtain the promise of the hand of one who had seen enough of the vices of nobility to have reasonably disenchanted her of all its baubles of honor. But every woman has a right to be a little foolish on that subject of marriage and Lola Montez, (I hope she will forgive me for telling family secrets) did engage herself to marry Prince Schulkoski; but alas for the constancy, or inconstancy, of human love, whilst the noble Prince was furiously telegraphing kisses three times a day to his affianced bride, he was merrily travelling through the South, with a celebrated singer. Putting his own name and title in his pocket and

conveniently assuming that of the Prima Donna, they booking themselves as plain Mr and Mrs – at the hotels.

She added that when she discovered the truth:

I leave you who probably have some general knowledge of Lola Montez, to judge of what followed. If the course of true-love never did run smooth it is more than probable that it was not particularly so when the Prince returned from his musical journey to the South.[41]

Nothing about transatlantic crossings and Paris hats.

Apologists for Lola present the affair as a cruel hoax, either by Sulkowski or an unidentified third party, but this begs a number of questions. How did she come into contact again with Sulkowski and get so close to him that marriage was even a possibility? Did she make no inquiries about him? There were plenty of detective agencies operating, including Pinkertons. Why on earth did he – after all these years – participate in such a cruel hoax? Just what had she done to him that he bore such resentment as to send her across the Atlantic in midwinter on a fool's errand? There is nothing whatsoever to show that she had treated him so badly that he and his friends had devised this long-term revenge. Much more likely is that Lola was beginning to suffer from delusions and that this whole affair was a manifestation of them.

The press had no doubt that the Prince was innocent: 'The Prince Sulkowski who is residing quietly in Lewis Co., New York with his wife and five children is somewhat surprised to find the papers intent on marrying him to Lola Montez, an arrangement in which he has not been consulted.'[42]

On her return Lola, now once again apparently in financial straits, took a room at 25 Bayard Street in the Bowery with Otto von Hoym, the manager of the German Stadttheater, and his family. It was back to lecturing for a living at the Hope Chapel, where in the first eight days of February she spoke three times, twice on 'Beautiful Women' followed up by 'Wits and Women of Paris'.

Meanwhile she took to travelling on public transport, where her portmanteau was stolen by a pickpocket. He escaped but dropped the wallet, and she remarked she was pleased he had avoided arrest. It did him little good. Tommy Hogan was caught and identified a few days later.[43]

Then, wreathed in the bosom of religion, Lola gave one of the worst displays of behaviour of her latter years. In London in the 1840s she had known the charlatan historian, dentist and would-be politician David Wemyss Jobson, with whom she had once casually discussed writing her memoirs. They would probably never have appeared, because although Jobson claimed to have written a *History of the French Revolution* in thirty-seven volumes it was never published. Now she was called as a character witness for the defence to discredit Jobson in an action brought against a Norman Griffin for work allegedly done in a court case on his behalf. Jobson thought he should receive $25 a day. The claim was heard by Referee John N. Whiting. The New York courts of the day were far more informal than their British counterparts and, before the proceedings degenerated entirely into farce, the cross-examination was good knockabout stuff. Lola set off in style with her first remark from the witness box:

> Before I answer any questions I wish to be guaranteed that I shall not be insulted by this person, Mr Jobson, Attorney of London. I have been in his clutches before.
> Whiting: I will guarantee that you shall be protected here.
> LM: I want to be protected from insolence, violence and black-mailing.

When C. B. Schermerhorn for Jobson referred to his client as 'Doctor', Lola wanted to know:

> LM: *Dr Jobson!* Who is Dr Jobson? I don't know any Dr Jobson. Are you a Dr Jobson? How long since? You introduced yourself to me as Jobson Attorney at Law in London.

When Schermerhorn objected, she responded, 'There are some women who have more brains than some men who are fools.' She then corrected Schermerhorn's pronunciation, saying she could not bear to hear bad English spoken, and adding:

LM: You may examine my character and I hope you can show as clean hands as I. I would not believe [Jobson] on his oath; he was known as a jail bird in London: I knew him in Paris; he asked my husband for two guineas blackmail; I have heard of him in New York from two or three people whom he has very much annoyed.

Jobson: [to reporter] Sit between me and Lola; she'll scratch my face before she's through.

She proceeded to give a somewhat fanciful resumé of her life:

LM: . . . I was married to James near Dublin; he ran away with another lady about a year after I was married. I was living in Mugeer, India. I lived there about seven years. From there I came to England I think in 1842. I don't know how long I remained in London after I returned.

Her father was adjutant-general of the Bengal army. She married in 1840 and came to England in about 1842 where she had lodged with an old Scotchman and his wife. Her husband had falsely accused her of an intrigue with Lennox. She had been practising ballet under Espa. Asked about Munich:

LM: I was engaged in political business. You might call me a prime-minister if you please. Or as the king said I was the king. There was a man of straw there as prime-minister but he was only a man of straw.

The hearing was adjourned and the next night she gave a lecture on 'Gallantry' at the Hope Chapel. She returned there a few days later, when on 15 February, in front of a large audience, she spoke on 'Strong-minded Women'. Then it was back in court on 18 February.

In view of the allegations Lola had made, the *New York Daily Times* wondered whether it would be prudent to send a commission to examine the police archives in London and Paris. The suggestion was not taken up. At the resumed hearing Lola was at her most magnificent and mendacious, her evidence a mixture of repartee, reconstruction and downright lies. Straight away C. B. Schermerhorn went for the throat. First came some truth:

LM: My name is Lola Montez; my family name was Maria Rosanna Gilbert.

S: Where were you born?

LM: In the beautiful town of Limerick.

S: How old are you?

LM: Thirty-three.

S: When were you born?

LM: Count, I cannot tell; I wasn't present when I was born. I have two husbands and I am on the point of having a third; my first husband was Captain James.

Of course, strictly speaking, she could not say what her age was; it is hearsay evidence. As to the remainder of the answer, Lola, despite overwhelming evidence to the contrary, must have still been persisting in the myth that she was going to marry Sulkowski. Hull, as the current third husband, had clearly been forgotten. Lola must have had something of the Mormon in her:

S: Were you married to James?

LM: The ring was put on my finger by a clergyman, but my spirit was never united to him.

S: What other husbands have you had?

LM: Now, wait a moment; I'd never have you, be sure.

Now Lola appears to have switched into the third-person persona she adopted for her lectures. Not surprisingly, Schermerhorn was confused:

LM: I remained in Spain a few months, learning to dance; I was travelling perfectly alone, as I travel now; there was a charming little girl named Dolores, whose husband had deserted her.

S: For you?

LM: No, no, I never did any of that sort of thing.

And, to be fair, with the possible exceptions of Liszt, whose mistress took great exception to Lola, and Ludwig, who was a serial adulterer himself, snatching other people's husbands was not in her line of work. Lola borrowed rather than stole the men. The cross-examination moved to her time in Munich; count the number of lies in her next replies:

LM: Mr Wittelsbacher he was called – that was his family name.

S: Were you the mistress of the king?

LM: [rising] What! [Emphatically] No, Sir. You are a villain, Sir; I'll take my oath on that book [the Bible], which I read every night, I had no intrigue with that old man; I knew the king and molded the mind of the king in the love of freedom; he took me before the whole court with his wife, and presented me as his best friend. I was in Bavaria in 1847 and 1848; in 1849 the Revolution occurred and liberty and I fled.

Now the questioning moved back to Lola's character generally and Schermerhorn turned to smearing her. He would have been pulled up smartly by an English judge unless he had evidence with which to back his claims:

S: Didn't Mr Jobson subscribe a guinea to prevent you from being taken to the watchhouse?

LM: He hadn't a guinea.

S: Did he not give you a guinea to keep you from taking to the streets for a living?

LM: [Indignantly rising] Am I to be insulted? Gentlemen, will you not protect me?

Referee: Mr Schermerhorn should not have asked the question.

LM: Schermerhorn! Is that his name? Oh, ho! I shall have some questions to ask of *him*.

Admission for the evening session was by ticket only, with two policemen in attendance. Neither Schermerhorn nor his client, who carried a silver-topped riding crop, had a happy time. First:

S: Madame, was your name not originally Betsy Watson?

LM: I don't choose to answer. I will answer no unimportant questions, or untrue questions . . . I will answer, if you please, whatever is right; but when I don't answer a question, remember, it is one which is a falsehood in the minds of those men. [Pointing to Jobson and Schermerhorn]

Schermerhorn then suggested she had been born in Montrose and that her mother was Mary or Molly Watson:

LM: It is not a very pretty name, Sir. Anybody would have chosen a better name for a tinker.

And when the questions became repetitive:

LM: There is no use my answering most absurd questions. He might ask me whether I did not murder Mrs Cunningham or Dr Burdell.[44]

LM: May I answer Yankee fashion one question with another back? . . . I have much to ask this Mr Schermerhorn, or Skrekhorn, or whatever his name is. I have some little questions about a lady that you beat the other day, when you were brought before the Police Court.

And so it degenerated, with Schermerhorn asking whether she had been an assistant chambermaid in the Star Hotel in Montrose. After interventions by Whiting and Frederick Seeley, acting for the defendant, Lola finally replied:

LM: I was not born there; you cannot make me out a chambermaid; it is not a dishonest thing, either, if I was; I should have considered myself a far greater woman if I had been born a chambermaid than I am today. Why, Sir, how do you know anything about me, or that I was a chambermaid?

S: I would say to this woman – this lady, I will call her –

LM: Pray call me a woman – I am proud to be a woman. Your mother was a woman! [Laughter].

The hearing broke up completely after Seeley referred to Jobson as 'that fellow'. Jobson shouted, 'If you call me a fellow again, you vagabond shyster, I'll let you see!' Lola now provided a running if indiscriminate commentary: 'You won't lay a hand on me as you did on that other woman that you were brought up for the other day to the police . . . Do take him off to The Tombs. He was there before.'

Seeley then threatened to throw Jobson through the window. Jobson struck at him with his whip and fighting broke out, the importunate Whiting scurrying back and forth in terror. Meanwhile:

Madame Montez . . . exhibited her customary coolness, but by the flashing of her eyes, and an involuntary movement towards Mr Jobson's *caput*, when it was suffering sore infliction at the hands of Mr Seeley, it was evident that she would have had no object whatever to furnish herself with a souvenir snatched from that unfortunate peri-cranium.

The fighting ended with Jobson upsetting a bottle of ink over a reporter's shirt, while Whiting refused to hear any further evidence and threatened both Seeley and Jobson with contempt of court. Jobson then asked Seeley to pass him his hat. Lola went on the attack again:

> LM: Is it his own? Mind he is Jobson the jail-bird.
> Jobson: Oh, you are too low to be noticed.
> LM: Ah, but I was 'My Lady' in London.

The unfortunate Jobson had taken the wrong hat. Lola was triumphant: 'I knew it. Don't let him steal that hat again.'

Jobson was removed and Lola gave an impromptu press conference about her dealings with him in London. She had, she said, been obliged to have two police officers guard her house in Half Moon Street after he had begun visiting and she feared for her jewellery. She continued that she had been left the ward of Lord Brougham. When some of the first noblemen in London who were her friends had heard Jobson was prowling about, they had arranged for police protection.

The last part of the Lola–Jobson clash came on 26 February when she was a witness in the contempt proceedings brought against both Seeley and Jobson, pointing out to Schermerhorn that it was he rather than she who was afraid during the fight. Seeley joined Jobson in Edridge Street prison, serving two days for contempt; in a show of solidarity, Lola visited him there. All in all, however, it was a most un-Christian performance by the Countess.[45]

But Jobson was by no means finished with Lola. On the evening of 18 March he gave a lecture in Stuyvesant Hall entitled 'Lola Montez and her Fancies'. It was attended by some forty people, of whom two were women; they both walked out and demanded their money back. The correspondent of the *New York Times* thought it was not worth reporting, 'for that portion of it that was not too vulgar to be heard, was altogether too stupid to be read'. The lecture was a complete fiasco. Such audience as remained gave up after Jobson sang a song and then threatened to give a lecture on Louis Napoleon.[46]

Down the road in the Bowery that night, Lola was basking in the glory of the revival in German of *Lola Montez in Bavaria*, with Mrs Hoym in the title role. When she arrived on stage after the play to give her talk 'Comic Aspects of Love', Lola was greeted with several rounds of applause, and she received further applause throughout her lecture. In fact, Lola had played herself in German twice in St Louis. Since her German was poor at best, presumably the performance was adapted and she relied heavily on mime.

During the spring of 1858 she became reacquainted with an old friend. Maria Thomson, from Montrose, was the daughter of an officer in the 100th Foot. She had first married a sergeant in the 71st and been widowed; moving to New York, she had married a florist named Isaac Buchanan who had come from Philadelphia. One fanciful story which circulated after Lola's death was that Buchanan was originally named Buch. He had helped her escape from Munich and in reward she had established him in America.[47] Now, with Lola about to give the first of her autobiographical lectures, Maria Buchanan sent flowers and wrote inviting Lola to call. She replied saying that the splendid bouquet had given her 'an additional courage for the arduous task I had inflicted upon myself of telling my history to a thousand curious people who cared actually no more for me than the man in the moon'. She would call on them on 10 April. The lecture itself was the usual mishmash of Lola's prevarications, improvements and downright lies, but the renewed friendship lasted until her death.

Lola's stage career ended on a low key when on 29 May she appeared in *Morning Call* at the Broadway Theatre. She had, by now, realised her talents lay in lecturing. The performance was followed by a lecture on 'Wits and Women', and she was back there on 31 May for a run of five nights of lectures. The next year, her book *The Arts and Secrets of Beauty or Secrets of a Lady's Toilet with Hints to Gentlemen on the Art of Fascinating*, based in part on her lectures, was to become a raging success. The secrets included a note that the fat of a stag kept the form elastic, and that binding thin slivers of raw beef around the face helped to stave off wrinkles. A pomade of rosemary and nutmeg prevented baldness and patent cosmetics were dangerous. Would-be beauties should mix their own formulas. One of these formulas was for prompting the growth of the bosom. For those who think they might wish to adopt it in the twenty-first century, the recipe was half an ounce of tincture of myrrh, four ounces of pimpernel water, four ounces of elderflower water, one gram of musk and six ounces of rectified spirits of wine. The mixture was to be very softly rubbed upon the bosom for five or ten minutes two or three times a day.[48]

Her autobiography appeared in the summer of 1858 to great acclaim in America, but it had a mixed reception when it was published in London. Lola lost money; since there was no copyright, some of the less reputable publishers brought out three simultaneous editions to suit all pockets. The *Athenaeum* was most enthusiastic, expressing what the *Illustrated News of the World* described as 'absurd laudation'. For its part the paper was less than impressed with her heavily bowdlerised story. It pointed out erroneously that the Polish count with whom Lola had been entangled had not only skipped off with a rival but had also taken her trinkets and valuables. It was then, said the paper, that she had fallen into the hands of Chauncey Burr, who became her 'guide, secretary, philosopher and friend' and as the compiler of the autobiography for whom most criticism was reserved.

There is perhaps a grain of truth in this misanthropic review. According to an anonymous reminiscence published immediately after her death, 'I may here mention that she did not write her lectures, nor any of the books that are ascribed to her – not one of them, as she has often told me.'[49] Certainly there were those, such as an editor of the *Cleveland Plain Dealer*, always supportive of Lola, who believed she had written the book and lectures. 'Lola Montez not write? Tell it to the Marines. She can set type too.' This was a reference to him having come across her, composing stick in hand, setting up a letter to the press.[50]

Despite her protestations of having been saved and brought to Jesus, which had begun with the commencement of her lecture tour, Lola was still mixing with the most louche of characters – certainly not people in whose company a newly converted woman now approaching middle age should be found. That summer she went to live in a summer cottage in Yorkville, on a knoll at the corner of Nine-teenth Street and Third Avenue. There a motley collection of guests – including freethinkers, spiritualists and, it was claimed, advocates of free love – were welcome. Some even odder characters lurked there as well. A report by a Corporal Trim in the *San Francisco Evening Bulletin* contained the story of a dinner party in the summer of 1858: 'Her great blue eyes were "sunk in caverns" but her white teeth were as flashing as ever. The guests included three or four wealthy young Creoles from Havana, several "bohemiens", two or three seedy lawyers, a nephew of a French general and a couple of women, one of whom was decidedly déclasseé.' Also on hand was a Capitaine Henri de Rivière, 'notorious at that point for his connection with some scandal or other'.

At eight o'clock the group was ushered into a rather small base-ment dining room hung with cages of birds, decked with flowers and furnished with quaint sideboards 'rich in ornaments gathered from all corners of the earth'. Conversation turned to the mysterious Burdell murder. De Rivière rummaged in drawers – something which indi-cated to Trim that he knew his way around the house – and produced a dagger. He proceeded to re-enact the stabbing so enthusiastically – showing how, since it was an upward thrust that killed the dentist, it must have been made by a woman – that Lola called a halt and changed the subject.[51]

If we accept Trim's account of his intimate knowledge of Lola's fur-niture, the twenty-nine-year-old de Rivière was probably one of Lola's last lovers. Appropriately enough, he was quite as unsuitable as most of the previous ones. He was, he maintained, Henry Guillaume Marie Arnous de Rivière and claimed to be a count, to have commanded a Zouave regiment and to have been a hero of Sebastopol, on which subject he lectured in New York. Lola had possibly met him on the *Orizaba* on the way from San Francisco to New York, when he was a member of General William Walker's Panamanian expedition. Clearly in the Lola mould, he had gone through a ceremony of marriage with a Jane Bouche at the Church of St Vincent de Paul on Canal Street on 8 November 1857. Curiously, one witness had been Antoine Maury, a man whom he would fight in a duel within the year. When ques-tioned, as with Lola and her marriage to James, he would deny the marriage was legal. There had only been one witness, there was no licence and he had gone through the ceremony with the greatest repugnance. All or any of these was, in his view, enough to have it declared void. There was also the matter of a seven-year sentence for fraud passed in France in his absence.

De Rivière's fall from grace began when he fought Maury in Mobile in March 1858. Accounts vary; either de Rivière had been wearing a vest of chain mail under his shirt and a shot from his opponent had struck him and ricocheted away, or he was trying to draw ahead of the requisite signal. But what is clear is that Maury promptly shot him in the face. De Rivière had earlier been befriended by a Colonel Frederick S. Blount, and probably more particularly by the colonel's wife and Emily, his seventeen-year-old daughter. De Rivière stayed with them during his recovery and the inevitable happened. After all, which romantically inclined teenager can resist the charms of a handsome – if cowardly – Frenchman?

By now Blount was beginning to think his guest was an imposter, but it was all too late. Mrs Blount, her daughter and de Rivière went to New Orleans, then to Havana and finally to New York, to try to find someone who would marry the happy couple. It all echoes James's attempt to find someone to marry him and Lola. In the first two instances the gallant colonel turned up in time to thwart their ambitions. Then, in New York, things took a more serious turn. Mother and daughter disappeared in suspicious circumstances. The colonel arrived to have de Rivière charged with seduction. De Rivière escaped from custody – given some money and a little ingenuity, not a very difficult thing to do in New York at the time. Mother reappeared, totally supportive of the gallant Zouave, but Emily did not. De Rivière and Emily were sighted in Canada; in Philadelphia; then 'not 200 miles from Hoboken, New Jersey'; they were in France; they were in Havana; she had been kidnapped by her father's men. The courts issued warrants against de Rivière, a hotel manager, his lawyer and the captain of the Hoboken police who, curiously, had stood de Rivière's bail. Finally a settlement was negotiated. De Rivière would produce Emily, after which he would return to France, a free man, to have his conviction there quashed and his marriage annulled; Emily would return with her parents to Mobile. The newspapers passed a happy July recounting the farce.

In fact de Rivière did not return to France. He was next reported as living at Lola's in Yorkville and there was speculation that the pair would go into partnership, giving lectures on alternate nights. The papers were convinced that she and de Rivière were 'very intimate'.[52]

While with Lola, he began his preparations for a return to the lecture circuit, beginning on 10 October 1858 at the Hope Chapel – this time on 'Love not War'. It was not a great success. As he entered he was arrested for once more proposing a duel. The lecture was cancelled. When he finally spoke on the Friday, in the audience of 100 there were only six women. It is not recorded if Lola was among them. The affair petered out and with it disappeared any possible partnership. The next year it was reported that the gallant Zouave's 'grief for the loss of the Countess has partially subsided'. He had been seen with the wife of a Boston banker both in that city and in Aiken, South Carolina.[53]

If Lola truly believed the Jesuits were persecuting her, from time to time there were grounds to think that they, and indeed other *religieux*, were not amused by her antics and attacks. In the summer of 1858 the Reverend Ralph Hoyt's Chapel of the Good Shepherd was destroyed by a tornado, causing some $15,000 of damage. Hoyt had been ordained in 1840 and soon afterwards established a mission at Market and Monroe Streets, in a furnished room over a liquor store. Over the years he had catered for the poor both spiritually and literally, providing clothes and a food kitchen, and by 1854 he had put together sufficient funds to buy some lots on Fifty-fourth Street between Second and Third Avenues and build a church. It had been destroyed shortly before completion and now he appealed for funds to help in the rebuilding.[54]

In response, not hiding her light under a bushel and doubtless well aware of the publicity it would bring, Lola wrote an open letter volunteering to give a lecture in aid of the fund: 'Had I not been prostrated with sickness, I should have expressed this sympathy at an earlier day; but I am now, by the blessing of Heaven, so far recovered as to be able to lecture again . . .'[55]

Perhaps she would have done well not to have chosen Rome as the topic for her address on 13 October 1858, again at the Hope Chapel. The advertising blurb cannot have helped either:

It is a narration of what she has
Personally observed
Of the Character and Power of the
Church of Rome
During a Life of Pilgrimage which has led her Through Every
Country in Europe.

There was an outcry. The Bishop of the diocese forbade Hoyt to receive the proceeds of the lecture under pain of excommunication. Other promised donations were withdrawn. Lola retaliated by saying that if Hoyt was not allowed to take the proceeds she would devote them to the building of a second Church of the Good Shepherd, this time in Yorkville. And, by the way, the Bishop was nothing but a Jesuit in disguise. As usual, opinion was divided. *The Tablet* and other Roman Catholic papers were naturally delighted, referring to this 'scandalous' alliance between the rector and the 'strange woman'.

One newspaper came out in her support, pointing out that when some years earlier a Mrs Brown had taken a pew for her lady boarders – which may itself have been a euphemism – at Grace Church, she had been given no peace, and Isaac Brown, the sexton, had been obliged to hustle her out. 'So it would thus seem, after all, that Christ did not come to call sinners but the righteous, to repentance.'[56] A broadside published on 5 October took a completely opposite view:

How deep must be their love for the sanctity of Religion, when they denounce its appointed ministers – its leading authorities – by means of a woman whose early maturity was graced by the possession of two living husbands, who figured so amiably in the Court of the King of Bavaria; the theatrical danseuse; the haranguer of the New York stage; the bar-room cow-herder of California; the heroine of an Australian campaign; the authoress of a work on Court intrigue?[57]

Naturally Lola sprang to her own defence. She had not expected to find:

even in the benighted regions of clerical bigotry and intolerance, one so stupid and so shameless as to find fault with a truly philanthropic clergyman for his willingness to receive a donation from me to feed and instruct the poor. I did remember that it was the doctors of theology and the pious folks who crucified the Master, and my wide experience has taught me that it is not to that class of people that we may generally look for good and charitable deeds; but I was not prepared to expect such an insulting interference of bishops and clergy in what is only a humble offer of mine to the poor.[58]

There were rumours that her lecture would be cancelled. But, in competition with Laura Keene and her former ballet master George Smith, who were appearing at Keene's Theatre at 624 Broadway, Lola gave her talk. Entrance was 50 cents – half the cost of seeing the organist Mlle Emma Wells, the pupil of Adolphe Adam, to whose music Lola had first danced *Betley the Tyrolean*.

Despite the poor weather there was a good and certainly very enthusiastic audience to hear her lambast bigotry. She thought the Catholic Church was the result of an effete civilisation, that it was now *de trop* and must eventually succumb to the progressive spirit of the age. To loud applause, she gave her usual line that Protestantism, which had brought the railway and the telegraph as well as American democracy, was the real thing. Then she turned her attention to Hoyt's critics:

> This is certainly a piece of bigotry, intolerance and cruelty to the poor and of meddlesome impertinence which I certainly have never witnessed – aye, even in the most illiberal Catholic countries of the world [Loud applause]. It may be that I will give a course of lectures to raise a fund to send missionaries to Christianise these clerical Pharisees.

The lecture ended to tumultuous and prolonged applause.[59] Three weeks later she left America for a lecture tour of Britain arranged by the Burrs.

→>-<+-

CHAPTER EIGHTEEN

Lola's Last Days

IN OCTOBER 1858 LOLA SAILED on the *Pacific* for Dublin and then England. With Heald dead there was no lingering problem with either the bigamy or bail. When she arrived in Ireland:

> The Countess was received with every attention and respect by the offi-
> cial and a few friends who went on board on the arrival of the vessel. She
> wore a flowered black silk dress – sans crinoline – and over it a rich fur
> mantle, trimmed with beaver fur. Her lecture was to be America, Its
> People and its Social Institutions. She would speak about them as they
> were and not as represented by Mr Dickens, Mr Mackay and Mr Thack-
> eray. She was very keen to visit Limerick, her birthplace.[1]

The lectures themselves were also generally well received, even if ticket prices, particularly for the reserved seats, were higher than those commanded by Charles Dickens. Occasionally this thinned the audience, but her share of the gate in Liverpool, where she lectured on 21 January 1859 at the Concert Hall on 'Comic Aspects of Fashion', was said to be £250.

There was one slight hiccup in York when she was greeted with almost continuous laughter and applause for her lecture on fashion. One man in the front row was chatting with his friend and not paying attention. The *Sunday Times* reported that he was actually thumbing his nose, although the local paper omitted this detail. Lola turned on him: 'Sir, you must excuse me but you must not behave in that way. This is a respectable audience.' She pointed out that this was the first time in either Scotland or England that she had been shown disrespect and she was sorry it came from a fashionable man. There were cries of 'Shame' and 'Turn him out'. Leaving the hall to return to the Black Swan, where she was staying, she was cheered by the crowd, to whom she made a graceful bow.[2]

In London, she lived at 49 Weymouth Street for a time, from where she wrote a long letter full of religious guff to a Miss Mitchell. Lola was still quite incapable of telling the truth. 'I was never a hypocrite. I believe Mr Harris is a true servant of the Lord.[3] Tell him I am brought to Jesus. Oh never again to be lost.' This letter can be used to support the argument that extracts from her diaries are genuine.

The *Pittsfield Sun* in Boston was by no means convinced of her conversion, likening it to that of Mother Cole in Samuel Foote's play *The Minor* and rather sourly referring to 'the earnings of her peccadilloes'. With that, and no doubt some of the money from her lectures, she bought the lease of a house in Piccadilly, at 26 Park Lane West, in which she intended to take paying guests:

> [It] is the resort of a large number of wealthy and pious enthusiasts of London, male and female. Amongst her most constant and intimate visitors is Mrs Thistlethwayte, formerly an actress who was familiarly known as Laura Bell and was about as notorious as Lola herself.
>
> It is said that Mrs Thistlethwayte drives her chariot with four milk white horses attached through the streets of London on missions of mercy and religious teachings.[4]

After Lola's lover Jung Bahadur had returned to Nepal, Laura ran through a string of men, including Sir Edwin Landseer and Arthur Thistlethwayte. She then married Arthur's brother, Frederick, to whom he had effectively bequeathed her before going to the Crimea. It was not a happy marriage; Laura was just as profligate with money as Lola. Then, in 1856, she became a lay preacher, at the same time continuing to hold all-male dinner parties in her husband's absence. After her conversion she declined on religious grounds to give evidence at Bow Street Police Court against a Jacob Levy, who was said to have stolen her jewellery when she was in Switzerland. She and Lola made a likely pair.[5]

Lola's first lecture in London, on 7 April, drew a respectable house. The stalls seats were five shillings, a shilling more than the best seats for a reading by Dickens, who was in town at the same time. Her accent still wandered across Europe. The *Era*, recording that she was 'a good looking lady in the bloom of womanhood', thought 'Her foreign accent might belong to any language from Irish to Bavarian' and that 'The lecture might have been a newspaper article'. The following week the critic was no more impressed. Certainly the audience had laughed and applauded, but 'Latin grammar never came under her notice' and he thought the lecture would 'have given Dr Arnold toothache'.[6] The Burrs returned to America and Lola remained in London, presumably to manage her boarding house.

Possibly because she needed to raise money to support the boarding house, she gave two more lectures in London, both at the St James's Hall. The first, 'Slavery in America' on 10 June, was completely new and presumably written entirely by herself. It was an equivocal talk. Lola thought slaves to be fat, lazy and content, full of pity for workers in England (if, that is, they had ever heard of them). On the other hand, she believed that slavery was a sin and one day America's national flag would 'flutter in the breezes of heaven as free and proud an ensign of universal liberty as the banners that wave from the mastheads of the ships of free England!'[7]

For her pains the lecture was roundly condemned by a 'lady of colour' when Sarah P. Remond refuted Lola's claims about slavery – 'Words are inadequate to express the depths of the infamy . . .' – in an address to the American Anti-Slavery Society.[8]

Lola's last lectures in London, 'Strong-minded Women' and, as a supplemental bonne-bouche, 'Women's Rights Movement in America', were given on 15 June, before she began a tour of the provinces. The *Era* was now completely in her favour, reporting that the audience for her lecture had risen en masse, with men cheering and waving their hats. She made a graceful little speech thanking the press and the 'brave-hearted Englishmen', saying she hoped she had entertained them for an hour and that one day she might come back and lecture on Bavaria and Hungary.[9] But there was to be no tour of the provinces. Lola simply disappeared.

It is amazing that Lola, the apple of the eye of the press, could vanish without any apparent sighting. Yet so she did until, travelling as Mrs Heald, she left Southampton on 4 October 1859 on the *Hammonia*. She arrived in New York at 6.30 pm on 18 October, the same evening the newspapers reported John Brown's attack on Harper's Ferry, an event which made a significant contribution to the commencement of the Civil War. Not everyone was pleased to have her back in America: 'Particularly unfortunate. Among the arrivals at New York from Europe by the steamer *Hammonia* is Madame Lola Montez. We had hoped that she had "gone from us – gone forever".'[10]

Where had she been for those four months? There really is only one account. It comes from some anonymous reminiscences, published in the *New York Herald* shortly after her death, by a man who claimed he had met her and her dog Gyp in Regent's Park, and is supported by a letter to a woman she refers to as Camille.

In the article the man recalls meeting Lola one afternoon in the summer of 1859 when Gyp had frightened some stray and shabby children. Lola, assuming something of a Christ-like figure, told them and their mothers not to be afraid. Soon they were patting the dog while she read passages from the Bible, by which time all were crying with pleasure. Later he took a walk in the park with her. She said she had been in the habit of visiting the most poor and abandoned people in the city, telling him: 'There was not a wicked thing I did not do and although I had plenty of money and friends yet I was never happy until I found out the beautiful truths of this little book.'

He then left London for some months. When they met again in America, she told him she had fallen on hard times. She had invested £900 of her own money and another £200 lent by lady friends in a house in Park Lane West, intending to take in lodgers. There was no housekeeper, the lodgers did not come and she quarrelled with the staff. The whole venture failed; the bailiffs were called in, she was forced to sell up and left with £56 6s. She took to her bed with a brain fever, until a kindly elderly Methodist gentleman from Derby who had heard of her plight came to London and took her by train back to his country home, where he and his wife devotedly nursed her back to health.

They then returned to Derby, leaving her in the country. She had the run of their estate, horses to ride, servants to look after her. There were herds of deer, swans, and beds brimming with flowers. Indeed there was even some talk that the childless couple would leave her their fortune. The woman had no real friends in this idyllic life, just gypsies who roamed around, and the disturbed wife of the local librarian who believed that a Jew had cast a spell on her and there was a devil in her stomach. She and Lola had been praying and reading the scriptures together. In October 1859, 'without sufficient reason she left her happy bower and once more launched her bark on the rude waters of chance and adventure'.[11]

There is some support for the story in the form of a diary supposedly kept by Lola while she was in the country and in the throes of religious fervour. Unfortunately it was not published before her death and the original does not survive. Indeed, there are less than half a dozen entries. They begin on 10 September 1859 but no other is dated, though one is marked Saturday. Then suddenly on another Saturday she is back in London. Nevertheless the missing diary has had a huge influence on the later belief that Lola was indeed a penitent.

Unfortunately this idyll was interrupted by an unhappy incident, which she recounted obliquely in a letter to a woman named as Camille when she was in Cleveland the following year. It claims that she 'would have been there now had it not unfortunately happened that mankind who are forever sinning and who in the person of the gentleman took too much upon himself, you understand what I mean … It was cruel indeed of Mr E to have said what he did; but I am afraid I was so hasty also.'[12]

What goes against the whole story is that there was not a word about her financial collapse or serious illness in any of the London – or for that matter American – papers. For the first six months of the year she had been headline news in the weekly papers, at the very least. Although Lola had the capacity to disappear from the eye of the press and the public, it is beyond belief that not a single newspaper would have picked up the story of the compulsory sale of her lease, or indeed of her illness. Such items would have been grist to the mill of the *Era*, but there is nothing.

Then, surely, her friend Laura Thistlethwayte, who by now had money coming out of her ears, would have come to her financial aid? How on earth does an elderly and unidentifiable couple in Derbyshire come to hear of her unreported plight and whisk her off to their home? The story smacks of another *religieuse*, Aimee Semple Macpherson, who went off the rails and provided a cover story for her lapse.

The anonymous reminiscer, by no means a wholehearted admirer, wrote of her quick temper and her unwillingness to acknowledge she was in the wrong and how dinner parties would be broken up because of her temper and incalcitrance:

> She had no real gratitude and was quite regardless of the truth; even in these last years when her ardent desire was to be a good Christian, native character was stronger than her new resolves. She was very kind to the humble and poor but oftentimes impertinent and insulting to the middle class.
>
> Like all people born in England or who have spent the early part of their life there, she was a worshiper of the aristocracy and in her giddy moments would boast of former friendships with titled people.

Lola was back in America two months before she delivered her first lecture in New York. On 15 December she appeared at Mozart Hall, on the corner of Bond Street and Broadway, to speak on 'John Bull at Home' before an estimated audience of 3,000. If she had been ill she was clearly fully recovered and still well capable of making admirers gush. The writer Mary Clemmer Ames, who contributed to the *New York Independent* and had, it seems, a reputation for being brusque at times, was one who was left quite breathless. After describing Lola's appearance in adulatory detail she gushed:

> Not an element of popularity was wanting in this lecture. Wit, satire, sarcasm double-edged yet sheathed in smiles, history, politics, religion;

quotations from Scripture; anecdotes of society all followed each other in brilliant succession.

She mixed in her careless gossip a strange quantity of sagacious thought, and of earnest, humane reflection. Rarely a man, and very rarely a woman, holds so complete a control over the modulation of voice as did Lola. Ever changing, its intonations were perfect and sweet as they were infinite. In her physique, in the perfect abandon of her manner, in her voice, were hidden the secrets of her power. The rest was centred in her head, rather than in her heart. She had a most subtle perception of character, a crystal intellect and any quantity of sang-froid. The delicate skill with which she played upon that harp of many strings, a popular audience, proved her to be the natural diplomat. She carried the audience with her completely; and when at last the velvet robe, the laces, the bouquet of radiant flowers, and the rarely radiant face made their courtesying exit it was amidst the most enthusiastic applause.[13]

As the *New York Herald* had ironically suggested so many years earlier, Lola had finally found her métier. Under the Burr regime she continued lecturing throughout the winter – New York, Philadelphia, Baltimore, Boston, Cleveland, Washington, again back to Baltimore and on to Pittsburgh and Cincinnati, from where she wrote to her friend Camille on 11 February 1860. Her health was better, the winter was not as cold as might have been. She had not heard from Laura Thistlethwayte, nor from a Mrs Palmer. She had plans for another English trip but meanwhile she was going down South and endeavouring to save some money – a little 'boire pour la soif' as she put it. She would be back in New York in six weeks' time. In Baltimore she had obviously been quite comfortable, writing to a Dr Robert Sheldon Mackenzie on 30 January 1860 that she had 'devilled crabs and a lazy bed' at Barnums Hotel.[14]

The tour continued to Louisville, where there were hundreds of ladies present; Chicago – no seats vacant and very little standing room; Detroit by early April; across the lake to Toronto; and on to Buffalo and Rochester, until she made her final appearance in Albany on 11 April. The Burrs were certainly making the most of their investment while she lasted, but she should have been managing to put away a number of *boires*. It was thought 'the Jesuit expeller' had received $800 for her three appearances in Chicago alone.[15]

From Louisville she wrote on 7 March 1860 to Maria Buchanan, saying she hoped that Burr was going to set her up in a quarter share of a weekly paper; and she was to receive $20 a week besides: 'This is a capital affair, as I do not invest a penny myself and I think it will be a better affair than the Candy Store. I am going to write the whole history of my life in an extended form and old Burr is capable of making it the best weekly in the country.'

Unfortunately nothing came of the Burr proposal. Lola's swan was another goose. By now she may well have been suffering something of a breakdown from the strain of overwork and travel. The actor Charles Warwick, who knew her from Grass Valley days, met her in Chicago, probably during her visit there at the end of March 1860:

> I met Lola Montez in Chicago some years afterwards evidently suffering from severe mental depression. It was one Sunday evening at the house of a mutual friend. Before leaving a violent storm had set in and I volunteered to go to the nearest stable and get a carriage to convey her to her hotel but she would not listen to the proposition and insisted on walking through the rain. She was elegantly dressed and wore a black-lace bonnet ornamented with artificial flowers. When we arrived at the hotel she was a sight to behold. Her hat had degenerated to an undefined pulp, while the colors of the variegated flowers had run down her face in irregular streaks giving her the appearance of a Commanche chief on the warpath. As I left her in the doorway of the hotel, so I must leave her to my readers for I never saw her more.[16]

By that summer Lola had a really good and lasting dose of religion. It had been coming on since Follin's death. Afterwards she began to take a closer interest in spiritualism, which from the 1850s had been gaining popularity, first in America and then in England. While living in Grass Valley she had read Andrew Jackson Davis's *The Principles of Nature, the Divine Revelation and Voice to Mankind.* Davis was a spiritualist who had dictated the book in a series of hypnotic trances over a fifteen-month period. It was, said Lola, the book which inspired her to read the Bible. She also attended seances by the medium Stephen

Andrews; she was, she believed, an excellent and susceptible subject. She abandoned the movement when another of the spirit mediums, who had not paid close enough attention to European affairs, to give Lola further solace summoned the spirit of Ludwig I who was very much alive and reasonably well.[17] Soon after that she fell into the waiting arms of the Evangelical movement. 'In her days of spiritual-ism she liked to regard herself as an illuminée and not one ungifted with glimpses into the inner world.'[18]

It was not that Lola was in any way insincere in her temporary belief in spiritualism, rather that she was disingenuous. Some twenty years after her death a recollection appeared in the *Chicago Daily News*:

> At that time, like most women who have led fast lives, [Lola] had become garrulously, if not deeply, religious, and, above all religions in the world, she had taken to what is called 'Swedenborgianism' or the doctrines of the Church of the New Jerusalem ...
>
> The fact was the woman was so badly ignorant of the subject which she professed to thoroughly understand that she would, woman-like, put forward propositions to me which were utterly absurd on the face of them with a cock-sureness which was delightfully refreshing.[19]

In 1894 an anonymous *Eagle* reader claimed that she had been in the same boarding house as Lola, on what was then old Clove Road, Brooklyn, in the year that she died. She had two nicely furnished rooms; she went to church and made friends with the minister's wife and children, read the psalms and sang 'Rock of Ages' on a Sunday afternoon, went walking in the evening, bought cream from the milkman and gave away copies of Pope's *Essay on Man* to the local children.

This letter has been discredited on the basis that according to the census of June Lola was living in Manhattan. However, she might have lived there before moving to Manhattan. It has also been used rather extravagantly by Helen Holdredge to boost the argument that Lola was now deranged, probably through syphilis. It may well be that the writer of the letter simply had the year or months wrong; but if talking to the local vicar, buying milk, taking walks, trying to interest children in literature and singing hymns on a Sunday is evidence of brain disease, then there must be a far greater number of sufferers than has previously been thought.[20]

In the summer, Lola was taken desperately ill. On Saturday, 30 June 1860 she suffered a stroke at 15 Clinton Place, Manhattan, where she was living. Getting up in the morning she complained of dizziness and collapsed. Early reports said she would not survive the night; she rallied, however, but then relapsed. By Tuesday she had lost all consciousness and obituaries appeared in the German papers. Like those for Mark Twain half a century later, they were an exaggeration. Again she rallied and now the Buchanans had her moved to Astoria, Long Island, where they lived when not in Manhattan. A woman journalist who visited her there in September reported that she was unable to utter a single intelligible word except spasmodically and after repeated effort. She drooled, wiping the froth away with the sleeve of her dress: 'But alas! In what condition of body and mind . . . In fact she had the strange, wild appearance and behaviour of a quiet idiot, and is evidently lost to all future interest in the world around her and its affairs. And so ends her eventful history! What a story for the brilliant and thoughtless! What a sermon on human vanity!'[21]

Once again she pulled round. She was moved back to Manhattan and 194 West Seventeenth Street, near Eighth Avenue – in the area now known as Hell's Kitchen, which was not then as bad an area as it later became. There she was placed in the care of Nurse Margaret Hamilton.

It was now that Mrs Buchanan asked the religious firebrand, the charismatic Reverend Francis Hawks, to visit Lola. When in town the Buchanans themselves lived just off fashionable Fifth Avenue, on West Seventeenth Street, and the Reverend Hawks and Maria travelled the few blocks farther west to no. 194, on the south side of the street, just short of Eighth Avenue. Curiously, Hawks thought it necessary to write that all his visits were made in the company of Mrs Buchanan and Lola's nurse. Lola was a great catch. Once he had met her he quickly developed and exploited the religious streak in her:

She read the blessed volume for herself, also, when I was not present. It was always within reach of her hand; and, on my first visit, when I took up her Bible from the table the fact struck me that it opened of its own accord to the touching story of Christ's forgiveness of the Magdalene in the house of Simon.

I spoke to her of Christ's gentle pity and pardon for this poor woman. 'Ah!' she replied, 'but she loved much. Can I love enough?'[22]

Hawks was convinced that her repentance and conversion was genuine:

> In the course of long experience as a Christian minister I do not think I ever saw deeper penitence and humility, more real contrition of soul and more of bitter self-reproach than in this poor woman.

Certainly she was able to make a substantial contribution to the cause. As she recovered, Lola was put to work visiting the women in the Magdalen Asylum on Fifth at Eighty-eighth Street, 'warning them and instructing them with a spirit which yearned over them, that they, too, might be brought into the fold'.

Writing after her death, the minister perhaps gave a hint that she might indeed have been suffering from syphilis:

> She strove to impress upon them not only the awful guilt of breaking the divine law, but the inevitable earthly sorrow which those who persisted with thoughtless desperation in sinful courses were treasuring up for themselves.

He concluded sanctimoniously:

> Her effort was thus to redeem the time as far as she could; and the results of her labours can only be known on that day when she will meet her erring sisters at the impartial tribunal of the Eternal Judge.[23]

How much is true, how much was his wishful thinking and how much written with one eye on the convert market is difficult to distinguish. Perhaps it is a little of each. Lola, ever the great enthusiast, was great conversion material. Certainly, over the years, penitents seem to have acquired the same self-flagellating phraseology. 'Lord, Thy mercies are great to me. Oh! How little they are deserved, filthy worm that I am!' wrote Lola.

There was almost a required style for penitential writing. The actress Eve Lavalière, who fifty years after Lola gave up a life of sin to undertake missionary work in North Africa, might almost have copied her: 'Here at your feet lies the vilest, lowest and most contemptible object on earth, a woman from the dung heap, the most infamous, the most soiled of all creatures. Lord, I am but a poor sheep in your flock.'[24]

There were of course stories about Lola and her whereabouts during these months. One was that she had left the Buchanans, refusing to give her address to her most intimate friends, and was living on Seventeenth Street under the name of Fanny Gibbons in meditation and prayer.[25] Another was that she was living in Brooklyn, going for walks at night, buying milk and handing out tracts.

Certainly her mother heard of Lola's illness and paid a quick visit, possibly to find out if there was any sort of estate to come to her. She found there was not and left as swiftly as she had arrived. She did, however, continue to write to the doctor and to Mrs Buchanan.

On 9 January 1861 came the moment for which the Buchanans no doubt devoutly wished: Lola amended her will in favour of Mrs Buchanan. Three hundred dollars went to the Magdalen Asylum and the rest to Mrs Buchanan, 'absolutely requesting however that she will distribute the same for charitable uses as she thinks best'. The author and actor Edward P. Hingston, who had also known Lola in Grass Valley, went to see her:

> Poor Wayward Lola! In the city of New York I called upon her a few days before she died. She who had lived in a palace in Munich, had become the occupant of an upstairs back-room in a small house; Consumption had reft her face of its beauty while it had added to the brilliancy of her wondrous eyes. Her couch was a humble one, and round her room were Scriptural texts in large, legible characters. It is to be hoped that as her feverish, burning eyes gazed upon them the heart of the contrite woman derived consolation.[26]

At least two different stories emerged about her treatment after the will was signed. On the one hand there were the kindly Buchanans, arranging for her every comfort and care by Margaret Hamilton. On the other there were the much less than kindly Buchanans; they had kept Lola more or less a prisoner in a tenement room in which there was no bed, simply an old mattress with dirty blankets and a piece of carpet nailed over the window, accompanied by a harpy named Margaret Hamilton who pulled what remained of Lola's hair.

A most curious letter which tends to support the poverty theory appeared in the London *Morning Post* on 7 February 1861, after Lola's death. Written by George Harrison FRCS of Grosvenor Square, it was to the effect that Lola Montez had died of pneumonia following a severe attack of paralysis. She had, he added, 'latterly subsisted entirely on charity which I was selected to dispense'. Is it possible that at the end Mrs Craigie did pay for her daughter's welfare?

There are a variety of stories about Lola's death, including one that Miriam Follin snubbed her on the street, so provoking her final stroke. It would seem to be apocryphal. Certainly Mrs Buchanan wrote to Mrs Craigie to tell her of her daughter's illness, but said that she was improving rapidly and able to walk without help. The improvement was only temporary. Out walking on Christmas Day, Lola had caught a cold and died on 17 January 1861.

There is also a third version, most romantic if highly improbable. It is based on a letter written to her son by the wife of Dr John Cooper. Cooper, apparently the son of a judge, certainly treated Lola and signed her death certificate. According to his wife's letter, written nearly fifty years after Lola's death:

> She was troubled by reporters and I suppose by her old mother – though I believe she did not stay around when she found there was nothing to be gotten out of her. Then she begged the doctor to get her away somewhere where she could die in peace. So one night he hired a boat and boatman and smuggled her across the north river to some woman who took care of her.[27]

Unfortunately the story doesn't quite stand up. First, it is doubtful she would have survived the crossing in a skiff in the middle of winter. Second, although this is not fatal to the story, there seems to be no evidence that reporters were beating a path to her door.

But Cooper was undoubtedly her doctor, and a letter to him from Mrs Craigie lends some support to the theory that Lola was suffering from syphilis. 'In a conversation I had with you one day you said she had what is called Softening of the brain.' After she sealed the letter, Mrs Craigie heard from Mrs Buchanan that 'Your daughter is recovering her health fast – she is now able to walk alone with very little lameness and looks in better health than I have ever seen her.' Mrs Craigie wrote a postscript to Cooper saying she was surprised he had not been mentioned. Whether Mrs Buchanan was simply stringing Lola's mother along or whether it was a calm before the storm, Lola lasted only three more days. According to legend, her last words on Thursday 17 January were 'Tell me, tell me more of my dear Saviour.' The Dyer/Hawks version has her speechless but relates that, motioning towards the bible, the good Pastor 'asked her to let him know by a sign whether her soul was at peace and she still felt Christ would save her. She fixed her eyes on mine and nodded her head affirmatively.'[28]

A burial permit in the name of Eliza Gilbert was issued the next day and she was buried on the Saturday. Again differing stories have arisen about the conduct of the service. There is the official version: the mourning Buchanans were present, while the undertaker and sexton of the fashionable Grace Church, Isaac H. Brown – the same man who had earlier evicted the unrelated Mrs Brown's ladies – shed a tear at the graveside as he made fervent responses to Hawks's prayers.[29] Set against this is the story from Mrs Cooper, whose husband was one of the few mourners, that Brown told the gravedigger, 'Hurry up with that dirt, damn you.' Certainly the Buchanans had wasted no time in burying her at Green-Wood cemetery, Brooklyn, early in the morning before a handful of spectators. Nor did they circulate the news of her death:

> Lola Montez's death was kept secret until it leaked out at noon on Saturday as her remains were being conveyed to Green-Wood. She was thin as a skeleton and it was difficult to recognise in her attenuated face the late brilliant favourite of the King of Bavaria.[30]

It might be thought that a number of theatricals in the city would have attended. Why was there such a hurry to bury Lola? Perhaps the kindest interpretation is that the Buchanans did not want the funeral to be turned into a three-ring circus. Lola had, apparently, renounced her worldly life on the stage and they may have felt that the small, ill-attended service was more suitable for a penitent. Probably the official account of her death and burial is the more correct, but it is impossible not to feel that Lola, now she had done her work, was shovelled out of the way with undue haste and a certain lack of ceremony.

Overall Lola received a good crop of obituaries. The *New York Herald*, while wildly inaccurate in many respects – it stated that Follin had drowned in Melbourne harbour – thought she had 'plenty of animal spirits, pluck, talked well and could dance a little . . . Notwithstanding her infirmities of temper Lola was very much liked by those who knew her best.' The *New York Times*, never her greatest supporter, said of her: 'She was generous and high-tempered to a fault; irritable, too, as such natures are apt to be, but forgiving and affectionate. Her natural talents were of the highest order; her accomplishments manifold, and in some respects, marvellous.' The *New York Post* thought, 'One of the most remarkable and versatile women of the present age, one whose life is a romance. "Let him who is without sin . . ."'

The other side of the coin came from the *Albion*: 'This notorious woman died in the neighbourhood of this city last week. Such portions of her wild career as had any influence on public affairs in Bavaria are well known to the public. Otherwise, we do not think it desirable to narrate the adventures of the unfortunates of her class, however prominent the position they may assume.' The Boston newspaper the *Pilot* was not happy at the way she had attacked the Jesuits, and added, 'Doubtless her four or five surviving husbands are praying for the beautiful, gifted, unfortunate daughter of virtuous Ireland.'

In London some of the papers, such as the *Era*, merely reprinted the obituary from the *New York Herald*, while the *Daily Telegraph* delivered a wonderful rant:

Her deathbed was one of lingering pain – the agony of her disease aggravated by her Magdalen-like remorse, for like Pompadour, Emma Hamilton and other celebrated favourites – who all had her personal charms without her glimpses of a better human nature – she upbraided herself in the last moments with the profligacy of a wasted life, and then, when all her ambition and vanity had turned to ashes, she understood what it was like to have been the toy of men and the scorn of women . . .

The minister of Calvary Church, New York, soothing her last moments, heard from her a confession of her sins and a declaration of penitence; her tomb is in the Greenwood cemetery, and those who look upon it may well reflect upon the frightful sacrifice which a woman makes when she forgets her virtue. But this unhappy creature was the victim of a worthless parent. It was to avoid virtual prostitution that she eloped at the age of 14; it was as a deserted wife that she went upon the stage; and then began the 'madly miserable' excitement of her career, now shining on the horizon of the demi-monde then trafficking as a fortune hunter, falling by degrees to lower depths, and at last a phantom of herself grown common in the sight of the world, her name a scoff and her beauty a tradition, she took rank among the most neglected and forsaken of her sex, and our involuntary reflection is, upon hearing of her abject death, that it was no unnatural termination to a life in which every brilliant hour of infamy had been purchased.[31]

The *Athenaeum*, which thought her a 'pretty picaroon woman', concluded with the quote from the *New York Herald*, 'she died in the odour of sanctity'.

Some years after her death there, perhaps the most acute epitaph appeared in *Records of the New York Stage:*

Born with a ruler's mind and a warrior's will she became the very plaything of circumstances and sank broken-hearted and poverty stricken into the humblest of all graves . . . Lola was not all bad. To the poor she was kind and charitable to a fault, ever ready to give to the needful one, half of her last dollar. In this regard there are some interesting stories told of her by those who knew her. And while her biographers have not forgotten all the bad they know of her, they fail to remember and grace her grave with any of her good.[32]

Of those who did know her, Edward De Leon thought 'She was a modern Magdalen – poor Lola – for if there was evil in her, there was also much good. Her heart was ever warm, although her head was a treacherous guide, and she was capable of acts of generosity and self-sacrifice, which many who would be called better women would never have performed.'[33] On the distaff side Mary Clemmer Ames wrote of her death: 'A beautiful intrigante, the clever diplomatist, the erring, wilful wayward woman, the generous and living woman is dead.'[34]

According to the journalist Charles Leland, who wrote her obituary for *Frank Leslie's Weekly*, she once proposed that they 'bolt' to Europe together, but he declined. A friend was in the room when she did so and asked:

> 'But, Madame, by what means can you two live?'
>
> 'Oh,' replied Lola, innocently and confidingly, 'people like us (or who know as much as we) can get a living anywhere.' And she rolled us each a cigarette, with one for herself.
>
> I must have had a great moral influence on her for so far as I know I am the only friend whom she ever had at whom she never threw a plate or a book or attacked with a dagger, poker, broom, chair or other deadly weapon.

Leland believed her to be extremely well read; she had a trunk full of books in which she would rummage for one which would support her current argument, but she 'romanced and embroidered so much in conversation that she did not get credit for what she really knew'. He thought that there were very few indeed, if any, 'who really knew the depths of her wild Irish soul. Men generally were fascinated by her, and then as suddenly disenchanted, and with that detracted from her in every way.'

Perhaps the depth of the affection felt for Lola by Mrs Buchanan can be gauged by the inscription on the tombstone. 'Mrs Eliza Gilbert' she never was; it was probably the one name in her life she never used. Mrs Buchanan's defenders suggest that she did this to avoid gawkers and to mark Lola's abandonment of her former life.

Where did all Lola's money go, and how did she live her last few months? According to one account, she had a dread of the almshouse and on her lecture tours sent a woman in New York $25 a day to bank for her, so that by April 1860 she had over $1,500.[35] But she is said only to have left a little over $1,000. There have, of course, been countless stories of her extravagances and generosity. She was 'The most generous person I ever met,' reminisced Thad Phillips, who had been employed as a messenger at the American Theatre in Sacramento in 1854. Many of the stories were apocryphal including his one, used to show she did not die in poverty – in which she gave a visitor – not Hawks – a costly diamond ring some hours before her death.[36]

There is no doubt that over the years she was profligate with money, when she had it, and equally little doubt that she was generous. There had of course been medical expenses during the last six months of her life, but it would seem that she had had no great extravagances for some years. It may be that the venture of the house in London had damaged her savings, but on the other hand, she had since given many lectures. Throughout the first four months of 1860 she was on stage between five and ten times a month, and possibly sent $25 a lecture back to New York.[37] There should also have been royalties from her books, which supposedly were enormously successful. And what happened to her jewellery? The inescapable conclusions are that someone had either helped him or herself to her money or had not accounted properly.

Certainly the Buchanans were not going to waste money on a fence surrounding the grave; the expense for that could fall on Ludwig. On 8 April 1861 Mrs Buchanan penned a suitably sanctimonious, and probably mendacious, note to the ex-monarch. From the letter it is easy to see how – if indeed she did – Lola had fallen into the penitential style of writing in her last months:

In early childhood having been school companion in Scotland with a young girl who I little thought would ever have requested me on her death bed to write to your Majesty . . .

Two years ago hearing I was in New York she called on me and although many years had passed since we met and in that peace of time, our paths in life had been very different – Still were we both coming nearer to that day, when we both would be required to render up an account of our Stewardship . . .

How beautiful it was to see this woman so long of the world imploring at the mercy seat of Him who said, 'Come unto me all Ye who are heavy laden and I will give you rest'. Nor did she ask in vain . . .

> She died a true penitent relying on her Saviour for pardon and accept-
> ance – triumphing in His merits . . .

Ludwig replied in fractured English to 'Mistress Maria Buchanan' –
signing himself 'Your affect Lewis' – that he was pleased Lola had
found religion and peace: 'With a great satisfaction I was hearing the
repentance of LM [sic] of her former behaviour, and I'm very fond of
it that she has given the confiance to inform me. It is a great consolation to hear her deying as a cristian. LM was a much distinguished
lady.'

Encouraged, Mrs Buchanan wrote pointing out that she had borne
the medical expenses, and that nothing had come from Lola's mother
towards the cost of the grave. Would Ludwig fulfil 'one last act of
friendship'?

> She herself called you her friend nearly with her dying breath to send a
> sum sufficient to put up a simple railing round the grave.
>
> I ask it as a boon of friendship from your Majesty, as a token of good
> will to the memory of one, who was brilliant, gifted and honored with
> the personal friendship of your Majesty.

But, sadly, she found the monarch's pockets finally to be sewn up. He
certainly received the letter, but there was to be no reply.[38]

* * * *

Lola is buried in Plot 12730, Section 8, to the south of the cross paths
of Summit Avenue and Andean at Green-Wood Cemetery in Brooklyn. Over the years the inscription on her grave weathered away and
by 1935 the headstone itself had almost disappeared. It was not until
Bruce Seymour used some of the royalties from his biography of her
that a new headstone was inaugurated on 25 April 1998. One side
maintains the inscription 'Mrs Eliza Gilbert', the other reads 'Lola
Montez, Countess of Landsfeld'. As is the custom of the cemetery, the
original headstone is now buried in the grave.[39]

➤➤◄◄

CHAPTER NINETEEN

What Happened to Them All?

IT IS IMPOSSIBLE to know just how many lovers Lola had during her lifetime. What happened to those who played a major part in her life, and also to her family?

Of her family, her stepfather, Patrick Craigie, did not survive her. He died in Dinapore on either 3 or 8 October 1843. Lola's despised mother never remarried. At the time of her death she was living in a boarding house at 36 Queen's Road, Bayswater, where in November 1875 she accidentally set fire to herself. Mrs Craigie's death was reported under the name Louisa Crawshay; she was described as aged seventy, the widow of a Madras officer. At around 6 pm on 15 November the police were called to Queen's Road, where a fire had broken out. She had seemingly locked herself in her room and at first an ineffectual attempt was made to pick the lock. When the door was finally broken down, she was found unconscious with her clothing almost wholly burned. Taken to St Mary's Hospital, Paddington, she did not regain consciousness and died on 21 November, leaving an estate of just under £3,000. Her executors were Patrick George Craigie of Hartley House, Lower Heath, Hampstead and John Gray of the Union Bank of Scotland.[1]

To give some indication of her wealth, on the day of the fire *The Times* was advertising a bedroom suite in pine for six guineas; a 'bijou residence' with four bedrooms, two drawing rooms, library, dining room and offices overlooking Regent's Park was for rent at £130 a year. The freehold of a six-bedroom house in Stockwell was for sale at £850. The best cabin on a crossing to New York was seventeen guineas.

Lola's only real husband, Thomas James, survived his ill-health and the inquiry into the loss of the mess funds, retiring from the army on 28 February 1856. He does not seem to have been a popular man, spending twelve years in Kotah with only two brother officers for company and, despite his seniority, being regularly passed over for promotion. At the end of his career, however, no doubt in a generous effort to increase his pension, he was promoted to major and given the honorary rank of half-colonel. His bookkeeping did not improve over the years; after he left Kotah it proved impossible to reconstruct the accounts of the regiment and the disposal of the funds under his care.

His romantic life post-Lola was curious. Until his retirement he never returned to England, although a period of convalescence was spent in South Africa. While in India he adopted a Catherine Haveland, who may of course have been his own illegitimate offspring, and sent her to his unmarried sister Wilhelmina in Cheltenham for her upbringing. During his retirement he met a Louisa Banning, who already had an illegitimate child, and they had two more before he finally did the right thing and married her on 1 January 1870 while she was pregnant with their third. He died suddenly following a stroke on 18 May 1871 at 1 Kildare Terrace, Bayswater, leaving an estate of a little under £4,000.[2]

Franz Liszt lived in some fear that Lola's predecessor, his mistress the comtesse d'Angoult, who wrote a number of novels and philosophical treatises such as *Nélida*, would carry out her threat and publish her memoirs during his lifetime. In the event she predeceased him, dying in 1876. In 1849 he conducted Wagner's *Tannhäuser* at Weimar, where he was court conductor, and began a long affair with Princess Caroline of Sayn-Wittgenstein, who like Lola smoked cigars. When she was ordered to leave Weimar, Liszt took minor clerical orders. It was not the comtesse he should have feared for his unauthorised biography, because in later life he became involved with his pupil, the fiery young Cossack Olga de Janina. Adopting an approach worthy of Lola, not only did she threaten to kill him and then take poison but she wrote two books about their affair. *Souvenirs d'un Cosaque* was followed by *Mémoires d'un Pianiste*, both under the name of a composer, Robert Franz. She also wrote two novels, again based on their relationship, this time under the name Sylvia Zorelli. When a Paris newspaper refused to send a critic to a recital by her, she took a horsewhip to him. Liszt died on 31 July 1886 at Bayreuth, three years after Wagner.

Lola's Parisian lover Pier-Angelo Fiorentino died on 31 May 1864 a rich man. He had come to the city with a mere 150 francs but now he left a fortune of 600,000 francs. He was the translator of Dante's *Inferno*, illustrated by Gustave Doré.

Sir Robert Peel was always thought to have lacked the qualities of his father, the Prime Minister. He sat as Liberal-Conservative MP for Tamworth for thirty years from 1850. Like his uncle Jonathan, he had extensive interests in the turf, which in his case contributed over the years to his financial ruin. He married in 1856, but Lady Emily Peel left him and went to live in Florence. In later years he was very much in favour of Home Rule for Ireland. He died following a brain haemorrhage at his home in Stratton Street, Mayfair, near Lola's old hunting grounds, on 9 May 1895. He left an estate of a little under £10,000.

In later life Lord Brougham, of whom it was said, 'Il n'y a pour lui qu'un pas entre le sublime et le ridicule'('For him it was only a step between the sublime and the ridiculous') and described by John Morley as having 'encyclopedic ignorance', was elected Chancellor of Edinburgh University and gave his name to black and white check trousers, in addition to the horse-drawn carriage named after him thirty years earlier. He believed men committed crime through passion not reason and argued strenuously for education rather than imprisonment; he was another who believed that drink was the curse of the working classes. He died at Château Eleanor-Louise in Cannes on 7 May 1868, where he was buried.

Ludwig I died in Nice on 29 February 1868 at the age of eighty-two. Following his abdication he was allowed to return to Munich, but after the death of the saintly Therese he spent a good deal of time in Italy. Indeed, one completely ridiculous story which has gained some credence is that Lola married Ludwig in Italy and that she contracted syphilis from him on their honeymoon.[3]

Ludwig had one more great love. Carlotta von Breidbach-Bürresheim was a lady-in-waiting of his daughter, the Grand Duchess Mathilde. His affection was not returned and Mathilde was obliged to intervene to put a stop to street gossip. The *Saturday Review* thought that while he was liberal with his money, 'he remained to the last what he always had been, indolent and selfish and was neither liked nor respected, though a certain interest was felt in him as a kind of chartered buffoon of the first rank.'[4]

The boulevardier Heinrich Maltzahn, suspected of being Lola's *souteneur* in her early days in Munich, survived only until 1851, dying of an eye cancer at the relatively early age of fifty-eight. Lola's young lover Friedrich Nüssbammer was yet another who had a short and unhappy life. After his exile from Munich he was placed on inactive duty, with the additional hardship that he must exist on his small pension and was not allowed to take up any trade or business. He went mad and died in an asylum on 18 March 1859. He was then thirty-nine.

Lola's other well-known Munich lover, Fritz Peissner, did rather better. After his confession of his relationship with Lola, Ludwig financed his emigration to America with his brother where he became a respected professor of languages at Union College, Schnectady. He married and had three children. There is no record of his ever having met Lola again in America. During the the Civil War, he fought with the rank of colonel on the Union side, leading a volunteer regiment in the 119th New York Light Infantry with a muster of German immigrants. At the battle of Chancellorville on 2 May 1863, the regiment was moved to a forward position at Peissner's request and almost immediately came under fire. He was riding the lines rallying his men when he was shot from his horse and died, allegedly calling out 'God protect my wife and children.'

The religious life of the shadowy Auguste Papon did not last long. Sadly ill-health prevented him remaining in the monastery, but happily he was able to continue his interest in the church. He took up insuring religious properties in France against theft and, to ensure a steady business, stole from them himself. He received ten years *in absentia*, but where he went remains a mystery. Since this information comes from the unreliable de Mirecourt it may not be wholly accurate.

Jung Bahadur, Lola's lover after Heald left Paris, remained a staunch friend to the British during the Indian Mutiny. There is a charming story that while he was with Laura Bell he gave her a ring, saying she should return it to him if she was ever in need. When the mutiny broke out she took it to the Foreign Office for it to be sent to the Prince. He died on 18 June 1877 on the banks of the Baghmati near Patharghatta. It is possible he was murdered.[5]

Savile Morton, Lola's lover after Bahadur, survived two duels, but soon afterwards his luck was to run out. Under the pretext of assisting in her divorce case, Morton took to comforting the wife of an old Cambridge acquaintance named Harold Elyot Bower, who was also living in Paris and was conducting an extra-marital affair. When Mrs Bower gave birth to a fifth child, Bower, believing it was Morton's, stabbed him in the neck at 2 rue de Sèze on 1 October 1852. It seems that in a delirium Mrs Bower had been raving that Morton had been her lover. Bower was acquitted in December, while for a time Morton joined Dujarier in the Montmartre cemetery.[6]

Lola's short-term lover Patrick O'Brien, who delivered her letters to Ludwig, reappeared in St Petersburg in the 1860s, again attempting to trade on his one-time association with *The Times*. On 12 December 1863 Mowbray Morris wrote to *The Times*'s correspondent in Poland, Sutherland Edwards, describing O'Brien as 'one of the most unintelligible scoundrels I ever knew. With little education, no great ability and a strong tinge of cowardice, he had contrived to make his way into places where really good men would be glad to find themselves. Long ago he corresponded with *The Times* from Greece, but was soon found out, and his official connection ceased absolutely.' He added, 'I hope you will never lose an opportunity of setting people right as regards this little blackleg.'[7]

Of Lola's many agents, managers and lovers, Joseph Scoville, 'Mr Pick', seems to have done the best for himself. He edited *The Pick* until 1855 and then, in 1857, the *Evening State Gazette*. Very much opposed to the Lincoln administration and the prosecution of the Civil War, he was warned as to his conduct over articles he published in the London *Morning Herald* and *Evening Standard*. He wrote a number of novels, including the heavily autobiographical *Vigor* (titled *Marion* in England). He is said to have made enough money from his literary work to leave his wife, Caroline, and daughter well provided for when he died in New York on 25 June 1864.

Lola's third husband, Patrick Hull, died on 21 May 1858, some three years after taking over the paper *Daily Town Talk*. According to the *Marysville Daily Examiner*, 'His sickness was long and painful. In November last he was suddenly struck down with paralysis and from that moment until he breathed his last he was helpless.'[8] The *Golden Era* wrote, 'he was as good-hearted and jovial a mortal as ever lived. Lightly rest the sod upon thy body, Pat.'[9]

The violinist Miska Hauser, who had been the cause of much of Hull's jealousy, lived long after Lola, dying in Vienna on 8 December 1888. *The Times* thought the style of playing he had employed twenty years earlier would not long have stood up against younger men such as Kreisler. He composed an operetta, *Der Blinder Leiermann*, and his *Songs without Words* and a transcription of Schubert's Lieder were well regarded.

The gallant Zouave, Henri de Rivière, who was apparently the brother of France's best-known chess player, finally married his Miss Blunt. But things did not go well and he was back in trouble in October 1869, when he was arrested on charges of swindling Mlle Hélène Stille, described as a wealthy and beautiful Parisian lady, out of some $7,500. She was not all she seemed and was a frequent visitor to a house of ill-fame at 102 East Twenty-second Street, run by one of New York's more famous and long-lasting madams, Mrs Van Ness. By consent the action was discontinued. After the case de Rivière disappeared from New York's view. There were unconfirmed accounts that he returned to France, where he was killed in the Franco-Prussian war.[10]

After Lola's death all manner of rumours and stories were published, particularly as the Gold Rush approached its half-century. Old-timers who may or may not have been in California were wheeled out to give their reminiscences of the good old days, and many of their stories included seeing Lola. One of the most ludicrous was published in the *San Francisco Examiner*, which should have known better.[11] It purported to be based on the recollections of F. N. Montez – the paper proudly printed that he had certified the truth of the story. He had, it seems, been a palmist who had impressed the actress, Ella Wheeler Wilcox. Montez claimed to be the son of the Frenchman Jean-François Montez, who from time to time featured in accounts of Lola. Montez senior, born in Pau, had met, fallen in love with, and supported Lola in London. He had later married, but when Lola reappeared it had nearly broken up the family. In Grass Valley Lola had taken a whip to a drover, who had in turn whipped her. She had shaken the man's hand, saying that no man had ever bested her before, but the incident had changed her luck. She soon took to opiates and was brought to the insane asylum at Randall's Island where she was murdered, her head being repeatedly banged on the stone floor. Young Montez did not record whether it was done by staff or inmates. Montez's name appeared occasionally in Lola stories. In an undated *Theatre Magazine*, a Dr Judd suggested she had taken her name from a Jean-François Montez, who met her in 1838 and supported her over the years until she went to Munich. It is possible, however, that Judd borrowed the story from the *Examiner* article.

At least Montez did not claim to be Lola's son. There were quite sufficient aspirants for that role already. She is said to have had at least seven children; almost certainly this is wholly incorrect.

Apart from the suggestion that Lola had two boys by Heald who drowned – itself a confabulation of the boating accident story – the first claimant to surface was Elise Montez, supposedly her child by Dujarier. Elise became an actress and made her debut in *Phèdre* at the Odéon in Paris in 1867. Another daughter was said to have appeared as a dancer in Germany in 1870.

In April the next year there was a report of a son by Ludwig who resigned his commission after inheriting a substantial sum from the ex-King. In September that year there was said to be a young man in Paris who claimed to be her son, but he may have been the same man who a few months earlier was spending his fortune.[12]

Further suggestions are that she had another daughter whose

names are variously given as Alice or Rosalind, by Patrick Hull. The child was said to have been given to the care of Mrs Samuel King of Sacramento, the wife of a rich gold miner. Lola would not allow the child to be adopted and said she would return to her after her tour to Australia. The Kings moved to Portland, Oregon; Rosalind married Louis Devereux of New Orleans at the age of eighteen, settling in Mexico City before moving to New Orleans in 1897 where she died leaving two children. On 28 December 1898 the *New York Times* announced the death in New Orleans, aged forty-four, of Lola's daughter Alice Devereux.[13]

Thad Phillips, a porter on the Oakland ferry service of the Southern Pacific Railroad who claimed that he had worked for Lola in 1854 and went to Australia as her baggage manager, maintained she had a child by Heald born in Sussex, asserting that the English consul visited Lola in Grass Valley to pay her £100 a month. The man had married and the payment was to ensure Lola never returned to England. Some years later the story reappeared as gospel, this time told, almost in Phillips' exact words, by a Colonel Daniel W. Preston of Los Angeles. He maintained he first met Lola when they travelled together from New York and that he had been a guest at the wedding. Much of the information in the article is correct. He names the Fiddes family as Lola's problem in Sydney and gives the name of Mrs Crosby (calling her Ormsby) as the woman she fought in Ballarat. He is certainly also correct when he says, 'No one could withstand the charm of Lola Montez' smile at close range. Her manners were delightful and her vivacity when she was pleased or when she wished to gain a point, was delightful. But she could change in an instant from the sweetest woman to the most violent and profane shrew.' He also thought she was conversant in no less than thirteen languages and stated, 'I never heard her claim the same nationality twice.'[14]

It is easy enough for men to father children and move on. It is much less so for women, particularly those in the public eye such as Lola. With the unlikely exception of the daughter said to be born during the period in which Lola disappeared following Dujarier's death, the dates and places simply do not tie in. Much more likely is that Lola had no children. When she was living in Grass Valley she often remarked that this was one of the regrets of her life. It is possible that she was barren from taking mercury and other medicines early in her life as cures for venereal diseases, although there is no supporting evidence.

The most venal and celebrated of the claimants is the 'spirit spook', Editha Lola Diss Debar, a fraudulent medium and swindler who plied her trade in America, South Africa and Europe. Just as Lola never could get it out of her head that she was Spanish and over the years went under a variety of names, so did Editha, or Della Ann O'Sullivan, Anne O'Delia, Solomon or Horos – after the Egyptian deity – and more often Diss Debar, as well as Vera. Throughout her life Diss Debar claimed, despite considerable evidence to the contrary, that she was the daughter of Lola's relationship with Ludwig and had been raised by nuns in Italy, before in 1855 being sent to America to a cruel foster family named Salomons.

There were other similarities between her and Lola. She was certainly her equal as a liar. In October 1890, echoing Lola and the Order of St Thérèse, she claimed that the Pope had given her a medal. 'I am the only woman in the world he has honoured with such a present.'[15] Editha also appeared on the stage, again with no great success, and like her putative mother it is difficult to know exactly how many marriage ceremonies she actually undertook. She certainly married Frank Jackson Dutton, who went under the title Theodore Horos, in a ceremony in 1889 in Louisiana, giving her title as Princess Editha Lolita and her parents as King Ludwig and Lola Montez.

On 25 September 1901 the pair were arrested in Birkenhead, where they had been lecturing, and brought to London to face charges of obtaining property by false pretences. To these, as the weeks went on, were added charges of rape and buggery. Jackson was sentenced to fifteen years and she to seven. Lola's long-time supporter the *New York Herald* was sure Diss Debar was a fake: 'She was altogether too able and too brilliant a woman to have foisted on her memory such an accusation as that of Ann O'Delia. Under no circumstances could Lola Montez have ever given birth to the frowsy, dismal apparition of Middle Age rural England . . .'[16]

Lola has remained a fascination for the world of the arts, making repeated appearances under a variety of guises. Over the years she has been played on screen by a number of actresses, many of whom failed to achieve recognition as long-standing as that of their subject. In 1918 a German black and white silent film directed by Robert Heyman was produced, with Leopoldine Konstantin as Lola. In the plot, based on an account in the version of her memoirs published in Grimma, Lola, a dancer at the Madrid theatres, is kidnapped by Madras, the leader of the Carlist movement. She falls for him and he proposes, but the English ambassador, who has been one of her admirers, wants information about the movement and sends spies to watch her. The story was repeated by Isaac Goldberg in his biography *Queen of Hearts*. The same year she was played by Claire du Brey in *Midnight Madness*. Four years after that Ellen Richter was in another German silent, *Lola Montez, die Tänzerin des Königs*, and in 1926 the very popular Betty Compson played her in *Palace of Pleasure*, again vaguely based on the Grimma memoirs. This time she escapes with Madras across the border into Portugal.

She was played in 1937 by Sheila Darcy, who also acted as Rebecca Wassen – she had been an extra and was picked as a lookalike – in a cameo role in *Wells Fargo*, starring Joel McCrea. A genuine star, Yvonne de Carlo, took the role in *Black Bart* in 1948. She persuades Dan Durea, as the real-life Californian bandit Charles E. Bolles, to give up robbing stagecoaches in return for true love. Yvonne de Carlo was not, however, universally well received in the part. Mae Tinee in the *Chicago Tribune* wrote that the role was 'far beyond her capabilities. Her singing and dancing were amateurish and her acting is the same.'[17] In fact, just like Lola.

Carmen D'Antonio played Lola in the 1951 *Golden Girl*; then came Max Ophüls' film, mentioned in the Introduction. Larissa Trembovel-skaya took over in the 1970 film *The Loves of Liszt*, while Ingrid Craven was in *Ludwig, Requiem for a Virgin King* in 1972. Anulka Dziubinska portrayed her as a sort of Marlene Dietrich in Ken Russell's absurd extravaganza *Lisztomania* in 1975, and Florinda Bolkan was a very mas-culine Lola in *Royal Flash* ten years later. In this adaptation of George Macdonald Fraser's novel, the rogue hero Flashman instigates the Betty James incident, as a result of which she plots a complicated and partially successful revenge. In Hitchcock's *Vertigo* the memory of Lola Montez in California played an important part in the plot.

On stage Olga Nethersole, who had something of a line in fallen women – she was prosecuted and acquitted in New York over her performance in the stage version of Daudet's *Sapho* – appeared as a character based on Lola in *The Silver Falls* in 1888, in which the hero is saved from the dominating temptress. Max Reinhardt put on a more sympathetic play by Joseph Reuderer in Berlin in 1904. It was banned from production in Munich for fear of offending Prince Regit Luitpold, King Ludwig's last surviving son.

In December 1939 the hugely popular Leo Carrillo, now best remembered as Pancho in the long-running television series opposite Duncan Renaldo's *Cisco Kid*, appeared in San Francisco as the bandit Joaquim Murietta with Tamara Geva in *The Red Bumblebee*, a comedy set in Grass Valley. Lola, with a Scots husband in tow, spends most of the piece scheming how she can get her hands on the $10,000 reward on Murietta, while enjoying a few perfunctory kisses with him. One reviewer thought the author Robert Craig 'shouldn't have named his drama after a bumble-bee without putting more sting in it'.[18] On 24 March 1982 the York Theatre Company presented *Lola*, a new musical by Claibe Richardson and Kenward Elmslie, at the Church of Heavenly Rest.[19]

Lola first appeared in ballet in *Bachanale*, based on the delirium of a dying Ludwig II. The score was the Venusberg music from Wagner's *Tannhäuser*, the decor was by Salvador Dali and the choreography by Leonide Massine, in a production for the Ballet Russe de Monte Carlo. It premiered in New York on 9 November 1939. Lola was danced in harem trousers with a hoop skirt decorated with false teeth. The piece played in repertory until 1942 and was revived in the 1990s. In 1947 the ballet *Lola Montez* by Edward Caton, with music by Fred Witt, was played in New York and then toured in America. It was described as dull.[20] In London *The Life and Death of Lola Montez* by J. Carter, with music adapted from Verdi, was danced by Anne Lascelles, with Michel de Lutry in all the male parts. It was first produced at the choreography workshop at the Mercury Theatre and then at Sadlers Wells.[21]

In the plot of the 1957 Australian musical *Lola Montez*, written by

Peter Stannard, Daniel Brady finds a gold nugget. When he sees Lola perform the Spider Dance he gives it to her and, in the original, sleeps with her. Then Jane Oliver, a young woman who nursed him in the Crimea, returns to Ballarat and he asks Lola to return it. Lola charms him into becoming her lover and manager, but another man promises to take her with him to America and restore her flagging career. She returns the nugget to Daniel, who gives it to his girl, but she returns it to him knowing he has overcome the double sins of promiscuity and greed. The play was more or less a complete failure, both critically and at the box office.[22]

In November 1997 the Hartford Ballet Company staged its Christmas *Nutcracker*, based on Petipa's choreography but with the location moved to the Sierra Nevada. Lotta Crabtree replaced Clara but retained her dreams, which naturally included toy soldiers and rats but also a grizzly bear and a spider. The new complement of characters included Lola, as well as Mark Twain and Joshua Norton, the fraudulent Emperor of the United States.[23] The next year, again in Connecticut, a new play, *Lola*, by Craig Safan and Kirby Tepper was produced.

Over the years there must have been more than a dozen now-forgotten novels written about Lola in a variety of languages, displaying various attitudes to the basic facts of her life. The best of them is probably Thomas Everett Harré's *The Heavenly Sinner*. Others include Joseph Ruederer's 1904 *Die Morgenrote*, in which Peissner is a scrounger who in the end deserts Lola. Her crossing of the ice-packed Hudson forms the opening of William Kennedy's *Quinn's Book* in his Albany series.

There have been suggestions that Thackeray's Rebecca Sharp has more than a little of Lola in her – though not Rebecca's hair, which is blonde. Thackeray certainly must have known her, if only through his friend Savile Morton, and throughout *Vanity Fair* there are incidents which mirror Lola's movements – the lying, the suggestions of spying, the gambling up and down the Rhine, the recognition of her, the benefit performance, flirting with her music teacher; all are the activities both of Lola and Becky Sharp. Certainly the *New York Evening Post* thought so: 'She was a Becky Sharp on a grand scale, only not quite as heartless as that imaginary character.'[24] Another unidentified obituary suggested that Becky Sharp sinned by *malice prepense*, while Lola simply erred from a fiery and ungovernable temper. 'Few women living were so incapable of anything like a deliberately evil action or of calmly injuring another.'

The novelist Anthony Trollope thought of Becky that 'there is no man so foul, so wicked, so unattractive, but that she can fawn over him for money and jewels. There are women to whom nothing is nasty either in person, language, scenes, actions or principle – and Becky is one of them; and yet she is herself attractive.'[25] He could have been writing of Lola. She herself was not wholly displeased with the suggestion that she had been the prototype for Becky Sharp, but said that any resemblance was because Thackeray had spoken only to her enemies in England.[26]

Lola was by no means the most successful of the *grandes horizon-tales*. She had far too restless a spirit for that. But, nevertheless, a remark attributed to Aldous Huxley is perhaps her best epitaph: 'When you met Lola Montez, her reputation made you automatically think of bedrooms.'

Endnotes

→>–<←

Introduction

1 *Bombay Telegraph*, 7 September 1852, reprinted in the *New York Daily Times*, 14 January 1853.
2 *Pittsfield Sun*, 21 January 1858.
3 *Brooklyn Daily Eagle*, 12 December 1886.
4 *Bayerische Eilbote* (Munich), 16 October 1846.
5 E. d'Auvergne, *Adventuresses*, p. 214.
6 A. Vandam, *An Englishman in Paris*, p. 145.
7 Quoted in Antoinette May, 'Mistress to an Era' in *San Francisco*, June 1976.
8 *Courrier de la Louisiane*, 7 January 1853.
9 Mary Clemmer Ames, *Outlines of Men, Women and Things*, pp. 124–5.
10 Isaac Goldberg, *Queen of Hearts. The Passionate Pilgrimage of Lola Montez*, p. 101.

1. Lola in Bud and Under Siege

1 A. Augustin-Thierry, 'Lola Montès favorite royale' in *La Revue des Deux Mondes*, 15 November, 1 December 1935.
2 National Archives, WO 42/18/81.
3 *Ennis Chronicle and Clare Advertiser*, 6 May 1820.
4 This research was carried out by Nicholas Shreeve, who passed the information on to Bruce Seymour. The note lodged by Mrs Gilbert seems to have been destroyed, possibly when the Public Records Office transferred the material it held in Chancery Lane to Kew.
5 Anon., *Cadet's Guide to India by a Lieutenant of the Bengal Establishment*; Journal of Capt. C. D. Aplin, Eur. Ms B208; Bessie Fenton, *The Journal of Mrs Fenton*.
6 National Archives, WO 25/1789.
7 Lola Montez, *Lectures of Lola Montez*, p. 7.
8 ibid., p. 8.

9   Ishbel Ross, *The Uncrowned Queen. Life of Lola Montez*, p. 4. Ross claimed that much of
     the early material in the book came from Anne Watson of Holly House, Montrose.

10   British Library, BLIO L/Mar/B/70B, Log of the *Malcolm*.

11   Lola Montez, *Lectures of Lola Montez*, p. 21.

12   *Edinburgh Evening Courant*, 20 August 1849.

13   J. G. Grant, letter to *Sunderland Herald*, 31 August 1849.

14   BLIO MSS Eur. F. 175, Jasper Nicolls' Journal, 14 September 1832.

15   ibid., 14 February 1834.

16   ibid., 18 April 1837.

17   *New York Daily Times*, 18 January 1861.

18   Lola Montez, *Lectures of Lola Montez*, p. 25.

19   Jasper Nicolls' Journal, 31 July 1837. In the margin he wrote 'Wretch Gilbert'.

20   Jasper Nicolls' Journal, 12 August 1837.

21   Lola Montez, Memoiren von Lola Montez, Gräfin von Landsfeld, aus dem französischen
     übertragen von Ludwig Fort Vol. 1, Ch 18, 161–3.

22   ibid.

23   Jasper Nicolls' Journal, 15 November 1837.

24   Emma Roberts, *The East India Voyager or Ten Minutes of Advice to the Outward Bound*.

25   Lola Montez, Memoiren von Lola Montez, Gräfin von Landsfeld, aus dem französischen
     übertragen von Ludwig Fort Vol. 1, 164–5.

26   ibid.

27   By comparison the Protestant chaplain at Bareilly had a stipend of 10,345 rupees or
     around £276 a year.

28   Lady Eden, letters to her sister, 8, 10 September, 13, 17 November 1839. See Emily Eden,
     Up the Country.

29   One of Lady Eden's diary entries records the death of the poetess Laetitia Elizabeth
     Landon (1802–38), who married George MacLean, Governor of Cape Coast Castle, and
     died regretting it. On 15 October 1838 she was found poisoned. Mrs Eden thought
     Landon's maid was the 'supposed murderer' but it is more likely she either deliberately
     or accidentally took laudanum.

2. Lola in India, London and on Her Toes

1   Lennox was the eldest son of the second son of the 5th Duke of Richmond. His father,
     Lord George Lennox, was Lord in Waiting to Prince Albert in June 1843.

2   *Hampshire Telegraph and Sussex Chronicle*, 1 March 1841. Lennox's local newspaper
     thought they went to Sussex: 'Lt. George Lennox, 4th Madras Cavalry, son of Lord
     George Lennox, landed here on the 20th instant, after an absence in India of nearly five
     years, and proceeded to Bognor.'

3   London Metropolitan Archives, Consistory Court, Accession 73.77.

4   It is good to be able to record that one of the pieces of flotsam discarded by Lola fetched
     up on a reasonably attractive beach. Charlotte Haddon eventually found work as a cook
     with Dr Devonald, a surgeon in Great Litchfield Street.

5   Harvard Theatre Collection, Boston.

6   Lawrence Stone quotes an 1802 example of £5,000 awarded without the jury leaving the
     box and another when in 1815 the jurors halved a £30,000 claim in an hour. *The Road to
     Divorce*, p. 234.

7   48 G. 3c 123; *Goodfellow v Robings* (1836) 3 Bingham N.C.

8   *Morning Herald, The Times*, 7 December 1843.

9 Paget was reputed to neglect his wife, and to be unfaithful as well as brutal. Not only that, but he rather unsportingly had Lady Frances watched. One day she left her country home for her house off Berkeley Square, called for Cardigan and took him into her drawing room. Winter, a known blackmailer employed by Lord William, had concealed himself under the drawing-room sofa and remained there for some two hours. Fortunately for her she took Cardigan into the back drawing room, and so the hidden Winter could not say exactly what did or did not happen. To the intense delight of the public, an action for 'crim con' was brought and appeared in the Guildhall list for 22 December 1843. As often happened, however, it was a damp squib. Winter failed to appear and the action failed with him.

10 London Metropolitan Archives, Consistory Court, Accession 73.77.

11 *Punch*, 12 July 1845.

12 *Edinburgh Courant*, quoted in *Weekly Chronicle*, 25 August 1849.

13 Bayerische Staatsbibiothek, Munich; Ludwig Archive 39.

14 See Emma Dickens, *Immaculate Contraception; The Extraordinary Story of Birth Control from the First Fumblings to the Present Day*; Ronald Pearsall, *The Worm in the Bud*.

15 Fanny Kelly continued with her drama school and to give Shakespearean readings. Later, apparently in increasing financial difficulties, she moved to Feltham, Middlesex and Prime Minister Gladstone was petitioned for help. She received a royal grant of £150 shortly before her death on 6 December 1882, the money being used to pay for a grave and headstone in Brompton cemetery. She either had an illegitimate child by Samuel Arnold or adopted the girl, Mary Ellen Thatcher Gerbini. She left £3,037. For a life of Fanny Kelly see Basil Francis, *Fanny Kelly of Drury Lane*.

16 Quoted in Jacques de Plunkett, *160 Ans de Théâtre*.

17 William Bennett, 'Mr Bennett's Letters from Europe' in *New York Herald*, 26 April 1847.

18 3rd Earl of Malmesbury, James Howard Harris, *Memoirs of an Ex-Minister. An Autobiography of the Rt. Honourable Earl of Malmesbury*.

19 *The Age*, 11 June 1843. James Howard Harris, 3rd Earl of Malmesbury, died on 17 May 1889. The little scandal about his having invited Lola into his home did not in any way affect his political career. He became Foreign Secretary in 1853 and again in 1858–9, and later Lord Privy Seal from 1874 to 1876. He is probably better remembered for his gossipy *Memoirs of an Ex-Minister* than for his political acumen. See *Dictionary of National Biography*.

20 Described as being a beauty and having an equally beautiful voice, Grisi was the star of the London and Paris opera from the 1820s to the end of the 1850s. In all she appeared in London on 925 nights, singing *Norma* seventy-nine times, *Lucretia Borgia* a hundred and making ninety-two appearances in *I Puritani*. She married the impoverished Viscount Gérard de Melcy, and so bought herself a title at what would prove to be great emotional and financial cost. For an account of her life see Elizabeth Forbes, *Mario and Grisi*.

21 *Morning Post*, 3 June 1843; 'Q', *You Have Heard of Them*, pp. 101–2.

22 See inter alia *Morning Post*, *Morning Herald*, *The Times*, *Evening Chronicle*, 5 June 1843; *Weekly Dispatch*, *Era*, 11 June 1843.

23 Thomas Ranelagh led something of a chequered career. A Lord-Lieutenant and prominent in the Military Volunteer Movement, he nevertheless made regular appearances in court as the accused in cases mostly involving police officers and railway officials. In 1868 he was involved in the scandal of a Madame Borrodaile, gulled by the fraudstress Madame Rachel who persuaded her that Ranelagh's one desire was to marry her. It was said that there were probably few men who had so many charges of the most varied and disagree-

able nature made against them and for a time he was banned from presentation at foreign courts. When he died unmarried on 13 November 1885 the title became extinct. For an account of the Madame Rachel case see Horace Wyndham, *Blotted 'Scutcheons*.

24 *Morning Post,* 16 June 1843.

25 *The Age,* 11 June 1843.

26 *Morning Post,* 13 June 1843.

27 Benjamin Lumley, *Reminiscences of the Opera*, pp. 77–8. Lumley qualified as a solicitor in 1835 and intended to read for the Bar. When two of his clients went to prison for debt he took over their lease of the Haymarket Theatre.

28 Edward Fitzball, *Thirty-Five Years of a Dramatic Author's Life*, Vol. II, pp. 90–2; *Theatrical Journal* (London), 4, no. 188.

29 Lola Montez, *Lectures of Lola Montez*, pg. 41.

30 For the lives of the Arbuthnots, see *Dictionary of National Biography*. In his extensive research Bruce Seymour was not able to establish which, if either, of the two Arbuthnots alive at the time was the admirer. Neither was on the passenger list for the *Larkins* and the second baronet does not seem to have left India until 1847.

31 *Morning Herald,* 16 June 1843 et seq.; *Era,* 9 July 1843.

3. Lola in Europe

1 K.G.M., 'Der erste Auftretung von Lola Montez in Deutschland'; Anon, 'Der Beherrscher eines Kleinstaates'. Lola also gives her version of events in her *Memoiren*.

2 *Era,* 15 October 1843.

3 Richard Moulin-Eckart, *Hans von Bülow*, pp. 29–30; Eduard von Bülow, 'Die Neue Melusine' in *Novellen* 1, pp. 281–328. Hans von Bülow later became Liszt's pupil and married his daughter Cosima before Wagner snatched her away. Not that this treachery prevented von Bülow from continuing to conduct the master's operas.

4 *Münchener Conversationsblatt,* 5 October 1843. Marie Taglioni, considered to be one of the greatest dancers of her era, retired in 1847 and died in obscurity in Marseilles on 24 April 1884, the day after her 80th birthday.

5 *Era,* 15 October 1843.

6 Bruce Seymour, *Lola Montez: A Life*, pp. 54–5.

7 *Berliner Illustrierte Zeitung,* 13 November 1927.

8 For accounts of the incident see for example *Era*, 15 October, 3 December 1843; *Journal des Débats* (which claims she had merely hired the horse), 7 October, 15 November 1843; *Allgemeine Deutsche Zeitung* (Leipzig), 25 November 1843; Montez, *Memoiren*, Vol. 2, pp. 201–6.

9 Ludwig Simon, 'L'Extraordinaire Aventure de Lola Montez' in *Archives Internationales de la Danse*, October 1939.

10 'The Warsaw Ballet 1832–1853' in *Dance Chronicle*; Kazimierz Skibinski, 'Pamietnik Aktora' in Dabrowski S., *Writer on the Theatre and Górshi*, 1925; 'Lola Montez in Warszawie' in *Tygodnik Illustrawany*, no. 21, 1912; Lola Montez, 'Autobiography' in *Lectures of Lola Montez*, pp. 45–6; *The Times*, 16 January 1844.

11 *Boston Times,* 3 April 1852.

12 Richard Wagner, *Mein Leben*, p. 283.

13 Cosima Wagner, *Cosima Wagner's Diaries*, Vol. I, p. 37, 13 January 1869.

14 Pantaleoni's son became a leading baritone at Milan while his daughter Romilda created Desdemona for Verdi. She was said to have a magnetic stage personality to be compared with the great actress Eleanor Duse.

15 *Königsbergische Staats-Kriegs-und-Friedens-Zeitung*, 26 March 1844; *Abend Zeitung* (Dresden), 19 March 1844.

16 Alan Walker in *Franz Liszt*, Vol. 1 discounts the story, suggesting that it first appeared in 1909.

4. LOLA IN PARIS

1 For the lives of these and other noted courtesans of the time see Joanna Richardson, *The Courtesans*.

2 M. Ryan, *Prostitution in London, with a Comparative View of that of Paris and New York*, p. 57.

3 Henry Murger, *La Vie Boheme* translated as *The Bohemians of the Latin Quarter*; Julien Teppe, *Vocabulaire de la vie amoureuse*.

4 Henri de Viel-Castel, *Mémoires d'un Bourgeois*, p. 29

5 Philibert Audebrand, *Derniers Jours de la Bohème*, pp. 234 et seq. In the chapter on Fiorentino there are some highly inaccurate memories of Lola. He falls for the story that she was born in Seville and, told by a gypsy she would make a fortune, fled from her father to Biarritz. There she met a German nobleman who took her to Berlin. He describes her as 'une belle entre les belles'.

6 *Courreur des Spectacles*, 11 September 1844. Other versions of the stories are that it was Petipa's brother Leon who was her lover and that it was a third brother, Jean-Claude, who was attacked rather than their father. Ivor Guest, *The Romantic Ballet in Paris*, pp. 230–1.

7 Guest, *The Romantic Ballet in Paris*, p. 232. A number of stories about Lola and the ballet in Paris come from Eugène de Mirecourt, an early biographer of Lola who sadly was not the most reliable of raconteurs.

8 *Le Siècle*, 2 May 1844; *Era*, 28 July 1844.

9 *Le Corsaire*, 29 July 1844. The previous day the *Era* had already reported the talent she had been showing at Lepage's.

10 *Era*, 28 July 1844.

11 Vandam, *An Englishman in Paris*, pp. 52, 57, 59.

12 Gustave Claudin, *Mes Souvenirs: Les Boulevards de 1840–1870*, p. 37.

13 Now Essouria.

14 The theatre was destroyed in the Franco-Prussian war but was rebuilt and stands around 100 metres from the Place de la République.

15 *Era*, 16 March 1845.

16 Frédéric Loliée, *The Gilded Beauties*.

17 Anais Liévenne was an expensive liability. In 1849 she was sued over her failure to pay for silks and crêpes de chine but, when the bailiffs appeared, all the property in her apartment at the Hôtel des Princes was claimed by her then lover the Baron d'Azzara, the Spanish ambassador to Paris. Things were much better in June 1852 when she had a hotel on the Champs-Elysées, in which she had 200,000 francs' worth of furniture and where she gave a grand ball costing 60,000 francs. By 1853 she was in Russia, again avoiding her creditors. At one time she ensnared Victor Hugo's son, François-Victor. He actually thought of marriage but she wrote, 'I think I am too weak to carry out this farewell to the light world in order to enter so serious a world.' She spent a little time in exile with him in Jersey and was also close to Dumas senior, but she was temperamentally unstable. She both suffered fits and was suicidal. Jules Janin, *735 lettres à sa femme*, letter, 27 June 1852.

18 For those interested in the technicalities of the game see Sir John Hall, *The Bravo Mystery and Other Cases.*

19 It was, however, a question of Faux le Vicomte; the *soi-disant* d'Ecquevilley was in fact Victor Vincent, formerly a mere militia captain in Spanish service. D'Ecquevilley was a known cheat and had been caught in the casino at Madrid with a card up his sleeve. After serving in Spain he had returned to France to become a cardsharp and general trickster.

20 Vandam, *An Englishman in Paris*, pp. 138–9. In fact this thoroughly entertaining book is something of a fraud. Some years later Vandam admitted that he had the notes for it from a M. de Maupas, who wrote *Mémoirs sur le Second Empire*, 'to whom I am, moreover, indebted for most of the rough notes that constituted the foundation of *An Englishman in Paris*. How they came into his possession and from his into mine, together with the name of the Englishman who entrusted them to him, I will relate one day, not very distant perhaps.' The whole of the notes apparently covered three very closely written quires of paper. Vandam was unrepentant: 'If after that I am not the author of the book, Stephenson is not the inventor of the locomotive, for he did not make his own materials any more than I did.' A. Vandam, *My Paris Notebook*, p. 273. In America *An Englishman in Paris* is attributed to Sir Richard Wallace.

21 Andrew Steinmetz, *The Romance of Duelling*, Vol. II, p. 127. In 1832 the very sparky Duchess, the idol of the Royalists and whose husband had been assassinated ten years earlier, led a rebellion in the Vendée. She was betrayed and imprisoned. See James Morton, *The First Detective.*

22 De Girardin was the illegitimate son of the Premier Veneur of Charles X. He founded *La Presse*, whose subscription success was due both to its low price and because it was the first of the Paris papers to take advertisements. He also published a fashion magazine, *La Mode*, which helped launch the careers of Balzac and George Sand. He was later exiled but returned to found *La Liberté* and in 1870 advocated annexing territories on the left bank of the Rhine, which contributed to the Franco-Prussian war.

23 Letter from S. François to *Figaro*, 3 October 1858.

24 *Era*, 30 March 1845.

25 *Rabelais* (Paris), 27 March 1845; *Era*, 30 March, 20 April 1845; *Revue des Théâtres*, 9 July 1845.

5. LOLA ON HER TRAVELS

1 *Le Courrier de l'Europe* (London), 6 September 1845, quoting an earlier article.

2 *The Athenaeum Journal of Literature, Science and the Fine Arts*, 23 August 1845.

3 Walker, *Franz Liszt.*

4 Henry Chorley, *Modern German Music*, Vol. II, p. 258; K. Schorn, *Lebenserinnerungen*, Vol. I, pp. 208–11.

5 *Mannheimer Abendzeitung*, no. 28, February 1847.

6 *Gazette des Tribunaux*, 19 December 1845.

7 Vandam, *An Englishman in Paris*, p. 146.

8 Toussaint Victor Vincent d'Ecquevilley, *Temoin das un duel ou la verité sur le proces Victor d'Ecquevilley.*

9 Lola to proprietress of Hôtel de Suède, 18 August 1846.

10 *Allgemeine Zeitung* (Augsburg), 1 September 1846.

11 *Sunday Times*, 12 July 1846.

12 *Gazette des Tribunaux*, 26 July 1846.

13 Norman Gash, *Sir Robert Peel*, p. 176.
14 *Frankfurter Journal*, 27 February 1847.

6. MR WITTELSBACH – LUIS Y LOLA

1 *Illustrated London News*, 30 October 1847.
2 *New York Herald*, 26 April 1847.
3 Mary S. Lovell, *A Scandalous Life*, pp. 101, 343; Lesley Blanch, *The Wilder Shores of Love*.
4 *Pictorial Times* (London), 11 March 1847.
5 *Dictionary of National Biography*, p. 332; London: Smith, Elder, 1888.
6 George Henry Francis, 'Lola Montez and the King of Bavaria' in *Fraser's Magazine*, 1848, p. 97.
7 August Fournier quoting reports by Hineis to Metternich, 'Lola Montez. Ein geheimer Bericht über Bayern im Jahre 1847', in *Deutsche Revue*, August 1902, pp. 214 et seq; Isaac Goldberg, 'Queen of Hearts' in *The Athenaeum Journal of Literature, Science and the Fine Arts*, 9 February 1861.
8 J. de Plunkett, *160 Ans de Théâtre* and *Les Théâtres de Paris*. According to Plunkett she had already set her cap at the King of Holland and when she failed turned her attentions to his son, Prince Citron, again unsuccessfully.
9 Fournier, 'Lola Montez' pp. 214–30.
10 Luise von Kobell, *Unter der Vier Ersten Könignen Bayers*, p. 134.
11 The painting is now in the Münchner Stadtmuseum. For an account of the commission see Josefa Dürck-Kaulbach, *Erinnerungen an Wilhelm von Kaulbach und sein Haus*, pp. 53–4.
12 Codicil to Will of King Ludwig, 20 November 1846.
13 Mon 2 660, Anonymous Diary, p. 4 in Monacensia-Sammlung, Stadtbibliothek, Munich.
14 G. Arentz (trans. J. Laver), *The Elegant Woman: From the Rococo Period to Modern Times*, p. 208.
15 *Merkur am Sonntag*, 4–5 February 1956.
16 Francis, 'Lola Montez and the King of Bavaria'.
17 BSB LA 41, Maltzahn to Lola, 15 November 1846.
18 The letter appeared in *Temps* (Paris), 26 February 1909.
19 BSB LA 38, Ludwig to Tann, 8 December 1846.
20 GHANLXXI 586B, Ludwig's handwritten note on a letter, Abel to Pechmann, 22 December 1846.
21 University of Southampton, PP/GC/SU/77, Sulivan to Palmerston, 18 November 1846.
22 PP/GC/SU/78, Sulivan to Palmerston, 20 December 1846.
23 Staatsarchiv München, RA 16177.
24 BSB LA 39, Maltzahn to Ludwig, 31 December 1846.
25 BSB LA 39, Tann to Ludwig, 5 February 1847.
26 Karl von Abel was appointed envoy to the Turin court in 1847 but only took up the appointment under Ludwig's son Maximilian II. He was recalled in March 1850 and withdrew completely from politics, living on his property in the Olbeplatz, which Ludwig had given him for life. He died on 3 September 1859.
27 BSB LA 33, Ludwig to Lola, 26 January 1847.
28 PP/GC/SU79, Sulivan to Palmerston, 13 February 1847; see also Nat. Arch. FO 149/39, Bavarian correspondence.
29 Milbanke, draft letter possibly never sent, February 1847.

30 The English Garden was one of a number of parks constructed in the eighteenth century to resemble the English countryside. It was created by Benjamin Thompson for Karl Theodore, the Elector of Bavaria.

31 BSB LA 39, Maltzahn to Ludwig; Staatsarchiv München, RA 16177.

32 *Brooklyn Daily Eagle*, 5 May 1852.

33 *The Times*, 2 March 1847.

34 Prince Metternich to Archbishop Diepenbrock, 29 March 1847, Anton Chroust (ed.), *Gestantschaftsberichte aus München, 1814–1848*, p. 435, fn 1.

7. Lola Triumphant

1 Pearsall, *The Worm in the Bud*, p. 285.

2 Anon [Michael Cannon], *Lola Montes: The Tragic Story of a 'Liberated Woman'*, p. 27; Count Corti, *Ludwig I of Bavaria*, p. 309.

3 *Pictorial Times*, 20 March 1847; *Le Journal des Débats*, 6 April 1847; *The Times*, 9 April 1847 etc.

4 *Allgemeine Augsburger Zeitung*, 1 May 1847.

5 William Bennett, 'Mr Bennett's Letters from Europe' in *New York Herald*, 26 April 1847.

6 For an account of the problems of the Jesuits in France see Geoffrey Cubitt, *The Jesuit Myth. Conspiracy Theory and Politics in 19th Century France*, pp. 105–42.

7 Ludwig to Tann, 14 June 1847.

8 BSB LA 33, Ludwig to Lola, 25 August 1847.

9 BSB LA 34, Lola to Ludwig, 2 September 1847.

10 Von Leiningen was a close friend of Prince Albert and with the help of the Prince reportedly assisted Wallerstein in his research into Lola's background in London.

11 BSB LA 39, Queen Therese file; Queen Therese to Ludwig, 13 October 1847.

12 *The Times*, quoting *Journal des Débats*, 22 September 1847.

13 *The Eclectic Magazine of Foreign Literature*, November 1847, p. 382, quoting an undated *Brighton Gazette*.

14 *Pittsfield Sun*, 7 October 1847.

15 A great rival of Robert-Houdin, Henri-Joseph Donckele (1811–74), whose stage name was Henri Robin, also toured Europe with a wax museum exhibiting such tasteful tableaux as 'The Grecian Daughter Visiting her Father in Prison and Giving him Nourishment from her Breast', and a 'Correct Representation of a Military Execution'. In 1862 he opened the Salle Robin on the boulevard du Temple in Paris.

16 BSB LA 39, Wallerstein to Ludwig, Maria Denker to Ludwig, Mussiman to Ludwig, Berks to Ludwig; LA 34, Lola to Ludwig.

17 BSB LA 39, Martin to Ludwig, 8 December 1847.

18 For a contemporary account by a student of Munich in the last weeks of 1847 and the first months of 1848, see the letters of Ludwig May to his parents in Lola Montez Papers, Volume 18, Bancroft Library.

19 BSB LA 39, Mark to Ludwig, 12 February 1848; Berks to Ludwig, 12 February 1848; Stieleriana I, 5, c.1; LA 24, Lola to Ludwig, 12 February 1848; *Sunday Times*, 20 February 1848.

20 BSB LA 33, Ludwig to Lola, 14 February 1848; Nat. Arch. FO 149/38.

21 BSB LA 33, Ludwig to Lola, 16, 18 February 1848; Lola to Ludwig, 17, 18, 22 February 1848.

22 BSB LA 42, Mussinan to Berks, 20 February 1848; LA 39, Mussinan to Ludwig, 22 February 1848.

23 BSB LA 34, Lola to Ludwig, 19, 22 February 1848.
24 BSB LA 34, Lola to Ludwig, 22 February 1848.
25 BSB LA 39, Mussinan to Ludwig, 23 February 1848; Denker to Ludwig (dated February 1848 in Ludwig's writing); LA 34, Lola to Ludwig, 23 February 1848.
26 Sir Jasper Nicolls' Journal, 14 February 1848.
27 'Q', *You Have Heard of Them*, p. 106.

8. Lola in Exile

1 BSB LA 41, Peel to Lola, 21 February 1848.
2 BSB LA 34, Lola to Ludwig, 25 February 1848. Anti-clerical material was regularly circulated in Britain, and in 1868 the publisher of *The Confessional Unmasked Showing the Depravity of the Romish Priesthood, the Iniquity of the Confessional and Questions Put to Females in Confession* was prosecuted for obscenity. The author recounted in some detail the physical pleasures undergone by the confessor. Lola would have been proud of it. Law Report, 3 Q.B. (1868).
3 *Pittsfield Sun*, 13 April 1848.
4 *The Times*, 17 October 1854.
5 BSB LM 36, Ludwig, 29 April 1854, 27 January 1858.
6 BSB LA 33, Ludwig to Lola, letter begun 12 March 1848.

9. Lola in Switzerland

1 BSB LA 40, Lola to Ludwig, 12 March 1848.
2 BSB LA 39, Robert Peel to Ludwig, 25 March 1848.
3 BSB LA 34, Lola to Ludwig, 9 May 1848.
4 BSB LA 39, Rufenacht to Ludwig, 31 August 1848.
5 BSB LA 33, Ludwig to Lola, 29 August 1848.
6 *Illustrated London News*, 29 April, 20 May 1848; *The Satirist*, 27 May 1848; *Weekly Dispatch*, 30 April, 27 May 1848.
7 Sir Jasper Nicolls' Journal, 17 August 1848. The choleric Sir Jasper did not live to see the later dénouements of Lola's career. He died in 1849 still in service in the army, which he had joined in 1793.
8 BSB LA 39, Rufenacht to Ludwig, 31 August 1848.
9 BSB LA 33, Ludwig to Lola, 29 August, 1, 9 September 1848.
10 BSB LA 33, Ludwig to Lola, 5, 6 October; LA 39, Rufenacht to Ludwig, 10 October 1848; LA 38, Ludwig to Papon, 30 October, 12 November 1848.
11 BSB LA 38, Papon to Ludwig, 23, 24, 26 October, 6 November 1848; LA 38, Ludwig to Papon, 28, 30 October 1848; LA 33, Lola to Ludwig, 1, 8 November 1848.
12 BSB LA 39, Peissner to Ludwig, 21, 29 December 1848, 5 January 1849, Ludwig to Peissner 17, 26 December 1848.
13 BSB LA 39, Papon to Ludwig, 1 December 1848.

10. London: Lola Remarried

1 George Sala, *The Life and Adventures of George Sala*, pp. 194–5.
2 *The Times*, 19 April 1842.
3 *The Satirist*, 5 March 1848.

4   *The Times*, 25 April 1848. Sardanopolous was a legendary King of Syria who lived in extreme luxury and was besieged by the Medes for two years. Finally he set fire to himself and his palace. His death is the subject of a painting by Delacroix. Charles James Mathews, actor and dramatist and son of the more famous comedian, was despite a life of bankruptcies and occasional imprisonment a much loved man. He was thought to be at his best in farce and light comedies. Born in 1803, he married the celebrated courtesan Mme Vectris, and died in 1878.
5   *Brooklyn Daily Eagle*, 1 February 1850.
6   *The Satirist*, 29 September 1849.
7   K. Bourne (ed.), *The Blackmailing of the Chancellor*, pp. 42–3.
8   J. B. Atlay, *The Victorian Chancellors*, Vol. I, p. 335.
9   Harriet Martineau, *Autobiography of Harriet Martineau*, Vol. I, p. 309; Vol. II, p. 137.
10 *Journal de Genève*, 12 January 1849.
11 BSB LA 33, Ludwig to Lola, 6 January 1849, Lola to Ludwig, 12, 19 January 1849; LA 39, Rufenacht file, Rufenacht to Ludwig, 13 January 1849; LA 38, Ludwig to Papon, 22 January 1849, Murray to Ludwig, 23 January 1849; *Journal de Genève*, 12 January 1849.
12 Auguste Papon, *Lola Montès. Mémoires accompagnés de lettres intimes de SM le roi de Bavière et de Lola Montès*. The English translation, August Papon, *The Memoirs and Private History of Lola Montes also, the Whole of her Correspondence between Her and the King of Bavaria*, was published by S. Y. Collins probably in 1851, since it ends with Heald and Lola in Spain.
13 BSB LA 38, Papon to Ludwig, 20 August 1849.
14 BSB LA 34, Lola to Ludwig, 12 May 1849.
15 *Sunday Times*, 25 March 1849.
16 BSB LA 33, Ludwig to Lola, 15 March 1849; LA 34, Lola to Ludwig, 19 March 1849.
17 E. A. Smith (ed.), *Letters of Princess Lieven to Lady Holland 1847–57*. The disease is also a recurring theme in Jasper Nicolls' Journal.
18 BSB LA 33, Ludwig to Lola, 9 April 1849.
19 BSB LA 34, Lola to Ludwig, 11 April, 6 June 1849.
20 BSB LA 34, Lola to Ludwig, 12 May 1848.
21 BSB LA 33, Ludwig to Lola, 23, 30 April 1849.
22 BSB LA 34, Lola to Ludwig, 12 July 1849; LA 33, Ludwig to Lola, 8 July and undated July 1849. It was a little presumptuous of Lola to compare herself, even obliquely, to Mme Sontag, whose delivery was said to be unsurpassed by any singer of her day. She had married the Italian Count Rossi but their money had been lost in the political unrest of 1848. Henriette Sontag died of cholera in Mexico in 1854.

11. Lola in Trouble

1   *Era*, 18 August 1849.
2   Disraeli thought the former sum while the *Weekly Dispatch* of 22 July 1849 reported the latter.
3   The most celebrated resident of the village has been the cobbler William Marwood, the public hangman from 1874 to 1883, who is credited with the invention of the long drop.
4   Barcelona Correspondent of the Assemblée Nationale reprinted in *Weekly Chronicle*, 27 October 1849.
5   *Weekly Chronicle*, 16 September 1849.
6   S. M. Ellis, *A Mid-Victorian Pepys*.

7   Benjamin Dismeli, *Home Letters*, p. 284.

8   *The Times*, 10 August 1849; letter from Vere Londonderry in *Weekly Dispatch*, 11 August 1849.

9   *Weekly Chronicle*, 12 August 1849.

10   *The Satirist*, 18 August 1849.

11   With her dark ringlets, the soprano Eugenia Tadolini (1809–after 1851) curiously resembled Lola. She sang throughout Europe, mainly in *bel canto* roles, and created the part of Linda di Chamonix for Donizetti. Verdi considered her voice too beautiful to sing Lady Macbeth. She retired in 1851 and lived in Naples.

12   Maria Manning had met the wealthy Irishman Patrick O'Connor on the Boulogne boat in 1846. Although she married the criminal Frederick Manning, she continued to see O'Connor. On 9 August 1849 Mrs Manning, who had invited O'Connor for dinner, shot him in the head. He was finished off by Manning with a chisel and they buried him under the kitchen floor. Each blamed the other, but both were convicted and hanged. At her execution she wore a black satin dress, which caused the garment to go out of fashion for some years.

13   *The Times*, 19 July, 13 September 1849.

14   *Weekly Chronicle*, 16 September 1849.

15   Sergeant Ballantine, *Some Experiences of a Barrister's Life*. A Sergeant was the equivalent of today's Queen's Counsel.

16   BSB LA 34, Lola to Ludwig, 15 September 1849.

17   *The Satirist*, 18 August 1849.

18   BSB LA 34, Lola to Ludwig, 15 September 1849.

19   *New York Herald*, 23 October 1849.

20   *New York Herald*, 17 July 1852.

21   Barcelona Correspondent of the Assemblée Nationale, 24 October 1849, reprinted in *Weekly Chronicle*, 27 October 1849.

22   *Illustrated London News*, 3 November 1849.

23   *Le Siècle*, 21 October 1849. The actress Baroness de Marguerites is said to have been the source of the story.

24   *Examiner*, 10 November 1849.

25   BSB LA 34, Lola to Ludwig, 16 November 1849.

26   BSB LA 34, Lola to Ludwig, 31 December 1849.

27   *Pittsfield Sun*, 29 November 1849.

28   BSB LA 34, Lola to Ludwig, 25 February 1850.

29   BSB LA 39, Cetto to Ludwig. August von Cetto was the Bavarian ambassador in London in 1848 and 1849 and was by no means supportive of Lola. He was another who reported regularly to Ludwig on her movements.

30   *New York Herald*, 20 May 1850.

31   Virginia Rounding, *Grandes Horizontales*, p. 18.

32   *New York Herald*, 10, 20 May, 7 June, 2 July 1850.

33   BSB LA 34, Lola to Ludwig, 26 June 1850.

34   George Duncan was born in Perthshire on 10 December 1815 and died of cholera caught in London on 20 September 1854. Described as a builder on the certificate, he married Emily Jones at St Martin's in the Fields on 4 March 1847. I am indebted to John Duncan, his great-grandson, for providing me with copies of the letters written home.

35   BSB LA 42, Henry Davies to George Heald, 2 August 1850.

36   *Examiner*, 17 August 1850.

37   Heald v Carey: *The Times*, 8 June, 6 November 1851, 15 January, 24 April 1852.

12. Lola Resurgent

1 *New York Herald*, 7 October 1850.

2 *Galignani's Messenger*, 17 February 1851.

3 *New York Herald*, 21 October 1850.

4 Frederick Leveson-Gower, *Bygone Years*, p. 175.

5 Laura Bell's career had many parallels with that of Lola. She was said to have had a relationship with Dr William Wilde, Oscar's father, before coming to London.

6 Jean Gilliland, *Gladstone's 'Dear Spirit' Laura Thistlethwayte*.

7 *Examiner*, 17, 24 August, 21 September, 5 October 1850.

8 Other suggestions as to the author include her friend Pier-Angelo Fiorentino.

9 BSB LA 39, Ludwig to Wendland, 2, 16, 28 December 1850; letters Wendland to Ludwig, 8, 15, 21 December 1850.

10 A *pair* was the very rough equivalent of a member of the House of Lords.

11 *New York Herald*, 23 December 1850.

12 Papers in Houghton Collection, Trinity College Cambridge.

13 The note bears the date 14 December 1850 ('14.12.50'), which almost certainly has been added. If it was that date, then she went to see *La Fille du Regiment* at the Italian Opera.

14 G. S. Venables to Savile Morton, 19 December 1850.

15 W. M. Thackeray, *Letters and Private Papers* Vol. 2, p. 726.

16 Lola Montez, 'Wits and Women of Paris' in *Lectures of Lola Montez*, p. 255.

17 Montez, 'Wits and Women of Paris', p. 257.

18 Franziska Elssler, called Fanny, (1810–84) was the daughter of Haydn's copyist. One of the most illustrious dancers of the age, she always denied she had an affair with Napoleon II, the duc de Reichstag. She retired after a performance in Vienna in 1851, dying in that city in 1884.

19 *New York Herald*, 23 December 1850; Montez, *Lectures of Lola Montez*, p. 255.

20 Benjamin Lumley's entrepreneurial career went from bad to worse. The French *coup d'état* of 1852 cost him a massive £14,400 and he found he could not manage both the Paris and London houses. Wages went unpaid and he fled to France to avoid his English creditors. His debts were bought up by Lord Ward, later the Earl of Dudley, who reinstated him as manager of Her Majesty's, but again he failed. He returned to the law and wrote both a legal textbook and a novel, *Sirenia*, as well as a pamphlet about his legal and financial disputes with Lord Ward. He died in Kensington on 17 May 1875 aged sixty-three, leaving less than £1,000.

21 In 1816, when Lamartine went to Aix-les-Bains for his health, he fell in love with the young wife of a doctor. She travelled with him to Paris but, too ill to go to the spa the next year, she died in the autumn. His work *Méditations poétiques*, inspired by her death, was immediately popular. He died in Paris in 1869.

22 BSB LA 39, Ludwig to Wendland, 12 March 1851.

23 BSB LA 33, Lola to Ludwig, received 26 March 1851.

24 Letter, Mowbray Morris to O'Brien, 25 July 1850.

25 BSB LA 39, O'Brien to Ludwig, dated Rome, Friday.

26 BSB LA 39, Ludwig to Wendland, 30 July 1851; Poci to Ludwig, 1 August 1851; O'Brien to Ludwig, 5 May, 6 July 1851.

27 Arthur Todd, ' . . . the Coming of Fanny Elssler and Lola Montez' in *Dance Magazine*, October 1950.

28 *New York Herald*, 1 November 1851.

29 *Sunday Times*, 10 August 1851; *Revue et Gazette des Théâtres*, 28 August 1851; *New York Herald*, 29 August 1851; *Le Courrier de l'Europe*, 7, 13, 14 September 1851.

30 *New York Times*, 26 September 1851.

31 Houghton Library, Harvard University. Given the date of her reappearance it is curious that the poem is dated 15 September 1851. Another copy is in the Bibliothèque de l'Arsenal, Paris.

32 *Le Courrier de Paris*, 19 September, 1851; *L'Independence Belge*, 20 September 1851; *Le Courrier de l'Europe*, 20 September 1851; *Sunday Times, Revue et Gazette des Théâtres*, 21 September 1851.

33 *Revue et Gazette des Théâtres*, 21 September 1851. *L'Impartial de Boulogne sur Mer*, 18 September 1851, was not so happy with her, commenting that the money which had passed through her hands could feed a hundred families for twenty years.

34 *Emancipation* (Brussels), 26 September 1851.

35 BSB LA 39, Ludwig to Wendland, 21 September 1851.

36 *Journal de la Belgique* (Brussels), 27 September 1851.

37 *Notice biographique sur Fieschi dit Gérard* (n.d., n.p.).

38 *Journal de la Belgique*, 27 September 1851.

39 *Gaglignani's Messenger*, 27 September 1851.

40 *Sunday Times*, 26 October 1851.

41 *Silesian Gazette*, 8 May 1847.

42 *Gazette des Tribunaux*, 19, 20 November 1851.

43 *New York Times*, 15 November 1851.

44 *New York Daily Tribune*, 6 December 1851.

45 *New York Herald*, 3 February 1852.

13. Lola on the Boards

1 Augusta Maywood appeared in Paris in 1839 at the age of fourteen dancing with Charles Mabille, with whom later she eloped. They were arrested after a telegraph was sent to Boulogne but were later allowed to marry. On 5 February 1845 she bolted with a Portuguese actor, by whom she had a child and lived in some style on the shores of Lake Como.

2 *New York Herald*, 3 January 1852; '*In re* Montes *Versus* Respectability' in *Albion*, 3 January 1852.

3 *New York Herald*, 5, 7, 10, 13, 15 January 1852; 8 April 1888; *Brooklyn Eagle* quoting *Washington Union*, 20 January 1852.

4 Quoted in M. M. Marberry, 'How New York Greeted King Ludwig's Girlfriend' in *American Heritage*, 6 February 1955.

5 For his death see *Boston Post*, 24 March 1853.

6 *The Pick*, 11 September 1852.

7 *New York Herald*, 5 January 1852.

8 *New York Herald*, 16 February 1852.

9 *New York Herald*, 23 February 1852.

10 Horace Wyndham, *The Magnificent Montez. From Courtesan to Convert*, p. 191.

11 Lilian Moore, 'George Washington Smith' in *Dance Index*, June–August 1945.

12 *New York Herald*, 17 January 1852.

13 *New York Herald*, 17 January 1852; *Courrier des Etats Unis*, 15, 16 January 1852.

14 Thomas Barry to J. B. Wright, 18 January 1852.

15   *Daily Pennsylvanian*, 24 January 1852.
16   *Public Ledger & Daily Transcript*, 3 February 1852; *New York Herald*, 5, 10 February 1852.
17   'Who is Colonel Bobo?' in *New York Herald*, 13 January 1852. William Seward, a militant abolitionist, later became Secretary of State. He survived an assassination attempt on the night John Wilkes Booth killed Lincoln and he was ruthless in hunting down and prosecuting the actor and his fellow conspirators.
18   *New York Daily Times*, 10 February 1852. In 1836 General Sam Houston had defeated the Mexican General Santa Ana and recaptured the Alamo.
19   Edwin De Leon, *Thirty Years of My Life in Three Continents*, p. 116.
20   *Sunday Dispatch* (Philadelphia), 25 January 1852.
21   *Richmond Dispatch*, *New York Herald*, 25 February 1852.
22   *Boston Herald*, 12 March 1852.
23   Undated and unidentified newspaper cutting in Harvard Theatre Collection; *Brooklyn Daily Eagle*, 22 July 1857.
24   *Boston Daily Evening Transcript*, 29 March 1852.
25   *New York Times*, 1 April 1852.
26   Edward Everett to Nathan Hale, 30 March 1852 in Edward Everett Papers, Massachusetts Historical Society.
27   *Boston Daily Transcript*, 2 April 1852.
28   For accounts of the quarrel see *New York Times,* 1 April 1852; *New York Herald*, 21, 27, 31 March, 1 April 1852.
29   *Boston Daily Mail*, 3 April 1852.
30   *New York Daily Times*, 15 November 1852.
31   *New York Herald*, 31 March 1852.
32   *Boston Daily Transcript*, 12 April 1852.
33   *Hartford Times*, 15 April 1852; *Boston Daily Mail*, 20 April 1852.
34   *New York Herald*, 14 April 1852.
35   *New Orleans Bee*, 9 April 1852; *Hartford Times*, 15 April 1852; *New York Herald*, 17 April 1852.
36   *New York Herald*, 22 April 1852.
37   ibid., 30 April 1852.
38   ibid., 9 May 1852.
39   ibid., 2 May 1852.
40   ibid.
41   *Missouri Republican*, 22 May 1852.
42   *Buffalo Daily Courier*, 11 May 1852; *Buffalo Daily Republic*, 12 May 1852.
43   *New York Herald*, 30 May, 1 June 1852.
44   ibid., 5 July 1852.
45   *Argus*, 31 August 1855.
46   *Sunday Dispatch* (Philadelphia), 15 October 1852.
47   *New York Herald*, 3 May 1852.
48   *Daily Argus* (Baltimore), 19 June 1852.
49   *New York Herald*, 12 June 1852.
50   Walt Whitman, *November Boughs*, p. 1189.
51   For an account of theatre in the Bowery in the nineteenth century see Luc Sante, *Low Life*, pp. 73–8.
52   *New York Herald*, 17 July 1852.
53   GHA Wendland NL 50/1, Ludwig to Wendland, 14 June 1852.
54   *New York Herald*, 26 August 1852.

55 *The Pick* (n.d.).
56 Michael W. Kauffman, *American Brutus*, pp. 98–9.

14. Lola in New Orleans, San Francisco and Sacramento

1   Letter, James Relfre Sprigg to his mother, Elizabeth A. R. Linn, 5 January 1853.
2   *New York Daily Times*, 14, 21, 25 January 1853.
3   *New Orleans Delta*, reprinted in *Boston Daily Mail*, 23 February 1853.
4   *Courrier de la Louisiane*, 10 February 1853.
5   Letter, Kate Field to her Aunt Corda, quoted in Lilian Whiting, *Kate Field, A Record*.
6   *Missouri Republican*, 21 March 1853.
7   *Louisville Daily Democrat*, 1 April 1853.
8   ibid.
9   *Courrier de la Louisiane*, 10 April 1853.
10 *New York Daily Times*, 21 April 1853.
11 ibid.; unidentified and undated newspaper.
12 Unknown newspaper quoted in *Boston Daily Mail*, 26 April 1853.
13 Sir William Don was an interesting character and one who would have appealed to Lola. Born in 1825, he inherited the baronetcy before his first birthday. Educated at Eton, he resigned his commission in the Dragoons in November 1845 in the face of huge debts. His estate was sold for £75,000 and he became an actor, playing mainly in America for five years. On his return to England he found he still owed £7,000 and began to tour again. Described as a good-hearted and able mimic, he died in Tasmania in 1862 after being reduced to playing travesty roles.
14 *New Orleans Delta*, 15 April 1853.
15 *Daily Picayune*, 10 April 1853.
16 Mary Jane Megquier, *Apron Full of Gold*; John Haskell Kemble, 'The Panama Route to the Pacific 1848–1869' in *Pacific Historical Review*, March 1938, pp. 1–13.
17 Flyer for the San Antonio and San Diego Mail-Line, c. 1850, in San Francisco History Center.
18 *Panama Herald*, 6 May 1853.
19 Mary Seacole (ed. W. J. Stead), *Wonderful Adventures of Mrs Seacole*; Montez, *Lectures*, pp. 78–80; unidentified cutting in Harvard Theatre Collection; *Chicago Tribune*, 28 February 1864.
20 Letter, Thomas Buchanan to his wife, 23 May 1853, Yale University Library.
21 Letter, H. B. Sheldon to 'Dear Friends', 25 June 1852. Henry B. Sheldon Collection, California Room, State Library, Sacramento.
22 Stuart Edward White, *Old California in Picture and Story*, p. 1.
23 B. E. Lloyd, *Lights and Shades in San Francisco*.
24 Herbert Asbury, *The Barbary Coast*; L. Estevan (ed.), *San Francisco Theatre Research*, Vol. 5.
25 *Golden Era*, 29 May 1853.
26 ibid., 27 May 1853; *Daily Alta California*, 27 May 1853.
27 *Daily Alta California*, 28 May 1853.
28 ibid.
29 George Horatio Derby [John Phoenix], 'Squibob at the Play' in *Phoenixiana or Sketches and Burlesques*, quoted by George R. MacMinn, *The Theatre of the Golden Age in California*, p. 484.
30 Estevan (ed.), *San Francisco Theatre Research*, Vol. 5, pp. 14–15.

31 Mary Jane Megquier, *Apron Full of Gold*, p. 80.
32 George Horatio Derby [John Phoenix], 'Squibob at the Play' in *Phoenixiana or Sketches and Burlesques*, quoted by MacMinn, *The Theatre of the Golden Age in California*, p. 327.
33 *Placer Times and Transcript* (San Francisco), 25 June 1853.
34 Andy Rogers, *A Hundred Years of Rip and Roarin' Rough and Ready*; *Daily Alta California*, 22 May 1853.
35 Estevan (ed.), *San Francisco Theatre Research*, Vol. 5, pp. 17–18.
36 Edwin V. Burkholder, 'The Girl with the Million Dollar Tag' in *Real Men*, August 1959.
37 'Grass Valley's famous Limerick Countess had high aspirations' in unidentified newspaper, 1 January 1915, quoted in Rogers, *A Hundred Years of Rip and Roarin' Rough and Ready*.
38 Walter Leman, *Memoirs of an Old Actor*, p. 253.
39 Letter from Librarian, Californian Historical Society to Clara Dills, San Mateo County Library, 24 November 1942.
40 *San Francisco Evening Journal*, 2 July 1853; *New York Daily Times*, 12 September 1853.
41 *Shasta Courier* (Oroville), 9 July 1853; *Pittsfield Sun*, 1 April 1852 quoting the *Boston Bee*.
42 Wyndham, *The Magnificent Montez*, p. 200.
43 Miska Hauser, *Diary of Miska Hauser*, Ch. 1; *Sacramento Union*, 7, 8 July 1853; *Daily Democratic State Journal* (Sacramento), 7, 8 July 1853; *Daily Californian*, 8 July 1853.

15. Lola at Pasture

1 *Golden Era*, 10 December 1853.
2 *Nevada (City) Journal*, 29 July 1853.
3 ibid., 5 August 1853. The story was written by Jonas Winchester. See Jonas Winchester papers, California State Library, Sacramento.
4 *Sacramento Union*, 18 July 1853.
5 *Sacramento Bee*, 16 March 1975.
6 Edward P. Hingston, *The Genial Showman*, p. 215.
7 Edward Vischer (translated from German by Ruth Frey Axe), 'A Trip to the Mining Regions in the Spring of 1859' in *Quarterly of the Californian Historical Society*, VII, no. 3, September 1932.
8 Unpublished notes of Helen Holdredge, Vol. 5, p. 10. In San Francisco History Center.
9 *Nevada (City) Journal*, 5 August 1853.
10 *Golden Era*, 4 September 1853.
11 *Brooklyn Daily Eagle*, 5 September 1853.
12 A variation is that Lola had bewitched the bandit Joaquim Murietta. Hull, away from home, heard of this and, hurrying back, was confronted by the bear, which he shot. [Anon], *Life and Adventures of Joaquim Murietta*.
13 Letter, Lola Montez to 'Paco', 14 September 1853.
14 *Nevada (City) Journal*, 7 October 1853.
15 *Marysville Evening Herald*, 7 November 1853; letter, Tallman Wright to his mother, 12 November 1853.
16 *Northampton Gazette* (undated), quoted in *New York Daily Times*, 27 May 1854.
17 *San Francisco Examiner*, 23 September 1888. This article pieced together reports from other papers, none of which appear to have survived. By no means a foul fighter, the Irish-born 'Yankee' Sullivan was defeated in a match on 10 January 1849 at Rock Point, Maryland by the far superior pugilist, Tom Hyer. Hyer died in New York on 26 June 1864.

18 Shipley lived only a few years after the whipping incident in Grass Valley. He had always been a great drinker and was never a settler. In October 1858 he was thrown from his horse at The Dalles and suffered severe injuries. He was in a coma for several weeks and at one time a coffin was brought to his room so his body could be shipped home. In the summer of the following year, after travelling in Canada, he edited the *Portland Times* (Oregon) and then returned to California planning to sail to Hawaii for his health. But in November he missed the ship and, in a fit of depression, took strychnine in the Merchant's Hotel, Sacramento. *Sacramento Union*, 15 November, 1 December 1858, 18 November 1859.

19 *Shasta Courier* (Oroville), 18 February 1854.

20 *Sacramento Bee*, 20 November 1960.

21 *New York Times*, 12 August 1877.

22 Edwin Franklin Morse, 'The Story of a Gold Miner in *California Historical Quarterly*, December 1927.

23 Undated *Nevada (City) Journal* quoted in Antoinette May, 'Mistress to an Era' in *San Francisco*, June 1978.

24 Stephen Massett, *'Drifting About' or What 'Jeems Pipes of Pipesville' Saw and Did*, p. 247.

25 Hingston, *The Genial Showman*, Vol. 2, pp. 215–16.

26 Frans Moos, 'Lola Montez' Schicksalsnacht in Kalifornien' in *Montrealer Nachrichten*, 11 November 1972.

27 Lucinda Linn Brown, 'Pioneer Letters' in *Historical Society of Southern California Quarterly*, March 1939, pp. 18–26.

28 *New York Sun*, 1897 (otherwise undated); Henry G. Tinsley, 'Mad Antics of Lola Montez in a Californian Mining Camp' in *San Francisco Examiner*, 19 February 1899.

29 *New York Clipper*, 5 July 1879.

30 *Boston Daily Globe*, 13 September 1891; B. G. Rousseau, 'The Sierra Lorelei', n.d., n.p.; other unidentified and undated clippings in Harvard Theatrical Collection.

31 Kauffman, *American Brutus*, pp. 95–7; Vernanne Bryan, *Laura Keene, A British Actress on the American Stage*, pp. 43–5.

32 *Grass Valley Telegraph*, 22 June 1854.

33 *Leslie Estate*, p. 379, see M.B. Stern, *Purple Passages*.

34 The one-time mistress of boxer John Heenan and friend of Swinburne, Menken later appeared as K. Klopper in *Pas de Fascination* in San Francisco on 19 September 1863.

35 *Placer Times and Transcript*, 6 June 1855.

36 Leman, *Memoirs of an Old Actor*, p. 251.

37 *California Chronicle*, 7 June 1855.

38 *Placer Times and Transcript*, 7 June 1855.

39 *New York Daily Times*, 19 July 1855; *Golden Era*, 10 June 1855.

40 *San Francisco Bulletin*, 2 November 1855.

16. LOLA DOWN UNDER

1 Letter, Hauser to his brother, 15 January 1855.

2 *Argus* (Melbourne), September 1855.

3 Born in Limerick in 1825, Catherine Hayes made her debut in Marseille in 1845 as Elvira in *I Puritani*. She first appeared at Covent Garden in 1849. Thackeray pays tribute to her in his *Irish-Sketch Book*. She died in London in August 1861, some seven months after Lola.

4 Frank Fowler, *Southern Lights and Shadows*, pp. 33–4.

5 *Chicago Tribune*, 18 March 1861.
6 ibid. Amelia Jenks Bloomer (1818–94), a temperance and suffragette reformer, introduced a modified trouser dress for women. Harriet Beecher Stowe first published her powerful anti-slavery and influential novel *Uncle Tom's Cabin* in serial form in *The National Era* in 1851–2, and then in book form. Throughout her life Lola's attitude to slavery was ambivalent.
7 *Bell's Life in Sydney*, 8 September 1855.
8 *Sydney Morning Herald*, 11 September 1855.
9 *Sydney Morning Herald*, 12, 14 September 1855.
10 Richard Horne, *Australian Facts*, pp. 87–9.
11 Quoted in Cyril Pearl, *Always Morning*, p. 171.
12 'Preliminary Essay to the Poor Artist' in Richard Horne papers, Melville Library, Sydney. Horne, who as a boy had thrown a snowball at Keats, lived long enough to challenge the poet Swinburne to a public swimming match. He died in poverty in London in 1884.
13 *Age*, 14 September 1855.
14 *Argus*, 15 September 1855.
15 ibid., 1 November 1855.
16 *Herald* (Melbourne), 21, 22 September 1855; *Age*, 22 September 1855; *New York Daily Times*, 3 January 1856; *Truth*, 12 August 1911.
17 MS in La Trobe Library, Melbourne.
18 Letter, Hauser to his brother, Melbourne, 4 August 1855.
19 *Bendigo Advertiser*, 26 September 1855; Isobel Massary, *Social Life and Manners in Australia*.
20 *Geelong Advertiser and Intelligencer*, 28 September 1855.
21 *South Australia Register*, 14 December 1855.
22 William Kelly, *Life in Victoria*, Vol. 2, pp. 133–4.
23 ibid., p. 135.
24 *Argus*, 24, 27 March 1855.
25 Massett, *'Drifting About' or What 'Jeems Pipes of Pipesville' Saw and Did*, pp. 282–3.
26 *Herald*, 14 January 1856.
27 W. B. Withers, *History of Ballarat*, p. 227.
28 *Herald*, 22 February 1856; *Age*, 23 February 1856; *Punch* (Melbourne), 21, 28 February 1856; Charles Eberlé, *Memoirs*, MS 7569.
29 *Punch* (Melbourne), 6 March 1856.
30 *Ballarat Times*, 5 March 1856.
31 *Age*, 8 March 1856; *Herald*, 10 March 1856.
32 Anon [Michael Cannon], *Lola Montes: The Tragic Story of a 'Liberated Woman'*, p. 74.
33 William Craig, *My Adventures on the Australian Goldfields*, pp. 225–9.
34 Kelly, *Life in Victoria*, Vol. 2, p. 283.
35 Craig, *My Adventures on the Australian Goldfields*, pp. 225–9.
36 *Mount Alexander Mail*, 11, 15 April 1856.
37 *Argus*, 28 May 1856.
38 *New York Daily Times*, 26 April 1856.

17. Lola Changes Jobs

1 Nat Arch. Prob 11/2236, pp. 581ff.
2 *Pacific Commercial Advertiser* (Honolulu), 10 July 1856.

3 *Mount Alexander Mail*, 11 April 1856.

4 John H. McCabe, 'Diary'.

5 *Golden Era*, 3 August 1856.

6 ibid.

7 *Extra*, pp. 5–6, see Holdredge.

8 See Asbury, *The Barbary Coast*; Jeremiah Lynch, *A Senator of the Fifties, David C. Broderick of California*.

9 C. Rourke, *Troupers of the Gold Coast or The Rise of Lotta Crabtree*, p. 119.

10 Gradually Caroline Chapman lost her power to charm. Tastes changed, she grew older and she was reduced to playing Topsy in blackface in *Uncle Tom's Cabin* with Junius B. Booth Jr. as Uncle Tom. She returned East to make an unsuccessful appearance in New York and finally retired in 1870, dying 'alone and forgotten' in San Francisco on 8 May 1876. Her brother-father Uncle Billy had died in 1857. During the Civil War she had a Confederate brig named after her.

11 *Daily Alta California*, 10 August 1856.

12 *San Francisco Daily Evening Bulletin*, 17 October 1856.

13 *Daily Alta California*, 10, 20 August 1856.

14 *San Francisco Daily Evening Bulletin*, 1, 8 September 1856; *San Francisco Call*, 22 October 1888. See also Lola Montez file in Performing Arts Library and Museum, San Francisco.

15 *San Francisco Alta California*, 9 September 1856.

16 See for example, Joseph Henry Jackson, *Gold Rush Album*.

17 Edwin Franklin Morse, 'The Story of a Gold Miner' in *California Historical Quarterly*, December 1927. The house was extensively modified by subsequent owners with a second storey being added. By the 1970s it was in complete disrepair and when it was condemned the then owner made it over to the community. It was completely gutted to the oak foundations before being rebuilt as the single-storey residence she owned. Rather appropriately, one of the first fundraising ventures by the community was to recreate an Oktoberfest featuring Bruce Mitchell and his Bavarian Schuhplattlers. *San Francisco Examiner*, 27 September 1974. The house now doubles as the Chamber of Commerce and the Visitor Centre.

18 Rourke, *Troupers of the Gold Coast*, p. 118.

19 British Library, BLIO E/4/840, ff171.

20 Susan Robinson, 'The Fairy Star', had a short and unhappy career in a life beset with personal and professional problems. Over the years of her brief career she was regarded as an outstanding Ophelia and as equally at home in burlesque and tragedy. In Sacramento she was Katherine Klopper in *Catching a Governor* while her father played Muffenpuff, her sister Clara was Joliejambe and her brother William the lovelorn Michael. She died in Sacramento at the age of twenty-six following an attack of gastritis. In contrast to Lola's funeral, the congregation spilled from the church on to the pavement. The inscription on her grave reads, 'A fallen rose, the fairest, sweetest but most transient of all the lovely sisterhood'.

On the other hand, Lotta Crabtree's career was a more or less unmitigated triumph. After her days as a child dancer she frequently appeared in melodramas, often in drag, working for the producer David Belasco and from time to time appearing in burlesques of Lola such as the 1866 production of *The Irish Diamond*. She retired in 1891 after investing her earnings in real estate across America. She died leaving over $4 million in 1924. Mary Pickford is said to have been greatly influenced by her acting.

21 David C. Peacock v. Miriam F. Peacock, Judgement Roll, Filed 24 March 1856, Superior Court, City and County of New York, EJ 1856 No. 444.

22 Charles Follin had a chequered career. A dealer in cotton, tobacco and hides, a linguist and adventurer, he had reputedly married a New Orleans heiress and run through her fortune. He then moved to New York and after his wife's death married Susan Danforth, said to be the owner of a brothel in the Bowery. She died on 26 June 1868. Miriam was their daughter.

23 *Albany Morning Times*, 4, 7 February 1857.

24 *Frank Leslie's Weekly News*, February 1857.

25 Of all the actresses who knew Lola, Miriam Follin was probably the greatest success – if not on the stage. She went from man to man and strength to strength, marrying publishing magnate Frank Leslie and on his death inheriting his empire. She was, however, little more successful with lasting relationships than Lola. After Leslie's death on 4 October 1871 she married Willie Wilde, Oscar's elder and alcoholic brother, after a courtship lasting all of two days. Later asked why he had married a woman some fifteen years his senior, Willie blew a ring of cigar smoke and replied, ''Pon my soul, I don't know. I really ought to have married Mrs Langtry I suppose.' She died in 1914 leaving $2 million to the suffragette movement, a legacy which was bitterly contested. For an account of Minnie Follin's life see Madeleine Stern, *Purple Passages, The Life of Mrs Frank B. Leslie*, Ch. 2, pp. 18–23.

26 *Golden Era*, 23 August 1857.

27 *Pittsburg Morning Post*, 28 February 1857.

28 *Louisville Daily Democrat*, 11 April 1857; *Louisville Daily Courier*, 11 April 1857; *Louisville Daily Journal*, 13 April 1857; *Enquirer* (Cincinnati), 18 April 1857.

29 *Golden Era*, 3 May 1857.

30 *Brooklyn Daily Eagle*, 24 July 1857.

31 *New York Times*, 3 May 1883.

32 'Old Time Facts and Fancies' in *Daily News* (Chicago), 21 July 1893.

33 *Chicago Tribune*, 22 April 1864.

34 *Illustrated News of the World*, 14 August 1858.

35 *Witness* (Montreal), 26 August 1857, *New York Times* (reprint), 7 September 1857; *Minèrve* (Montreal), 3, 8 September 1857.

36 Roger de Beauvoir squandered his father's fortune. A great bohemian, he was said to drink enough champagne each night to float a ship. Some thought him the most delightful dandy of his day but the sometimes malevolent Goncourt brothers thought him 'ruthless and sadistic'. He married a Mlle Doze, an actress of the Comédie Française, but neither was suited for marriage and years of litigation was the only offspring. Just before he died impoverished in 1866 he said, 'I have drunk 150,000 francs worth of champagne, and written 300 little poems, madrigals, epigrams and songs.' For anecdotes of de Beauvoir see Joanna Richardson, *The Bohemians*; Henri de Villemessant, *Mémoires d'un journalist*.

37 Montez, *Lectures*, pp. 263–4.

38 Montez, *Lectures*, pp. 176–7; Harvard Theatrical Collection. She omitted the summation in her later lectures.

39 *Philadelphia Press*, 5 December 1857.

40 It was not the only 'marriage' she had at the time. In September 1856 the French provincial actor Mauclerc denied an actual eight-day marriage to her. This must have been a hoax, because there is every indication that Lola was in California at the time she was purporting to write from St Jean de Luz. There have, however, been suggestions that he made up an entire correspondence with her as self-advertisement.

41 Montez, *Lectures*, pp. 44–5.

42 *Pittsfield Sun*, 7 January 1858.

43 *Brooklyn Daily Eagle*, 22 May 1858.

44 The Harvey Burdell murder was one of the most entertaining of New York's mid-nineteenth century unsolved murders and it fascinated the public for months. The thoroughly disagreeable forty-six-year-old dentist was found stabbed to death with twenty-seven wounds to the head on 31 January 1857 at 31 Bond Street. There had clearly been a great struggle, but curiously not one of the other ten boarders had heard anything. The killer was almost certainly an Emily Cunningham – who may or may not have been married to Burdell – possibly with the help of one or more of the other boarders. For an account of the case see James Morton, *A Who's Who of Unsolved Murder.*

45 *New York Times*, 10, 19, 27 February 1858.

46 ibid., 19 March 1858. David Weymss Jobson died on 29 May 1876 in the Insane Asylum on Ward's Island, New York. Immediately after his first case against John Allen, he tried unsuccessfully to have the dentist charged with attempting to poison him. He then returned to England, turning his attentions against a Sir James Ferguson whom he believed, completely without foundation, to be acting in concert with Lola against him. He was first bound over to keep the peace. The original sum was two sureties of £100 but Ferguson decently asked them to be reduced to £40. Jobson soon broke the terms and this time he was convicted of publishing a libel with intent to extort money. On 16 August 1860 he was sentenced to twelve months with hard labour and again bound over with two sureties for his future behaviour. Jobson was apparently in poor health and the kindly judge indicated that he would have full medical attention in prison. His claims that he had been Queen Victoria's dentist were most improbable, but he was never challenged on the subject. He was declared insolvent in New York in 1865 and on his arrest ten years later was sent to the asylum. In the days before he died he was confined in a crib, a form of straitjacket. The *New York Times* noted, 'The treatment he received at the hands of men who should have known better was often brutal in the extreme.'

47 Thad Spencer quoted in *San Francisco Examiner*, 11 June 1888.

48 Lola Montez, *The Arts and Secrets of Beauty or Secrets of a Lady's Toilet with Hints to Gentlemen on the Art of Fascinating.*

49 *Illustrated News of the World*, 14 August 1858; *New York Tribune*, 30 January 1861.

50 *New York Daily News*, 17 September 1858.

51 *New York Post*, November 1868; undated clipping in San Francisco Public Library.

52 *Mobile Register*, 16 March 1858; *New York Herald*, 3 to 26 July 1858; *Brooklyn Daily Eagle*, 27 August 1858; *Chicago Tribune*, 6 September 1858; *Sunday Dispatch* (Philadelphia), 3 October 1858; 'A Remarkable Woman' in *Chicago Tribune*, 15 April 1872.

53 *Chicago Tribune*, 7 June 1859.

54 *New York Times*, 22 June 1858.

55 ibid., 2 October 1858.

56 Unknown newspaper in the Manuscripts Collection, New York Public Library, 13 October 1858.

57 Unknown and undated newspaper in the Manuscripts Collection, New York Public Library.

58 ibid.

59 *New York Times*, 14 October 1858. Along with other contributions and money from a collection of poems Hoyt had written, the church was rebuilt. It was pulled down in 1871 to make way for housing and Hoyt resigned his rectorship, opening a second Church of the Good Shepherd in Fort Lee, New Jersey, which he also ran as a mission. He died on 11 October 1878 following a severe attack of bronchitis.

18. LOLA'S LAST DAYS

1   *Sacramento Daily Union Supplement*, 26 January 1859, reprinting the *Galway Vindicator*.

2   *York Herald*, 19 February 1859; *Sunday Times*, 27 February 1859. The nose-thumbing incident is almost identical to one in Washington seven years earlier, when on 9 February 1852 she told the audience about the offender, 'I did not come to dis country to be insulted.' There were cries of 'Put him out'. *Richmond Dispatch*, 16 February 1852.

3   This was a reference to Thomas Lake Harris, born in Fenny Stratford in 1816, who formed the community 'The Brotherhood of the New Life' as a Universalist preacher in 1844. He studied Spiritualism under Andrew Jackson Davis and had a New Church in New York to which Lola was attracted. He is described as being of slight build and moderate height, with a high forehead and overhanging eyebrows denoting substantial perceptive faculties. At one time the community had 1,600 acres at Wassaic in New York state, and 400 at Santa Rosa, California in 1875. In 1884 Harris withdrew from the community and lived in seclusion in New York, where he died on 23 March 1906.

4   *Pittsfield Sun*, 2 June 1859. *The Minor* by Samuel Foote (1720–77) was an anti-Methodist satire in which he played three parts, including Mother Cole. The redeemed lady, formerly a bawd, is reformed and converted by Mr Squintum, based on the illiterate, cross-eyed Methodist evangelist George Whitfield.

5   *The Times*, 22 January 1851, 27 July 1864.

6   Dr Arnold was the legendary reforming headmaster of Rugby School.

7   Bound lectures in Harvard Theatre Collection.

8   *New York Times*, 2 July 1859.

9   *Era*, 19 June 1859.

10   *Chicago Press and Tribune*, 24 October 1859.

11   *New York Tribune*, 30 January 1861.

12   Letter, Lola Montez to 'Camille', 11 February 1860 in Monacensia-Sammlung, Stadtbibliothek, Munich; *New York Evening Post*, 19 January 1861.

13   Mary Clemmer Ames, *Outlines of Men, Women and Things*, pp. 124–5.

14   *Boston Sunday Post*, 28 October 1891.

15   *Buffalo Daily Republic*, quoting *Chicago Journal*, 6 April 1860.

16   Charles Warwick, 'Lola Montez' in *New York Clipper*, 5 July 1879.

17   Wyndham, *The Magnificent Montez*, p. 232.

18   Unidentified and undated cutting in Harvard Theatre Collection.

19   'Old Time Facts and Fancies' in *Daily News* (Chicago), 21 July 1883.

20   *Brooklyn Daily Eagle*, 16 April 1894.

21   'Closing Career of a Bad Woman' in *Sunday Dispatch* (Philadelphia), 9 September 1861.

22   Heman Dyer, *The Story of a Penitent: Lola Montez, A Brand Plucked From The Fire*, p. 38. The book is often attributed to Francis Hawks, on whose recollection it is based. However, Hawks was dead by the time it appeared in print.

23   ibid., p. 36.

24   Quotations from Wyndham, *The Magnificent Montez*, pp. 256–7.

25   *Chicago Tribune*, 7 December 1860, quoting the *Cincinnati Gazette*.

26   Hingston, *The Genial Showman*, pp. 215–16.

27   Letter, Mrs Cooper to her son Harley B. Cooper, 13 January 1909.

28   Dyer, *The Story of a Penitent*, p. 36.

29   In 1862 Hawks, very much a Southern gentleman and abolitionist, refused to let the Union flag fly from his Calvary Episcopal Church in Manhattan, relenting only when a mob threatened to burn it down. As a result he felt obliged to resign and left New York

to become Rector of Christ Church, Baltimore for the duration of the war. Before he took up religion he had been a lawyer and was regarded as equally powerful before a jury and a congregation. He was noted for the force, felicity and sincerity of his sermons. Like Lola he was quick tempered and inclined to unrestrained and angry speech; unlike Lola he was equally quick to repent. He died on 26 September 1866, having written 'Let my epitaph be "Died of New York"'.

30 *Sunday Dispatch* (Philadelphia), 27 January 1861.
31 *New York Times*, 18 January 1861; *New York Herald*, *New York Evening Post*, 19 January 1861; *Albion* (New York City), 22 January 1861; *Pilot* (Boston), 2 February 1861; *Daily Telegraph*, 9 February 1861.
32 Ireland (ed.), *Records of the New York Stage*.
33 De Leon, *Thirty Years of My Life in Three Continents*, Vol. I, pp. 112–16.
34 Ames, *Outlines of Men, Women and Things*, p. 125.
35 *New York Daily Clipper*, 16 September 1911.
36 *San Francisco Examiner*, 11 June 1888.
37 *New York Daily Clipper*, 16 September 1911.
38 Maria E. Buchanan to Ludwig, 8 April, 21 September 1861. Ludwig to Mrs Buchanan, Buchanan Papers, Harvard Theatre Collection. The papers are an eclectic collection including one from Lola, one from the Duke of Wellington and one from Joseph Mazzini. There is no record of how Maria Buchanan disposed of her legacy, but she does not seem to have benefited substantially from Lola's reputed wealth. She and her husband were buried in unmarked graves not far from that of Lola in Green-Wood cemetery, Brooklyn.
39 *New York Times*, 26 April 1998.

19. What happened to them all?

1 *Paddington Times*, 20, 27 November 1875; Probate, 29 November 1875.
2 Probate, 8 June 1871.
3 Helen Holdredge and Bob Reed, 'Lola Montez – The Woman in Black' in *California Voice*, 12 August 1983. The story is repeated in Holdredge's book on Lola.
4 'Old King Ludwig' in *Saturday Review*, reprinted in *New York Times*, 4 July 1886.
5 J. B. Rana, *The Life of Maharaja Sir Jung Bahadur*.
6 Morton's remains were moved to Père Lachaise in 1958. Although Thackeray also thought of him as 'the maddest, wildest and gentlest of creatures – scarce answerable for his actions or passions', he used him as the villain in his 'A Shabby Story'. Wyndham, *The Magnificent Montez*; K. H. Varnhagen von Ense, *Tagebücher*; *Gazette des Tribunaux*, December 1852; Letter, G. M. Crawford to Morton's sister, 7 October 1852.
7 Letter, Mowbray Morris to Sutherland Edwards, 12 December 1863, see [Anon], *The History of The Times: The Tradition Established 1841–1884*.
8 *Marysville Daily Examiner*, 28 May 1858.
9 *Golden Era*, 30 May 1858.
10 *New York Times*, 4, 10 October 1869.
11 *San Francisco Examiner*, 29 April 1888.
12 *Brooklyn Daily Eagle*, 8 April 1868, 19 July 1870.
13 *San Francisco Call*, 17 June 1900.
14 *San Francisco Examiner*, 11 June 1893; *New York Herald*, 18 July 1897.
15 *Chicago Tribune*, 23 October 1890.
16 *New York Herald*, 8 April 1888.

17 *Chicago Times*, 28 February 1948.
18 *San Francisco Chronicle*, 15 December 1939.
19 *New York Times*, 14 March 1982.
20 *Chicago Times*, 6 October 1947.
21 *The Times*, 16 March, 18 June 1954.
22 Richard Waterhouse, 'Lola Montez and High Culture' in *Journal of Australian Studies*, no. 52, 1997.
23 *New York Times*, 22 November 1998.
24 *New York Evening Post*, 21 January 1861.
25 Anthony Trollope, *Thackeray*.
26 *Frank Leslie's Illustrated Newspaper*, 2 February 1861.

Note: All references to BSB LA are to documents in the King Ludwig I Archiv, Bayerside Staatsbibliothek, Munich.

Bibliography

➤‑◄‑

BOOKS

Ames, M. C., *Outlines of Men, Women and Things*, New York: Hurd & Houghton, 1873

[Anon], *The History of The Times: The Tradition Established 1841–1884*, London, 1939

[Anon], *Life and Adventures of Joaquim Murietta*, Oklahoma: University of Oklahoma, 1854 (reprinted 1955)

[Anon], *Mola oder Tanz und Weltgeschichte*, Leipzig: Ernst Keil, 1847

[Anon], *Notes on Duels and Duelling, Alphabetically Arranged with a Preliminary Historical Essay*, Boston: Crosby, Nichols & Co., 1855

[Anon], *Procès de Beauvallon*, Paris: Moquet, 1846

[Anon (Henry Vigo Carey?)], *Cadet's Guide to India by a Lieutenant of the Bengal Establishment*, London: Blade Kingsbury, Parbury & Allen, 1820

[Anon (Michael Cannon)], *Lola Montes: The Tragic Story of a 'Liberated Woman'*, Melbourne: Heritage Publications, 1973

Arentz, G. (trans. J. Laver), *The Elegant Woman: From the Rococo Period to Modern Times*, London: George G. Harrap & Co., 1932

Asbury, H., *The Barbary Coast*, London: Robert Hale & Co., 1937

Atlay, J. B., *The Victorian Chancellors*, Vols I and II, London: Smith Elder, 1906, 1908

Audebrand, P., *Derniers Jours de la Bohème*, Paris: Calman-Levy, 1905

Ballantine, Sergeant, *Some Experiences of a Barrister's Life*, London: Richard Bentley & Son, 1882

Bate, W., *Lucky City: The First Generation at Ballarat 1851–1901*, Carlton, Victoria: University of Melbourne Press, 1978

Beyer, L., *Glorreiches Leben und Taten der edelen Sennora Dolores*, Leipzig: E.O. Weller, 1847

Blainey, A., *The Farthing Poet*, London: Longmans, 1968

Blake, C., *An Historical Account of the Providence Stage*, New York: G. H. Whitney, 1868

Blanch, L., *The Wilder Shores of Love*, London: John Murray, 1954

Borthwick, J. D., *Three Years in California*, Harr, San Francisco: Wagner Publishing Co., 1857, 1908

Bourchardon, P., *Le Duel du Chemin de la Favorite*, Paris: Albin Michel, 1927

Bourne, K. (ed.), *The Blackmailing of the Chancellor*, London: Lemon Tree Press, 1975

Boyd, A. B., *Old Colonials*, Sydney: Sydney University Press, 1974

Bradfield, R. A., *Lola Montez and Castlemaine*, Castlemaine: Castlemaine Mall., n.d.

Brown, J. H., *Reminiscences and Incidents of Early Days in San Francisco: 1845–50*, San Francisco: The Grabhorn Press, 1933

Brown, T. A., *The History of the New York Stage*, New York: Dodd, Mead & Co., 1903

Bryan, V., *Laura Keene, A British Actress on the American Stage*, Jefferson, NC: McFarland, 1993

Certegny, H., *Lola Montès d'un trône à un cirque*, Paris, 1959

Chambers, J., *Palmerston: The People's Darling*, London: John Murray, 2004

Channon, H., *The Ludwigs of Bavaria*, London: Methuen, 1934

Chapman-Huston, D., *Bavarian Fantasy. The Story of Ludwig II*, London: John Murray, 1955

Chorley, H., *Modern German Music*, Vol. II, New York: Da Capo Press, 1973

Chroust, A. (ed.), *Gesandtschaftsberichte aus München, 1814–1848*, Munich

Clarke, A. B., *The Elder and Younger Booth*, London: David Bogne, 1882

Claudin, G., *Mes Souvenirs: Les Boulevards de 1840–1870*, Paris: C. Lévy, 1884

Corti, Count (trans. Evelyn B. Graham Stamper), *Ludwig I of Bavaria*, London: Eyre & Spottiswood, 1938

Coyne, J. S., *Pas de Fascination or Catching a Governor*, London: Nassau Steam Press, 1849

Craig, W., *My Adventures on the Australian Goldfields*, London: Cassell & Co, 1903

Crawford, M. C., *The Romance of the American Theatre*, Boston: Little, Brown & Co., 1925

Crow, D., *Henry Wikoff, the American Chevalier*, London: Macgibbon & Kee, 1963

Cubitt, Geoffrey, *The Jesuit Myth. Conspiracy Theory and Politics in 19th Century France*, Oxford: Clarendon Press, 1993

d'Ariste, P., *La vie et le monde du Boulevard*, Paris: Jules Tallandier, 1930

Darling, A., *Lola Montez*, New York: Stein & Day, 1972

d'Auvergne, E. B. F. D., *Lola Montez*, London: 1909

— *Adventuresses*, London: Hutchinson, 1927

de Beaumont–Vassy, *Salons de Paris sous Louis-Philippe*

d' Ecquevilley, T. V. V., *Temoin das un duel ou la verité sur le proces Victor d'Equevilley*, Frankfurt on Main, 1848

Delano, A., *A Live Woman in the Mines*, New York: J. Lane, 1909

— *Across the Plains and Among the Diggings*, New York: Wilson-Erickson, 1936

— *A Sojourn with Royalty and other sketches by 'Old Block'*, San Francisco: George Fields, 1936

De Leon, E., *Thirty Years of My Life in Three Continents*, London: Ward & Downey, 1890

Dickens, W., *Immaculate Contraception: The Extraordinary Story of Birth Control From the First Fumblings to the Present Day*, London: Robson Books, 2000

Disraeli, B. (Lord Beaconsfield), *Home Letters*, London: Cassell & Co., 1928

Dunbar, J., *Golden Interlude*, London: John Murray, 1955

Dürck-Kaulback, J., *Erinnerungen an Wilhelm von Kaulbach und sein Haus*, Munich: Delfin, 1917

Eden, E., *Up the Country*, London, 1876; also Oxford: Oxford University Press, 1930

Ellis, S. M., *A Mid-Victorian Pepys*, London: C. Palmer, 1923

Equiros, A., *Les Vierges Folles*, Paris: P. Delavigne, 1842

Estevan. L. (ed.), *San Francisco Theatre Research*, San Francisco: WPA Project, 1938

Fenton, B., *The Journal of Mrs Fenton*, London: Edward Arnold, 1901

Fitzball, E., *Thirty-Five Years of a Dramatic Author's Life*, London: T. C. Newby, 1859

Foley, D., *The Divine Eccentric, Lola Montez and the Newspapers*, Los Angeles: Westernlore Press, 1969

Forbes, E., *Mario and Grisi*, London: Victor Gollancz, 1985

Ford, George D., *These Were Actors*, New York: Library Publishers, 1955

Fowler, F., *Southern Lights and Shadows*, London: Sampson Low, Son & Co., 1859

Francis, B., *Fanny Kelly of Drury Lane*, London: Rockliff, 1950

Gaer, Joseph, 'Theatre of the Gold Rush Decade in San Francisco', Monograph no. 5, San Francisco: Works Progress Administration, 1938

Gagey, E., *The San Francisco Stage*, New York: Columbia Press, 1950

Garraty, J, A. and Carnes, M. C., *American National Biography*, New York: Oxford University Press, 1999

Gash, N., *Sir Robert Peel*, London: Longman, 1972

Gilliland, J., *Gladstone's 'Dear Spirit' Laura Thistlethwayte*, Oxford: private, 1994

Glasscock, G. B., *A Golden Highway*, Indianapolis: The Bobbs-Merrill Co., 1934

Goldberg, I., *Queen of Hearts. The Passionate Pilgrimage of Lola Montez*, New York, 1936

Gordeaux, P. (ed.), *Les Amours Célèbres*, Paris, Trévise, 1976

Guest, I., *The Romantic Ballet in Paris*, London: Dance Books, 1980

Haldane, C., *Daughter of Paris*, London: Hutchinson, 1961

Hall, J. R., *The Bravo Mystery and Other Cases*, London: John Lane, The Bodley Head, 1923.

Hauser, M., *Letters from Australia 1854–1857*, Melbourne: Red Roaster Press, 1988

Hawks, F. L., *The Story of a Penitent*, New York: Protestant Episcopal Society for the Promotion of Evangelical Knowledge, 1861

Hickman, J., *Courtesans*, London: Harper Perennial, 2003

Hingston, E. P., *The Genial Showman*, Vol. 1, London: John Camden, n.d.

Holdredge, H., *The Woman in Black; The Life of Lola Montez*, London: Alvin Redman, 1957

Holmes, R., *The British Soldier in India*, London: HarperCollins, 2005

Horne, R. H., *Australian Facts*, London: Smith, Elder & Co., 1859

Horstman, A., *Victorian Divorce*, New York: St Martin's Press, 1985

Hurtado, A. L., *Intimate Frontiers – Sex, Gender and Culture in Old California*, Albuquerque: University of New Mexico Press, 1999

Ireland, J. N. (ed.), *Records of the New York Stage*, New York: T. H. Morris, 1867

Jackson, J. H., *Gold Rush Album*, New York: Scribner's Sons, 1941

Janin, J., *735 Lettres à sa Femme*, Paris: Literature Klinckseck, 1973–79

— *Mlle Rachel et la tragédie*, Paris: Amyot, 1858

Johnson, S. L., *Roaring Camp: the Social World of the California Gold Rush*, New York: W. W. Norton, 2000

Kauffman, M. W., *American Brutus*, New York: Random House, 2004

Kelly, W., *Life in Victoria*, London: Chapman and Hall, 1859

Kitchen, M., *Kaspar Hauser: Europe's Child*, Basingstoke: Palgrave, 2001

Knepler, K., *The Gilded Stage: The Years of the Great International Actresses*, London: Constable, 1968

Latour, G. and Claval, F., *Les Théâtres de Paris*, Paris: Delegation à l'Action Artistique de la Ville de Paris, 1991

Leland, C. G., *Memoirs*, New York: D. Appleton, 1893

Leman, W., *Memoirs of an Old Actor*, San Francisco: A. Roman & Co., 1886

Leveson-Gower, E. F., *Bygone Years*, London, 1905

Lewis, O., *Lola Montez in California*, San Francisco: The Colt Press, 1938

Lieven, D.K. (ed. Quennell, P.C.), *Private Letters of Princess Lieven to Metternich*, London: Hutchinson, 1935

Lloyd, B. E., *Lights and Shades in San Francisco*, San Francisco: A. L. Bancroft & Co., 1876

Loliée, F., *The Gilded Beauties*, London: John Long, 1909

Lovell, M. S., *A Scandalous Life*, London: Richard Cohen Books, 1995

Ludlow, N. M., *Dramatic Life as I Found It*, St Louis: G. I. Jones & Co., 1880

Lumley, B., *Reminiscences of the Opera*, London: Hurst & Blackett, 1864

Lynch, J., *A Senator of the Fifties, David C. Broderick of California*, San Francisco: A.M. Robertson, 1911

MacAlister, C., *Old Pioneering Days in the Sunny South*, Sydney, 1977

MacMinn, G. R., *The Theatre of the Golden Era in California*, Caldwell, Idaho: The Caxton Printers, 1941

Maillier, C., *Trois Journalistes Drouais: Brisset, Dujarier, Bure*, Paris: Promotion et Edition, 1968

Malmesbury, 3rd Earl of, James Howard Harris, *Memoirs of an Ex-Minister. An Autobiography of the Rt. Honourable Earl of Malmesbury*, London: Longman, Green and Co., 1884

Marguerittes, J. de, *The Ins and Outs of Paris*, Philadelphia: William White Smith, 1855

Martineau, H., *Autobiography of Harriet Martineau*, London: M. W. Chapman, 1887

Massary, I., *Social Life and Manners in Australia*, London: Longman, Green & Co., 1861

Massett, S., *'Drifting About' or What 'Jeems Pipes of Pipesville' Saw and Did*, New York: G. W. Carlton, 1863

Maurois, A., *The Three Musketeers: A Study of the Dumas Family*, London, 1957

Maury, D. H., *Recollections of a Virginian in the Mexican, Indian and Civil Wars*, New York: Charles Scribner, 1894

McCabe, J. *Diary* (nd) Manuscript in Sutro Library, San Francisco. Unpublished.

Megquier, M.J. , *Apron Full of Gold*, Whitefish, Montana: Kessinger Publishing, 2005

Metternich, Graf von, *Aus Metternich's nachgelassen Papieren Dritter Teil, In der Ruhezeit 1848–1859*, Vienna: Wilhelm Braumüller, 1884

Milligan, R., *A History of Duelling*, London: Richard Bentley, 1841

Mirecourt, E. de, *Lola Montès*, Paris: Gustave Harvard, 1857

Montès, L., *Aventures de la célèbre danseuse raconté par elle-même avec son portrait et un fac-simile de son écriture*, Paris: Baruche, 1847

Montes, L., *The Arts and Secrets of Beauty or Secrets of a Lady's Toilet with Hints to Gentlemen on the Art of Fascinating*, New York: Dick & Fitzgerald, 1858

Montez, L., *Lectures of Lola Montez*, New York: Rudd & Carleton, 1858

— *Memoiren von Lola Montez, Gräfin von Landsfeld, aus dem französischen übertragen von Ludwig Fort*, Grimma und Leipzig: Verlag des Verlags-Comptoirs, 1851

Morton, J., *A Who's Who of Unsolved Murder*, London: Kyle Cathie, 1994

—*The First Detective*, London: Ebury Press, 2004

Moulin-Eckart, R., *Hans von Bülow*, Munich: Rosl, 1921

Mourot, S., *This was Sydney*, Sydney: Ure Smith, 1969

Muger, H., *La Vie Bohème*, [trans. as] *The Bohemians of the Latin Quarter*, University of Pennsylvaia Press, 2004

Neville, A., *The Fantastic City*, Boston: Houghton Mifflin, 1932

Odell, G. C. D., *Annals of the New York Stage*, Vol. VI, New York: Columbia University Press, 1931

Papon, A., *Lola Montez: Memoiren in begleitung vertrauter briefe Sr Majesté des Königs Ludwig von Bayern und Lola Montez*, London: Hrsg von Auguste Papon, 1849

— *The Memoirs and Private History of Lola Montes also the Whole of her Correspondence between Her and the King of Bavaria*, S. Y. Collins, 1851?

Parent-Duchâtelet, A. J. B., *De la prostitution dans la ville de Paris*, Paris: J. B. Baillière, 1836

Pearl, C., *Always Morning. The Life of Richard Henry 'Orian' Horne*, Melbourne: F. W. Cheshire, 1960

Pearsall, R., *The Table Rappers*, London: Michael Joseph, 1972

— *The Worm in the Bud*, Harmondsworth: Penguin Books, 1983

Plunkett, J. de, *160 Ans de théâtres de Paris*, Paris: Latour, 1941

— *160 Ans de théâtre: Fantômes et souvenirs de la Porte Saint-Martin*, Paris: Ariane, 1946

Q. [C. G. Rosenberg], *You Have Heard of Them*, New York: Redfield, 1854

Rana, P. J. B., *The Life of Maharaja Sir Jung Bahadur*, Katmandu: Ratna Pustak Bhandar, 1980

Reclus, Maurice, *Émile de Rirardin. Le Créateur de la Press moderne*, Paris: Hachette, 1934

Richardson, J., *Rachel*, London: Reinhard, 1958

— *The Bohemians*, London: Macmillan, 1969

— *The Courtesans*, London: Phoenix, 2000

Roberts, E., *The East India Voyager or Ten Minutes of Advice to the Outward bound*, London: J. Madden & Co., 1839

Rogers, A., *A Hundred Years of Rip and Roarin' Rough and Ready*, Rough and Ready, California: private, 1952

Ross, Ishbel, *The Uncrowned Queen. Life of Lola Montez*, New York: Harper & Row, 1972

Rounding, V., *Grandes Horizontales*, London: Bloomsbury, 2003

Rourke, C., *Troupers of the Gold Coast or The Rise of Lotta Crabtree*, New York: Harcourt, Brace & Co., 1928

Ryan, M., *Prostitution in London, with a Comparative View of that of Paris and New York*, London: H. Baillière, 1839

Sala, G. A., *The Life and Adventures of George Sala*, London: Cassell, 1895

Sante, L., *Low Life*, New York: Vintage Departures, 1992

Saxon, A. H., *P. T. Barnum, The Legend and the Man*, New York: Columbia University Press, 1989

Schorn, K., *Lebenserinnerungen*, Bonn: P. Hanstein, 1898

Seacole, M. (ed. W. J. Stead), *Wonderful Adventures of Mrs Seacole*, London: James Blackwood, 1853

Seymour, B., *Lola Montez: A Life*, New Haven: Yale University Press, 1996

Shultz, G. D., *Jenny Lind: The Swedish Nightingale*, Philadelphia and New York: J. B. Lippincott, 1962

Skibinski , K., 'Pamietnik Aktora' in Dabrowski, S., *Writer on the Theatre and Górshi*, Warsaw, 1925

Smith, E. A. (ed.), *Letters of Princess Lieven to Lady Holland 1847–57*, London: The Roxburghe Club, 1956

Steinmetz, A., *The Romance of Duelling*, London: Chapman & Hall, 1868

Stellman, L. J., *Sam Brannan, Builder of San Francisco*, New York: Exposition Press, 1996

Stern, M. B., *Purple Passages. The Life of Mrs Frank B. Leslie*, Norman: University of Oklahoma Press, 1953

Stewart, Leslie, *The Rise and Fall of Little Betty Gilbert*, Grass Valley, 1994

Stone, L., *The Road to Divorce: England 1530 to 1987*, Oxford: Oxford University Press, 1990

— *Uncertain Unions and Broken Lives: Intimate and Revealing Accounts of Marriage and Divorce in England 1600–1857*, Oxford: Oxford University Press, 1995

Taylor, D. J., *Thackeray*, London: Chatto & Windus, 1999

Taylor, R., *Franz Liszt*, London: Grafton, 1986

Teppe, J., *Vocabulaire de la vie amoureuse*, Paris: Le Pavillon, 1973

Thackeray, W. M., *A Collection of Letters of William Makepeace Thackeray 1847-1855*, London: Smith & Elder, 1887

Thompson, F. M. L., *The Rise of Respectable Society: A Social History of Victorian Britain*, London: Fontana, 1988

Tinling, M., *Lola Montez in Grass Valley*, Carmichael, California, 1980

Train, G. F., *A Yankee Merchant in Goldrush Australia: The Letters of George Francis Train*, Melbourne: Heinemann, 1970

Trollope, A., *Thackeray*, London: The Trollope Society/Macmillan & Co, 1997

Trowbridge, W. R. H., *Seven Splendid Sinners*, London: T. Fisher Unwin, 1908

Trueman, B. C., *The Field of Honour*, New York: Fors, Howard & Hulbert, 1884

Vandam, A., *An Englishman in Paris*, London: Chapman and Hall, 1892

— *My Paris Notebook*, London: William Heinemann, 1894

Varley, J. F., *The Legend of Joaquim Murietta*, Twin Falls, Idaho: Big Lost River Press, 1995

— *Lola Montez*, Spokane: Arthur H. Clarke Co., 1997

Varnhagen von Ense, K. H., *Tagebücher*, Bern: Lang, 1972

Veron, L. M., *Mémoires d'un Bourgeois*, Paris: Librairie Nouvelle, 1853–5

Viel-Castel, H., *Mémoires*, Paris: Jules Lévy, 1886

Villemessant, H. de, *Mémoires d'un journaliste*, Paris: Dentu, 1872–5

Von Kobell, L., *Under der Vier Ersten Königen Bayers* Munich: Beck, 1894

Wagner, C. (ed. Martin Gregor-Dellin and Dietrich Mack), *Die Tagebucher 1. 32*, Munich: R. Piper, 1976–8. (trans. by Geoffrey Skelton as) *Cosima Wagner's Diaries*, New York: Harcourt Brace Jovanich, 1978

Wagner, R., *Mein Leben*, Munich: Wilhelm Goldman Verlag, 1983, (trans. by Andrew Grey as) *My Life*, London: Cambridge University Press, 1911

Walker, A., *Franz Liszt*, New York: Alfred A. Knopf, 1983

White, S. E., *Old California in Picture and Story*, New York: Doubleday, Doran & Co., 1937

Whiting, K.F., *Kate Field, A Record*, Boston: Little, Brown, 1899

Whitman, W., *November Boughs*, New York: Alexander Gardner, 1889

Williams, A., *Portrait of Liszt*, Oxford: Clarendon Press, 1990

Winter, W., *Life and Art of Edwin Booth*, London: T. Fisher Unwin, 1893

Withers, W. B., *History of Ballarat*, Ballarat: Niven, 1870

Wyndham, H., *The Magnificent Montez. From Courtesan to Convert*, London: Hutchinson, 1935

— *Blotted 'Scutcheons*, London: Hutchinson & Co., n.d.

— *Feminine Frailty*, London: Ernest Benn, 1929

Zes, *La Société Parisienne*, Paris: Librairie Illustrée, 1888

— *Parisiens et Parisiennes en Déshabillé*, Paris: Ernest Kolb, 1889

— *Le Demi-Monde sous le Second Empire, Souvenirs d'un Sybarite*, Paris: Ernest Kolb, 1892

ARTICLES ETC.

Amédée, Augustin-Thierry, 'Lola Montes' in *La Review des Deux Mondes*, no. 30, 15 November, 1 December 1935

Annan, Gabriele, 'Lola, Ludwig and Lord Malmesbury' in *Times Literary Supplement*, 7 June 1996

[Anon], 'A Beautiful Fiend' in *San Francisco Examiner*, 29 April 1888

— Larousse, *Grand Dictionnaire* vi., pp. 1365–6

— 'Lola Montès et Les Catholiques de la Bavère' in *Le Correspondant*, no. 17, 1847

— 'Lola Montez' in *The Athenaeum Journal of Literature, Science and the Fine Arts*, no. 9, February 1861

— 'Lola Montez in Warszawie' in *Tygodnik Illustrawany*, no. 21, 1912

— 'Reminiscences of Lola Montez' in *New York Tribune*, 30 January 1861

— 'Trial for Murder in France – Lola Montez' in *American Law Journal*, July 1848, Philadelphia

— 'The Warsaw Ballet 1832–1853' in *Dance Chronicle*, Vol. 10

— 'Flying Sheets From Our Travelling Contributor' in *Illustrated London News*, 27 November 1847

[Anon (Richardson, Johnson?)], *Lola Montes: A Reply to the 'Private History and Memoirs' of that Celebrated Lady Recently Published by the Marquis of Papon*, 1851

Avedisian, Louise Joanne, 'Lola Montez in California', unpublished dissertation, UCLA, 1971

Berson, Misha, 'The San Francisco Stage Pt 1. From Gold Rush To Golden Spike 1849–1869' in *San Francisco Performing Arts Library and Museum Journal*, no. 2, Fall 1989

Brown, Lucinda Linn, 'Pioneer Letters' in *Historical Society of Southern California Quarterly*, March 1939

Buckbee, Edna Bryan, 'Swan of Erin' in *Touring Topics*, XXII, no. 12

Burkholder, Edwin V., 'The Girl with the Million Dollar Tag' in *Real Men*, August 1959

Burns, J. F., 'From Whoredom to Evangelism' in *Lisburn Historical Society Journal*, no. 2, 1979

Carr, Raymond, 'Many are the Ways of Love' in *The Spectator*, 25 May 1996

Celeste, Mabel, 'Gold Rush Theatre in Nevada City, California', unpublished thesis, Stanford University, 1967

Danton, George H., 'Elias Peissner' in *Monatschefte für Deutschen Unterricht*, XXXII, no. 7, November 1940, University of Wisconsin

Day, Diane L., 'Lola Montez and her American Image' in *History of Photography*, October 1981

Dornberg, John, untitled article in *New York Times*, 19 June 1988

Duyckinck, E. A., 'A Memorial to Francis Hawks', New York Historical Society, 7 May 1867

Eberlé, C. (trans. J. E. Petraki), 'Reminiscences of Charles Eberlé (1854–1864)' in La Trobe Library, Melbourne

Fournier, August, 'Lola Montez. Ein geheimer Bericht über Bayern im Jahre 1847' in *Deutsche Revue*, August 1902

Francis, George Henry, 'Lola Montez and the King of Bavaria' in *Fraser's Magazine*, January 1848

Goldberg, I., 'Queen of Hearts' in *The Athenaeum Journal of Literature, Science and the Fine Arts*, 9 February 1861

Kemble, John Haskell, 'The Panama Route to the Pacific 1848–1869' in *Pacific Historical Review*, March 1938

Kirkpatrick, Rod, 'Eureka and the Editor: A Reappraisal 150 Years On' in *Journalist Review* 26 (2), 2004, pp 31–42

K. G. M., 'Der erste Auftretung von Lola Montez in Deutschland'; Anon, 'Der Beherrscher eines Kleinstates'

Marberry, M. M., 'How New York Greeted King Ludwig's Girlfriend' in *American Heritage*, no. 6, February 1955

May, Antoinette, 'Mistress to an Era' in *San Francisco*, June 1978

McCarthy, Michael, 'Lola Montez Down Under' in *The Old Limerick Journal*, n.d.

Moore, Lilian, 'George Washington Smith' in *Dance Index*, June–August 1945

Moos, Frans, 'Lola Montez' Schicksalsnacht in Kalifornien' in *Montrealer Nachrichten*, 11 November 1972

Morice, Polly, 'Whatever Lola Wanted' in *Cosmopolitan*, August 1983

Morse, Edwin Franklin, 'The Story of a Gold Miner' in *California Historical Quarterly*, December 1927

Murname, K., 'The History of Theatre in Ballarat, Decade by Decade', unpublished thesis in Australiana Collection in Ballarat Public Library, n.d.

Robb, Graham, 'Lola Montès et la Fanfarlo' in *Études Baudelairiennes*, no. 12, Neuchâtel

Rousseau, B. G., 'Sierra Lorelei', unidentified newspaper clipping, Harvard Collection

Simon, Ludwig, 'L'Extraordinaire Aventure de Lola Montez' in *Archives Internationales de la Danse*, October 1939

Stevenson, Lionel, 'Vanity Fair and Lord Morgan' in *Publications of the Modern Language Association*, 24 June 1933, Wisconsin

Thackeray, William Makepeace, 'Shrove Tuesday in Paris' in *Britannia*, 5 June 1841

Todd, Arthur, '. . . the Coming of Fanny Elssler and Lola Montez' in *Dance Magazine*, October 1950

Vischer, Edward (trans. from German by Ruth Frey Axe), 'A Trip to the Mining Regions in the Spring of 1859' in *Quarterly of the Californian Historical Society*, VII, no. 3, September 1932

Von Bülow, Eduard, 'Die Nieue Melusine' in *Novellen*

Waterhouse, Richard, 'Lola Montez and High Culture' in *Journal of Australian Studies*, no. 52, 1997

Archival Papers

Aplin, Capt. Christopher, Journal kept in India December 1829 to October 1831, British Library India Office, MSS EurB208

Nicolls, Sir Jasper, Journals and Correspondence, India Office, British Library, MSS Eur. F.175 et seq.

The Palmerston Papers, University of Southampton

Seymour, Bruce, Lola Montez papers, University of California, Berkeley

Index

→>—<←